Theory and Practice of Development in
THE THIRDWORLD

Department of World Economy
Karl Marx University of Economic Sciences, Budapest

n/a

Theory and Practice of Development in THE THIRD WORLD

edited by
Professor JÓZSEF NYILAS
D. Sci. (econ.)

1977

A. W. SIJTHOFF · LEYDEN

AKADÉMIAI KIADÓ · BUDAPEST

This book is based on *Korunk Világgazdasága* Vol.
Közgazdasági és Jogi Könyvkiadó, Budapest

English translation by
ISTVÁN VÉGES

ISBN 90 286 0597 5 (Sijthoff)
ISBN 963 05 1248 3 (Akadémiai Kiadó)

© Akadémiai Kiadó, Budapest 1977

Printed in Hungary

CONTENTS

PREFACE

The research team of the Department of World Economy at the Karl Marx University of Economics, Budapest, recently set about publishing in English the results of their scientific work done during the past two and a half decades. Two collections of studies on the general and theoretical problems of the world economy appeared under the auspices of the publishers of the present work early in 1976 under the titles "Theoretical Problems, Current Structural Changes in the World Economy" and "Integration in the World Economy, East-West and Inter-State Relations". These studies represent a comprehensive theoretical background to the present work, as well as to the subsequent one soon to be published under the title "The Changing Face of the Third World: Regional and National Studies".

Research into the socio-economic problem of the developing countries has been conducted in our Department for quite a long time. For some time, from the mid-1950s on, it was the process of the disintegration of the colonial system, the emergence of new independent states as well as the rapidly expanding relations between socialist and developing countries that put the problems of the group of countries in question into the forefront of interest. Relevant Marxist research in Hungary, just as in the other socialist countries, was focused at that time primarily on the foundations of scientific knowledge relating to the developing world. These foundations, however, are to be interpreted in a rather broad sense in that they required not only a thorough analysis of the socio-economic problems of the countries concerned, but also of the social, economic, ideological, etc. factors inherent in their ancient history and colonial past and those still working in their present conditions. Therefore, the socio-economic problems cannot be understood without the knowledge of their historical heritage. It is for these reasons that special attention had to be paid to the analysis of their pre-colonial socio-economic structure, their institutional set-up, as well as of the changes that, under the compulsion of the colonial rule, have taken place in the economies and societies of present-day developing countries. This endeavour had already found expression in the first studies prepared in Hungarian by the author's collective in Volume II of *Korunk kapitalizmusa* (The Capitalism of Our Age) published in 1961.

In Volume III of *Korunk világgazdasága* (The World Economy of Our Age), published in 1966 and entirely devoted to the theoretical and practical issues of the devel-

9

oping world, sufficient attention was also paid, though to a lesser extent, to the problems discussed above.

During the past ten years, however, the study of the developing countries has assumed very significant proportions in the socialist countries, among them in Hungary, too. For this purpose special institutes with adequately qualified research personnel have been established. As a result, the number of contributions to a Marxist presentation of the present state and the history of the developing countries has increased tremendously. All this has made it possible for us to re-orientate the original concept of our research, notably in the sense that now we are making efforts to concentrate our work more than before on analysing the actual position and increasing role of the developing countries in the world economy, the special features of their socio-economic development and international relations. It stands to reason that the attainment of this objective presupposes the discussion of the historical socio-political background and the present national and international political implications of the subject.

This line of thought manifests itself in the second, revised edition of Volume III published in Hungarian in 1974 of the work *Korunk világgazdasága* (The World Economy of Our Age), which constitutes the basis of the present English book.

The authors of this volume – internationally known and highly qualified specialists with first-hand experience – present an analysis in depth of the characteristics, causes and consequences of economic underdevelopment, as well as of the problems of economic growth and planning in the Third World countries. Their investigations and experiences also allow important conclusions to be drawn for economic practice. All this serves as a sort of theoretical basis for another work soon to be published in English and written by the staff members of our Department on certain developing regions (Latin America and Tropical Africa) and some highly important developing countries.

The countries of the Third World have attained, with the active support of the socialist states, appreciable results in their anti-imperialist struggle. Yet, they still continue to be faced with the extremely hard task to gain, in addition to their political independence, economic independence, too. Obviously, it is inconceivable to accomplish this objective without creating a really new international economic order, which is tantamount to breaking away from the imperialist system of exploitation and dependence. It follows from this that the developing countries still have an immensely difficult phase of struggle ahead of them. The decisive breakthrough, the gaining of economic independence, can only be achieved if these countries have already built up their own economies capable of self-sustained growth. This radical change, however, is bound to affect the very existence of the huge monopoly organizations, veritable world powers in our days, still exercising control over the natural and other resources of the developing countries, besides being harmful to the interests of the various imperialist powers as well. Thus it is likely that the struggle being waged for the economic emancipation of the developing countries will enter in the decades to come into its decisive stage, which, in all probability, will impose extremely great tasks on the developing world and also on the socialist countries, the main force of social progress, in their anti-imperialist struggle.

At the same time, it should not be ignored that the colonial forces will elaborate and pursue a more "scientific", a better thought-out policy than before to preserve their privileges. Disquieting in this respect is the fact alone that they have succeeded, at the cost of not insignificant efforts and in face of the disintegration of the colonial system, in maintaining, in no small measure, their economic positions and in ensuring further possibilities of exploitation of the developing countries. Their methods applied to this end include "granting" independence with strings attached to it, creation of small countries incapable of existing in themselves, the rapid building up of the many-sided and intricate system of neo-colonialism, etc.

The colonialists continue to resort to arms in many parts of the world against peoples fighting for their independence, and violence and aggression must be reckoned with in future, too. There is, however, no doubt about it that the imperialist powers will also increasingly apply economic means (trade, extending grants, participation in the development process, etc.) to ensure their privileges. They have already brought about several institutions, mobilized and employed hosts of highly qualified personnel to realize this aim.

The developing countries and the progressive forces of the world must also make conscious efforts to prevent as soon as possible that the tendencies that have become apparent in the past decades should further be continued, tendencies as a result of which the position of the developing countries, accounting for half the world population and for more than 70 per cent of the population living in non-socialist countries, has rapidly deteriorated.

It is increasingly realized that economic theory and practical economic knowledge are powerful aids for the solution of the burning problems of the day. Not even the implementation of certain UN, UNCTAD and other resolutions to this end is conceivable without adequate scientific foundations, theoretical and practical knowledge. Our work is aimed at contributing, by scientific means, to the just and rightful struggle of the peoples of the developing countries for attaining economic independence.

József Nyilas
editor

11

PART ONE

THE MAIN THEORETICAL QUESTIONS OF "UNDERDEVELOPMENT"

by

Tamás Szentes

I. THE INTERPRETATION OF "UNDERDEVELOPMENT"

The inherited economy of the countries liberated from colonial oppression presents a rather heterogeneous picture. There are immense differences not only between individual countries or rather continents such as Asia and Africa, or the formally long independent Latin America, but also within the economy of a single country. We can find in it side by side modern productive plants and primitive subsistence economy; up-to-date airports and harbours together with camels, mules, or even "human means of transport"; supermarkets full of luxuries and not far from them street vendors selling rags as clothing and roots as foodstuffs. Under the helicopters carrying plantation owners, we can see the army of indigenous labourers working almost exclusively manually. And this list could be continued at will for pages.

But our task is to explore and reveal the real situation, the internal state of the economy, under this multi-coloured and confusing surface. There are statistical indices available making it possible for us to classify and systematize these phenomena. It is commonly known that *per capita national income* is generally used as the most comprehensive indicator of economic development of a given country. No doubt, this index number provides invaluable information on the economy of a country. And if we apply it to the countries of Asia, Africa and Latin America, the low level of national income per capita proves to be characteristic of most of them. While in the developed capitalist countries per capita national income is above § 2,000, it is, as a rule, under § 200 in most of the above-mentioned countries. Thus, one may think to have found in it the most characteristic manifestation and factor of economic underdevelopment.

And since present-day developed capitalist countries used to stand at about the income level of the developing countries of today, it appears as if there were a difference in the phase of development only, the developing countries being merely at an earlier stage of the general development process. This view is rather widespread in Western bourgeois economics.[1] It serves as an evidence and

---

[1] For a more detailed critical analysis of bourgeois theories explaining underdevelopment, especially those including – explicitly or implicitly – the apology of colonialism, see T. Szentes: *The Political Economy of Underdevelopment*. Akadémiai Kiadó, Budapest, 1971, 1973; and T. Szentes: *Theories of Underdevelopment*. Paper presented at the Conference on the Teaching of Economics, University College, Dar es Salaam, March, 1969.

ideological argument to show that developing countries have to proceed along the same road of development covered by the developed capitalist countries. (There is no space for us to deal here with the question what role these Western theories of the stages of development play in the ideological struggle against socialism.)

For this and other reasons, this index number is in the centre of the underdevelopment theories of Western apologetic economies,[2] also applied for the purpose of defining "underdeveloped" countries.

This indicator, however, may prove extremely misleading. It conceals essential differences existing in the socio-economic relations of individual countries and do not reveal anything about the actual distribution of national income and the methods of its utilization. But it is even more deceptive if used to define underdevelopment, to disclose its true causes and to delineate the group of developing countries. Thus, if we regard underdevelopment as a *temporary state* characterized by a statistical index number, we cannot understand its causes and cannot answer the questions what impediments hamper rapid economic development in the countries concerned, and, consequently, what obstacles have to be removed in order to liquidate this state in the shortest possible time.[3]

Using the level of per capita national income as a basis for categorization, we could put countries in which rapid economic development is hindered or slowed down by quite different factors. Thus, e. g., as commonly known, there are also a number of socialist countries (e. g. some Asian countries and Cuba in America), which, according to this statistical indicator, could be classified as belonging to the developing countries, whereas the promoting and retarding forces of their economic growth, following the radical socio-economic changes effected there, have been considerably different from those in developing countries. At the same time there are a few countries (e. g. Venezuela or Kuwait) which, on the basis of their national income levels, fall into the category of advanced countries, while their economic growth is hindered by the same factors as those hampering the other developing countries.

Therefore, if we want to find an answer to the question what main tasks the ex-colonial countries have to perform in order to ensure economic advance, we cannot be satisfied with quantitative criteria as indicators of their state, not even with such an important index number as per capita national income. We must reveal the *qualitative criteria* of their position, those basic factors which paralyze their sound and rapid development.

These countries have gone through a peculiar development process which was part of the development process of imperialism, of the world capitalist system as a whole. That is, they *have not developed independently,* and therefore the emergence of their present conditions cannot be explained by internal causes

---

[2] Very typical of this is the so-called vicious-circle theory. (For details on this question see subsequent chapters.)

[3] This state can be explained at best from itself as done by the vicious-circle theory already referred to.

either. Since the time they came into their state of colonial or semi-colonial dependence, they have ceased to develop independently. True, prior to colonialization this independent development had made very slow progress in many countries, and by breaking up obsolete social systems, colonialism integrated these countries into the world market, speeding up thereby their development.

But this faster development served the interests of the colonizing countries and was accompanied by consequences which, in the last analysis, have been the main obstacles on the road of the further development of the colonies up to this time.

Consequently, *underdevelopment* – despite the original sense of the word – does not mean either a dropping out of and lagging behind development or an earlier stage of the general process of evolution: but just the contrary: *it is the result of a specific, distorted development.* It is for this reason that no analogy can be drawn between the present conditions of these countries and the former state of the developed capitalist countries (as done by the initiators of the theory of the "stages and development"), since it is also due to this distorted development – despite all appearances – that the "modern" capitalist sector with its often surprisingly up-to-date phenomena exists side by side with the primitive conditions of the "pre-capitalist" sector.

Apologetic bourgeois economics does not examine this specific development, does not analyse the *historical* circumstances of the emergence of underdevelopment, but accepts it as a given state, as a starting-point. In this way it conceals the fact and role of colonialism.

Since it does not concern itself with the historical roots of underdevelopment which are closely connected with colonialism, that is with *external* influences and factors, bourgeois economics tries to explain underdevelopment from itself, from its existing forms, predominantly from internal factors.[4] In doing so it prefers to emphasize such internal factors, or makes them appear as the basic causes of underdevelopment, which can be conceived of either as objective facts or can be traced back to the peculiar way of life and unfavourable qualities of the people concerned and can by no means be connected with colonialism.

It is a rather popular variety of the theories of underdevelopment which offers an explanation of underdevelopment by means of a summary of certain "typical" features or *factors hindering or limiting* development. This usually specifies the "typical" features and limiting factors by comparing the given "static" state of the most developed capitalist countries together with a number of surface phenome-

---

[4] Besides the apologetic views and approaches in question there is also of course a critical school in Western non-Marxist economics, which for an explanation of the present state of developing countries refers to the effects of external, international factors such as the detrimental consequences of colonialism, the disadvantages and losses suffered by these countries in international trade and division of labour. This school includes such prominent economists as R. Prebisch, G. Myrdal, A. Lewis, H. Singer, etc.

na.[5] What, as a result of comparison, appears as a "plus" or "minus" for the developing countries, constitutes the aggregate of deficiencies or limiting factors that makes up the definition of underdevelopment.

This "subtraction approach" – or "ideal typical index approach"[6] (as it is called by A.G. Frank) or "gap approach" (named so by Charles Kindleberger) – is so popular and general, indeed, that it can be found even with such economists who, as H. Leibenstein,[7] go beyond a summarized description and specification of these factors and their superficial interrelationships, and demonstrate underdevelopment as a peculiar qualitative "form of motion" or, more exactly, a "system", and not merely as a relative phenomenon. In other words, this approach is often a starting-point also for the theories concentrating on *relationships* between factors. On the other hand, it also offers some support for certain "historical" explanations,[8] and may serve those "historical" conceptions which interpret underdevelopment as an original (or at least earlier) general state from which the natural way of development leads towards the ideal type of the opposite pole. It is also utilized in those theories which, in compliance with, or independently of, the already mentioned "historical" approaches, concentrate on the sociological and psychological differences and regard underdevelopment as the consequence of a closed, stagnant, traditional society.[9]

Of the factors limiting development, the one which is most frequently referred to is the unfavourable *demographic* situation, more exactly the high birth rate and the resulting "population pressure" in these countries.[10]

There is no reason for denying the importance of this factor. However, the space and time aspects of the phenomenon of "demographic explosion", the causes of its incidence and particularly its causal relationship with underdevelopment require a more thorough investigation.

[5] This confrontation remains a comparison of "static states" even if it happens to include some dynamic factors (such as the rate of population growth, the rate of accumulation, etc.), as it compares a movement observed within a certain period of time with a movement and stagnation within a certain period of time. That is, the two states or movements as *related to each other are static*, and therefore there is no dynamic relationship between them. This shows at the same time the unhistorical character of the comparison.

[6] A.G. Frank: Sociology of Development and Underdevelopment of Sociology. *Catalyst*, No. 3, University of Buffalo, 1967.

[7] See H. Leibenstein: *Economic Backwardness and Economic Growth*. New York, 1957.

[8] See, e.g., W.W. Rostow's or R. Aron's theory. (*The Stages of Economic Growth. A Non-Communist Manifesto*. Cambridge, 1960; *Dix-huit leçons sur la société industrielle*. Gallimard, 1962.)

[9] See, e.g., B.F. Hoselitz: Social Structure and Economic Growth. *Economia Internazionale*, Vol. 6, No. 3, 1953; E.E. Hagen: *On the Theory of Social Change*. Dorsey Press, Homewood, 1962; D. McClelland: *The Achieving Society*. Van Nostrand, Princeton, 1961.

[10] The demographic factor is accorded a prominent place in the whole theory of Leibenstein but also among the characteristics of A. Sauvy, J. Viner, G.M. Meier and R.E. Baldwin. (See H. Leibenstein: *op. cit.;* A. Sauvy: *Theorie générale de la population*. Vol. I, Paris, 1956; E. Gannagé: *Economie du Développement*. Paris, 1962; J. Viner: *International Trade and Economic Development*. Oxford, 1963; G.M. Meier and R.E. Baldwin: *Economic Development. Theory, History, Policy*. New York, 1956, etc.)

18

On the one hand, the perspective aspect of the problem of population growth is quite different in the densely populated countries (particularly in those with poor natural resources) from that in the sparsely populated countries. It is true that 50 per cent of the total population of the underdeveloped world is concentrated in five countries (India, Pakistan, Bangla Desh, Indonesia and Nigeria), and that the first three of them (India, Pakistan and Bangla Desh) and certain regions of the fourth (Indonesia) are very densely populated, but this does not justify us in appraising all developing countries, including the very sparsely populated ones, in a uniform way, on the basis of high population growth. In a considerable part of the underdeveloped world (mainly in Tropical Africa and some regions of Latin America) labour shortage is one of the causes of the underutilization of natural resources.

On the other hand, the phenomenon itself, namely the rise in the rate of population growth, must be accounted for. It is not enough to relate – as it is often done – the notions of the two rates and explain the fall of the mortality rate by improving health service and protection against epidemics. The heart of the matter is whether or not such a divergence of the two rates is a natural demographic phenomenon.

If the answer is an *affirmative* one, then the divergence also ought to be discovered in the history of the present-day developed countries. And this raises the other question: why did it not bring about economic backwardness in those countries, why did it not hamper their development?

If, however, the answer is a *negative* one (or if the measure of the divergence as regards its order of magnitude is substantially different from what it was in the case of the developed countries), then how can we account for this more or less new phenomenon?

Apologetic economists explain the slow growth of the productive forces, the low level of labour productivity of developing countries, by their *unfavourable natural endowments* (poor-quality soil, virgin forests, deserts, lack of mineral resources and water power, unfavourable climatic and precipitation conditions, poor transport facilities, unfavourable geographic situation with respect to foreign trade, etc.), or by the underutilization of existing natural resources, and partly by the poor quality of the working population (in respect of culture, education, health and nutrition) or the "backwardness" of the people.[11]

No doubt, unfavourable natural conditions may, and in certain regions do, hinder economic development, but they can hardly be regarded as universal. It is common knowledge that Africa, Latin America, India, Indonesia and the countries of the Middle East are very rich in mineral resources, and some of them

---

[11] H. Myint e. g. distinguishes two aspects of economic underdevelopment: the underdevelopment of natural resources (the inadequate utilization of potential resources owing to the shortage of capital) and the backwardness of population (economic ignorance, lack of enterprise, limited specialization, etc.) (H. Myint: An Interpretation of Economic Backwardness. Oxford Economic Papers, IV, 1954. *The Economics of Underdevelopment*. Ed. by A. N. Agarwala and A. P. Singh, London, 1958.)

have very high potentials of water power. And the climatic conditions, though disadvantageous in a number of countries, are definitely favourable in others.

The *poor quality of the working population* and the backwardness and ignorance of the people cannot provide an acceptable explanation of economic underdevelopment either, as it is the consequence rather than the cause of backwardness. Incidentally, the quality of the working population – whether in its physical sense, i.e. relating to the nutrition and health level, or in its intellectual sense, i.e. relating to the cultural and educational level – is almost entirely a function of economic development. The same applies to the social, cultural and hygienic conditions of the whole population. Moreover, in the colonial countries the question is put just the other way round: What prevented the quality of the working population from improving even within the given limitations of economic development; why could the technical and professional skills of manpower not make any appreciable progress; why did its physical and intellectual energy not develop?

The most widespread variety of the apologetic interpretations of underdevelopment is – as mentioned already – the *vicious-circle theory*.

The substitution of interdependence for causal relationships has perhaps never found such an independent theoretical manifestation, and pure tautology has never stepped on such a high pedestal as in the vicious-circle idea. The explanation of underdevelopment by itself means of course – at least seemingly – an escape from the necessity of a historical analysis. If, by inserting a few interdependent factors, the direct relationship of underdevelopment to itself can be made indirect, even the appearance of an obvious tautology can be avoided. And the question of the causes of individual inhibiting or limiting factors can be evaded by reference to another factor, and so on, until we come back to where we started from.

Though it would be possible to set up a number of circular relationships and interdependences for any advanced country and any historical period, they have become popular and widespread particularly in the various underdevelopment theories so that underdevelopment seems to be, at least in economic literature, a separate world and an independent system of various vicious circles.

Underdevelopment in these theories is no longer the simple aggregate of individual deficiencies and obstacles, but an interdependent system of their relationships. The explanation of a characteristic deficiency or obstacle is provided by another, and that, in turn, is explained by a third and so on, or *vice versa*.

What is the cause of capital shortage, for instance, as one of the obstacles to development?

– It is the insufficiency of domestic capital accumulation which, in turn, is the result of low per capita savings ratio. And the latter is low because per capita national income is low, which again cannot grow quickly because of capital shortage.

20

These and similar circular relationships and "magic" circles could be drawn up in any number, and they really crop up with the followers of the most different schools.[12] As simplified patterns of the results of some partial analyses, these vicious circles undoubtedly reflect actually existing relationships and dialectic contradictions. It is beyond doubt, e. g., that a low national income also limits the volume of accumulation, which, in turn, restricts the growth of national income by means of productive investments. Similarly, a chain of interrelationships does exist indeed in many other cases, too.

But these chains of relationships are never complete. Highly important factors are often disregarded, and the missing links make the continuity of the chain very doubtful.

Not only can the inaccuracy and deficiency of the chain of relationships be demonstrated – in the case of all vicious circles as well as in the case of the one just discussed – but what is more important is that any factors of the vicious circle can change without the preceding factor being changed, or it can remain unchanged even after the preceding one has changed. Thus the vicious circle, despite the seemingly dialectical character of mutual relationships, is in fact *metaphysical* and *mechanical*. No process, apart from processes under laboratory conditions, can be repeated or actually repeats itself unchanged in time, especially not the process of social motion. If there is any circular cause-effect relationship – and it certainly does exist – it can only move *spirally* upwards and downwards,[13] and, therefore, has a *starting-point,* too (just like a spiral spring but unlike a ring). Now, if it has a starting-point, then it is exactly this, the *fundamental cause* of circular relationship, the *historical root* of underdevelopment that must be explored.

Despite their realistic appearance, the main weakness of the vicious-circle theories is that they reveal neither the historical circumstances out of which the assumed "magic" circle originated, nor the underlying socio-economic relations and the fundamental determinant causes.

[12] See, e.g., J. Viner: *op. cit.;* G.M. Meier and R.E. Baldwin: *op. cit.;* E. Gannagé: *op. cit.;* R. Nurkse: Some International Aspects of the Problem of Economic Underdevelopment. *The American Economic Review,* May 1952, and *Some Aspects of Capital Accumulation in Underdeveloped Countries,* Cairo, 1952; N.S. Buchanan: Deliberate Industrialization for Higher Incomes. *Economic Journal,* Vol. 56, 1946; R.T. Gill: *Economic Development, Past and Present.* Prentice-Hall, New Jersey, 1963, etc.
[13] G. Myrdal has transcended the static conception of the vicious circle and investigates in a dialectic way the interrelation between the factors that promote and those which hinder development, and describes a cumulative, ascending or descending spiral motion: "If either of the two factors should change, this is bound to bring a change in the other factor, too, and start a cumulative process of mutual interaction in which the change in one factor would continuously be supported by the reaction of the other factor and so on in a circular way." (The great progress Myrdal made seems to be vitiated by his statement which, by the way, reveals the influence of the vicious circle idea, that it is absolutely useless to look for one basic, primary factor "as everything is cause to everything else in an interlocking circular manner".) To illustrate the ascending spiral motion, Myrdal gives the following example: "Quite obviously, a circular relationship between less poverty, more food, improved health and higher working capacity would sustain a cumulative process upwards." (G. Myrdal: *Economic Theory and Underdeveloped Regions.* London, 1957, pp. 16, 19 and 12.)

Trying to explain the vicious circle by itself, these theories look at it as a natural, given phenomenon. But if that is the case, the question to be answered is this: how did the present-day developed countries succeed in getting over this natural phenomenon, i.e. the vicious circle of poverty? That is, even if they avoid answering the historical question of how the vicious circle came into existence, they still must answer the no less historical question of how it was broken.

As a condition of breaking the vicious circle, the supporters of the theory usually point to an external factor, the increased influx of capital and foreign skilled personnel. By this they want to strengthen the illusion that societies incapable for internal reasons of any development by themselves, must rely on the developed capitalist countries for their progress. This is the conception which, in accordance with the subtraction approach, imagines the advance of developing countries like this: "The West diffuses knowledge, skills, organization, values, technology and capital to the poor nations, until over time its society, culture and personnel become variants of that which made the Atlantic community economically successful."[14]

It is in fact this "diffusion" theory which also finds its reflection in *Rostow's "historical" explanation* already mentioned. Though he is not specifically concerned with underdevelopment, and merely touches upon it within his theoretical system, but his impact on the underdevelopment theories is very significant, and his own theory is the ideological summary of all apologetic interpretations.

Rostow purposefully confronts his historical explanation with that of Marxism. He endeavours to present the state and development of all possible societies of the past and present as a certain stage or part of a single, uniform development process. In other words, he wishes to offer a comprehensive historical explanation, just as Marxism does. However, unlike Marxism, he sees in the highest stage of this process not socialism or communism, but some kind of an ideal of developed capitalism.

Rostow distinguishes five main stages:
1. traditional society;
2. the traditional stage providing the preconditions for the take-off;
3. "take-off" stage;
4. drive to maturity;
5. the stage of a high-level mass consumption.

Rostow attempts to define the various stages of economic growth by certain economic *and* social characteristics. However, the economic characteristics appear oversimplified and restricted as quantitative indices or just simple descriptions of the state of productive forces, while the social characteristics are narrowed down to the motivations and propensities of society or the actual

---

[14] M. Nash: Introduction to the Study of Economic Growth. Quoted by A. G. Frank (*op. cit.*) who gives an excellent critique of this sort of "diffusionist approach".

positions and roles of individuals as members of society endowed with certain propensities.

As regards the *former*, it is scarcely possible to distinguish objectively between the different stages or societies on the basis of the *quantitative* evolution of productive forces. Unlike *qualitative* differences in ownership and distribution relations, i. e. production relations, which provide an objective basis for marking out the individual socio-economic systems or "stages", distinctions made on the basis of quantitative statistical indices are hopelessly arbitrary and artificial.

As to the *latter:* if we conceive of social propensities as variables independent of production relations, their very nature and the cause of their change become inexplicable. Since these social propensities, whose nature and change seem to be due to some accident or *deus ex machina* (or some sort of predestination), constitute in the last analysis the motive forces of growth in Rostow's theory, the sequence of stages remains, as a matter of fact, scientifically undetermined (or just fatalistic).

Consequently, as the individual "stages" do not constitute an organic and qualitative unity either historically or logically, they can hardly be regarded as scientifically defined, and the interrelationship between the individual stages is indeterminate, too.

The inaccurate, superficial and sloppy nature of Rostow's definitions is pointed out by several critics of his.[15]

Besides the faulty interpretation of the relationship of economy and society, of the essence of social development and, thus, the superficial or sometimes even tautological definition of the arbitrary stages, there is still a very important and fundamental *methodological* error in Rostow's theory. He outlines the imagined process of social development in such a way that he places societies existing side by side in space one after the other in time, or one before the other, as representing different "stages" of a general process of growth (not according to their inner substance and historical content, but simply on the basis of the given level of their productive forces), while the mutual relationships of their development, particularly their close intertwining since the emergence of world capitalist economy, find scarcely any appreciation in the analysis, and if it does, it is strongly biased.

There exist the present-day societies, each with their peculiar, variegated aspects, their different socio-economic set-ups, historical backgrounds and natural-geographic environments, and, above all, with their interrelationships different in scope and direction. But apart from all these differences and interrelationships the societies can, indeed, be classified at discretion into certain categories according to economic indices representing the *levels of their*

---

[15] See, e. g., H. J. Habakukk's Review on Rostow's Stages of Economic Growth. *Economic Journal*, September 1961; S. Kurnets: Notes on the Take-off. Paper reprinted in *Leading Issues in Development Economics*. Ed. by G. M. Meier, New York, 1964; A. K. Cairncross: Essays in Bibliography and Criticism, XLV. The Stages of Economic Growth. In *Economic History Review*, April 1961, etc.

productive forces. Thus, irrespective of all differences between them, some countries may be put into the highest, some into the lowest, and many others into the intermediate groups. And then comes the logical "salto mortale": the individual features of societies already classified, reappear, but this time no longer as indicators – mostly very superficial as that – of a certain phase of their own specific development, but as characteristics of a certain stage of general historical development. If a society classified among the highest group has certain characteristic features, then every society that reaches this stage owing to the development of its productive forces, will assume the same features. Moreover, in order to reach this higher stage, on the strength of its productive forces, it must develop these very characteristics. Thus, from groups classified by a narrow and one-sided criterion, Rostow forms historical "stages": a society in a lower group corresponds to the earlier "stage" of growth of a society in a higher group, while a society in a higher group represents but a stage to be reached by a low-ranking society in the further course of its development. After that all that remains to be done is to illustrate this process by historical analogies picked out, and to point out the phenomena which seem to be really similar in the past of the more developed and the present of the less developed countries – and the logical "somersault" appears justified and acceptable.

By this method not only the socialist countries can be classified, irrespective of their social system, into one or another stage of general development, but even the colonial areas can be treated as "one of the variants" of the general case and allotted to a specific stage of growth.

Of course, all this is not presented by Rostow in such an open, unambiguous way. The individual "stages" are shown to be far more complex and varied, the historical illustrations given are far more numerous, with the result that it is not easy to find out at first sight the basically unhistorical nature and real purport of this "historical" approach.

Obviously, from the point of view of our study, the first three stages, particularly the second one, will be of special interest as the picture Rostow draws of the societies in the pre-take-off stage is intended to resemble, in one way or another, most of the developing countries. Moreover, some of the characteristics of the transitional stage[16] are such that they are far more or even exclusively (unless occasionally and to an insignificant extent) typical of the developing countries, than of any earlier historical period in the development of the now developed countries. Thus, e. g., it would be useless to seek in history a "stage" *in general* which was characterized by one-sided dependence on trade and foreign capital and, at the same time, by a more rapid development of agriculture than industry. And, anyway, foreign capital needed to set development in motion, the export of raw materials adjusted to the interests of other countries, together with

---

[16] As e.g. the development of agriculture, foreign trade and transport, which is usually characterized by primary production and exports "financed" by foreign capital, and in which other nations have an economic interest. Further: penetration from abroad of new ideas and mentality.

import sensitivity, and new ideas penetrating from outside – all *presuppose* a more advanced external environment, that is, the *existence* of more developed countries. And if we presuppose this *ad infinitum,* even for the latter countries, we shall inevitably come, in the end, to a *single* country which is an *exception* to the outlined process of general development.

But apart from the details, what should be thought of a theory of growth which makes an exception to the law of general process of growth in the case of the very country which first started on the road of growth?!

As a matter of fact, Rostow's "historical" explanation and similar theories of the present state of the former colonial countries provide the theoretical basis for the use of the terms *"economically backward"* or *"underdeveloped"* country.[17] Then, if what these countries pass through – though belatedly, owing to several internal factors – is the same natural and general stage of economic growth that the more developed countries had passed through earlier, then their present state is backwardness indeed in the strict sense of the word. If this is true, colonialism cannot be made responsible for that condition. On the contrary, it appears to be exclusively the accelerator of progress.

The interpretation of "underdevelopment" as simple lagging behind may be a more or less correct and acceptable explanation of the historical past which preceded the formation of the *world economy,* or more exactly the building up of a system of lasting economic relations and massive interactions of various parts of the world.

Nevertheless, the characteristic features of the present-day state of developing countries are no longer the consequence of those long-standing internal limiting factors hindering development – even if they happen to be their remnants – which provided the basis for and the possibility of creating a relationship of dependence, but the consequence of the fact that the oppressed and dependent countries have developed since that time together with the world system of imperialism as its constituent parts. It is true that imperialist penetration, the power of foreign capital, has also yielded the positive result of fitting these countries into the circulation of world capitalist trade and has given a tremendous boost to the development of commodity production as opposed to subsistence economy, yet by this very act and in the course of its implementation it has brought about such distortions in their economic structure which presently constitute the main obstacles to their further development. It is true that it started the exploitation of

[17] We wish to emphasize that the expression "developing" country used – for lack of a better term – in this book, as also widely accepted in international diplomacy, is in line with the false ideological conception mentioned which denies the previous development of the countries in question, that is, that their present state is the result of a specific dialectical development. In so far as this terminological distinction is merely the consequence of a *de facto* habit of general customs, which accords, by way of a euphemism, a polite gesture, the name of "developing" countries to ex-colonial, semi-colonial and dependent countries, there is no trouble with the practice. (Perhaps only in so far as these countries belong to the *least developing* part of the world economy. For this reason it would be more appropriate to speak of "countries most needing development".)

previously unutilized natural resources, but it robbed them of these resources and subordinated and tied them to the economic development of the developed countries. It is true that it broke up in quite a few subjugated countries the obsolete social structure and substituted more up-to-date relations for it, but preserved at the same time the remnants of the broken-up structure in a symbiosis with "modern" formations.

Thus the present-day socio-economic state of developing countries is not simply "underdevelopment", not just a sign of their dropping out of and falling behind development, but it is indeed the product of a peculiar development most closely connected with and deriving from the development of world capitalist economy.

II. THE IMPACT OF WORLD CAPITALIST ECONOMY

It follows from the foregoing that the analysis of the present state of developing countries must be started both *historically and logically* with the examination and evaluation of colonialism, or more precisely, world capitalist economy and the international division of labour.

The colonial system established in the last third of the 19th and at the beginning of the 20th century was but the specific manifestation of the world-wide expansion of the already developed capitalist mode of production, which had outgrown its national limits, the form of a peculiar international division of labour in the unfolding world capitalist economy. The building up of the colonial system, the economic establishment and transformation of the colonies was a highly important moment in the development of world capitalist economy.

The coming into being of the world economy was undoubtedly a highly significant step forward in the historical development of human society, proving that capitalism was of a definitely higher and more developed character than any other previous socio-economic systems. But it follows from the very substance of the capitalist system that this essentially positive historical fact has become the source of the sharpest conflicts and most striking inequalities, subjugation and exploitation being its intrinsic features.

It is true of course that the integration into the world economy, the world market, the breaking up of the old, often rigid, stagnant or only rather slowly developing socio-economic systems, the introduction of the elements of a definitely more developed mode of production, the expansion of commodity production and market relations, the abrupt growth of certain branches of production, the transfer of more developed technological, scientific, cultural, sanitary and other infrastructural elements, etc., which are based on higher-level forces of production, are all undoubtedly positive achievements for the development of the colonial and dependent countries as well. Since, however, these results are but parts of a motion wholly governed by the *internal laws of capitalism,* they cannot be evaluated by themselves, but only together with the whole motion and process. These achievements are the consequences of the penetration of foreign capitalist powers, of the activity of foreign capital, and this very penetration and activity – apart from the violence used – has had, besides the achievements, or just because of them, the gravest consequences. In so far as the achievements themselves have turned into detrimental consequences, we are faced with a *specific dialectics of development* in which the steps taken forward give rise to ever newer obstacles to further development, which, in turn, require incessantly additional energy to be overcome.

What are the serious consequences which the colonial and dependent countries taking part in the international division of labour unfolding in the wake of emerging world capitalism, have come to suffer, and which have determined the main, essential features of their present state, their so-called "underdevelopment"? In other words, what are the consequences of the fact that the above-mentioned achievements are connected with the activities of foreign powers and capital? And what are the consequences in general of the participation in the capitalist international division of labour?

As the activities of colonial powers and foreign capital cannot be explained by personal motivations, but are also determined by the objective relations of the international division of labour of capitalism (a historical category), let us begin our answer with the examination of this division of labour.

1. INTERNATIONAL DIVISION OF LABOUR UNDER THE SYSTEM OF COLONIALISM

The international division of labour as embodied in the colonial system (also including the semi-colonial and other dependent countries) was the exact expression and equivalent of the historical development of capitalism in a given period of time. We might also say that it was the specific – and in this sense almost "classical" – division of labour of capitalism grown over into imperialism. What determined the concrete structure and operation of this division of labour in the given historical period? Those internal relations and external power relations which were characteristic of the countries of the developed sector of the world capitalist order and of their position in the world economy.

In the period of establishing the colonial system the most developed, the leading country of world capitalism was Great Britain, with France and Germany following behind. In these countries, but especially in Britain, a very rapid industrial development took place, while agriculture lagged behind in development. The mineral raw material basis also proved more or less inadequate. Rapid industrial growth, especially in its extensive stage, was accompanied by an increase in the number of the employed (mainly wage workers recruited from the formerly self-sufficient rural population) and, consequently, by the growing demand for foodstuffs as well as by a rapidly expanding demand for mineral and agricultural raw materials for industrial use. It also called for an adequately expanding market for manufactured goods. The rather backward agriculture was not able to ensure a sufficient supply of goods, nor was it able to meet – together with the extractive industries – the demand for raw materials. On the other hand, the population being at a very low income level could not provide a large and sufficiently expanding market for the industrial products. And Britain, the leading industrial power, depended *especially* heavily on external food and raw material sources as well as on foreign markets for carrying on her industrial development. The more the internal laws of capital accumulation asserted themselves, the more the strange twins of unemployment and the underutilization of part of the accumulated capital as concomitants of the new development – along with the falling tendency of the rate of profit – became apparent. Thus, besides the acquisition of external sources of raw materials and foodstuffs and of foreign markets, an outward-oriented *capital drain* (which, through the emigration to the colonies, took also the form of labour drain) as well as the search for investment opportunities promising a higher rate of profit became natural imperatives.

The increasingly powerful monopolies and the militarily strengthened states succeeded in satisfying these imperative needs. (The fact that the way to it was marked by rivalry, bargaining and ruthless wars is relevant to our subject only to the extent that the subjugated territories were "balkanized", cut up and differentiated even in language and culture.)

The satisfaction of these needs determined the economic functions of the subjugated territories. Thus the colonies, apart from having a strategic role, became

– the suppliers of mineral and agricultural raw materials to the metropolitan countries;

– secure markets for their industrial products;

– the territories of their capital drain and investment activities and thereby

– their regular source of income.

It was in accordance with this division of labour and these functions that the economies of the colonial and dependent countries were shaped and transformed. The present-day developing countries bear the marks of this division of labour.

But before analysing one by one these marks and the internal socio-economic consequences of transformation, let us point out right away that this typical form and system of capitalist international division of labour has since that time *undergone substantial changes,* especially after the World War II, and that, after the emergence of a new kind of division of labour due to the development of productive forces, its operation has come up against considerable difficulties.

2. CHANGES IN THE PATTERN OF CAPITALIST INTERNATIONAL DIVISION OF LABOUR

These changes and their consequences may be summed up briefly[1] in the following way:

The development of productive forces, with the unfolding of the scientific and technological revolution, has brought about rapid and far-reaching changes in the

[1] For details see the relevant chapters of Parts Two, Three and Four in *Theoretical Problems and Structural Changes in the World Economy* (ed. J. Nyilas), Akadémiai Kiadó, Budapest 1976, and Parts One and Two in *Integration in the Word Economy. East-West and Inter-State Relations* (ed. J. Nyilas), Akadémiai Kiadó, Budapest 1976.

pattern of international trade. It has increased the significance and proportion of industrial products based on qualified intellectual labour, while diminishing at the same time the importance of many natural raw materials and primary products.

The leadership in the developed sector of the world capitalist economy has shifted from Britain, a traditionally and more or less naturally raw-material and food-importing country, to the USA, a country with rich raw material resources, the most developed agriculture, a much wider internal market and an economy less susceptible to foreign trade.

State intervention and the unfolding and advance of state monopoly capitalism in the most developed capitalist countries (partly in connection with the scientific and technological revolution) have widened and ensured the opportunities for profitable private investments also within national boundaries. They have set about developing backward agriculture in several countries (e.g. in France and Germany) by artificial protectionist means.

Increasing private and state monopoly co-operation among the developed capitalist countries, especially in the framework of the European Economic Community, has given a great impetus to the widening of the division of labour among the developed industrial countries.

As a result of the shift in the power relations of the world economy, of the collapse of the colonial system, as well as of increasing capital concentration, the advance made by international monopolies, multinational corporations in the developed capitalist countries, the structure of capital export to developing countries and the investment policy of foreign capital, too, have undergone substantial changes.

The development programmes in the ex-colonial countries and the "population explosion" have made the question of expanding their import capacities especially acute and have intensified marketing and pricing problems of their exports, whilst in the capitalist sector of the world economy the processes of marketing and price formation have come to be controlled more and more by the international monopolies.

The rise in the general income level in the developed capitalist countries has brought about a certain shift in the pattern of consumption, viz. towards the more sophisticated durable consumer goods.[2]

As a result of all these and other changes, the realization of the export products of many developing countries in the world market meets with ever greater difficulties. The significance of many of the traditional primary products has drastically diminished, the dependence of the developed capitalist countries on a number of "colonial" products has ceased or weakened (owing to new artificial

---

[2] In this shift in the pattern of consumption the well-known Engel's law finds expression. The rise in income levels results primarily in the relative fall in the demand for foodstuffs, the effect of which makes itself felt gradually, especially under a protectionist policy, in food *imports*. According to the data of the UN World Economic Survey (1967) the income elasticity of imports from the developing countries is as follows: agricultural raw materials: 0.60, foodstuffs: 0.76, fuels: 1.40, manufactured goods: 1.24.

30

raw materials or shifts in the consumption pattern).[3] The development of West-European agriculture and the immense agricultural reserves of the US and Canada, as well as the shifts in the consumption pattern, have increasingly limited the agrarian export possibilities of the developing countries, and, what is more, a number of developing countries have to rely, owing to the extremely rapid population growth, on agricultural imports from the developed capitalist countries to an ever greater extent. The expansion of capital investment opportunities in the advanced sector of the world capitalist economy – owing to state intervention, the scientific and technological revolution and international co-operation and integration – have greatly curbed the earlier rapid rise in private capital export to the developing countries. And since, parallel to this development, the political risk, the danger of nationalization, has generally increased in the newly independent countries, the interest of foreign private capital (especially foreign private capital independent of international monopolies) in the developing countries has relatively dwindled.[4]

Hence the present state of the developing countries, the so-called "underdevelopment", bears not only the marks and consequences of the international division of labour which materialized in the colonial system, but it also reflects the detrimental effects of recent *changes* in this division of labour. In other words, most of the developing countries suffer today not only from the fact that they have become appendages to a special kind of international division of labour, but also from the substantial changes this division of labour is undergoing in our days, and from the increasing troubles it is faced with.

Let us examine now more concretely what consequences have resulted from the fact that the developing countries as colonies and dependent territories joined in the capitalist international division of labour, and to what extent the inherited situation has changed owing to recent shifts in this division of labour.

3. THE DETRIMENTAL CONSEQUENCES OF THE COLONIAL SYSTEM OF INTERNATIONAL DIVISION OF LABOUR

Under the colonial system *political power* was concentrated naturally in the colonial representations of the metropolitan countries or their puppet governments. Thus the direction of the economic development in the dependent countries, their social and institutional systems, their cultural development, including even the question of language, etc., could be controlled or influenced

[3] In this way, differentiation between developing countries has also increased.

[4] These changes and consequences are of course far from being of absolute value, equal measure or effect. By no means do they mean that all sources of raw materials of the developing countries have lost their significance for them. Just the contrary. Nor do they mean that the growth of the inflow of foreign private capital has suffered a setback, and primarily not that the importance of earlier capital investments and profit-making has diminished. And as to the late 1960s and early 1970, a certain revival of the interest of foreign private capital can be observed, though of a different nature and orientation as compared with the colonial investment pattern.

directly by foreign powers. In most cases even the boundaries of the country were determined artificially by them.

This situation enabled the metropolitan powers to develop or suppress in their own interests certain economic sectors, that is, to determine the *economic structure,* and by fixing the boundaries of the country they could even lay down the framework in which, after achieving independence, the internal economic and social processes could start. In consequence, they were in a position also to determine the size of the "national" economy.

The rivalry leading to the fixing by the imperialist colonial powers of the boundaries of countries, artificial both geographically and ethnically, economically and culturally, influenced not only the political processes and conflicts after independence, but also gave rise, in many cases, to such *dwarf states* which are incapable of ensuring the preconditions appropriate in dimensions for any real economic development and industrialization. This, incidentally, also shows how limited or even misleading the sense is of any comparisons trying, by means of statistical indices, to measure and compare the "underdevelopment" of a number of countries endowed with formal political independence but lacking the rudimental prerequisites of a national economy. It also demonstrates the fact that contemporary development problems can hardly be explained by the characteristics of pre-colonial traditional societies.

Foreign private capital flowing into the colonized territories and supported by a purposeful economic policy, but also independently of it, influenced by the play of spontaneous market forces, developed, according to given production and market conditions, the leading export sectors of the dependent countries: the agricultural one-crop economy and mineral raw material production. The limited capacity of the local market, coupled with the then very strong demand induction of the world market justified from the outset an export-oriented economy. And the inducement of this external demand towards the production of mineral and agricultural primary products, as well as the lack of local skilled labour and the high costs of procuring machines (from overseas), stimulated at the beginning capital investments in agriculture and mining, i.e. investments of usually low capital-intensity requiring only cheap unskilled labour. The marketing problem of the industrial products of the metropolitan countries as well as the importance of suppressing possible rivalry also worked in the same direction.

Foreign capital not only distorted the *economic structure* of the developing countries with its investments, but within the limits of its operation it also built into it the elements of the capitalist mode of production. Furthermore, it suppressed, or at least limited to certain fields, the rise and development of the local, "national" capital and occupied the key sectors of the economy and also its most important potential sources. At the same time it put these sources into the service of its activity and made use of them in the process of profit-making.

In this way, foreign capital created, in conformity with the activity of political power, the foundations and mechanisms of *direct economic dependence* and *income drain.* It also became responsible, and in no small measure at that, for

32

socio-economic disintegration, in addition to the sectoral distortions of the economic structure.

Apart from the dispersion of the internal cohesive forces of natural communities and the eccentric effect of artificial boundaries, this disintegration and distortion manifest themselves mainly in the *dualistic structure* of the economy and society. Actually this is the result of the fact that capitalist transformation under the system of colonialism started, or was given a new direction, from outside. Its motive force was foreign capital, which, beyond the scope of its operation, was not interested in the capitalist transformation of the economy and society as a whole, and at the same time prevented by its very predominance the development of the local force (national capital) which could have been naturally interested in carrying out such a transformation.

Foreign capital, while turning part of the economy and society into a capitalist one, developed capitalist commodity production in the agricultural plantations, farms, mines, etc., and introduced new strata of wageworkers and paid employees, while it preserved the remnants of the old mode of production and the traditional society. It preserved them not only because the survival of these remnants did not clash with its own interests, did not disturb its own activity, but also because, and to the extent to which, it could make use of them in its own interests. The latter can be observed when the labour supply of the capitalist sector (plantations, mines) is based originally on the "traditional", i.e. "pre-capitalist" sector as its source, which enables the "modern",[5] more exactly the capitalist sector, to keep wages at a low level, as the "pre-capitalist" sector proves a nearly unlimited source of manpower, and also because it plays an important supplementary role in the subsistence of the families of wageworkers.

But the conservation of the old pre-capitalist elements is often and in many places the consequence of the fact that the primary interest of preserving foreign political (or only economic) rule forced the colonial power and foreign capital to enter into alliance with the leading strata of "pre-capitalist" society.[6]

The development and intensification of bilateral *trade relations* between the metropolitan countries and their colonies touched off, according to the world-market situation or, more exactly, according to the needs of the leading capitalist powers of the time, appropriate impulses in the colonial economies. These external demand and supply inducements and spontaneous market forces

[5] International literature usually prefers the terms *traditional* and *modern* sector. Since, however, "traditional" may imply reference to Rostow's first stage and, consequently, give rise to a confusing interpretation, and "modern" can be used, in the given case, only in a very relative sense, i.e. in relation to the other sector, but by no means in the sense that it means something new leading to a sound development, I find it more appropriate to distinguish between *"pre-capitalist"* and *"capitalist"* sectors, and also in the restricted sense that the former, being part of, and functioning for the latter, is no longer a real, genuine "pre-capitalist" sector.

[6] "For political reasons the great capitalist power supported the feudal elements in the underdeveloped countries as an instrument of maintaining their economic and political influence." (O. Lange: Economic Development, Planning and International Co-operation. *Booklet of the Central Bank of Egypt.*)

channelled, from the outset, economic activities and investments into a direction to which even the local investors, capitalist entrepreneurs and manufacturers, often independently of external, foreign aims and means, used to influence them, were compelled to adapt themselves. Thus, along with foreign capital, also local capital, where there was any, took an active part in the development of the one-crop economy and the branches serving it.

The process causing the distortion of the economic structure and the outward orientation of part of the economy and its isolation from the rest of the economy made headway as a *cumulative* process. While foreign capital, with its overwhelming predominance and vitality, suppressed and stifled rivalling local private capital, and while the new cumulative economic process suppressed and stifled local economic activity deviating from or countering its direction (e.g. efforts to create a national economy), there sprang up, one after the other, as appendages to foreign capital, or in the wake of the spontaneous cumulative process conforming to the activity of foreign capital, those secondary forms of domestic capital and the corresponding strata of local society (the so-called comprador capital and comprador bourgeoisie), which were directly interested in co-operation with foreign capital and in carrying on the new economic process. (In Africa it was mostly from non-European minorities – in East-Africa, e.g., from Asian immigrants – that the stratum of these middlemen evolved and fulfilled this role.)

Thus the trade relations established between the developed industrial countries and their primary-producing colonies and dependent territories increased in a cumulative way the primary-exporting character of the latter and distorted their internal economic and social structure accordingly. At the same time the expansion of a one-sided and one-way commodity production brought about a certain decline and suppression of earlier, relatively wide-ranged subsistence economy (mainly food production). Owing to this as well as to the predominance of import articles absorbing an increasing ratio of purchasing power and privileged against local products, import-sensitivity increased and the range of import needs widened.

But the more the whole economic and social structure of a dependent area adjusted itself to these trade relations and to the international division of labour embodied in them, the more it became objectively and *sponte sua* dependent, owing to both its export orientation and import-sensitivity, on the country at the opposite end of these trade relations. Thus, the political dependence as imposed by the colonial system and the "direct" economic dependence as manifested in the economic positions taken by the inflowing capital, were increasingly complemented by "indirect" dependence as materialized in the direction and structure of external trade relations. (It is justified to call it "indirect" in so far that it is based on, and becomes effective through, the distorted economic and foreign-trade structure.)

In so far and as long as these commodity relations of a one-sided and distorted structure are linked to the direct forms of dependence, and the very process of commodity relations and even the way and conditions of transacting them are under the control and pressure of foreign economic powers,[7] they provide, by the monopolistic determination of trade conditions, the possibility of an income drain supplementing the profit repatriation of working capital. This income drain is based on the monopolistic violation of the equality of exchange.

The bilateral capital and commodity flow under the system of the colonial division of labour was organically supplemented – though to a different extent in various countries – by the movement of *human resources*. This manifested itself, on the one hand, in the "precipitation" in the colonies of part of the surplus labour of developed capitalist countries, a surplus created especially in the post-war period (including, among others, small capitalists, clerks, army officers who had lost their jobs in the crises and after the wars),[8] as well as in the exportation of skilled labour, technicians, foremen and clerical personnel needed for colonial investments (not to speak of the personnel of colonial administrations and armies). On the other hand, the movement of human resources also involved to some extent cheap, unskilled and mainly unorganized (!) labour of the colonies, which were transferred to the advanced economies in a volume varying from country to country and from time to time.[9]

Due to the labour-inflow (or more exactly the influx of skilled and administrative personnel) from the metropolitan countries to the colonies, the jobs with higher salaries have been monopolized by European expatriates. At the same time, the development and expansion of the local educational system has not received any stimulation, as the supply of skilled labour was ensured from foreign sources. Thus indigenous labour force has been "frozen" into cheap, unskilled categories.

4. THE NEGATIVE EFFECTS OF CHANGES IN THE INTERNATIONAL DIVISION OF LABOUR

Changes in the system of the capitalist international division of labour as well as the disintegration of colonialism have brought about of course certain shifts in the relations outlined above. It is a peculiar feature of these changes, however, that they are accompanied, at least in several respects, by a further accumulation of the detrimental consequences of the division of labour of colonialism. This again underlines the necessity of also considering, when examining the *present* state, i. e. the "underdevelopment", of developing countries, the character and direction of the processes begun in the colonial period. This does not mean, however, that the

[7] The market conditions for a number of countries and commodities are still controlled or influenced by powerful international companies.

[8] After World War I, in 1921, the number of white settlers in Kenya rose to 10,000, in 1935–1938 to 18,000 and after World War II, in 1946, it reached 23,000.

[9] As an example we may mention the role of Arab manpower recruited for the French economy from Algeria.

cessation of colonial rule and the gaining of political independence have not brought also *radical changes,* if not in the character and direction of economic relations and processes, but at least in the *possibility* of their transformation!

The most fundamental change resulting from the disintegration of the colonial system is the *changed character of political power* and with it the disappearance of the most overt, most direct form of dependence. This does not mean of course that the more concealed forms of political or even military dependence do not survive or replace the other one in a number of countries!

When formerly it was the military-political rule that provided the basis for establishing economic dependence, now it is only a usually hidden form of political (and military) dependence that can be maintained – apart from a few gross exceptions – where and in so far as it is based on economic dependence.

The more concealed, mostly economic methods of preserving or acquiring political influence are usually called *neo-colonialism.* This term comprises not only the new methods and policies applied by the old colonial powers in their struggle for preserving their earlier spheres of interest, but – in no small measure – also the activities and policies of those "new" imperialist powers which try to gain economic and political control over the newly independent territories having gained sovereignty, making use of the weakened monopoly positions of the "old" colonialists and of those economic and social difficulties, including national, "racial", religious and tribal conflicts, which these territories have inherited from colonialism.

All this, however, would not reveal the specific *new* character of neo-colonialism. Similar methods and policies had also been applied earlier, well before the world-wide collapse of the colonial system. Examples could be cited primarily from the history of Latin American countries, which had gained formal political independence as early as one and a half centuries ago and came under the semi-colonial rule of the USA. It is true, however, that what was formerly regarded as an exception, has now become a general phenomenon, that is, instead of open military-political oppression it is *economic* dependence, and through it *indirect* political influence, that has become typical. This is primarily due to changes in *international* relations. The successes of the national liberation movements and the emergence, development and increasing international weight of the world socialist system have made it increasingly more difficult and expensive to maintain open military rule. In addition, American monopolies penetrating formerly protected territories were also interested in decolonization.

The United States aspiring to world dominance has substituted for the obsolete and ever less effective system of maintaining colonial order the idea of a *collective* defence of the so-called "free world", i.e. world capitalism, and the practice of its own role as the gendarme of the world, for which the system of formally independent but economically dependent countries, held under military-political pressure and bound by "legal" treaties, has proved or at least seemed more suitable than the too rigid and conspicuous colonial system.

36

Neo-colonialism differs from "old" colonialism not only in respect of the means applied, of preferring indirect to direct methods, but also in its *content*. Just as colonialism was the reflection and adequate manifestation of a given period of capitalist economic development and international division of labour, so neo-colonialism reflects the new features and needs of capitalist development and the changes that international division of labour has undergone. It reflects, above all, the fact that the achievements of economic, mainly industrial and technical development make it possible for the developed capitalist countries to loosen their monopolistic control over manufacturing industries in general in relation to the developing countries. Moreover, the rapid growth of their capital-goods production and their increasing marketing problems induce them to transfer certain manufacturing industries applying their technology and machinery into the developing countries. Thus, instead of the colonial pattern of division of labour between industrial centres and primary-producing peripheries, the outlines of a new, neo-colonialist pattern of division of labour are beginning to take shape. Namely, a division of labour between those few highly developed capitalist countries (or rather their multinational companies) which monopolize the centres of industrial technology and research, on the one hand, and, on the other, countries which are compelled to rely on imported new technology, only to apply but unable to develop it, and have available certain industrial enclaves, in addition to the "old" primary-producing sectors.

Though the manifestations of capital export are manifold and contradictory, the market interests (as one of these manifestations) of those metropolitan companies which are rooted in the new dynamic industries of the scientific and technical revolution, clearly suggest the "double bias" (as G. Arrighi calls it) in their foreign investments: bias for applying (relatively) capital-intensive tech-niques, whose installation, operation, replacement and expansion are based upon supplies from the centre, and bias against local sources of independent capital-goods production and technical development. To meet this double bias, a kind of "industrialization" seems to be adequate which, instead of the central links of the industry with capacities for technical progress, research and experiments, establishes in the periphery only surface elements, "enclave" branches of industry relying on imported techniques and producing import-sub-stitutive luxury goods of consumption for the local élite, or are built as spare-part producing links or assembly plants into the vertical chain of the production process of the companies themselves.

Neo-colonialism further reflects the shift which has taken place in the developing countries in the composition of foreign capital investments at the expense of the so-called settlers' capital, and in fact of the "independent" capital of smaller foreign companies also operating in the colonies, and, to an increasing extent, in favour of the capital investments of vertically integrated multinational corporations and their subsidiaries. Owing to their economic power and the threatening weight of *"collective"* imperialism backing them, the latter are much less bound to resort to the colonial measures of unconcealed political and military oppression, i.e. to *"de jure"* colonial administration than settlers' capital or the smaller foreign companies. With their industrial investments made in the developing countries aimed at creating technologically dependent industrial enclaves, these vertical monopolies pave the way for unfolding the above-mentioned new type of division of labour. They often resort to the method of making their capital investments in the form of joint ventures or even in partnership with the state.[10]

Owing to the strengthening of the forces of socialism and the successes of the national liberation movements, it is that aim of neo-colonialist policy which comes increasingly to the fore, which seeks to make use of its influence in the interest of not simply ousting other capitalist great powers but rather of *controlling the direction and course of further social development.* It is in this really new feature that the basic change in the socio-political situation of the whole world finds its reflection, a transformation of international relations which has offered socialist development to the developing world as a possible (and attractive) alternative. The prevention of this alternative, i.e. the defence of the world capitalist system, has become a high-priority central aim of neo-colonialist policy, which often compels the capitalist power – especially in the "endangered relations" – to start *collective* actions and co-operation rather than to compete with one another.

It is mainly this new content of neo-colonialism which provides the answer to the question why *aid and grants* have become such important economic methods, why the otherwise so hard-hearted capitalists are willing to make financial sacrifices and neglect – at least for some time – profit considerations if they are to "save" a country flirting with socialism and pregnant with revolution.

With this political, that is, not directly economic, or even, at least in the short run, anti-economic viewpoint becoming evident, it is possible for the developing countries to expand their manoeuvring possibilities in their external, international economic relations.

The changes in *capital movement* already mentioned have made the problem of capital supply in a number of newly independent colonial countries an acute one. In the increased orientation of capital towards the developed countries it is not only its natural attraction to the less risky and more profitable spheres of investment, or the improvement for capital of the economic and political conditions in the developed countries – in relation to the conditions of the developing countries – that finds expression.

[10] For more detail on this question see G. Arrighi: International Corporations, Labour Aristocracies and Economic Development in Tropical Africa. *The Corporations and the Cold War.* Ed. by. D. Horowitz. Mimeographed, University College, Dar es Salaam, 1967; Ann Seidman: Old Motives, New Methods: Foreign Enterprise in Africa Today. *African Perspectives.* Ed. by C. H. Allen and R. W. Johnson. Cambridge University Press, 1970, pp. 251–272; M. Kidron: *Foreign Investment in India.* Oxford University Press, 1965; I. G. Shivji: Tanzania: The Silent Class Struggle. *Cheche.* University College of Dar es Salaam, 1970; T. Szentes: *Socio-Economic Effects of Two Patterns of Foreign Capital Investments.* I. D. E. P. Seminar on the Use of Foreign Funds in Developing Countries. Dar as Salaam, April 1972.

Over and above this, a less "healthy" but nonetheless natural propensity of capital is also manifest in the re-orientation of the capital flow. It is namely its propensity to use, in the interest of the "individual" solution of the market problem, such means as lead to the further intensification of the common and general market problems. To be more concrete: the strengthening and increasing competitiveness of the monopolies of the countries integrated into the West-European Common Market, together with the customs barriers against outsiders, threatens the markets of US capital, whose counter-manoeuvre consists of the outflanking of the European customs barriers by means of direct capital investments, of buying up foreign firms, of establishing foreign subsidiaries. This step of US capital is stimulated, among other things, by the generally increasing significance of the intra-sectoral division of labour and the assertion of US technical superiority. "This kind of capital export tends to increase superprofits but, at the same time, intensifies abruptly the market problem and international competition as capital being invested in the very countries and the very industries whose competitiveness on the world market is regarded as the most effective and the most dangerous."[11]

As far as the investment climate in developing countries is concerned, the determining factor is not only, and often not even primarily, a change in the political climate, the pushing into the foreground of a radical nationalism or of socialist tendencies endangering foreign capital (or capital in general), its expropriation, nationalization for political reasons, the regulation of profit reinvestment, etc. This is of course the most direct and gravest danger to the capital investments of small foreign capital and expatriate settlers, but much less to the capital-strong international monopolies, partly because they have at their disposal a whole arsenal of retaliatory measures with which they can enforce at least financial compensation, and partly (this being the decisive factor) because they enjoy the protection and support of those capitalist countries on which the aid and loan supply of the developing countries depends.

But there is also an objective and originally *non*-political factor which constitutes a cumulatively increasing danger to foreign investors: the deteriorating balance of payments position of the country in question. The export of investment capital, owing to the concomitant profit-repatriation and the typical investment policy of this capital, is in itself one of the principal factors of the deterioration of the balance of payments of the capital-importing developing countries. In so far as investments are made in the "enclave" sector producing for export without the expansion of the production and market relations with the other sectors of the economy, including the "traditonal" rural sector, this practice will inevitably lead to such an increase in imports which regularly exceeds, i.e. overcompensates, the growth of exports by means of investments. This follows partly from the import-sensitivity of the investments themselves and the import-sensitivity of the productive units thus created. This import-sensitivity is

[11] Gy. Göncöl: On the Transformation of the Capitalist World Economy. *Studies in International Economics*. Akadémiai Kiadó, Budapest, 1966, p. 47.

especially high when capital-intensive technology is applied. It further follows from the consumption pattern of those employed in the "modern" sector, in which, for various reasons, the ratio of import goods is usually very high.

Therefore, by its effect on the balance of trade, such an investment policy exerts a detrimental influence on the balance of payments. This, together with other factors listed below, may lead to such a cumulative and acute shortage of foreign exchange that either the repayment of the grants and long-term government loans extended as some kind of remedy becomes illusory (and prejudices, in this respect, the interest of the metropolitan government also supporting the capital-exporting monopolies with its aid policy), or else the freedom to repatriate profits and capital cannot be maintained any longer without the collapse of the whole state budget and the domestic economy. Thus the risk of the expropriation of assets and nationalization without "full" compensation may increase even independently of changes in the political climate, though such economic changes are usually accompanied by political crises.

The situation has been aggravated by the abrupt increase in both international and external expenditure, due to the establishment of the machinery of the newly independent state (diplomatic representations, army, public administration, etc.), to the objectives of economic development with its plans and industrialization programmes (often oversized for political reasons), to social and cultural policy (e. g. luxurious expenditures on public education), etc. As a rule, the former colonial mechanism of money and capital supply ceased to work (which can of course also be regarded as a first step towards economic independence), causing acute financial difficulties.

Where the efforts to attain economic independence did not prove strong enough, or even came to a halt, or political independence itself remained a formal, illusory or sometimes even a neo-colonialist act only, the mechanism of money and capital supply has not changed substantially (if at all) either. A change took place here only to the extent that the increase in expenditure made it even more necessary for the developing country to draw on the old metropolitan financial resources, and that the more or less general change in the direction[12] of the interest of foreign capital became a greater inducement to grant privileges and guarantees rendered to foreign investors. Thus, an earlier form of financial and "direct" economic dependence embodied in the positions of foreign capital has been strengthened here, ensuring thereby the maintenance of the mechanism of income drain (profit-repatriation) and through it the increasing dependence on foreign financial resources.

Where, on the other hand, as a result of independence and the subsequent political changes or measures taken in economic policy to achieve economic independence, the earlier (colonial) mechanism of capital supply collapsed abruptly – especially if it coincided with the panicky flight of metropolitan private

---

[12] Not insignificant are of course the exceptions, that is, the areas of capital investments favoured earlier but invariably highly important, e. g. oil production.

capital –, the acute payments difficulties usually created such a *financial vacuum* that its filling out, that is, the elimination of the budget and balance of payments deficits, induced a number of countries to draw on other, but likewise foreign resources. If in such cases the developing country committed itself, in the interest of the rapid acquisition of these resources, to another capitalist power and succeeded, by making concessions, in winning over other groups of foreign private capital for investments in the country, then a new, neo-colonialist form of financial and "direct" economic dependence (not infrequently even a military-political dependence) usually replaced the earlier dependence.

This picture of course seems rather too pessimistic and overdrawn. Actually the disintegration of the colonial mechanism of capital supply is also a necessary precondition for progress, and the concomitant difficulties are only temporary and do not necessarily lead to the above-mentioned consequences. This is especially true if the acquisition of the new foreign capital and money resources is made less urgent by the greater volume and reasonable utilization of the domestic resources, and if the foreign resources are drawn on in a relatively wide sphere, including several capitalist countries at a time, as well as the international organizations and particularly also the socialist countries, which ensures from the outset greater bargaining possibilities and a more independent financial policy towards the capitalist powers. The increased volume and share of international donations, government loans and grants (as compared with the inflow of foreign private capital in the form of investments)[13] may doubtless mean a more favourable situation, the repression, depending on their conditions, of the direct, more open forms of dependence and income drain.

Nevertheless, the reality of the danger outlined above is convincingly demonstrated by a number of instances and also by the fact in general that the necessity of coping quickly with the financial difficulties will usually cause the country to drift into the sphere of the very country, the mightiest capitalist power, the USA, which has taken over the leading role of the former colonizing countries in world capitalist economy.

On the other hand, the pointing out of these dangers in connection with the explanation of "underdevelopment" provides exactly the evidence that the present-day problems of developing countries are direct consequences of the mechanism of the colonial division of labour and the recent changes in the world economy.

There are also changes in the structure and direction of the *flow of commodities,* of trade relations. The share of developing countries in the foreign trade of the industrially advanced capitalist countries has decreased considera-

[13] After a considerable shift in favour of the share of public versus private funds, in the pattern of total capital inflow, recently the share of private capital export has increased again, which shows a certain consolidation of the investment "climate" on neo-colonial lines in many countries and also the business-serving (defending or door-opening) character of Western aid. The share of private capital in total inflow increased again from the rather low level of 34 per cent in 1960 to 1962 to 48 per cent in 1969 to 1971. (1972 *Review*. Development Co-operation, *OECD*, 1972, p. 46.)

bly.[14] This is connected with changes that have taken place in the *structure of production* of the world economy and with the shifting of the leading role in world capitalist economy.

Significant changes have taken place in the world production of manufactured goods and raw materials – in favour of the former. Between 1928 and 1960 world trade in manufactured products achieved an annual average growth rate of 3.1 per cent, while that of the trade in primary products averaged only 2 per cent, and the increase in the trade in these commodities, without crude oil, represented only 1 per cent.[15] It is worth mentioning that the decline in the share of primary products in total world exports manifested itself in the 1960s, too. While in 1960 the shares of industrial raw materials and foodstuffs were 26.7 and 17.5 per cent, by 1969 they dropped to 20.1 and 13.5 per cent, respectively. Thus the share of raw material exporting countries in world trade is of a decreasing trend in the long run. In addition, the share of industrial countries in the world production and export of raw materials shows a rising tendency, and thus the share of raw material exporting developing countries is decreasing even within that relatively diminishing share: In the period 1950 to 1961, e.g., the share of the developed capitalist countries in the raw material export of the world rose from 47 per cent to 55 per cent, while that of developing countries fell from 41 per cent to 20 per cent. Between 1960 and 1968 the annual average value of the raw material exports of developing countries increased only by 1.4 per cent, while the developed capitalist countries were able to raise the value of their raw material exports by an annual average of 4.2 per cent.[16]

These shifts in the proportions of world production and exports have been aggravated even more by the increasing internationalization of the monopolies and the expanding productive co-operation in the advanced sector of the world economy, which rather promoted the intra-trade of the developed capitalist countries at the expense of their trade with the developing countries. This tendency is illustrated by the fact that between 1960 and 1969 the share of the intra-trade of the developed capitalist countries in total world export rose from 47 per cent to 55 per cent, and in 1969 this trade turnover increased by 17 per cent as against the 14 per cent annual average increase of world trade.[17]

The shift in the production and export shares of the world economy in favour of manufactured products, and within them in favour of industrial goods embodying more intellectual work, is an objective process, in which the general tendency of the development of productive forces and the rise in consumption demands finds

---

[14] Their share in world total exports was 31.2 per cent in 1950, which dropped to 19.1 per cent in 1966. It decreased further in the late 1960s. It was 18.6 per cent in 1968, 18.2 per cent in 1969 and 17.4 per cent in 1970. *Review of International Trade and Development*, 1967 and 1970; *UN Statistical Yearbook*, 1969 and *UN Monthly Bulletin of Statistics*, June 1971.

[15] See Prebisch Report (Towards a New Trade Policy for Development). UNCTAD Conference, New York, 1964.

[16] *Review of International Trade and Development*, UN. New York, 1970, pp. 16–17.

[17] Ibid., p. 9.

expression. The increased role and expanded production co-operation of international monopolies as well as the growing inequalities in the world economy are but manifestations of the *capitalist* framework of this process.

The so-called *"energy crisis"* and the rapid increase in 1973–74 of the world-market prices of crude oil and some other raw materials, with the concomitant "rush" (again) for raw material resources have somewhat reversed the above-outlined tendencies, but hardly for the long run and in general. The need of Western countries for compensating the increased oil-import costs may re-orientate trade and co-operation relations, while the enormous amounts of oil revenues accumulated in the hands of Arab oil-exporters have, no doubt, brought about a new factor and reshaped conditions in the centre-periphery relations of world capitalist economy. But on the whole, the economic position of the Third World has not improved, the benefits from raw material price increases have been shared by a few countries only, while the majority of developing countries, particularly those relying on heavy oil and food imports, have been facing cumulatively growing troubles of foreign trade and finance. Their economic structure continues to favour the export of primary products which, apart from a few exceptions, generally meets with increasing long-run marketing difficulties. At the same time, the development of the economy and the transformation of its structure – in addition to the defence purchases of the young states and the problems relating to the food supply of the population, etc. – raise increasing and acute import requirements. To satisfy them, additional foreign-exchange earnings are needed, which, in turn, make export an even more crucial factor, and usually lead to a forced export resulting, for lack of other export possibilities, in the oversupply of the traditional (mono-) product. Thus, owing to the structural changes in the world economy, there is a decrease, apart from a few but not insignificant exceptions[18], on the one hand, in the dependence of the former metropolitan countries on the primary commodities of the developing countries, and, on the other hand, there is an increase, as a legacy of the old structure and division of labour of the world capitalist economy, in the dependence of primary-producing countries on the principal buyers of these products.

It is true that in so far as there is real progress in the transformation of the economic structure of developing countries, all these troubles may be regarded as temporary, even though they involve not inconsiderable difficulties and dangers. On the basis of the old mechanism, and as its legacy, the commercial form of dependence will survive and in fact strengthen, just as the mechanism of income drain and losses through indirect or hidden channels in international trade will remain in operation. The opening up of new markets (e. g. in socialist countries), the conclusion of international agreements, etc., may have mitigating effects, but the final solution can only be expected from *structural* changes.

---

[18] One of the most significant exceptions is oil. Oil imports from the developing countries of the OECD member countries rose from 56.6 million tons to 167 million tons during the period 1950 to 1960. Scientific-technical progress may further increase reliance on new raw materials (e. g. uranium).

In addition, though in close connection with the internal structure and the deteriorating foreign-trade position, nutrition problems develop increasing dependence on imports and aid. This is all the more dangerous as it makes itself felt especially in relation to the United States, a country possessing huge grain surpluses.

The changes in the *movement of human resources* are not negligible either. Following independence or as a result of subsequent political changes, the *reflux* of colonial settlers, businessmen, skilled workers, technicians, professionals, doctors, teachers and administrative personnel has created an even larger vacuum[19] than the withdrawal of capital, putting in bold relief the underdevelopment of human resources and making the shortage of experts in various fields an even acuter problem. The building up of the new states and the launching of development programmes have generally increased this shortage and made it necessary to fall back, at least temporarily, on further foreign resources in this field, too.

The gradual, or occasionally abrupt withdrawal of the old colonial personnel is complemented in many countries by the flight of forced emigration of "racial" minorities.

The reflux of the ex-colonial personnel and minorities who, owing to their intermediate position, had an important part to play, has made of course the shortage of qualified personnel an even more acute problem. As a stop-gap solution appeared to be the enticement of new foreign personnel (or the "taking over" of part of the old staff) which, however, involved employment conditions equal to or even more favourable than the original ones (salaries, paid holidays, benefits, etc.), thus imposing heavy burdens on the young states. The income level of qualified manpower was determined, or at least affected, by the income brackets of the privileged colonial leading stratum of the former period and not by the actual economic possibilities of the country concerned. And since, from the point of view of easing the ever graver financial burdens, it could not and cannot be indifferent to the young states what part of the payments made to the newly recruited foreign labour is on their own account, and what part of these payments come to the country as a "grant", in the framework of technical aid, the practice tended to prevail that in the recruitment of foreign qualified personnel the candidates of the principal capitalist donor countries enjoy a certain degre of priority.[20] Thus, for instance, American experts, advisers, educators and research workers literally flood the African countries, taking over in this field, too, the positions held earlier by the British or French.

Another factor has been the increasing flow of cadres sent for higher education to the developed countries. This means their breaking away from the domestic environment for a shorter or longer period of time, their temporary or lasting alienation from their society, and not infrequently their final loss to the country.

[19] As in Guinea, following its breaking away from France.

[20] This tendency is restricted only in such countries where, and to the extent to which, a conscious struggle is carried on for political considerations against one-sided foreign influence.

The system of *foreign scholarships* paves the way for the penetration of foreign influences and habits, and threatens to increase the direct impact of the powerful foundations (Ford, Rockefeller, as well as other foundations and organizations).

It is true that all these changes may prepare the way for a transition to a more independent development and the creation of a national intelligentsia, and are thus, even with the attendant problems and difficulties, in line with progress. And since this aid is available also from several other countries, including the smaller European capitalist countries with less capital supply, and above all the socialist countries, the acute difficulties and negative effects are also easier to overcome. Yet a real danger, which has arisen as the inheritance of the earlier mechanism and as a result of its disintegration, must not be overlooked: the danger of a new type of dependence, the dependence on "technical assistance". This is becoming the more pronounced, the more its direction falls in line with that of financial and commercial dependence, the more it is one-sided and the more it is connected with the leading capitalist powers.

5. THE TWO ASPECTS OF "UNDERDEVELOPMENT" AND ITS MAIN QUALITATIVE CRITERIA

Our roughly outlined survey has made it clear that the present state of the developing countries derives basically from external factors related to the movement of world capitalist economy, and that the earlier mechanism and the division of labour of the latter resulted for the developing countries in a tendency of increasing economic dependence and income drain, which, strangely enough, has been reinforced, at least temporarily and in certain aspects, even by the recent disturbances and transformation of this mechanism. At the same time, as a result of the external factors, a peculiarly distorted and internally disintegrated economic and social structure has come into being, which in turn has become, even independently to a certain extent of the external factors, the determinant of, and the basis for, the system of external relations, of the mechanism of dependence and exploitation.

Thus there are *two aspects*, two sides of "underdevelopment": the basically external, international aspect, which, from the historical point of view of the emergence of the present state of affairs, is the primary aspect; and the internal aspect, which, historically of secondary significance, is increasingly important from the point of view of future development. A clear distinction between the two, and at the same time the awareness of their close interrelationship are of great importance for the assessment of the perspectives of development. It is self-evident that the further development of the world economy and of international politics will continue to exert a great influence on the internal life and external relations of the developing countries, but the direction and the intensity of influence will depend *to a decisive degree* on the progress of the internal changes and on the results of the transformation of the inherited structure.

The main, *qualitative* criteria and at the same time the causes of the present state of the developing countries, of the so-called "underdevelopment", leaving here out of account the quantitative differences,[21] may be summed up briefly under the following sub-headings:

1. *economic dependence* on foreign capitalist powers;

2. income losses to, or systematic income drain by foreign capitalist powers, that is, a *state of exploitation;*

3. internally disintegrated economy with a (functionally) *dualistic, distorted structure;* ·

4. heterogeneous *society of a dualistic structure.*

As we can see, the first two criteria are related to the international aspect, the system of external economic relations, while the other two affect the internal aspect, the structural features within the country. While the first two involve the problems of losses and outward orientation, the other two are concerned with the questions of the immobility of potential energies and internal tensions. While from the point of view of further development, i. e. for overcoming "underdevelopment", the first two call for changes in the world economy, for the solution of the problems of world trade and international aid, and external struggles for their attainment, for further changes in power relations and the building up of new relations, the other two necessitate an internal transformation, structural and institutional reforms.

These are the *most general* characteristics of the present state of developing countries and at the same time the main causes of that peculiar phenomenon, called "underdevelopment". These criteria and causes do not appear of course with the same intensity, nor do they assert themselves in a similar way in relation to each developing country.

Along with the general qualitative identical features, there are of course substantial differences between individual countries and even between groups of countries. Thus, there are differences not only in the size of the area of the country, the number, density and composition and growth rate of the population, the natural resources and geographical endowments, etc., but also in respect of the socio-economic indices in their strict sense, such as the developmental level of productive forces, per capita national income, degree of industrialization, the character of the key sector of the economy, the content and interrelationship of the "modern" and "traditional" sectors, the concrete class structure of society, the position of national minorities, tribes and religious groups, the cultural level, the economic, political, cultural and other ties with, and the degree of dependence on, the metropolitan country, and of course the development achieved and the direction of the politics pursued after independence, etc. In many respects, neo-colonialist policy and the investment policy of international corporations may have a differentiating effect, too.

[21] Such an abstraction can of course be justified only by the aim of providing a historical explanation of the present state and by pointing to the most general identical features, but can by no means exonerate the underestimation of quantitative differences and other secondary characteristics.

Though there is no scope for us to go into a thorough analysis of the differences, we wish to cite a few examples to demonstrate the dimensions of these divergences.

The Sudan and Zaire are among the largest countries in *Africa*. (The area of the former is 2.5 million, that of the latter 2.3 million square kilometres, the number of population, however, is only 14.8 and 17 millions, respectively.) At the same time, of the big *Asian* countries there live in India 524 million people on an area of 3.3 million square kilometres, and in Indonesia, more than 112 millions on an area of 1.9 million square kilometres. The large countries in *Latin America* take an intermediate position in respect of population between these two extremes: there are only 88 millions on 8.5 million square kilometres of Brazil, and about 24 millions on 2.8 million square kilometres of Argentine.

There are also immense differences within the continent of Africa: in contrast to a density of 6 and 7 per square kilometre in the Sudan and Zaire respectively, one of the smallest countries, Burundi, (0.03 million square kilometres) has a density of 117 per square kilometre, roughly identical with that of Rwanda, and Togo (0.06 million square kilometres) has a density of 30 per square kilometre.

In the tropical countries of Latin America per capita gross national product is, as a rule, many times over 100 dollars (the 332 dollar level of gross national product in Brazil belongs to the lowest extreme values, while the 1,000 dollar level in Venezuela represents the upper extreme). On the other hand, in a number of tropical countries in Africa and Asia per capita national product is below the annual 100 dollar average. Yet, differences between individual countries of the two continents are significant. Let us contrast two series of countries in Africa and in Asia in respect of their annual gross national product. *Africa:* Burundi 53, Rwanda 43, Upper Volta 50, Malawi 58, Ethiopia 63, Somalia 64 dollars, and Libya 1,644, Gambia 417, Zambia 325, Ivory Coast 303, Algeria 260, Ghana 238, Rhodesia 230 dollars. *Asia:* West-Irian 50, Burma 71, Laos 72, India 85, Afghanistan 85, Indonesia 97 dollars, and Singapore 700, Malaysia 384 dollars.[22] Kuwait, a country with a small area and population, would fall with its over 4,000 dollars of gross national income into a category of the most advanced industrial countries if we were to measure development or underdevelopment in terms of per capita national income only.

It is also worthwhile to compare the sizes of aggregate output per square kilometre. While in Latin America about 2,500 dollars' worth of output is realized per 1 square kilometre, it is only 930 dollars in Africa.[23]

There are also wide differences in respect to annual average growth rate. While in the 54 countries comprising 87 per cent of the "Third World" annual growth rate registered 4.5 per cent between 1960 and 1965, 18 of these 54 countries averaged 7.5 per cent, and other 15 countries achieved only an average of 2.7 per

---

[22] The data refer to 1967 or 1968. Source: *Review of International Trade and Development*, 1970. UN TD (B) 30, New York, 1970, pp. 48–50.

[23] Source: A. M. Kamarck: *The Economics of African Development*. Frederick A. Graeger, 1967, p. IX.

cent over the same period. Differences in growth rate are also substantial within Africa. With Dahomey, Mali, Upper Volta, Burundi, Chad and Madagascar registering increases in gross national product ranging from 1.4 to 2.8 per cent, other countries (e.g. Gabon and the Arab Republic of Egypt) achieve or even surpass an annual 5 per cent, and the rates of Ivory Coast, Zambia and Gambia move between 7 and 10 per cent, and that of Libya even exceeds 30 per cent.[24] During the 1960s, i.e. the whole "Development Decade", less than half the developing countries exceeded the 5 per cent target rate of growth. About one-fourth of them had a much lower growth rate in total output, which failed to keep pace even with population growth.

There are great differences in respect of the present state and the development possibilities of the economy resulting from the character of the leading sector and depending first of all on whether the still more or less characteristic primary production for exports is based on agrarian produce, or rather on mineral extraction. It is also of decisive importance which agrarian or mining sector is represented by these basic economic activities. As a rule, countries with extractive industries, especially oil- (and non-ferrous metal-) producing countries, are in a more favourable situation than the agricultural countries, while those among them which specialize in one single crop are the most disadvantaged.

Though equally characterized by the dualism of the "pre-capitalistic" sectors, the economic and social structure may be very different depending on whether this dualism itself means the duality of "tribal" rural communities and of capitalist plantations and the urban sector, as in a number of countries in Tropical Africa, or the duality of "traditional" semi-feudalism, or semi-feudal large estates, and of foreign capital controlling urban industry and commerce, as in Asia in general, or in a number of Latin American countries.

As far as the different directions of development, the differences in foreign relations and the actual measure of independence, as well as the dissimilarities in the politics pursued or chosen are concerned, it will suffice to refer to a group of countries (e.g. Tanzania, Algeria, etc.) which are making serious efforts to strengthen their economic independence and to ensure development in a socialist direction, and to such countries as South Vietnam, Thailand, which are dependencies, both economically, politically and militarily, of capitalist great powers.

Despite all these differences, however, the qualitative criteria listed above as the characteristics of "underdevelopment", are general, common and determining features typical of almost all African, Asian and Latin American countries, ex-colonies and semi-colonies, except those countries, in which the socialist transformation of the economy and society has already been carried out, or has made appreciable progress, and whose economic dependence on world capitalism

---

[24] The comparison is of a rather relative value owing to large-scale fluctuations and to the fact that the data do not always refer to the same periods of time. Therefore, they serve rather as illustrations of differences. (Source: *Review of International Trade and Development* 1970, op. cit., ibid.)

has ceased, and also those countries in which the build-up of a national capitalism with its own industrial bourgeoisie has reached a relatively high level of development (as in Japan).

Let us examine now in more detail first the content of the first two criteria (external dependence and income drain), i.e. the international aspect of "underdevelopment", and then the internal factors and mechanism of "underdevelopment".

III. THE EXTERNAL ASPECT OF THE SYSTEM OF UNDER-DEVELOPMENT: DEPENDENCE AND INCOME DRAIN

1. DEPENDENCE AND VULNERABILITY

The relations of dependence are rooted in the system of international capitalism. They came into being, or became general, on the basis of early conquests, and were built into a system when, in the last third of the 19th century, classical capitalism turned into monopoly capitalism, and the finance capital of the developed capitalist countries carved up the whole world into spheres of interest.

One-sided dependence gained its most extreme form under the colonial system, which meant complete administrative, military, legal, economic and political dependence. But along with the colonies proper and the various protectorates and trusteeship territories hardly differing from them, there came into being the merely *formally* independent semi-colonial and dependent territories.

The collapse of the colonial system brought about the disappearance of the most extreme form of dependence: legally independent and sovereign countries have come into existence in the territories liberated from the colonial yoke. But this in itself has not yet put an end to the relations of dependence. On the one hand, the economic and social structure itself, transformed according to the colonial functions, provides to a certain extent the very basis for, and the possibilities of, maintaining the relations of dependence and the above-mentioned functions, and even produces objectively new ties of dependence, while, on the other hand, the imperialist countries and their monopolies, taking advantage of these possibilities, are producing new forms and methods of reorganizing and consolidating the relations of dependence.

(a) ECONOMIC KEY POSITIONS IN FOREIGN HANDS

In the developing countries, partly as a legacy of the colonial and semi-colonial past, partly as a result of a more recent, neo-colonialist penetration, the key positions of the economy, the most important economic sectors, are held or controlled as a rule by foreign capital. This dominant role of foreign (monopoly or settlers') capital represents of course the most direct form of economic dependence.

Though in the past few years deliberate efforts have been made in several countries to break the hegemony of foreign capital and to push back foreign ownership to some extent, and the weight and role of the public sector as well as the share of national capital in the economic processes, in general, have undoubtedly grown,[1] yet foreign control over the key positions of the economy and the influencing of economic activities from outside, i. e. abroad, are still fairly general characteristics of developing countries. This is all the more so as their economic dependence is by far not fully expressed by the actual share of foreign ownership. The most direct method of dependence is complemented or substituted for by the trade, financial, foreign-exchange, "technological" and other forms of dependence.

(b) FOREIGN-TRADE SUBORDINATION AND VULNERABILITY

Developing countries play a subordinate role in international capitalist trade. Moreover, their *trading* with the developed capitalist countries makes them *extremely vulnerable,* as their external trade and through it their whole economy are very sensitive to the cyclical fluctuations of the capitalist world market and to the slightest changes in the commercial policy of capitalist powers.

The subordinate position and sensitivity of their foreign trade are partly due to the fact that foreign trade plays a disproportionately prominent role in the reproduction and accumulation processes of their "national economies", while at the same time this foreign trade is of a distorted, unhealthy structure – reflecting thereby the distorted structure of the whole economy – and of a too one-sided direction, channelled into the metropolitan country,[2] reflecting the inheritance of colonial functions and the dominant role of foreign capital in the domestic economy.

Thus Latin America exports about 30 to 40 per cent of its total commodity production, but there are countries whose export ratio reaches as much as 60 per cent. The export ratio in Saudi Arabia amounts to about 75 per cent, in Iraq to about 50 to 60 per cent, in Kuwait to 90 per cent of their national incomes.

Especially great is the importance of foreign trade in the economic life of the African countries. Exports account here for a sizeable proportion of the commodity-producing sector. This proportion is around 25 per cent of the gross national product in the average of Tropical Africa. In the larger countries of East-

---

[1] These phenomena reflect incidentally not only the results of nationalistic economic policies but in a sense and in certain countries also the shifted interests of neo-colonialism. In other words, they are not necessarily realized against the interests of international monopoly capital.

[2] Here and in the following by metropolitan countries we understand, for simplicity's sake, not only the colonizing countries but *generally* the particular developed country with which the developing country in question upholds a relationship for one-sided dependence, even if this dependence has not assumed, and did not even assume earlier a colonial form.

and Central-Africa it ranges from 20 per cent (Kenya, Uganda, Tanzania, the Sudan, Ethiopia) to 50 per cent (Mauritius, Zambia).[3]

Foreign-trade vulnerability, the excessively great role of foreign trade in the national economy, however, cannot be reduced simply to the ratio of the export-import trade to gross national product or total commodity production and investment expenditures. It is much more important to examine the role foreign trade plays, together with other factors promoting or inhibiting development, in the *dynamics* of the national economy. The fact that, e.g., the import requirements of the African economies have been increasing as a rule at a higher rate[4] – at least over the past few years – than the national product itself and the exports, clearly indicates the limitations of economic development in foreign trade as well as the internal disequilibrium of the economy as a whole.

Though the importance of foreign trade for the national economy is evidently more limited in countries with a large number of population and a large internal market, it must be taken into account that "even a very small share of foreign trade in the national income can go hand in hand with an almost complete dependence of the growth process on imports of capital goods (means of production) if the country has no engineering industry of its own".[5] And it is exactly the engineering industry which is the most backward in the developing countries.

But the disproportionately great role of foreign trade in the national economy is an unfavourable phenomenon not in itself, but only owing to the distorted structure, one-sided orientation of foreign trade and the underdevelopment and biased character of the economy as a whole.

As far as one-sided orientation, the disproportionately one-way link-up – generally with the metropolitan country – is concerned, it is obviously the consequence of the colonial heritage as well as of the predominant position of foreign capital in the main sectors of the economy.

It is self-evident that a country whose most important economic sectors are controlled by foreign capital will primarily or exclusively carry on trade with the country of this capital, i. e. the metropolitan country, will produce goods that the metropolitan country needs, and will buy such products as the firms of the metropolitan country wish to sell.

Very often even the actual transaction of foreign trade is effected or controlled by foreign monopolies, which can determine thereby the direction of foreign trade, too. But even if this case does not obtain, and if – let us assume – foreign trade is directly controlled by the state and transacted through state agencies,

---

[3] A.M. Kamarck: *op. cit.*, p. 72; R.H. Green: *African Economic Development and the World Economy: Four Essays*. Carnegie Institute in Diplomacy. CIG, 20/65.

[4] According to Green's estimation a 6 to 8 per cent rate of growth of the national income is usually accompanied by an 8 to 12 per cent growth rate of imports in Africa. (*Ibid.*)

[5] I. Sachs: *Foreign Trade and Economic Development of Underdeveloped Countries*, London 1965, p. 100.

even then there are numerous possibilities for foreign capital exercising control over the other economic key positions of the country to divert trade in the desired direction and prevent the establishment of expansion of trade relations with other countries, in other words, to maintain the country's relational trade dependence. In addition to such means as bribery, sanctions, blackmail, it can make use of the banks under its control and their credit policy in order to promote trade with the metropolitan country, or to discourage establishing new trade relations. It can ensure relational trade dependence by specializing the industrial and agricultural sectors under its control, i.e. by determining their production structure and composition according to the needs of the market of the metropolitan country. It can also ensure the maintenance of relational trade dependence by making investments and introducing the production of equipment which can only be purchased or replaced (standardized products!) from firms in the metropolitan country.

From this point of view, the recent bias in the direction and pattern of foreign capital investment in favour of certain capital-intensive branches of the light industry also plays a significant role. While favouring capital-intensive techniques, foreign capital continues to refuse the development of capital-goods industries, capital-intensive investments in the light industries necessarily result in the increasing imports of machines and equipment and also in a more intensive trade dependence on the metropolitan country.

But the metropolitan state itself has various means at its disposal to establish and maintain relational trade dependence. Among those of the highest importance are the system of preferential customs duties, financing policy (export crediting, loans and aids), and monetary relations (monetary areas).

The dependence on the foreign trade partner is particularly intensive in the case of countries where the narrowness of the domestic market is coupled with extensive one-crop exports. In general, the smaller the domestic market and the less the number and variety of export goods of a country on the one hand, and the greater the economic power of the partner country on the other, the stronger and the more dangerous will be this form of trade dependence. The resulting disadvantages and dangers are manifold: the stronger partner-country can determine – or at least influence – the conditions of exchange (its volume, price relations and points of time) according to her own interests, and can use this form of dependence in order to exert political pressure upon the dependent country when trying e.g. to influence the economic policy or even the foreign policy of the country concerned by a sort of trading blackmail. (By way of example, we might cite one of the many cases when e.g. the United States – in order to take revenge on Brazil for the contract concluded by President Quadros with several socialist countries – had recourse to open blackmail and, immediately after the conclusion of the contracts, drastically reduced the quantity of coffee, Brazil's principal export commodity, to be purchased. Between February and June 1961, the United States bought 613 thousand bags less coffee from Brazil than in the corresponding period of the previous year, buying at the same time 737 thousand bags more coffee from other countries.)[6]

Owing to this close and one-sided trade connection and dependence, the economy of the dependent country becomes sensitive to and defenceless against cyclical slumps and crises of the partner country. Moreover, the latter can shift the burden of any incidental crisis on to the dependent country. (It will suffice to remind of the effect of the recession of US economy in 1957–58 on the Latin American economies.)

As far as the *distorted structure*, the composition of *foreign trade* and the resulting trade dependence are concerned, it is obvious that the biased, distorted structure of exports in itself makes the balance of payments and the foreign-exchange position of the country concerned defenceless against the cyclical changes of the world market. If for some reason the world-market demand for the main or almost exclusive export commodities in question drops, there is no or hardly any possibility for the country affected to offset the resulting loss of her export earnings by stepping up the export of other commodities. In addition, most of these export products are usually unprocessed primary products or raw materials, and, as a rule, the same as exported by other developing countries, which affects them unfavourably from the point of view of their terms of trade.

Some economists explain the biased, one-sided structure of exports and in general the unduly high export ration simply by the narrowness of the domestic market, and attribute a natural, positive role to foreign trade which, by its income-generating effect, partly expands the domestic market and leads thereby to the liquidation of its own disproportion, and speeds up economic growth by transforming part of the potential consumption fund into a source of accumulation. No doubt, the narrowness and unfavourable pattern of the domestic market exert a negative inducement towards branches producing for the domestic market, and really justify in this respect export-orientation. It is also theoretically undebatable that foreign trade may perform a transformation function which "takes the form of an exchange of part of the potential consumption fund into the accumulation fund, by means of trading goods produced in Department II (sectors producing consumer goods) for foreign goods in Department I (sectors producing capital goods)".[7]

But as far as the assumption of this spontaneous, automatic market-expanding effect of foreign trade is concerned, this is not only refuted in practice by the decades-old experience of developing countries, but it is even in theory the result of a rather biased outlook. This is the outlook which reduces the market problem to the question of incomes (and consumption propensities) instead of recognizing

[6] P. Halatbari: A marxi újratermelési modell alkalmazása a fejlődő országok esetében (The Application of the Marxian Model of Reproduction to the Developing Countries). *Studies on Developing Countries*, No. 31, Budapest 1969, p. 23. Centre for Afro-Asian Research of the Hungarian Academy of Sciences.

[7] I. Sachs: (*loc. cit.*)

its real essence: the commodity metamorphosis built on the *division of labour in production,* the system of linkages between the productive sectors. Yet, the market-expanding effect of foreign trade depends on whether linkage effects come into being and multiply between the export sector and the other sectors of the national economy, and not only indirectly through incomes, but largely directly, through productive co-operation. And it is exactly in this respect that a peculiar mechanism can be observed in most of the developing countries, a mechanism, which – owing partly to the inherited economic (and social) structure, partly to the activity of foreign capital controlling foreign trade and the key positions of the economy – includes the reproduction of the enclave-character of the export sector. The expansion of the export sector, namely, deprives production for the domestic market of necessary resources, and the competition of import commodities keeps domestic (industrial) production under pressure. And even the distribution and spending of incomes, as well as the consumption propensities, are such that they induce a growth in import-consumption and compel the country to increase export production. Consequently, foreign trade, contrary to the market-expanding effect attributed to it, may limit the expansion of the domestic market by means of its specific structure, and may therefore exert a directly negative effect.

As regards the "transformation function",[8] its assertion is limited not only by the deterioration of the terms of trade, but, even if they improved, by other factors, too. Part of the export earnings gets lost to the national economy through profit repatriation by foreign capitalists transacting foreign trade and through other channels. And the utilization of export earnings does not usually serve the purposes of a rational economic development, but those of non-productive consumption, first of all the luxury consumption of foreigners and the local élite. This is the case even in countries where foreign trade has come under state control. But even if this transformation happens to take place, it is usually of such a character and direction that it does not *sponte sua* result in the expansion of the capital-goods producing sector (Department I). Instead, it includes the spontaneous tendency, reinforced by the conscious business policy of the international monopolies,[9] on the basis of which the maintenance of the results of the transformation makes further transformation necessary, i.e. increases export orientation and import sensitivity.

As it is evident from the foregoing, dependence on the capitalist world market has its roots deep in the very structure of the economy. That is why it is much more

[8] This means of course in the case of the developing countries not simply the use of the exports of consumer goods for the purposes of importing means of production but the conversion in general of the export earnings of raw materials (including raw materials that cannot be considered as belonging to the potential consumption fund) into buying machinery and equipment.

[9] This manifests itself in the phenomenon already referred to, i.e. that their industrial capital investments made in developing countries also aim at expanding the imports of capital goods and equipment (or restrict at least the sphere of import substitution for these products), i.e. which work against the coming into being of a genuine Department I.

difficult to abolish than relational dependence. It is even possible that the very economic measures taken to liquidate direct economic dependence and relational dependence arising partly from the latter give rise, temporarily, to increased dependence on the world market. This may be the case, e.g., when a newly independent country embarks upon the creation of a self-contained national industry and the expansion of state investments, and is consequently compelled substantially to step up machinery imports. However, to offset the growth of imports it has – at least *temporarily* – hardly any other possibility but to enforce the raw-material exports to the one-crop sector.

Thus the one-sided foreign-trade dependence of developing countries implies that the development of these countries is determined to a very great extent by foreign-trade relations, the absorbing capacity of the market of the former metropolitan countries, as well as the cyclical changes of the world economy. The domestic economy is actually rather defenceless against the detrimental effects of international trade, and so the economic growth achieved by internal efforts may be easily counteracted by external effects, sometimes as a result of conscious neo-colonial interference.

In addition to, and in connection with, taking possession of, or exercising control over, the main commodity-producing branches of the economy, and directly or indirectly influencing foreign trade, the capital of the advanced industrial countries, primarily metropolitan capital, has linked the developing countries to itself with a thousand ties of dependence also in the field of the money and credit system.

(c) FINANCIAL DEPENDENCE

The possibilities of internal accumulation in the developing countries are limited by the very size of surplus product,[10] which, owing to the unfavourable utilization of social labour, is also restricted in its absolute sense. In addition, the utilization of the potential surplus product for the expansion of production is also limited by a number of other factors. Further limiting factors are the systematic skimming of a substantial proportion of the actual surplus product by the profit and capital repatriation of foreign capital and by losses through the system of external economic relations. As a result, most of the developing countries are faced with acute capital shortage, aggravated by the increasing demands of economic development and even by the mere fact of population growth, and are trying to draw on foreign financial resources to finance their economic development

[10] Here we use the term "surplus" not simply in the Marxian sense as connected with the revealing and analysing of exploitation but in the wider sense of "economic surplus" as used by Baran. Paul Baran distinguishes "actual economic surplus" and "potential economic surplus". By the former he means the difference between actual current production and consumption, and by the latter the difference between "potential" production and "essential" (that is minimum) consumption. (The Political Economy of Growth. Prometheus, New York, 1957.)

programmes, to eliminate their budget deficits and offset their adverse balance of payments.

Though no massive aid programme (even if we disregard the difficulties arising from its implementation[11]) can solve those basic problems inherent in structural and productive relations which constitute the very roots of "underdevelopment", it is beyond doubt that the demand and real need of the developing countries themselves and the ever-widening gap between the living standards of peoples lend the question of foreign loans and aids a paramount significance in international economic and political relations.

They very fact, however, that the leading capitalist countries are making an increasing use of economic loans and grants in order to keep the developing countries in a state of dependence, is indicative of the considerable changes that have taken place in their relations with the developing countries since the emergence of the socialist countries and the disintegration of the colonial system. At the same time it also puts in bold relief the lack of equilibrium in world capitalist economy as it is now less and less possible to maintain its internal mechanism without these loans and grants.

The practice of extending loans and grants has become today the organic constituent of the mechanism of international capitalist economy, reacting with great sensitivity to the changes of this mechanism, while exercising at the same time considerable influence on the process of the world economy. In the United States the debate and voting on the aid programme, the budget appropriations for foreign aid affect not only the internal economy and the balance of international payments of the USA, as well as the economies of the recipient countries, but also, owing to their spread effects, international capitalist economy as a whole.

Loans and grants serve as a device to solve or ease temporarily the sharpening of the internal contradictions of world capitalist economy, while making the mechanism of the world economy itself more sensitive to and defenceless against fluctuations.

Loans and grants have manysided and contradictory implications both for the donor and the recipient countries, implications the non-understanding of which

---

[11] "It is a simple fact" – writes B. W. Hodder – "that the total amount of such external capital is unlikely ever to be of the scale to allow even a moderate rate of growth in developing countries." (B. W. Hodder: *Economic Development in the Tropics*. Methuen, London, 1968, p. 226.) – Hodder's view may seem a bit too pessimistic. The facts, however, are these. The sum total of average annual investments in the developing countries has been around 30,000 million dollars in the mid-1960s of which about 10,000 million has been provided from external sources. This sum of investment has been able to ensure only an average growth rate of somewhat less than 3 per cent. In order to ensure the very modest 5 per cent growth rate set for the "Development Decade" (assuming an unchanged capital-output ratio), an investment level of at least 45 to 50,000 million dollars, i. e. a 50 per cent expansion of both the internal and external resources, would have been necessary. An increase of aid by 5,000 million dollars per annum appears, however, simply impossible unless a general international disarmament is realized. (Problems of Economic Management on the Government Level in Developing Countries and the Implementation of Central Decisions.) *Studies on Developing Countries*. No. 21, Budapest, 1968, p. 209. Centre for Afro-Asian Research of the Hungarian Academy of Sciences.

may result in dangerously biased value judgements. Only the internal contradictions of loans and grants provide answers to such questions as what causes the conflict of capitalist interests even within the donor country, and why the developing countries of different, often contradictory socio-political orientation, among them those which have embarked upon the road of socialist development, are keen to receive loans and grants.

For the advanced capitalist countries the provision of loans and grants – taken in itself – undoubtedly represents a financial burden. Even if fully borne, through increased taxation, by the working population, loans and grants may detrimentally affect, owing to their limiting effect on domestic purchasing power, the interests of capitalist business circles producing for the home market. On the other hand, aid policy has become definitely advantageous and indispensable for a number of reasons.

Disregarding for the time being its political implications, the extension of loans and grants is advantageous even from the point of view of economy and business, since the resulting *expansion of commodity exports* usually has a boost effect on the economy. Even the financial sacrifice involved in extending outright donations may be compensated owing to the export-multiplier effect, that is, to the income-generating chain reaction of expanding production and employment. In addition, in so far as the expansion of exports takes place in favour of the most dynamic industries, it will further improve the position in the international division of labour of the advanced country concerned, and will make the internal division of social labour more effective by regrouping the productive forces in the interest of the most dynamic industries. And if expanded exports release the accumulated stock of certain commodities, it may prove a factor of crucial importance for staving off a threatening recession, for preventing a crisis from becoming general.

Providing aid, especially credits, is usually tied directly to the expansion of commodity exports (and thus to aggravate dependence on foreign trade).[12]

Talking on the advantages of the aid programmes, Eugen R. Black, former director of the World Bank, has pointed out that they provide significant and immediate markets for US products, stimulate the development of new overseas markets for American companies, and orientate the national economies affected towards the system of free enterprise, in which the American companies may prosper.[13]

Export crediting, which has become general practice in transacting export deals, is absolutely indispensable in the case of a significant part of exports to the developing countries. Owing to the chronic, in fact ever-increasing balance of

---

[12] In 1967, i.e., over five-sixth of Western financial aid from government resources were tied. In 1970, about 98 per cent of the assistance funds of IDA, the American aid organization, were used for purchases in the United States. (V. Rymalov: Western Aid to the Third World: Statistics and Reality. *International Affairs,* 1972, No. 4, pp. 22–23.)

[13] See H. Magdoff: Economic Aspects of US Imperialism. *Monthly Review* Vol. 18. No. 6, p. 5.

payments difficulties of most of these countries, the developed capitalist countries have been forced over the past few years to raise substantially the proportion of export crediting (from an average 50 to 60 per cent in the 1950s to the present 80 to 90 per cent). The growth in the proportion of credit-financing is to a certain extent also connected with a shift in the import structure of the developing countries in the direction of investment goods, as well as with an increased competition among the developed capitalist countries. The crediting of commodity exports serves the ousting of competitors from, and the monopolistic control over, markets and the expansion of export opportunities in general. Over and above the repayment of credits – and the advantages gained in the development of the export sectors – credits are "returned", more exactly, they yield surplus income in the form of income drain through foreign-trade channels.

The extension of loans and grants is often tied to certain *development projects* in the developing countries. The realization and operation of such projects are usually in accordance, directly or indirectly, with the capitalist interests of the donor country. The aid itself is extended in order to influence the socio-political decision on the project in favour of foreign companies. What is involved here is not merely the implementation of the project, but the direct participation and deliveries of metropolitan firms, and also the requirement that the operation of the finished project should be in harmony with the interests involved.

The investments in infrastructure (e. g. harbours, roads, railways, airports, post and communication services, urban development, etc.) do not endanger the productive investments of private capital and the export interests of the monopolies. On the contrary, they usually improve the conditions for metropolitan working capital involved, i. e. its profitability (e. g. they decrease the operating costs and the time of return), or improve the conditions for the new investments of working capital (e. g. relieving them of a number of complementary investments.) Investments in the sphere of export enclaves may be directly connected with the raw-material needs of metropolitan corporations, or may be favourable for the donor country simply because they improve the solvency of the developing country. And the financial support for setting up industrial establishments may not only be justified but also profitable for the developed capitalist country because in this way it can exert its influence upon their production profile, technical level of equipment and supply. It may prevent thereby the appearance and strengthening of competitors and ensure that the new project can be kept going only by imported machinery (or even necessary semi-manufactures). It further ensures continuous export opportunities for metropolitan companies, and in case "managerial aid" is also extended, the investment project can be run directly from the metropolitan country.

But even in the case of "discretional government loans and grants" direct economic interest, i.e. advantages accruing to the metropolitan capitalist countries from extending aid, are usually easy to trace. On the one hand, the easing of the balance of payments position itself alleviates objectively profit and

59

capital repatriation,[14] and, on the other, the developing countries are compelled, at least "morally", to provide, in return for the loans and grants received, guarantees and certain benefits to the metropolitan capital and staff, and to create a "favourable investment climate" for foreign capital.[15] These guarantees cover e. g. the freedom for foreign companies to operate, free repatriation of capital and profits, guarantees against expropriation and/or full indemnity in the case of nationalization, various tax and customs exemptions, free income transfer for foreign investors and the staff of technical assistance.

Last but not least, the *political* considerations of aid cannot fully be separated from economic interests either. The political considerations of aid have increasingly come into prominence lately as evidenced, among other things, by the preference given to politically important "key countries" as against those which would perhaps be in a greater need of aid.[16] But political considerations are given increased attention in the distribution of aid not only in space but also in time, in that not only the politically endangered "posts" but also "points of time" deemed to be dangerous seem to attract of course not only safety-conscious private capital, but the government aids of the great power willing even to take risks in the defence of capitalist interests. Putting pressure on the political leadership and decisions, on the socio-economic conception and development strategy as well as on external socio-political orientation serves not simply the aim of curbing the spread of socialism, but represents at the same time the direct defence of the sphere of operation of capital, i. e. the safeguarding of capitalist economic interests.

Looking at capitalist loans and grants from the angle of the recipient countries, we are faced, on the one hand, with the fact of their actual dependence on and real need of them, and, on the other, with inherent disadvantages and dangers.

We can of course regard the utilization of external financial resources by no means as an absolute and general condition for the economic development of

[14] "... these financial flows, other than for military purposes, are, for the most part, a dependent factor, i. e. it is likely that they are determined by the flows of direct private investment. In the first place, this financial assistance is more and more made available on the basis of the "economic viability" of the projects which it is supposed to support. This, in general, means that the private capital must be forthcoming to make use of the overhead capital financed by public capital. In the second place, a large proportion of bilateral assistance aims at easing the balance of payments position of Tropical-African economies in order to make possible either the importation of capital goods or the repatriation of profits and capital." (G. Arrighi: *op. cit.*, p. 28.)

[15] M. Strong, President of the Canadian Aid Programme Agency (CIDA), quite openly declared at the OECD Seminar in Dar es Salaam that the large-scale capital flow from the rich to the poor countries made it necessary for the latter to pursue a *policy stimulating private investments.* (Mimeographed abstract of his paper. – *Author's italics.*)

[16] As the average for the period 1965 to 1968, the aggregate amount of per capita loans, export credits and aid for Laos, amounting to 72 dollars of per capita gross national product in 1958, was 24.37 dollars, while the corresponding figures for Rwanda, Upper Volta and Burundi were 3.92, 3.82 and 2.88 dollars respectively, though their per capita gross national incomes are the same as or even lower than those of Laos. (Source: *Review of International Trade and Development* 1970, *UNCTAD*, TD/B/30: New York, 1970, pp. 51–61.)

each developing country. Such a proposition would imply the tacit assumption that the present internal and international structures or mechanisms hindering the expansion of internal accumulation remained unchanged in the long run. It is a historically[17] and logically[18] demonstrated fact that it is never the bottleneck of financial resources, i.e. capital shortage, but the social limitations of production and of the growth of productive forces that constitute the basic impediments to development.

But it is also true that *the earliest possible* bridging of the international gap and the urgent solution of the nutrition problem actually make it imperative to draw on foreign aid, and the transformation processes expanding accumulation of internal structures can also develop at a higher rate if external resources are also made a temporary use of.

Owing to the structure of the developing economy, the conversion of internal accumulation into productive investments – as well as the transformation of the structure itself – presupposes in no small measure (in the majority of developing countries to a much greater extent than it did in the case of the socialist countries of Eastern Europe) the "transformation function" of foreign trade, i.e. the import of machinery and equipment. And such imports – owing to the slower rate of return – usually necessitate crediting and the supply of loans.

On the other hand, with export earnings declining in absolute, or only in relative terms, and with the balance of payments lacking other significant sources of income, the financing of the growing imports also make it necessary to rely on external resources if internal accumulation is making rapid progress. In this way, reliance on loans and grants may make it possible to bridge, if only temporarily, acute difficulties. Depending on its conditions and the way of utilizing it, foreign aid may be beneficial to the recipient economy in other respects, too, namely be promoting the earliest possible realization of important projects, the expansion of employment, the improvement of the sanitary and socio-cultural situation of the recipient country.

The dangers and disadvantages resulting from capitalist loans and grants follow obviously from the above-mentioned advantages and considerations that govern the policy of developed capitalist countries.

It is self-evident that any country that bases the financing of its economic development programme primarily on foreign resources and is able to maintain the temporary balance of the state budget only by foreign aid, and make good the recurrent deficit of its foreign-trade balance only by foreign loans, will be left to the mercy of the countries supplying grants and loans. This holds the more true, the more one single capitalist country monopolizes the role of creditor.

By stopping these credits and freezing the amounts earmarked for aid, the creditor country may cause unexpected difficulties in the debtor country, may

---

[17] See the history of Soviet industrialization or the example of the socialist countries starting reconstruction and industrialization after World War II without foreign capital.

[18] That is, by means of the labour theory of value.

hinder the implementation of its development programme, and can use all these methods, according to its purposes, for economic, political or military blackmail. When supporting the budget of the debtor country and undertaking the financing of its economic development programme or covering the deficit of its foreign trade, the donor-creditor country will usually claim the right to interfere to a considerable extent in the fiscal policy, the elaboration of the development plan and the foreign trade policy of that country. Thus, what is involved here is not merely the fact that the implementation of the budget estimates and the fulfilment of the targets of the development plan depend to a great extent on the financial support of the creditor country, but also the fact that the fiscal policy and the development plan themselves have to be adjusted to its interests. Consequently, financial dependence is one of the most serious obstacles to an economic policy aimed at the fulfilment of national interests.

In addition, dependence on foreign financial resources has a *self-reinforcing, cumulative* tendency,[19] which is connected partly with the credit and aid policy and practice of the leading capitalist countries, partly with the concrete credit conditions themselves.

Before discussing the latter, let us briefly survey some data on the volume and structure of aid.

The volume of these aids, i. e. of the external financial resources available to the developing countries, shows an abrupt growth in the second half of the 1950s and increased about two-and-half-fold within a single decade, which is largely due to an increasing number of African countries gaining independence. In the period 1950 to 1955 the total amount of credits, grants and private capital influx averaged an annual $ 3,500 million, while in 1965 it amounted already to $ 10,000 million. But in the second half of the 1960s this tendency of growth slowed down. In the early 1970s the total annual inflow of all foreign funds (loans, credits, grants, investment capital, donations, etc.) was only around 18,000 million US dollars, while the total outflow of income (in the form of repatriations, losses and payments) far exceeded $ 20,000 million a year.

Over 70 per cent of all loans and grants flowing from the developed capitalist countries to the developing countries originate from the three "big": the USA, Great Britain and France. The USA, representing more than 50 per cent of the combined gross national product of the OECD countries, accounts for about 50 per cent of all capitalist loans and grants. In the second half of the 1960s, it uas exactly these three countries whose assistance activities did not further develop. The amounts provided by them in 1968 remained essentially the same as in 1963,

---

[19] "Recent years have witnessed, on the one hand, an increase in the proportion of exports which developing countries have to set aside for this servicing of external debts, and, on the other hand, a hardening of the terms on which further loans are obtained: the proportion rose from less than 4 per cent in the mid-1950s to 9 per cent in 1965." (Report by the Secretary-General of UNCTAD. New York, 1968.) During the 1960s the debt service of the developing countries rose by about 9 per cent, while the average growth of their export earnings was only 7.5 per cent. (1972 Review, Development Co-operation, *OECD,* 1972, p. 71).

and the contribution of the USA even declined in absolute terms. (The USA makes available to the developing countries loans and grants corresponding to only 0.65 per cent of its gross national product, and even that is mainly military aid.[20])

The stagnation or decline in providing financial assistance in the case of all three countries is primarily connected with the deterioration of their own balance of payments position. Therefore, it is in the first place aid in the strict sense of the term, i. e. assistance extended from government funds that experiences a decline. The share of government assistance in all financial resources made available fell to 50 per cent. This is partly connected with certain changes that have taken place in US foreign aid policy (Public Law 480, Foreign Aid Program, etc.) as a result of an economy drive, and partly with a certain renewal of the interest of private capital in "Third World" investments.

Prior to these recent changes, setbacks and shifts, it was the growth in the ratio of exactly these government credits and grants (primarily those of the USA) that was characteristic of the *structure* of external assistance and capital flow.

The volume of commercial credits and long-term direct investments from private sources dropped significantly after 1957, and has begun to rise again only since 1965. In 1957 about half the capital flow to the developing countries derived from private sources. Between 1960 and 1965 it was less than one-third. It is obvious that in the early 1960s it was the uncertain political (and economic) situation resulting from a number of countries gaining independence that detained private capital from making new investments, while it was the very same factor that made the capitalist governments (especially those of the United States of America and the two main colonial powers, Great Britain and France) provide increased assistance of a mainly political nature. Then in the second half of the 1960s partly the confidence of private capital towards several countries was restored, partly, and mainly, the three great powers adopted the new policy of decreasing the burden of assistance and distributing it more evenly among all capitalist countries (together with or within the international organizations, too), in order to ease their own budget and balance of payments difficulties.

The flow of assistance from the rest of the capitalist countries is increasing, which is partly due to their competitive struggle for strengthening their own positions – and this applies mainly to Japan and West Germany –, and partly to the "mediating" role the smaller capitalist states play. Especially characteristic of this "mediating" role is the case of *Canada,* which between 1964 and 1969 raised the sum of its development assistance from $ 65 million to almost $ 340 million, while 90 cents in each Canadian aid dollar is of American origin! Similar motives can also be detected in the aid policy of the governments of Sweden, Denmark, Norway, etc., with certain moral motives: to help poor peoples, and with a sense

[20] Source of data: *The Outlook for Aid*. A speech made by E. Martin, Chairman of the OECD Assistance Committee, at the OECD Seminar in Dar es Salaam. Mimeographed. January 1970.

of international responsibility also, under democratic pressure, playing some role in it.

As regards the concrete credit conditions, the credit policy of the leading capitalist countries was until recently very unfavourable for the developing countries. Incidentally, long-term credits were generally provided on usual commercial terms, with maturities ranging at most from 10 to 12 years, at interest rates of 4 to 6 per cent, and repayable in hard currency.

In the case of developing countries this time-limit of repayment is usually short as perspective planning calculates already with a period of 15 to 20 years, and this is necessary, too, because of the long gestation period of big investment projects and the immense task of implementing their industrialization programmes and the reorganization of agriculture. And if the bulk of credits is extended for less than 10 to 15 years, the obligation to repay them imposes heavy burdens on the recipient countries long before the results of the economic development started by means of these credits could be apparent.

In this case they can often fulfil their repayment obligations only by raising new loans. They may be compelled to do so also by the high interest rates charged by the developed capitalist countries and by the obligation imposed on them of repaying the credit together with their service charges in the same hard currency in which they received the loan.

But in the terms of loans and credits certain improvements were experienced in the 1960s. This manifested itself first of all in the longer maturity of credits, more exactly, in a shift in the composition of credits towards long-term credits, but also in other conditions of repayment. While, e. g., in 1959 and 1960 credits with more than 10 years of maturity accounted for hardly 10 to 15 per cent of all external assistance, over two-thirds of all credits were of more than 10 years of maturity in the period 1961 to 1963, and the share of total government loans was 80 per cent. The period of grace, that is the time between disbursement and the first instalment of repayment, also became longer, rising from an average of 3 years to 6, or even 10 years in the case of loans made to international institutions. The rate of interest dropped, at least in the case of certain forms of credits. The average rate for medium- and long-term credit was 6 per cent in the period 1955 to 1960, while in 1962 and 1963 some 40 per cent of all loans by the OECD countries were given at a rate of interest lower than 3 per cent. Furthermore, the number of credits repayable in local currency also increased.[21]

The improvement in credit terms was obviously connected partly with competition among the developed capitalist countries themselves (which is apparent mainly in the extension of commodity credits), and partly, and mainly with the pressure which made itself felt in the increasing dissatisfaction of the newly independent countries with credit conditions, and became apparent in the form of demands (see e. g. the UNCTAD Conferences), further strengthened by

[21] Source: Problems of Economic Management ... *Studies on Developing Countries*, No. 21, *op. cit.*, pp. 196–199. (See Footnote 11.)

64

the credit policy of the socialist countries and their participation in foreign aid programmes.[22]

In spite of all these developments there is *no fundamental* change in credit terms. Moreover, in the 1970s, owing to the accelerating inflation and aggravating monetary problems of the main donor countries, a certain worsening of the credit terms could be observed again. As a result of the accumulation of previous credit and interest charges, of the worsening of their foreign-trade position, as well as the growing share of foreign property through re-investment and new investments, the financial position of most of the developing countries is deteriorating and their financial dependence is increasing to such an extent that they are threatened by a cumulative process of indebtedness.

While in 1962 the total debt of developing countries amounted to 24,000 million US dollars, with an annual debt service of less than 3,000 million, by the end of 1971 the total public debt of 80 developing countries was around 74,000 million dollars, with the total debt-service payments reaching 7,000 million. At the beginning of 1973, the total indebtedness of "Third World" countries exceeded 80,000 million dollars, which is almost equal to one-fourth of their GDP. According to conservative UNCTAD estimates, the total indebtedness of developing countries may exceed 150,000 million dollars by 1980, with an annual debt-service charge of more than 15,000 million. While the average annual growth rate of the export earnings of developing countries was only 7.5 per cent between 1960 and 1970, that of indebtedness reached 14 per cent.

This *increasing indebtedness* of developing countries is favourable in some respects for the leading capitalist countries in that they are able to reduce the former to a more and more dependent position, which falls completely into line with their neo-colonialist endeavours. Beyond a certain point, however, this cumulative process makes repayment itself illusory, and this intolerable situation also involves economic (e.g. expropriation of foreign capital) and political

[22] The great advantage of credits and grants provided by the socialist countries is that repayment is usually made at a low, generally 2 to 2.5 per cent rate of interest, and in most cases either in *national currency*, or mainly by *deliveries* by the recipient country, though the use of credits is, as a rule, tied, for foreign exchange reasons, to deliveries and services by the creditor country. Thus, the shortage of convertible ("hard") currency is not increased. And repayment by exports usually opens up external market possibilities for industrial establishments built with foreign assistance, which is not only of special importance in the years of running-in of the newly commissioned plants – owing to the narrowness of the internal market – but also because otherwise marketing would hardly be possible at all in view of external competitors in the world market. The direction of the utilization of credits and grants is also such that – instead of expanding one-crop economy and of promoting infrastructural investments in favour of foreign capital – they serve industrial development, usually the creation of basic industries. In the 1960s, 35 per cent of credits were used e.g. for building power plants, metallurgical works and opening new mines, and 25 per cent were devoted to developing the chemical and building industries. Source of data: M. Balogh, A. Inotai, K. Iványi, S. Surányi and M. Szilágyi: A Szovjetunió segítsége a fejlődő országok számára (Assistance of the Soviet Union to the Developing Countries). *Studies on Developing Countries*. No. 17, Budapest 1968, p. 8. Centre for Afro-Asian Research of the Hungarian Academy of Sciences.

dangers, which may cause the donor countries to write off part of the credits extended.

It is mainly the danger of such risks and of course the already mentioned intention of eliminating competition among themselves, together with the endeavour to conceal their neo-colonialist aspirations, that compel the leading capitalist countries to make loans and grants available to developing countries through various *international organizations*.[23] Of these organizations (Colombo Plan, Technical Assistance Programmes of the OAS, EEC Development Fund, the affiliates of the UNO: IBRD, IFC, IDA, UNICEF, EFTA, UN Special Fund, etc.) it is especially the World Bank (IBRD) and its two subsidiaries, the International Finance Corporation and the International Development Association (IDA), which are of great importance.

The financial dependence of the developing countries on loans and grants provided to them by the leading capitalist countries and the international organizations controlled by the latter, is determined of course not only by the size of these amounts, the credit conditions and the political and economic strings attached to them. To the extent that the *internal* sources of accumulation increase, that the role of the state in guiding the economy and controlling international finance grows, that the independent state-capitalistic sector is consolidated in the developing countries, and that the external sources of loans and grants expand (in no small measure by the aid from the socialist countries and also by the mutual assistance of the developing countries), the intensity of this form of financial dependence may diminish, even if the flow of foreign loans and grants from the leading capitalist countries increases either in absolute terms or in relation to the size of the state budget. Thus, in spite of the fact that this form of financial dependence is becoming an increasingly important form of the economic dependence of developing countries and the principal means of neo-colonialism, this form itself may lose much of its intensity and one-sidedness according to how the *internal* growth of the developing countries makes advance, and how the shifts in the power relations in the *world economy* and world politics develop.

Thus it is evident that dependence on foreign loans and grants is primarily effective in countries with little economic power and internal accumulation potentials, but with a significant budgetary expenditure. Most of the countries of Tropical Africa belong to this category.

[23] Incidentally, it is in the interest of the developing countries, too, that they should, if possible, receive assistance from international organizations (UN agencies) which do not bring them into a one-sided dependence on individual imperialist countries and in whose activities they themselves as well as the socialist countries can also have a say. But today several UN institutions do not meet yet this requirement. Despite the increasing role of multilateral institutions, about 90 per cent of all financial resources are available on a bilateral basis.

The distribution of the world's intellectual resources and of the institutions serving their utilization is even more unfavourable than that of the material resources for the developing countries. The gap between the development levels of the educational network is much wider than that between per capita incomes.[24] And as to the scientific capacities, more than 90 per cent of them is concentrated in 30 countries, while it is common knowledge today that the development of human resources, the availability of well-trained manpower and research apparatus play an extremely important role in economic growth.

The dependence of developing countries on the technical assistance of more developed countries, that is their "technical dependence", is therefore even greater than their financial dependence.

By "technical dependence" we actually mean dependence on "intellectual imports", whether in their *materialized* form (as the import of technology, standardization systems, patents and licences or the results of scientific and technical research), or in its *"live"* form (as the import of experts, advisers, teachers, or the sending to developed countries of students on foreign scholarships). The developed capitalist countries and their monopolies are also trying to tie to themselves the countries in their spheres of interest "technologically" and "intellectually". This endeavour of theirs undoubtedly coincides with the actual needs of the developing countries for "technical" assistance. And just as capital supply, that is long-term credits and grants, is a two-faced phenomenon, being built, on the one hand, on a *real* need for capital and as such it may have, subject to appropriate conditions, a *positive* effect, and, on the other hand, being accompanied, as we have seen, by *dangers and negative consequences*, in the same way "technical assistance" also has, often to a greater extent, a mixed character, and may either promote or hinder development.

This specific form of dependence has come to the fore quite recently, following the effort of developing countries in industrialization and public education, etc., and owing to the technical assistance of the developed capitalist countries and the industrial investment policy of international monopolies.

This does not mean of course that the transfer of technology and qualified personnel to the developing countries was not determined by the metropolitan countries and their monopolies even long before.[25] While previously, however, this dependence manifested itself in the general retardation of industrial

---

[24] See on this question – among others – the computations made by F. Harbison and Ch. A. Myers: *Education, Manpower and Economic Growth.* New York, 1964.

[25] "During the course of the historical development of the capitalist system" – writes A. G. Frank – "the developed countries have always diffused out to their satellite colonial dependencies the technology whose employment in the colonial and now underdeveloped countries has served the interests of the metropolis; and the metropolis has always suppressed the technology in the now underdeveloped countries which conflicted with the interests of the metropolis." (A. G. Frank: *op. cit.,* p. 52.)

development and technical education, and thus it could by no means assume – at least in industry – the form of technical assistance, today it appears that the metropolitan countries have somewhat relinquished their monopoly in industrial production and technology, as well as in technical education, and are ready to support, to a certain degree, industrialization in the developing countries by promoting technical education and sharing with them their own technology. What is really involved here – among other factors –, however, is the fact that on the one hand, the foreign firms taking part in "industrialization" or selling technology gain enormous profits from this activity, and, on the other, the industrial countries have a strong monopoly position in the developing countries in heavy industry today, which makes it not only possible but even necessary for them to give up their monopoly in manufacturing industry because of the adequate expansion of the market of capital-goods production.[26] Moreover, we are witnessing today the emergence of a sort of monopoly which is the more dangerous, the more concentrated it is,[27] namely the monopoly in electronics, automation, cybernetics and, to an ever greater extent, in the scientific and research capacities in general of the capitalist world. (As, however, the process of scientific and technological revolution is also making progress in the socialist world, the scope of the above-mentioned monopoly has been limited to a certain extent even in relation to the developing countries.)

For their industrial development the developing countries need patents and licences, blueprints, standards, technological specifications, equipment and their component parts, special raw materials and, last but not least, specialists (engineers, geologists, economists, etc.) and teaching staffs. When the metropolitan capitalist countries grant these countries "technical assistance", they see to it that it is done in such a way that the exploitation of the patents and licences, blueprints, standards and technological specifications, etc., provided and the smooth operation of plants installed by them, and the working and repairing of the machinery and equipment are dependent exclusively on deliveries by the metropolitan companies. They also take care that the production of new plants does not embrace the whole cycle of manufacturing and thus the component parts, standard equipment, motors and machines can be supplied by metropolitan firms only. They arrange things so that the management of production and technological leadership should be concentrated in the hands of specialists sent from the metropolitan country, or should be transferred to local cadres trained in the metropolitan country.

[26] This change is reflected to a considerable extent in the investment policy of the multinational corporations in developing countries. Though the application of capital-intensive technology is also connected with other factors, but determinant is the shift referred to above.

[27] This monopoly, on account of the economies of large-scale capital supply and accumulated scientific capacities, is more and more concentrated in the USA. This is the prophecy of the *Newsweek:* "European industries will function more and more under foreign licensing agreements; they will become subsidiaries of US parent companies, which will sell them their know-how and manage Europe's production... Research costs are too high. The transatlantic technological gap is a fact of life." (Quoted by A. G. Frank: *op. cit.,* p. 52.)

While formerly the nearly complete blockade of industrial development impeded from the very outset the development of education in general and technical education in particular, now this kind of industrialization, with the basic national sectors (e. g. the capital-goods producing sector) lacking, and relying on imported capital-intensive technology, retards the "learning process" of the broad masses of population. "In addition, even in the state-owned enterprises, it considerably limits the range of experiences that can be undergone in the periphery, as the crucial economic and technical decisions are made in the industrial countries."[28] That is, among other things, how the materialized forms of "intellectual import", i. e. the import of technology, is connected with the demand for "live intellectual import", i. e. the import of specialists, teachers, etc.

Very often the new plants built in developing countries perform only the production of the component parts of the main product manufactured in the metropolitan country, or the assembly of parts supplied from the metropolitan country. They are virtually nothing but subsidiary units of the metropolitan firm, only appendages, not independent industrial plants. Such co-operation is one of the most suitable means of tax and customs evasion. Since, however, foreign capital establishes such plants manufacturing for the narrow domestic market and often protected with high tariff walls and other government subsidies (e. g. tax reduction) with the same profile in several neighbouring countries, it often also impedes the integration of these economies.[29]

These production relations between metropolitan countries and the newly established local enterprises – an unnatural and economically hardly justifiable form of co-operation – in addition to the leading role of specialists from the metropolitan country, show that production in certain industrial branches, or most important industrial plants, can, depending on foreign interests, be paralysed overnight. This may have serious consequences for employment, the meeting of export commitments, the fulfilment of envisaged plan targets, the satisfaction of the production needs of their branches, etc. With the unexpected withdrawal of specialists immense difficulties may be caused in economic management or in any other fields of life.

Through these productive linkages the monopolies of the metropolitan countries can control the development of individual industries of developing countries, and the experts and advisers made available to them in the framework of techncial assistance can play a decisive role in determining the direction and spirit of economic policy, public education, etc.

The direction and spirit of public education are of special interest for the economic, social and political development of these countries. The assertion of the demonstration effect via education may result, through increased salary claims, a changed way of living and consumption propensities, etc., in serious tensions, of which we shall have to say more later on. And since the development

[28] G. Arrighi: *op. cit.*, p. 33.
[29] For such and other implications of this sort of "industrialization", see the author's study: *op. cit.*

of education in these countries is characterized not by a proportionate widening and increase of the pyramid of public education but, as in industrial development, by some spectacular establishments of superstructure without an adequate basis and intermediate elements, the danger of alienation of highly qualified cadres from local society is accordingly greater. All this exerts a negative effect on the cohesive forces of society. It is hardly surprising then that the cadres trained in the framework of technical assistance often also become "physically" alienated from their own society and, yielding to the temptation of better living conditions and a different way of life, and perhaps as a result of marriage, they prefer to settle down in the advanced country ("brain-drain").

The danger of emigration is the greatest in the case of the professionally most talented and best qualified people as it is easier for them to find rewarding jobs in the developed countries, where the possibilities of further development (research institutes, experimental laboratories, scientific societies and the atmosphere of scientific life in general, etc.) represent greater attraction for them. Such "brain-drain", that is the skimming of human resources, constitutes a much greater loss than the number of emigrant specialists or the cost of their training would suggest. Actually, the qualitative loss cannot be expressed in terms of figures, even less can it be determined what direct and mainly indirect spread effect would have resulted from their operation in their country, and to what extent they would have eased this form of dependence and the attendant dangers, among them the danger of emigration.

But even if no actual emigration takes place, the cadres settling down after their education abroad often get alienated in their ways of thinking and habits, that is, they become "intellectual emigrants". They find it usually hard to readjust themselves to their native environment and often take their wives from abroad. They tend to orientate themselves toward the "European" world of cities or university campuses, and wish by no means to return to their earlier rural environment. Even so, owing to their experiences and knowledge, they might be the vanguards of enlightenment against traditional superstition, and of the new technology and organization, the transformation of the obsolete order in general. But in many cases they look upon their environment with a passive dissatisfaction, or even regard the scene of their studies abroad uncritically as a model country. The greater the contrast between the living standards enjoyed abroad and at home, the greater the danger of alienation.

2. INCOME DRAIN AND LOSSES

Another, similarly basic impediment to the economic development of "Third World" countries is income drain, that is, the systematic appropriation of a significant part of the national income and the sources of accumulation, as well as those disadvantages and losses sustained by them in international economic

70

relations which are connected partly with the above-discussed economic dependence and partly with the distortion of their economic and social structure.

Formerly, the fact of these income losses was revealed by Marxist literature only, while bourgeois economics was either silent about the exploitation of the developing countries, or simply denied it, branding it as Marxist propaganda. Nowadays the reader need not turn to Marxist authors to get information on the fact of exploitation. The official publications of the United Nations Organization and the writings of a host of non-Marxist authors deal with the income losses sustained by the developing countries in their systems of relations with the metropolitan capitalist countries.

These income losses have a large number of forms and "channels". Some of them are rather apparent and directly observable, manifest themselves in a more or less open way. Others are more concealed, or assert themselves indirectly, through various transmissions.

The transfer, the so-called repatriation into the metropolitan country of profits, dividends, interests on loan capital, capital reinvested and reproduced many times over, as well as of personal incomes and fortunes gained in the developing country (disregarding here the accounting manoeuvres and illegal actions) usually take place overtly, and are therefore statistically more or less accessible. And not only the fact of losses is obvious but also their direction, i.e. the countries benefiting from them at the other end.

The losses arising from changes in world-market price proportions can be defined much less unambiguously, in that, among other things, they also depend on the choice of the base year, the basis for comparison and also on shifts in the export and import structures. Therefore, owing to the intricate transmissions of world trade, the actual beneficiary countries are also difficult to identify.

The disadvantages and losses, which arise from the uneven international distribution of activities and from sectors of different types and efficiency from the point of view of the dynamics of economic development manifesting themselves mainly in the limitations of further income-generating effects and in the lack of positive chain reactions, can no longer be measured statistically, and can only be pointed out by an abstract analysis and logical conclusions. Though the secondary and spread effects, the so-called linkage effects, are already dealt with by a rich literature today, and though it is almost a commonplace to say that, from the point of view of economic development, the activities and sectors with the largest number of linkages and of a great many directions are the most important, yet nobody can undertake to determine quantitatively how much *indirect* income increment a country is deprived of which has not got its own engineering and instruments industry providing the basis for technical development, education and research, and giving rise to a host of demand and supply inductions of several directions.

Concealed income drains and indirect losses certainly have many varieties, which for the time being are not or hardly known to us, and will perhaps be revealed, if at all, only by future research. A thorough analysis of these losses and disadvantages is of extraordinary importance for the economic policy of developing countries.

(a) PROFIT REPATRIATION

It follows from the very nature of capital that the aim and function of capital export to the developing countries is profit-making. But profit repatriation is not only, and not primarily, the direct result of repeated capital export, but also of the operation of capital increased by reinvestment, or more exactly, the result of capital increment achieved in the developing country. On the other hand, owing to the very fact of reinvestment, the actual loss manifests itself not only in the volume of repatriated profit but also in the local increase of foreign capital. The accumulation resulting from the utilization of local manpower and natural resources does not constitute part of actual national accumulation but an element of the indebtedness of the country to foreign capital. This becomes evident and appears on the list of measurable losses when foreign capital, together with its increment achieved *in situ*, leaves the country, that is, when the national government has to pay compensation for the capital expropriated. (Of course, not only capital increment but the "original" capital itself, too, owing to its multiple reproduction, is in fact a local production, the product of the labour of the developing country.)

The significance of reinvestment in strengthening the position of foreign capital and in profit-making is much greater than generally assumed. Current capital interests can be regarded as the result of new capital investments. For example in the period 1870 to 1913, when total British investments abroad inreased from about 1,000 million to almost 4,000 million pound sterling, the total amount of *new* investments hardly accounted for 40 per cent of the income from past investments. And in the case of Brazil, about 50 per cent of direct US investments derived from the reinvestment of profits.[30]

The degree of exploitation by foreign capital is the highest in countries where the economic positions of foreign capital are the strongest, and its operative freedom is the greatest, that is, where direct economic dependence is the most intensive.

Foreign monopolies usually transfer by far more profits and dividends from the developing countries than the capital they export to them. According to official data, *British* monopolies made in the period 1952 to 1963 a profit of about 7,600 million pounds sterling from their investments in developing countries, which was about two and a half times the amount of capital exported there over the same period. Between 1950 and 1965, profit repatriation by *American* companies from

[30] I. Sachs: *op. cit.*

72

developing countries amounted to 25,600 million US dollars, while American capital export to the developing countries was only 9,000 million dollars.[31]

According to the data of GATT,[32] in 1956, 1957 and 1958 foreign capital investors repatriated about 2,500 million dollars annually. This sum seems not only to have risen since that time, but it was certainly underestimated, too, in the past. According to the data of UNCTAD,[33] in 1967 the developing countries paid 5,800 million dollars to foreign investors as the yield of their investments (together with 8,000 million dollars as amortization). Of the former amount 73 per cent was made up of profits and dividends. Incidentally, in the period 1963 to 1967 the income of foreign investors increased by an annual average of 12 per cent.

By the end of the 1960s, the total outflow of investment incomes from the developing countries had exceeded 6,000 million dollars, and in the early 1970s it was around 8,000 million. The average profit rate of e.g. American mining companies in the developing countries exceeded 19 per cent and that of oil companies 27 per cent in 1969. According to official US data, the profits of US companies in developing countries reached more than 3,700 million dollars in the same year. From one single country, Peru e.g., the mining companies repatriated 790 million dollars in profits in the period 1950 to 1970 (of which 699 million during the 1960s), while their total investments in Peruvian subsidiaries were less than 290 million in the same period.[34]

Along with direct, mostly inconcealed income drains (profit and interest repatriation), a whole system of *indirect* income drain effected through foreign-trade of financial-monetary relations has been built up in world capitalist economy. These drains, owing to their "natural" character adjusting itself to the movement of the world economy (disregarding a few exceptions as marginal cases), appear in a "depersonalized" form, which means that, contrary to the transaction of profit-making and repatriation taking place between two or more, but identifiable partners, they usually appear as losses sustained by the whole of the world economy. (That is, looking at it from the other side, they appear as advantages for the developed countries received from the whole of the world economy.)

A specific form of concealed income drain, or often only relational losses, can be found in the transfer or uneven distribution of the advantages of productive specialization adjusting itself to foreign trade, and of the benefits arising out of

[31] See E. Khesin's paper in the booklet *"Soviet Economists Discuss: Parent States and Colonies"*. Novosty Press Agency Publishing House, Moscow 1968, and H. Magdoff: Economic Aspects of US Imperialism. *Monthly Review,* Vol. 18, No. 6.

[32] *G.A.T.T. International Trade, 1959.* Geneva, 1960.

[33] *Review of International Trade and Development,* 1970. UNCTAD, U.N., New York, 1970, p. 100.

[34] Sources of data: V. Rymalov: *op. cit.,* pp. 18, 21; C. Brundenius: The Anatomy of Imperialism: The Case of the Multinational Mining Corporations in Peru. *Journal of Peace Research,* No. 3, 1972, p. 196.

the increased productivity of the export sectors. This is of course impossible to identify and measure *per se*, since its consequences manifest themselves only in the joint effect of many other factors.

As far as the uneven distribution of the results of technical progress and increased productivity is concerned, we may refer to the theses elaborated first of all by R. Prebisch, G. Myrdal, A. Lewis and H. Singer.

The uneven distribution of benefits deriving from foreign trade and the subsequent specialization consists in the fact that the secondary and cumulative effects of investments made in the export sector (either in the export sector of the advanced industrial countries or in that of the primary-producing developing countries) will be concentrated mostly in the developed industrial countries. The character of specialization itself offers less scope for technical progress, for the emergence of the so-called "internal and external economies", i.e. for the benefits of large-scale production and highly developed economic environment (infrastructure).

By their vary nature, the primary-producing sectors are accompanied by considerably fewer and weaker linkage effects than the manufacturing sectors. Consequently, they do not require and induce such an expansion of economic activity. Moreover, in contrast to heavy industries manufacturing machines, tools, instruments and chemicals, they can become neither the dynamic motive force of technical progress, nor the active generators and transmitters, but merely the passive beneficiaries of technical development.

These disadvantages in respect to the external and internal economies, the generation and spread of technical progress manifest themselves, among other things, in the higher costs of investment and operation and in the lower level of productivity, together with the tendency of widening the existing gap. This means that they narrow down "vertically" the potential sources of accumulation. At the same time, as a result of the less required and induced, i.e. retarded expansion of the scope of economic activity, the potential sources of accumulation are also narrowed down "horizontally", in that the creation of profit, more exactly of economic surplus, is confined to a few branches only. The transfer to the industrial metropolitan countries of the final manufacturing of primary products, usually together with concentrating in the same countries the transporting and marketing apparatus serving the manufacturing process, has also resulted in the reduction and transfer to the same countries of the potential income formation and accumulation for which the product itself provides the material basis.

A further and, from this aspect, indirect consequence of all that is the relatively limited scope of profitable investment possibilities and state revenue sources.

Contrary to all this, the capitalist industrial countries fully enjoy (not just in a reduced way as the primary-producing countries) not only the benefits[35]

---

[35] Such benefits are, e. g. according to Singer: "1. Possibility of building up export of manufactures and thus transferring their population from low-productivity occupations to high-productivity occupations; 2. enjoyment of internal economies of expanded manufacturing industries; 3. enjoy-

resulting from their *own* specialization, but also a considerable proportion of the benefits deriving from the specialization of the other, i.e. the primary-producing developing countries, in that part of the economic activities based on, or complementary to, primary production is also controlled by them. In this way, they have access to such sources of income and accumulation which lie beyond their own potentialities. The expansion of their own sphere of economic activity beyond its "original" limit means at the same time the expansion of profitable investment possibilities and the potential extension of the revenue sources of the state.

Another form of indirect and disguised income drain is connected with the mechanism of "internal" price formation and accountancy manipulation, or bookkeeping techniques of the usually vertically structured multinational corporations, international monopolies.

Accountancy manipulations are manifold, and it is not only monopoly companies which prefer to make use of such practices. Putting part of actual profits on the account of costs and especially hiding them behind the higher amortization ratio, reserve funds, managerial fees and losses arising from force majeure, etc., is an old-established and widely used practice also applied by smaller private enterprises. It is simply impossible to estimate what enourmous sums eváde taxation thereby, or, in the case of foreign capital, what losses are sustained by the national economy. For the application of such and similar accountancy manipulations, however, the vertically integrated multinational corporations have by far more possibilities than small and medium capital, and, exactly owing to their verticality, they are in a position to supplement it by their own price systems and price manipulations. Incidentally, in respect to their own products, they are free to introduce a price system deviating almost arbitrarily from actual costs. Even though this means for them only a system of internal accounting prices, i.e. the higher the profits on the one side, the lower the profits on the other, yet for the national economy concerned this practice fixes a significant, usually the most important part of the export and import prices.

Perhaps one of the most characteristic examples of the price-formation manoeuvres of international monopolies was the so-called *posted-price system* imposed on the oil-producing Arab countries by the International Oil Cartel. It was a highly artificial pricing system calculated on the basis of the higher extracting costs of American oil wells and the mostly fictive transportation costs of oil to the American market. It skimmed off imperceptibly the differential rent of the Arab oil fields and kept down the basis for calculating share of the local states (i.e. the profits deriving from the lower cost level). (It should be noted that the accounting price of the oil of the Arab East was calculated on the basis of the

ment of the general dynamic impulse radiating from industries in a progressive society; 4. enjoyment of the fruits of technical progress in primary production as main consumers of primary commodities; 5. enjoyment of a contribution from foreign consumers of manufactured articles." (H.W. Singer: *International Development: Growth and Change.* McGraw-Hill, 1964, p. 168.)

New York accounting price in such a way that the tax imposed on it by the USA and the cost of freight to New York were deducted from it, though the main market for the oil of the Arab East was not the USA, but Western Europe.) Due to the manipulated monopoly-price system, the OPEC countries had actually lost about 215,000 million US dollars in the twenty years before the recent "oil-crisis". In one year, 1967, e. g., they were able to realize only about 8 per cent of the total oil revenues from their own natural resources.

In addition to the price manipulation another sources of disguised losses is the transfer, usually by a simple bookkeeping operation, of part of the profits gained in extraction to the costs or gains of transportation, refining and marketing. The possibility of this practice is proved by the fact that all these processes extending over several countries are also controlled by the very same monopoly organizations.

An exquisite analysis of the operation of international oil-price mechanism and the exploitation disguised in the posted-price system was given in a dissertation by F. A. Hasab (Hungarian Academy of Sciences, 1966), the relevant parts of which were summarized in his study published in the Acta Oeconomica.[36]

As a result of the increasingly intensive and successful struggle of the Arab oil-producing countries versus international companies for increasing their control over, and share in, their own natural resources, and also in connection with the Middle East crisis, considerable changes have taken place in oil-business relations and also in the price and profit-sharing system since the late 1960s. As commonly known, in 1973–74 crude-oil prices were increased more and more (exceeding approximately four times the previous level). This practically meant the explosion of the former price system and, though increasing considerably the profits of the companies, too, has eventually led to the growing accumulation of enormous oil revenues in the hands of OPEC governments. The progressive regimes of these countries have even made efforts to take over or control oil production.

(b) LOSSES ARISING FROM THE DETERIORATION OF THE TERMS OF TRADE

The form of income loss through foreign trade most frequently referred to is the one arising from the deterioration of the terms of trade.

The tendency of shifts in the terms of trade at the expense of primary producers was already inherent in the division of labour between the industrial and primary-producing countries, even in its "classical" variety evolved originally under the colonial rule and operating in a relatively "smooth" way, when the industrial centres still absorbed eagerly and voraciously all types of raw materials and foodstuffs of the colonial countries. During the period between the end of the last century and the beginning of World War II, i.e. prior to the shifts in the

[36] The International Oil Prices Mechanism. *Acta Oeconomica Academiae Scientiarum Hungaricae.* Tomus 3, Fasc. 1, Budapest, 1968, pp. 91–107.

structure of international economy and division of labour, the terms of trade of primary producers had already been unfavourable as a whole. By the end of that period, i. e. immediately before World War II, one unit of exported raw materials could only purchase 60 per cent of manufactured goods previously exchanged for the same unit.[37]

Thus, the deteriorating trade position of primary producers can hardly be regarded as a transitory phenomenon, as a consequence of temporary or special factors. Illusory are also the assumptions based on the future prosperity of certain agricultural model countries. One of the most instructive and unambiguous lesson of the past centuries has been the recognition that only industrial countries have a perspective, and agriculture is capable of vigorous development only in countries with an advanced industry.

The determinating tendency of the terms of trade for primary-producing developing countries became apparent in a marked form particularly in the late 1950s and early 1960s.

The sharpening of the long-run deteriorating tendency was connected with "the *one-sided policy* of *the concentrated economic powers*" (monopolies supported by the leading capitalist countries),[38] and partly with those changes already mentioned that have taken place in the economies of the developed capitalist and developing countries in the post-war period, but especially in the 1960s.

As far as the policy of "concentrated economic powers" is concerned, the state monopolies or sometimes even the supra-state monopolistic associations and integrational organizations interfere in the economy and system of economic relations in such a way that the measures taken by them (e. g. in the fields of customs rates, export subsidies and import restrictions, etc.) hamper or retard the adequate expansion of the exports of developing countries.

It is especially agricultural *protectionism* of the highly developed capitalist countries which does serious harm to the developing countries. The agricultural organization of the European Economic Community is spending e. g. an annual 2,000 million dollars on subsidizing the prices of the agricultural products of the six countries of the Common Market. The USA alone subsidizes its agriculture by 7,000 million dollars annually. This, in the first place, provides the explanation why the price index of the agricultural products of the industrially developed countries rose by 11 points during the period 1958 to 1965, while that of the developing countries fell by 12 points during the same period.[39] Thus, in spite of

[37] See I. Sachs: *Patterns of Public Sectors in Underdeveloped Economies*. Asia Publishing House, 1964, p. 27.

[38] J. Bognár: Gazdasági kapcsolataink távlatai a fejlődő országokkal (The Perspectives of Hungarian Economic Relations with Developing Countries). *Közgazdasági Szemle*, May, 1968, p. 515.

[39] F. Kane: Afrikai országok társulása a Közös Piachoz (The Association of African Countries with the Common Market). *Studies on Developing Countries*. No. 30, 1969, p. 7. Centre for Afro-Asian Research of the Hungarian Academy of Sciences.

the general declining tendency of the prices of most primary products, the "concentrated economic powers" proved strong enough. This becomes even clearer if we compare the price indices of all primary products exported. While the average export price of the primary products of the developing countries fell by 7 per cent between 1958 and 1966, the export price of the raw materials of the developed countries went up by 10 per cent.[40]

No less unfavourable and for future development even more serious is the *industrial protectionism* of the developed capitalist countries. Their monopoly position in the complex heavy industries has strengthened to a very considerable extent in relation to the developing countries, which makes it not only possible but to a certain degree also necessary for them to loosen their monopoly position towards the developing countries in the light industries (the manifestation of which can be witnessed primarily in a certain shift in the investment policy of vertical monopolies). Nevertheless, their trade policy protecting the domestic light industry and hitting the exports of the light industry of developing countries continues to assert itself all along. The import duties grow generally progressively with the degree of processing in the developed capitalist countries.

It is not only indirectly, through the market-contracting effect that the protectionism of the developed capitalist countries deteriorates the trade position and the terms of trade of the developing countries and hampers at the same time the abolition of one-sided specialization and the introduction to their export structure of new (industrial) products more favourable from the point of view of the terms of trade, but also causes them damage directly as they can maintain the competitiveness of their products, heavily burdened by customs duty, only by a reduction of their export prices.

Through their effect on the trend of world-market prices, the capital-strong big international monopolies also prevent the assertion of the opposite tendency which, owing to the more rapid rate of increase in productivity, would divert the price of manufactured goods downwards in relation to raw materials. Besides influencing the prices directly, they also exert an indirect effect on the prices of manufactures in that the same monopolies of their "peers" in the metropolitan country further increase the import needs of the latter by their investment policy pursued in the developing countries (see also the shift towards capital-intensive light industries discussed above). At the same time, the export of manufactured goods of the developing countries is also restricted, besides discriminatory customs regulations and the oppressive competition of the cheaper or higher-quality products of the monopolies, by the fact that these countries are also handicapped in respect of the so-called "extra-price factors" (e. g. trade-marks, models, network of servicing stations, publicity, advertising, etc.).

The *scientific and technological revolution* evolving in the developed countries has relatively reduced – with certain exceptions – the needs of the metropolitan countries for natural raw materials and agrarian imports, and has even resulted,

[40] *Review of International Trade and Development*, 1967, Part I, TD/15, pp. 1–2.

together with other factors, in the fact that the share of the developed countries in the raw-material export of the capitalist world has grown at the expense of the developing countries.

The share of the developing countries in the world export of primary products has dropped to less than 40 per cent, while that of the advanced capitalist countries is now about 55 per cent. But the reliance of the former on primary production is still heavy, since nearly 80 per cent of their total export earnings arise from primary exports, while the proportion of the latter is only about 25 per cent. On the supply side the position of the developing countries is further aggravated by the fact that they are usually also competing with each other on the world market by putting up for sale the same few products and are increasingly dependent, in proportion to their growing import needs, on marketing their mono-products at any price.

In these countries, especially in those recently liberated from colonial oppression, the emergence of pressing tasks, such as the creation of an independent national economy, industrialization, the urgent need for raising the living standards, or simply the tasks of supplying the increasing numbers of population, rapidly expanded their import needs. In this way, most of the "export economies" have changed into "import-sensitive economies".

In this process an important part has also been played by the population explosion, which has turned former grain-exporting countries into grain-importing ones. In the late 1930s, the developing countries exported about 11 million tons of grain a year, but by the end of the 1940s these countries, taken as a whole, had become net grain-importers, and in 1964 their grain imports reached an annual 25 million tons.

The inviability of their economic structure and their deteriorating economic position can also be seen from the fact that, in spite of their one-sidedly agricultural specialization, most of the developing countries depend not only on grain imports, but also on substantial agricultural, mainly food imports.

Per-capita food production of the developing countries has averaged only a 0.5 per cent annual rate of increase in the last two decades (with an absolute decrease e. g. in Africa since 1961). The food-supply situation became particularly serious and tragic in 1972–73, when the famine zones destroyed all the hopes and illusions of the former years created by the "green revolution".

Considerable impact on import-sensitivity has also been exerted by the double shift in the investment pattern already referred to, which has increased, together with the simultaneous retarding of the development of the capital-goods industries, the expansion of the capital-intensive techniques.

But the developing countries are harmfully affected not only by the long-term tendency of a general deterioration, but also by the frequent *fluctuations* of the terms of trade. Reliable planning is well-nigh impossible because of these fluctuations.

The world-market prices of industrial raw materials are, as a rule, highly sensitive to cyclical changes in the economies of the developed capitalist countries constituting their most important market. The prices of these products generally increase rapidly in boom periods – due to a considerable extent to speculative hoarding, which encourages fictive demand divorced from actual industrial needs – and drop faster and deeper than any other goods in times of recession.

From the mid-1960s on, the terms of trade for the "Third World" as a whole showed greater stability up to the sudden price increases in 1972–1974. But behind the averages considerable differences can be found in the terms of trade for the individual countries or groups of countries exporting different products.

Between the mid-1950s and 1970, due to the rather stagnant prices of the export products (excepting e.g. oil) of developing countries as against the increasing prices of (both primary and manufactured) export products of advanced capitalist countries, the terms of trade for the non-oil exporting developing countries deteriorated by 12 per cent (for the oil-exporters only by 10 per cent). In 1971, when the terms of trade for the "Third World" as a whole remained stable, it sharply deteriorated (from 107 to 99, if 1963 = 100) for the non-oil exporting countries.[41] In 1972 and 1973 there was an improvement (by about 6 per cent) for the latter, too, as a result of the raw-material price increases in the world market. The unfolding recession in 1974, however, resulted already in price drops for a number of primary products, while crude oil and a few other raw materials continued to command high or even further increasing prices. Since changes in technology and shifts in international trade and the division of labour, as well as in the capital export and investment pattern of the companies affect in a very different way and measure the various products and producers of the "Third World", a *further differentiation* can also be expected in respect of the terms of trade within the developing world.

The total loss of the developing countries resulting from the deterioration of the terms of trade amounted to 16,700 million dollars in the period 1951 to 1962. *Their annual loss in the mid-1960s averaged about 2,500 million dollars.*

The deterioration of the terms of trade is of course an additional aggravating factor in the balance of trade and balance of payments position of the developing countries. For most of them the rapidly increasing import needs (particularly those connected with the food supply problem of a growing population) and the limited export growth and facilities have resulted in a rather permanent and widening trade decifit, added to by further losses and drains in the balance of payments.

The aggregate balance of trade of all developing countries showed an annual deficit of 1,500 to 3,100 million dollars between 1958 and 1962. Their annual trade deficit with DAC countries exceeded 3,000 million dollars in 1968–1970 as well, but if the nine major oil-exporters (with their trade surplus of 6,600 million dollars a year) are excluded, the deficit was close to 10,000 million dollars.[42] While the world-market price changes (particularly those of oil) resulted in an

[41] 1972 Review, Development Co-operation, *OECD,* 1972. p. 91.
[42] *Ibidem,* p. 90.

enormous trade surplus for a small group of developing countries, for the majority the deficit grew cumulatively, and, as a consequence of price increases, the import bill reached almost twice the amount of the 8,000 million dollars of total development aid.

(c) SERVICE CHARGES

Another indirect form of income loss, also connected with foreign trade and export orientation resulting from the colonial division of labour, manifests itself in the net balance of payments for shipping freights, insurance and other services.

Besides its abnormal volume, which is in no proportion to the size and development of the national economy and its distorted structure, production for exports geared to foreign interests also has the harmful consequences that it presupposes mainly overseas deliveries. And since the developing countries have no fleets of their own, they are bound to make use of foreign merchant shipping.[43]

Though what is involved here is really payments for actual services, i.e. apparently "fair" business transactions, yet in fact we are faced here with a form of income drain, at least for two reasons. First and foremost because these services, or more exactly the overwhelming part of them, have become necessary on account of performing fuctions gained only on the system of the colonial division of labour, i.e. in the interest of the metropolitan countries and foreing capital, or, since the importance of these functions has decreased, owing to the colonial heritage of economic and foreign-trade structure. In case the development of the economies of the countries concerned were sound and normal, most of these services would hardly be necessary, at least not in overseas relations and at the given level of their economic development. If the external economic relations developed in a sound proportion to, and in harmony with, internal economic development, there would be a sort of balanced state between the need for these external services and the material conditions of satisfying them (own transport facilities, etc.), or between the use and the provision of these services. By no means is it possible that there develops by itself, without any external force or intervention, such a disproportionate, abnormal situation in which a national economy directs an overwhelming proportion of its export products to far-away overseas markets, while it is unable to provide the necessary transport facilities – not only in the case of overseas deliveries, but even of deliveries within the country.

Secondly, the service charges and the conditions of payments are again determined mostly by Western capitalist companies enjoying monopoly positions.

[43] The share of the developing countries (except for Liberia and Panama) in the world merchant fleet was 8.1 per cent only in 1964, and even less in the late 1960s, namely 7.6 per cent in 1969. This sharply contrasts with their high share in world sea-borne trade which exceeded 60 per cent for food loaded, and reached almost 20 per cent for goods unloaded in the 1960s. (*Review of Maritime Transport*, UN. New York, 1969 and *Review of International Trade and Development*, UN. New York 1970. p. 103.)

We could further lengthen the list of losses (e. g. with postal and communications services, banking operations, insurance, experts' and managerial fees, etc.)[44] which are reflected in the constant deficit of the "balance" of services, and result from the striking disproportion between the internal development and external relations of the economy.[45] But even this list of losses is apt to dispel any illusions. It dispels, e. g., the illusion that the gap between the developed and developing countries can appreciably be narrowed down by simply increasing aid, even to the extent of doubling the 1 per cent of national income required of the developed countries, or by expanding the market of the traditional export products of the developing countries. As long as the influx of material and intellectual resources is linked up with the increasing outflow of resources, a fact which follows from the spontaneous mechanism of world capitalist economy and the structural endowments of the developing countries and, consequently, as long as the uneven distribution of the factors of dynamic growth (science, technology and the closely related industries) survives or even increases, not only the narrowing down, but also the prevention of a further widening of the gap is hopeless.

It would be easy to advise the developing countries to prevent the drain of their incomes and the exploitation of their resources simply by an overnight expropriation of the expropriators, or to carry on trade with the socialist countries rather than with the developed capitalist ones, and ask credit and aid of the former. Such simplification not only underestimates the economic and technical conditions of nationalizations (not to speak of the social and political conditions) and the structural and monetary difficulties of trading with the socialist countries, but also disregards the actual state of international economic power relations.

Where the mechanism of exploitation is a spontaneous one based, on the one hand, on the internal structure of the countries exploited and, on the other, is part and consequence of the whole mechanism of world capitalist economy itself, there the *internal* solution can only be of a structural, and consequently also a political act, while the *international* solution can only be a political, and consequently also a structural one.

---

[44] On this question see the author's book: *The Political Economy of Underdevelopment*, Akadémiai Kiadó, Budapest 1976.

[45] In 1964, for example, the excess of payments for services over receipts from them amounted to 4,100 million dollars (10,400–6,300), and in addition to this, about 4,000 million dollars had to be paid by the developing countries for shipping charges, freight etc. The transport and insurance costs represent an increasing burden, particularly for the "least-developed countries". Ther net payments (i.e. payments exceeding receipts) for freight, insurance and other transport costs averaged 200 million dollars in the period 1964 to 1967, and more than trebled by the late 1960s, when, in the period 1968 to 1970, the annual average reached 700 million dollars. (1972 Review, Development Co-operation, *OECD*. 1972, p. 197.)

IV. THE DUALISM AND DISTORTIONS OF THE ECONOMIC STRUCTURE

The disintegration and the lack of internal unity of the socio-economic structure are due to the fact that it was not the internal evolution of their own economy which led these countries to become organic parts of the world economy but on the contrary: it was their integration into world capitalist economy that started growth in certain sectors of their economy. In this way, the elements of a more modern mode of production (and society) were imposed on the traditional economy (and society) *from outside,* as a strange and isolated element, generally within the framework of colonialism, and often by brute force. These well-known "enclaves" were *outwardly* oriented from the very beginning and also remained so subsequently, partly because their establishment and operation were attached to foreign interests, the interests of colonial powers and foreign capital in general, and partly because they were under the influence of spontaneous economic forces which stimulated even the national investors – if there were any – to engage in export-producing economic branches.

These enclaves could evidently not become the driving force of national economic development, *partly* because they embodied the sort of international division of labour which had, even at its height, a number of negative consequences for the countries in question (e.g. biased economic structure, different income drains, etc.). Moreover, since chronic difficulties arose (as a consequence of scientific and technical progress and the emergence of a new type of international division of labour), these enclave sectors, finding themselves face to face with marketing difficulties and an inelastically expanding and fluctuating world-market demand in general, lost in most cases even their initial dynamism. *On the other hand,* the enclaves could not become the driving force of the economy because they were scarcely in any production contact with their environment, with other sectors of the economy (and society) of the given country. Thus, the elements of the destroyed pre-capitalistic forms of the economy (and society) survived, in a subordinated position, along with the capitalistic sectors induced from outside.

This internally non-integrated character of the economy (and society) of the developing countries manifest itself in

(a) the dualism of the "capitalist" and "pre-capitalist" sectors of the economy (and society);

(b) the co-existence of the market sector producing directly for the world market and subsistence economies;

(c) the distorted sectoral structure and the inadequacy of sectoral relations.

Thus, this distorted, disintegrated structure actually means that the economy is composed of two diametrically opposed sectors. The individual branches of the economy did not develop side by side, connected with, and complementing, each other, but in a strikingly disproportionate way, so that some, usually identical or similar economic branches began to grow abruptly as "alien bodies", isolated from the development of the other economic branches, often hindering or even preventing their development. It is common knowledge that these "alien bodies" evolved in the fields of *raw material extraction* and *agricultural export production,* in accordance with the interests of the developed capitalist countries and as a result of their purposeful intervention.

In addition to this purposeful colonialistic intervention, the spontaneous economic forces set in motion also worked in the direction of establishing and perpetuating such primary-producing export enclaves.

Instead of expensive industrial investments, which necessitated imported machinery and qualified labour, agricultural production appeared to be quite naturally more attractive as it could be conducted successfully even in an extensive way by using masses of cheap, unskilled labour. Market relations also favoured agricultural (and mineral raw-materials) production as the industries of the developed capitalist countries promised rapidly expanding markets, while the structure and absorbing capacity of the local market were determined partly by the import and preference of more sophisticated manufactures. In addition, the infrastructure developed by the colonial administration and the whole system of economic, sanitary, cultural and legal institutions also served raw-material export production.

The one-sided development, the "outward orientation" of economic activity and the infrastructure serving it, as well as the network of institutions also provide the answer to the question why the so-called *"traditional"* or *"pre-capitalist"* *sector* could survive in the developing countries in such considerable proportions, and how it is possible that, along with the highest degree of commodity production, i.e. export production for the international market, the primitive mode of production separated even from the local, national market and not yet reaching the level of regular commodity production, i.e. subsistence economy, can still exist in a large measure.

1. IMPEDIMENTS TO EXPANDING THE HOME MARKET

A common and well-known problem of the developing countries is the narrowness of the home market. This phenomenon is due not only to the generally low income level and the unfavourable distribution of incomes but also to the distorted, dualistic structure of the economy.

Both the outwardly oriented capitalist sector and especially the "pre-capitalist" sector set, by their very nature, limits to the development of internal commodity relations.

84

The development of commodity relations depends, primarily, on the growth of the division of labour among individual productive units and the stimulating effect of the supply and demand relating to them. Such effects of supply or demand induction are called linkage effects in international economic literature, and a distinction is made between vertically downward and vertically upward operating linkage effects. The vertically downward operating effects (sometimes also called "forward" effects) actually represent the induction effects of supply, which means that they point from the consumer towards the producer, in the last analysis to the raw-material producer.

(a) THE INADEQUATE INDUCTIONS OF THE "MODERN" SECTOR

As far as the *"modern"*, or capitalist *sector* of the developing countries, i. e. the sector inherited from the colonial period, is concerned, which includes, as a rule, the production of agricultural raw materials for export and the exploitation of mineral resources, where there are any (together with the infrastructure and superstructure serving them), its productive units exert but a slight inductive effect on the internal economy.

The vertically downward operating effects appear only in such sidelines of industry, which supplement raw-material production or prepare its products for export (e. g. cleaning, packaging, etc.). They contribute at best to the expansion of the export sector but scarcely modify the commodity relations directed towards home trade. This is due to the fact that raw materials are manufactured abroad and, therefore, the positive effect of supply acts only on the manufacturing industries of foreign countries. The positive effect of supply manifests itself not only in the fact that the commodity is actually available, and in a growing volume at that, and stimulates by its very existence consumption or utilization, the exploitation of its potential economic possibilities, but beyond that also in the fact that the user of the commodity himself has his share in the advantages arising from recent changes in production (sophisticated technology, better quality, lower costs, etc.). The intensity of such supply effects depends of course to a large extent on the sphere in which the commodity is used. In the case of products like crude oil, whose sphere of utilization is not only extremely wide, as that of mineral raw materials in general (as a matter of fact much wider, being, at the moment, the most important source of energy), but further expands also vertically, on more than one level, according to the individual phases of manufacturing and to the by-products thus gained, the positive effects of supply stimulate the development of whole industries or even groups of industries. What the processing of their raw material abroad, in the developed capitalist countries, means for the developing world, has already been touched upon above. Here we only refer to the problem from the point of view of its effect on the home market. Over and above the fact that the benefits resulting from increased productivity and the decrease of prices for this or other reasons are enjoyed by the developed capitalist countries, the spread and multiplier effects, so important for the expansion of the market, are also transferred, together with the raw product, to the field of processing.

The vertically upward operating linkage effects of the export sectors of the "modern" enclave, however, owing to their primary-producing character, are insignificant. They do not require further raw and basic materials for production, at the very most fuels, lubricants, means of transport, and even machines only to a small extent because of the availability of large masses of cheap, unskilled manpower.

In addition, the demand induction of these sectors is, for several reasons, also outward-bound, directed towards foreign industries. It is possible, or even general, that the industries turning out the necessary products have not yet been developed in the economy concerned. Or they are at a disadvantage compared with the products of foreign industries, because the management of the export sectors is in the hands of those (e. g. foreign companies) who are used to foreign technology, to certain brands, or are even directly interested in importing the necessary products from abroad.

Also rather limited or disproportionate is the demand induction exerted by the primary-producing export sector towards the home production of basic consumer goods, i. e. the secondary, or indirect vertical effect, which also manifests itself in an "upward" direction, towards the producer, through the spending of the personal incomes of those belonging to this sector.

The demand for consumer goods and its structure depend, first of all, on income relations, on the size and distribution of incomes, i. e. in the case of the "modern" sector, on the production and distribution relations prevailing in it. Accordingly, a distinction must be made of course between such sectors of the various developing countries.

Where the capitalist sector includes a relatively developed *extractive industry* (mining and oil wells), the market effect of the consumption of the wage labourers engaged in mineral extraction is limited by their low rate of employment, their low wage level and, in the case of migrant workers, by their "double life", i. e. by the role the family subsistence economy still plays in supply. But the personal consumption requirements of capitalists, foreign managers, highly-paid officials and skilled workers engaged in the extractive industry usually induce demand for imported goods, or are largely transferred to foreign countries (profit and saving repatriation).

The market effect of the consumption of agricultural wage labourers employed on plantations is further limited, in addition to their low incomes, by the fact that the still largely existing family (traditional) economy continues to play a role in satisfying their needs.

Where the "modern" export sector embraces a large number of *small-* and *medium-sized farms,* owned by the local peasant population but controlled by commercial companies, the income level of the bulk of this peasant population is very low, owing to their exploitation by these companies, to the production method used, as well as to the deteriorating marketing possibilities. An additional factor, just as in the case of plantation workers, is the role that subsistence economy still plays in their consumption. In the years of boom, however, when the rich farmers getting prosperous by employing wage labour, increase their incomes to a sufficiently high level, they, too will prefer imported manufactures, partly because they want to imitate the example of rich foreigners and the urban élite, partly because they usually display less interest in exactly those simple, "everyday" goods which can be produced even by the less developed home industry.

Similar characteristics of the orientation of personal consumption can also be observed in the other, less typical productive branches of the capitalist sector, branches which are of different origin and have come into being largely as a result of recent changes, as well as in the related infrastructure network and superstructure system. In general, the growth of the urban élite generates a further shift in favour of important consumption. Ot the employees of public administration and public utilities, those in the lower income brackets have a limited demand, in absolute terms, for local goods, because their incomes are low, and those in the higher income brackets have no demand for them, because they prefer the more sophisticated imported goods.

The demand of strata with higher incomes for imports, i.e. goods that under the circumstances of the given economy are considered "luxuries", together with its demonstration effect even on the poorer social strata, provide the basis for a concept of economic policy which seeks the possibilities of an import-substituting industrialization along the line of this limited and disproportionate demand induction. It ensures thereby the possibility for foreign monopolies to establish subsidiaries in the secondary or even in the luxury industries producing or assembling their own "home" products by means of their own up-to-date technology. Thus, the distortion of the demand induction and of course the business policy of foreign monopolies will lead to an "import-substituting" type of industrialization which finds its expression in practically enclave-like industrial establishments which are uneconomical to operate, require lasting tariff protection, state subsidies, and lead to indirect import growth, and hardly promote the vertical structure of the national economy.

"The lack of the continuity of demand" is typical not only of the consumption of the rich peasant strata emerging from poor peasantry, but is a fairly general phenomenon in the lower and medium spheres of the societies of developing countries. In addition to the demonstration effect (i.e. the demonstration of consumer habits corresponding to a high income level), also manifested directly by foreign visitors and resident foreigners, stimulating to disproportionate efforts to reach at least some elements of high-level consumption thus leading to a disproportionate demand pattern, an important role is also played in the intermittent, discontinuous structure of demand by such factors as climate (tropical countries), reducing to a considerable extent the clothing needs, which, together with the "medium" housing demand, usually come second in the "normal" order of consumption. Further factors are the impact of the traditional

way of life, and the lack of "transitions", a general phenomenon which can be witnessed in the economy and infrastructure as a whole. (In Africa, e.g., the lack of the use of draught animals as a transition between human and motor-vehicle transport, or the lack of rural brick houses that could be built by native craftsmen using local products instead of the two extremes of well-equipped urban dwellings and rural mudhuts, etc.) But it could be the function of exactly these links missing in the development of needs and demands to ensure that, parallel with the expansion of commodity and money economy, with the transformation of the "pre-capitalist" sector, and with the increasing income levels either in the capitalist or urban sector, or in the more or less "pre-capitalist" rural sector, the "inward directed" induction effects manifesting themselves within the national economy can be multiplied.

Discontinuity in itself is of course neither a new, nor an unfavourable phenomenon. It is always the radical, progressive, revolutionary changes that have brought about breaks in continuity. Yet it is a rather peculiar phenomenon that the gradual rise in needs far exceeds, *on a massive scale,* the productive capacities of the national economy, and will, for a long time yet, be in excess of even its absolute possibilities.

This phenomenon was not experienced in the history of today's developed capitalist countries, because there the development of needs and the fairly continuous shift in the demand towards more sophisticated goods took place parallel with economic growth, and, in fact, it was the development of productive forces that led the way and opened up new areas for the emergence of needs, or created new demands. The relationship between the advance in the development of local productive forces and the expansion of effective consumer demand is a reverse one, also because it follows from the very essence of the developed capitalist system that the effective demand of masses relatively lags behind the expansion of productive capacities. Consequently, the growth of effective demand resulting from cyclical influences, a higher rate of employment and higher income levels or more favourable income distribution leads, as a rule, to the increased utilization or further expansion of local productive capacities, i.e. the domestic national economy is usually in a position also to satisfy the changed pattern of demand directly, in terms of both quantity and quality. It is, properly speaking, this boom effect of increased demand that finds its expression in the Keynesian principle of the multiplier effect, which Western economic textbooks, including those written for the universities of developing countries, describe as a general economic law, forgetting that it only reflects the peculiar circumstances of developed capitalism.

In the *socialist countries,* however, where the start from the basis of economic backwardness, or at least "underdevelopment", might have actually given rise, just as in the case of the present-day developing countries, to the massive emergence of the phenomenon in question,[1] this did not occur, primarily because

[1] The manifestations of this phenomenon are to be felt, though. Such is, e.g., the abrupt expansion

88

central economic policy, taking advantage of the public sector and the possibility of central management and planning, of the device of foreign-trade and foreign-exchange monopoly as well as of the non-economic means of eliminating the demonstration effects of the developed capitalist countries, made the economy, in the critical period of industrialization and structural transformation, a relatively "closed" economy. This was a temporarily justified and necessary policy towards the developed capitalist (but not the other socialist) countries, even independently of the elimination of the negative effects of the capitalist trade cycle and from the danger of war. (It is another question to what extent capitalist embargo policy was responsible for the excessive measure of this "closed" economy.) Though the restriction imposed on tourism and on the import of Western consumer goods has never been a popular measure, this and similar measures proved to be necessary merely from the point of view of economic development as long as the general level of domestic productive forces was not high enough to ensure that the demonstration effect could assert itself not only in the field of demand but also of production. (It is again a different thing that in practice serious errors were also made in economic policy, which sometimes prejudiced the satisfaction of justified consumer demands.)

The precondition for the demonstration effect also asserting itself in production, and in a positive way, is that the developmental level of domestic industry should approach the state of being able to satisfy more sophisticated consumer demands, i.e. it should be in a position to adopt the advanced technology and production methods of the more developed countries, and, under the pressure of domestic needs, can set about producing new and higher-quality consumer goods without giving rise to serious contradictions or larger disproportions either in respect to the level of manpower, or the general structure of industry (the existence of basic industries) and market relations. If this is the case, the very acquaintance with higher-quality products and technology will stimulate to follow the example and has, therefore, a positive challenging effect. The reaching of this level, however, also means that "discontinuity" can less and less occur in the further development of consumption and effective demand, and there is, in fact, a growing tendency to satisfy subsequently those needs that were either *relatively* neglected or met insufficiently earlier.[2]

Whether the developing countries should follow, or those which have already made the attempt, will succeed in following the practice of socialist countries (hopefully without the well-known errors made in economic policy) to limit, by artificial means in the critical period of structural transformation, the assertion of the demonstration effects and the subsequent disproportionate but not the *basic*

---

of the demand for motor-cars, quite out of proportion to the level of satisfaction of demands of a lower order – mainly as a result of the demonstration effect of the more developed Western countries.

[2] This can be experienced, on the other hand, when e.g. additional simple household articles are bought only after purchasing durable household utensils, or clothing needs are satisfied only after buying cameras, radios, tape recorders, television sets, etc.

demand, and cause effective demand to orientate increasingly towards locally manufactured products, is not so much a theoretical, not even simply a political-ideological, but rather a fairly complex practical question.

(b) THE IMPACT OF THE "PRE-CAPITALIST" SECTOR

The "pre-capitalist" sector is mostly composed of subsistence economies, which hardly generate or receive any induction effects except for those arising from the transmissions of the weak contacts with state administration and the neighbouring commodity-producing sectors (e. g. taxation, communal development in the district, migrant-labour system, etc.). However, economic units of a "pure" subsistence character have become rather rare, and a certain degree of market production and other additional income sources (e. g. in the form of migrant labour) are almost always attached, mostly as a result of taxation and certain "target" purchases, even to economies producing basically for self-consumption. But the growth of income or the decreasing effect of the outside factors inducing marketing (e. g. taxation) leads, as a rule, to the expansion of self-consumption, hence to the decrease of marketable surplus.[3]

The development of market relations within the "pre-capitalist" sector is limited by the fact that the division of labour between agricultural and non-agricultural activities is non-existent (or where it does exist, it is usually a division of labour merely *within* the family or community according to sex and age). Thus, the basic needs are satisfied, as a rule, by the own activity of the community and not by an exchange of products. The lack of a division of labour, the use of a primitive mode of production and the serious difficulty of satisfying even the most rudimentary needs (aggravated by the rising rate of population growth and the contradiction of arable land available) make the systematic building up of a (potential) marketable surplus ("surplus" in the sense used by Baran) increasingly difficult. And the lack of storage and transport facilities, of marketing institutions and knowledge, etc., prevents even the occasionally available surplus from entering the process of commodity exchange.

But the existence of the "pre-capitalist" sector sets limits not only directly, for the reasons listed above, but also indirectly, through its effect on the capitalist sector, to the development of the market relations of the national economy and the expansion of internal commodity relations. The indirect effect of the former manifests itself in the following:

(a) The "pre-capitalist" sector as an inexhaustible source of cheap unskilled labour exerts an incessant pressure on the income level and purchasing power of the wageworkers of the capitalistic sector.

[3] "In the case of an underdeveloped country, however" – says Rao – "household enterprises predominate, and production is much more for self-consumption than for the market, with the result that when there is an increase in income, the marginal propensity to consume leads to an increase in the demand for self-consumption rather than for purchases in the market." (V. J. R. V. Rao: *Essays in Economic Development.* Asia Publishing House, London, 1964, p. 46.)

90

(b) The families of many wageworkers of the capitalist sector still live within the "pre-capitalist" sector and are provided for by the subsistence economy. In this way, the purchasing power gained by wage labour is diverted from the market of basic necessities, and, in addition, a further pressure is put on the subsistence wage level.

(c) The "pre-capitalist" sector exerts – through traditional and treasured social customs – an influence on the consumer demands and the spending habits of its people, in general, and on those of migrant workers leading a "double life", in particular.

Thus, as we have seen, the outward orientation and internal sectoral pattern of the capitalist sector, as well as the isolation and indirect detrimental effects of the "pre-capitalist" sector, impede the unfolding of internal commodity relations and spread effects.

(c) SLIGHT CHANGES AND THE CONSEQUENCES OF A "FALSE" INDUSTRIALIZA-TION

It is obvious that in the last analysis only the abolition of the dualistic structure can bring about the intensification of internal market relations.

No doubt, some steps have already been taken in this direction even in countries whose economies are of a particularly distorted and strikingly dualistic character. Such steps taken in areas also comprising the "pre-capitalist" sector are, e. g., the creation of some manufacturing industries based either on domestic raw materials or at least on production for the domestic market; the development of infrastructure, making transport facilities available for the exchange of goods; the organization of marketing institutions and co-operatives; the implementation of re-settlement programmes, etc. Further steps of this type are the diversion towards the home market of the consumption of those enjoying higher incomes in the capitalist sector by employing foreign-exchange controls, customs regulations, the devices of price and tax policy, etc., and the adjustment, rather rare in practice, of the production profile of the new industrial establishments of the capitalist sector to the developmental requirements of the backward agricultural sector.

In addition to such more or less purposeful measures, the increasing flow of labour force into towns, the migrant-worker system itself, and primarily the influence exerted by a growing number of young people from the "pre-capitalist" sector enrolled in schools lead to the loosening of ties and the isolation of that sector.

But as long as the most important, intermediate links are missing in the chain of the vertical structure of national production, these steps and spontaneous relaxations are bound to produce only minor quantitative changes.

The missing intermediate and decisive links in the vertical structure of social production provide also the explanation why the system of inter-sectoral relations and linkage effects has *not* changed and cannot change in spite of the fact that the originally predominant labour-intensive techniques have been replaced in certain newly established branches of light industry by capital-intensive techniques. Where there is a lack of domestic industries manufacturing capital goods, machines, tools and equipment, the adopting of capital-intensive techniques leads to an intensification of import orientation. And since in the plants and assembly shops of capital-intensive light industry the so-called "training process" is confined to a narrow workers' élite only, it leaves, strangely enough, the mechanism in the rest of the economy unchanged, a mechanism ensuring the predominance of the sectors and branches using primitive, labour-intensive techniques, generating hardly any market effects and having no significance for internal commodity relations.

Thus, instead of creating the intermediate and decisive links which ensure the dynamism of industrial (and agrarian) development, of gradually building up the capital-goods industries, expanding the productive and labour-absorbing capacity as well as the market of the national economy, and determining the level of technology and productivity, this false method of "industrialization" implants only the secondary, surface elements of industry (as "alien" bodies like the enclave sectors) in the national economy. Therefore, it practically hinders in many respects the process of integrating society with the economy, and gives rise to or strengthens, among other things, the tendency of reducing inter-sectoral market relations and spread effects. This tendency manifests itself in the impact of this type of "industrialization" on

- the import sensitivity of the national economy;
- the volume and composition of the labour force employed;
- the "pre-capitalist" rural sector;
- the other branches and economic units of the urban sector.

The increase in import sensitivity, resulting from the fact that the use of capital-intensive technology depends on the import of machinery, equipment, means of transport and even of fuels and raw materials,[4] aggravates the export dependence of the national economy and thus results in the cumulative strengthening of the enclave character of the export sectors.

Owing to a shift towards capital-intensive technology, the employment of labour force, or the absorptive capacity of the capitalist sector, decreases in relative terms, while a change takes place in the composition of the working population in favour of the highly paid employees and élite workers. This leads to a decrease in exactly the purchasing power of those in the lower income brackets (owing to the relative drop in employment and the "freezing" or fall of their real wages), which would and could create demand for local products (and thereby inducement for the development of industries producing for the domestic market as well as for the transformation of the "traditional" economy). On the other hand, the purchasing power of expatriates directing or teaching the utilization of

---

[4] It is in this sense that this sort of import-substitution is termed "self-destructive".

92

advanced technology, and of the élite of local employees imitating the consumption habits of the former, i.e. the purchasing power interested in imported articles or goods manufactured locally with imported technology (luxuries), will increase.

The process of the transformation and integration of the "pre-capitalist" rural sector is strongly impeded by the relative contraction of employment opportunities of unskilled labour moving out of that sector, and by the structural shift in purchasing power and demand (at the expense of the potential market of the products of this sector). Even those relations have been reduced which came into being between the "pre-capitalist" rural and the capitalist urban sectors as a result of the migrant-labour system, or were realized in such a form that the occasional agricultural surplus and simple handicraft products of the rural sector were purchased by the urban low-income strata, among them the migrant workers.

This type of capital-intensive production of light manufactures also has its impact on the other spheres of the urban sector. Thus, first of all, the domain of local small-scale and handicraft industries continues to contract, and the small or medium capital belonging to a few indigenous entrepreneurs or local "racial" minorities engaged in the manufacturing or marketing of local products is either ousted from its activity or compelled to turn elsewhere. The labour force of the new plants of the light industry is recruited not from among the self-employed artisans or handicraft workers engaged in the same trade – even if they do exist, which is the case in the textile, clothing and shoe industries, etc. Thus, not only the periods of guilds and manufactories are missing (very plausibly, by the way) in the development process but also the phase of the labour-intensive handicraft co-operatives and small-scale plants of the light industry. As a result, the previously established forms of specialization become unviable and incapable of any further development. Products are ousted from the market and their producers cease to possess purchasing power of their own. This process is a negative one not simply because it is painful (other societies also had to undergo similar painful processes), but because, instead of promoting the expansion of the internal social division of labour, it leads to its contraction. The self-employed artisans, handicraft workers, as well as migrant workers who have lost their jobs are usually re-employed *not* by the rapidly developing productive branches, owing to the peculiar structure of the "modern" sector, but they either return to the sphere of the "traditional" economy or seek employment in the *non-productive* sectors (usually in the domestic services).

Due partly to the shift of demand towards imported goods or luxury articles manufactured locally with imported technology, and partly to its decreasing competitiveness against the mostly state-subsidized large-scale plants with a longer time horizon, employing capital-intensive technology and paying higher wages, small and medium capital engaged in producing local products is compelled either to retreat to other sectors of the economy (mainly to the service industries or the retail trade in imported goods), or usually comes under the

93

control of foreign big capital. The result is again *not* the expansion of the production and market relations between sectors and branches, a concomitant of the apparently similar process of concentration, but their narrowing down.

All this only goes to show that not any kind of change is capable of triggering off a positive chain reaction suitable to abolish the dualism of the economy.

In the foregoing we have examined the effects and consequences of this "false" industrialization rather "purely", disregarding the modifying role of such "subsidiary" and "external" factors as the measure and form of the participation of the state in the profits of these enterprises of light industry operating with capital-intensive technology (on the basis of title to ownership right and shares, or through taxation). We have also left out of account the offsetting or easing effect of the economic policy or intervention of the state (import restrictions, employment, educational and wage policy, price control, etc.).

But even the model of a dualistic economy outlined in this chapter is a fairly abstract one, which means that even when analysing from different angles its part-mechanisms, the effects and interactions arising from the two sectors, we have to disregard a number of secondary and incidental factors. Thus it is obvious, e.g., that the outlines of the two sectors cannot be drawn that sharply; that the character and composition of the "pre-capitalist" and capitalist sectors are not that homogeneous; that there exist within and between these two sectors several other, transitory, mixed and intermediate "sub-sectors"; that the urban sector cannot simply be identified with the capitalist sector, or the rural with the "pre-capitalist" sector; that the "pre-capitalist" sector as used by us means a genuine, intact and complete, i.e. a real pre-capitalist economy and society, since it is a part of the whole dominated by capitalism; that the existing and generally expanding public sector cannot simply be regarded as part of the "modern" sector having the characteristics described above, etc. Yet, the abstraction is justified as it is possible only in this way to separate the tendencies arising from the very *nature* of the phenomenon under examination from effects of different origin.

2. THE LIMITING EFFECT OF THE DUALISTIC STRUCTURE ON THE GROWTH OF ACCUMULATION

Another well-known pehnomenon often referred to in international economic literature as a major obstacle, together with the restricted character of the market, to the economic growth of developing countries is the lack of capital, the inadequacy of accumulation.

Obviously, capital shortage is not due simply to the low level of the national income, as apologetic literature, in order to avoid any thorough analysis, seeks to make it appear.[5] The unfavourable distribution and utilization of the national

[5] For more detail see Part One of *The Political Economy of Underdevelopment*. Op. cit.

94

income is at least as important as its level, and, in fact, is a much more important factor in preventing the expansion of accumulation than the index of per capita national income, which has hardly any relevance to the dynamics of development. This becomes apparent, e.g., in the fact that while a wide range of deviations (3- to 30-fold) can be found among developing countries in respect to the level of per capita national income, the percentage share of productive accumulation (i.e. for productive investments) in gross national income are roughly the same. It even occurs that the rate of accumulation in countries, classified on the basis of the level of per capita national income as the poorest, is higher than in some of the "richer" countries. From the point of view of the order of magnitude of development programmes and industrial projects to be realized it is of course primarily the absolute measure of accumulation that counts, which depends not only on the rate of accumulation but also, and primarily, on the absolute magnitude of the national income. Yet, the growth *rate* of the latter and thus the absolute magnitude of the national income are determined in the dynamics of development by the way the national income produced is distributed and utilized.

In addition to the circumstances of producing the national income in developing countries (remnants of the ancient mode of production, predominance of poorly qualified unskilled labour, insufficient utilization of social labour resources, underdevelopment of the division of labour and organization, lack of economic incentives, foreign property and control, etc.), the distribution and utilization of the national income are also unfavourable. On the one hand, a substantial part of the national income produced is leaking away, as we have seen, through international economic relations and is transferred to and consumed in the developed capitalist countries. On the other hand, the part that remains in the country does not contribute at all, or only to an insignificant extent, to the development of the national economy, as the prevailing production and social relations and the economic mechanism cause it to be utilized mostly in a non-productive way. This seems to characterize, in most cases, the enormous oil revenues accumulating in recent years.

The causes of the inadequacy of accumulation, that is, the circumstances of the production, distribution, and utilization of the national income, also unfavourable for the expansion of accumulation, are directly connected, and not only separately, with the peculiarities of the "modern" and "pre-capitalist" sector but also with the interactions of the two sectors.

(a) THE LIMITED ACCUMULATION CAPACITY OF THE "MODERN" SECTOR

In the "modern" (export) commodity-producing sector, saving and accumulation for reinvestment purposes are restricted *first of all* by the price movement of most export products of the developing countries on the world market, either directly by the profit margin or income decreasing incidentally or in the long run, or indirectly by the negative induction effect of the price decrease. A negative induction effect may be due not only to decreasing world-market prices. The uncertainty of price formation, the *fluctuation* of prices may also discourage productive reinvestments. Even a temporary rise in prices tends to induce the filling up of the consumption funds or the consumption of the surplus income as a whole rather than reinvestment.

Secondly, it is the profit repatriation of foreign capital operating in the "modern" sector and the income transfers of foreigners living in that country which heavily reduce the potential savings and accumulation funds.

Thirdly, the low level of savings and accumulation is connected with the weakness and lack of specialization of local capital. Local small capital (including small capital represented by the "racial" minorities) is usually characterized by the joint employment of family labour and wage labour, as well as by the combination of the most different activities, often commercial ones, with all kinds of artisan and even agricultural activities. This will lead of course to the complete dispersal of capital, labour and managerial resources. As a consequence, the economic efficiency of undertakings of this type is not only extremely low and stagnant but even its survey, observation and calculation are usually lacking. There is usually no accounting of the economic results achieved, and often no stock-taking is effected. The credit-worthiness of such undertakings is low, since the banks, even if they happen not to prefer big foreign companies, are understandably reluctant to extend credits to enterprises with such a shaky financial position. The employment of family labour is often justified not by the demand for labour or the desire to make savings on the wage bill but by the compelling force of the traditional ties of the clans, which clearly point to the impact of the "pre-capitalist" sector.

Fourthly, saving for productive purposes is hampered by the limited possibility of making profitable investments. According to Paul Baran, the narrowness of investment funds and the lack of investment possibilities are but two aspects of the same problem. Some authors even go to the length of speaking of the "illusion" of capital shortage or of a "false capital need".[6] The low level of the capital-absorbing capacity of the national economy also constitutes a frequent subject of the reports of UN institutions concerned with international aid, and of other official and semi-official surveys. The weakness of the capital- and aid-absorbing capacity is due to the obstacles to the growth of branches making up the "modern" sector, first of all to the export orientation getting "stuck", and, in relation to the national economy as a whole (and mainly outside the export sector), to the backwardness of infrastructure, the lack of external economies, the limited supply of skilled workers and managerial élite and the market limitations already referred to, etc.

Fifthly, an impediment to accumulation is the insufficient motivation for reinvestment of foreign capital in the (mainly export) branches of the "modern"

[6] See, e. g., S. P. Schatz: The Capital Shortage Illusion: Government Lending in Nigeria. (*Readings in the Applied Economics of Africa.* Vol. I, Cambridge University Press, 1967, pp. 93–101.)

sector, which, together with the already mentioned negative world-market induction, reflects the lack of the internal incentives of the national economy, or the presence of negative incentives working in the opposite direction. Here, too, a distinction must be made according to the actual composition of the capitalist sector (as to what particular branches and products it comprises), the character of capital operating in it (i. e. according to the ratio and role of vertically integrated foreign monopolies, "independent" foreign private capital, "settlers' capital", national or local capital), as well as to the political, etc. environment influencing investments. The (re)investment propensity of foreign capital and private settlers' capital, more or less independent of the vertical monopolies, has fallen back, especially where the risk of nationalization or foreign-exchange difficulties, due to the adverse balance of payments, have increased. The capital of the "racial" minorities (mostly merchant, partly industrial and bank capital, occasionally agrarian capital) is discouraged to invest or kept back from further investments by the uncertainty of the political position or even of the nationality rights of the minorities. (A typical case in point is that of the East-African Indians.)

The slackening activity of private capital and its decreasing propensity to invest cannot be termed.a negative phenomenon at all where, and to the extent that, they are attending factors of strengthening the public sector and of the positive changes taking place in production relations. But even this case raises two questions:

The first is this: What happens to private, especially foreign resident capital withdrawn or withheld from investments? If no expropriation, no nationalization of the accumulated surplus value and wealth takes place, or these potential investment resources are not mobilized by the government in another way (e. g. by saving accounts, state bonds, etc.), then this immobile capital is a definite loss to the national economy. The situation is still graver if the owners have the legal or illegal possibility to transfer abroad their withheld capital, which, owing to the "open" character of the economy, the complexity of external economic relations and the weakness of foreign-exchange control resulting largely from the above factors, is a rather regular practice in most countries being in this situation.

It is these objective possibilities of transferring capital abroad and of economic sabotage – together with the accompanying subjective possibilities (corruption) – that largely provide the explanation why nationalization has led to economic troubles in many countries.

The other question – no less critical as far as the evaluation of nationalization is concerned – is whether the extended public sector is able to replace the outstanding, non-effected investments of private capital, or even to carry on in practice a more intensive, sounder and more effective investment activity than private capital. The possibility itself is indisputable and evident, of which hardly anybody needs to be convinced today. Even the majority of the representatives of Western bourgeois economics admit that state ownership and direction can ensure such a concentration of scarce resources of which private capital is incapable, and further, at least in developing countries, the sphere and nature of private investment induced by spontaneous forces of the market mechanism do not usually coincide with the criteria of the fastest development of the national economy. But the real question is how and when this possibility materializes in practice. But this leads already on to the discussion of the following problem.

The *sixth* impediment to a fast rate of accumulation and productive investment is the low level of economic effectiveness and "surplus-value"-producing capacity of state-owned productive units or state-guided mixed companies in the "modern" sector. This is due not only to the poor quality of manpower, the lack of technical knowledge, the obstacles to enlarging the market needed to expand production, etc., i.e. the temporary factors deriving directly from economic underdevelopment, but to some less "direct" and "objective" factors as well. Such are the deficiencies of labour organization and management, which result from the negligence, irresponsibility and the lack of supervision of the otherwise highly qualified (often imported and highly paid) economic managers, and especially from the tendency which manifests itself within the public and semi-public, the so-called parastatal sector in the shift of activities and costs towards *non-productive activities, costs and investments,* and is a rather general phenomenon in nearly all developing countries.

The disproportionate increase in non-productive activities and expenses is of course characteristic not only of the state-owned productive units and their guiding organs but to a much greater extent of the development of the whole public administration, the public sector as well as of the entire structure of budget expenditures and indeed of the development programmes.

Seventhly, the unproductive squandering of potential accumulation resources in the whole public sector and in the spheres under the guidance and financing of the state in general must be regarded as one of the most serious obstacles to internal accumulation, growing in significance with the development of the public sector and central planning.

What is involved here is not merely the fact that *bureaucracy* has its own "law of growth".[7] It is the centralization of decisions, more exactly the extension of the decision-making authority of the centre to more and more questions and to their minute details, that entails the danger of an overgrowth of administrative work (information, reports, instructions, expertise, etc.), and that all "division of labour" in the centre of administration – contrary to the division of labour in the sphere of production – results, together with more and more desks, in the increased work and new burdens of administration. This "self-development" of bureaucracy is not limited, as we know, to the developing countries only. What is specific, however, to the developing countries is the fact that the bureaucracy and bureaucratic tendency of colonial administration have been taken over, mostly directly and more or less unchanged, by the public administration after independence. On the other hand, owing to the dualistic economic pattern and

---

[7] For a witty description of this phenomenon see *Parkinson's Law*, Houghton Mifflin Co., Boston.

the peculiar class structure, the wide gap, even within the "modern" sector, between the narrow élite and the lower social strata, as well as to other factors (e.g. "racial", minority, tribal, religious, etc. factors), the social and political forces that could take an active part in the never-ending struggle against bureaucracy are lacking.

Since the question of economies and potential investments are closely connected with the structure of consumption and the so-called consumption habits, it seems to be worthwhile to dwell here, in some detail but from another angle, on this question, too.

Consumption habits in developing countries do not adjust themselves to the average level of development (including both sectors) of the given national economy, but are under the influence of effects coming from different directions yet providing stimulation equally, or even in a cumulative way, to "overconsumption". This *"propensity to overconsumption"* manifests itself of course in a different way in the case of persons with high incomes and belonging to the leading stratum of the "modern" sector (foreign and local capitalists, landowners, plantation owners) and in the case of employees with low salaries. It is of course also motivated by religious and other factors.

The effects stimulating "overconsumption" and their cumulation derive, characteristically, from the nature and co-existence of the two sectors. As a subsidiary and more or less new factor may be mentioned the fairly general practice of the "nationalization" of colonial administration, in which, with the structure and mechanism of state administration left intact, the posts of colonial officials are gradually filled up by local cadres who inherit not only the payments and service scales[8] but also the way of life and consumption habits of their predecessors.

The "modern" sector represents, primarily, an open gate to the so-called *demonstration effect* related to the higher consumption level of the more developed countries and inducing, as already mentioned, the employees in higher income brackets, local capitalist entrepreneurs, plantation owners, farmers, merchants, etc., to imitate the higher consumption levels of the economically more developed countries. Especially strong is the demonstration effect, and the *"propensity to imitate"* following in its wake, when a large number of foreigners (capitalist entrepreneurs, officials, experts, high-salaried skilled workers, technicians) are engaged in the "modern" sector, who as a matter of routine try to imitate the consumption habits of the metropolitan country.

The existence and influence of the "pre-capitalist" sector and inherited social remnants, however, give rise to the "propensity to conspicuous consumption" also extending to the "modern" sector and leading to non-productive expenses on

[8] In connection with this Dumont writes: "During the past phase of colonization, the policy was to equalize salaries of Africans and Europeans in similar jobs, a defensible position only in the framework of 'assimilation' ... At independence, this pseudo-equality has led to flagrant disparity with the rest of population, whose standard of living is often a fifteenth of the French." (R. Dumont: *False Start in Africa*. Sphere Books, 1966, p. 67.)

luxuries. It is rooted in the authoritarian system of the traditional society, where a person's social status was determined by the relative degree of luxury and splendour he could afford. The "propensity to conspicuous consumption" manifests itself within the "pre-capitalist" sector in the fact that members of the rich upper stratum of that sector (reigning princes, maharajahs, tribal chiefs, etc.) waste their incomes on the ancient symbols of wealth, in addition to the new ones which came into fashion as a result of the demonstration effect (hoarding of gold and silver treasures,[9] luxury palaces, army of servants, luxury motor-cars, pleasure yachts, etc.). However, similar symptoms can also be observed among the poorer strata of this sector: they squander their meagre and relatively insignificant "surpluses" in order to raise their prestige and social status in the community, on the lavish entertainment of guests and the above-mentioned or similar symbols of wealth. This sometimes may also have a sort of inverted economic aim, e. g. of contracting an advantageous marriage, or gaining a public post.

Being members of the same (though by no means homogeneous) society and wishing to become well-established in the very same social hierarchy, the wealthy stratum of the "modern" sector is not immune from the "propensity to conspicuous consumption" either. Especially strong is the "propensity to conspicuous consumption" where there is a pronounced rivalry between the leading strata of the two sectors, and where the propensity to conspicuous consumption is intensified by the demonstration effect.[10]

But members of the low-income stratum of employees and wage workers of the "modern" sector are also subject to the above-mentioned effect of the "pre-capitalist" sector, especially where part of them are "migrant labourers" of the "pre-capitalist" sector. They also waste part of their earned income in a similar way, instead of satisfying their vital needs.

The saving possibilities of the members of the capitalist sector are also restricted by some effects stemming from the "pre-capitalist" sector that force people, in compliance with the *social habits* rooted in that sector, to spend a considerable part of their incomes on the excessive celebration of religious ceremonies and certain social events (e. g. marriages, funerals, common feasts, etc.), together with and even beyond the "propensity to conspicuous consumption".

The result, then, is that the capitalists of the "modern" sector, i.e. industrialists, businessmen, farmers, transport contractors, plantation owners,

[9] As an example of gold and silver hoarding let us mention the data quoted by B. Datta, according to which about 105 million ounces of gold and 4,235 million ounces of silver, the equivalent of almost half the total investments of the Third Five-Year Plan, were hoarded by private people in India. According to M. Poniatowski, a sum corresponding to about 10 per cent of the national income is hoarded up in the Arab countries. (Quoted by I. Sachs: *op. cit.,* p. 40.)

[10] This is typically the case where the élite of the state bureaucracy has been recruited from the leading stratum of the "traditional" society and has become assimilated to the group of colonial officials, or inherited their position.

100

etc., spend, as a result of the "propensity to conspicuous consumption" (and the demonstration effect), sums that are in no proportion to their actual economic position on consumption and non-productive expenses,[11] instead of saving money for productive purposes. Low-income employees often prefer luxuries instead of satisfying their basic needs in the reasonable order of their importance.

In addition, the propensity to "overconsumption" does not favour the expansion of the internal market either, and is usually associated with the increasing demand for imports or luxuries manufactured locally with imported technology.

The accumulation-restricting effect of the "pre-capitalist" sector also manifests itself in the capitalist sector in another way: the wide-spread institution of the *clan* of the "pre-capitalist" sector, but more or less common in the capitalist sector too, leads to a large-scale fragmentation of incomes.[12] This keeps under pressure both the capitalist accumulation possibilities maintaining the clan, and the higher consumption requirements, and saving possibilities of the low-income employees.

(b) THE ROLE OF THE "PRE-CAPITALIST" SECTOR IN LIMITING ACCUMULATION

The expansion of saving and productive accumulation within the "pre-capitalist" sector is limited from the very outset by the low and stagnant level of production. This is, in general, the consequence of
– the underdevelopment of the division of labour and its organization;
– inadequacy of the techniques and production methods applied;
– the predominance of the short "time-horizon" in economic decisions, and, in particular, of
– the effects resulting from the transplantation from outside and the operation of the
"modern" sector, bringing about, instead of the transformation of the "pre-capitalist" sector, only its decline.

The underdevelopment of the division of labour hampers not only the growth of productivity and the surplus-producing capacity, but also the unfolding of exchange. As a result, there is no possibility for the incentive to surplus production to develop, i. e. to produce in excess of one's own needs as long as one cannot meet them rationally at a higher level. As long as everybody produces for

---

[11] As e.g. on the purchase of uncultivated lands to demonstrate their wealth or just to amass or "freeze in" their assets in a peculiar way. These unproductive purchases of land by city dwellers are especially frequent in the Middle-East and Latin-American countries.

[12] "Whether deputy or civil servant, the African who has 'arrived' feels obliged to take his large family in charge, sometimes his friends and fellow-villagers. In the city a guest, he no longer does anything and becomes totally parasitic." (R. Dumont: *op. cit.*, p. 70.)

his own needs only and can turn out – for meeting his own needs – the same products as anybody else,[13] surplus production remains fully irrational.

The low level of the techniques and production methods applied follows of course already from the lack of the division of labour, as it is primarily the latter which provides both the subjective preconditions (accumulation of the professional experiences of a highly specialized labour force which enables it to produce technical innovations) and the objective preconditions of technical development (the breaking down to details of the production processes, which makes it possible to introduce specialized and thereby more developed tools of labour). If the production methods and techniques do not develop, the growth of labour productivity is also hampered. Under such circumstances the necessity to expand production motivated by "endogenous" factors (e. g. the growth[14] of population that is to be supplied) or "exogenous" factors (e. g. new needs arising from the existence of the "modern" sector, taxation, etc.) induces the *extensive* utilization of the factors of production. This takes place under constant and later diminishing returns, and leads, sooner or later, to a shortage of these factors (primarily of land) and results in the relative and in many respects only apparent phenomenon of "over-population" even in countries where originally the abundance of unutilized lands and natural resources was the typical case. As a consequence, the surplus-producing capacity of the "pre-capitalist" economic sector is not only incapable of any expansion but is bound to decrease.

The *short time-horizon* of economic decisions is generally unfavourable for productive accumulation. The more direct the relationship and interaction between the investment decisions and personal consumption of the decision-makers, the shorter is the time-horizon and the more the investment of savings appears as a "sacrifice" and "renunciation". Thus the time-horizon depends basically on the system of income distribution, i.e. on the production and distribution relations.

When the rather orthodox-minded authors of studies and textbooks complain about the short time-horizon of the peasant producers of developing countries, usually comparing it with the long time-horizon of Schumpeter's capitalist entrepreneurs endowed with exceptional abilities, they fail to mention this very relationship, i.e. the objective and material basis of the time-horizon.

The reason why the long time-horizon in capitalist economy could play a role at all in economic decisions, though only from the point of view of the individual

[13] Here we must distinguish of course between "pre-capitalist tribal" communities and "feudal-semifeudal" social structure. In the latter, in spite of the backwardness of exchange, there is a systematic surplus production and expropriation. Since, however, this expropriation is based on violence and not on exchange, the incentive referred to is missing just as it is in a primitive communal society.

[14] The increase in the rate of population growth cannot be actually regarded as an endogenous factor, as it is usually closely related to changes stemming from the existence of the "modern" sector. The fact that "population explosion" and the so-called "population pressure" are *not* natural phenomena but the consequences of a distorted development which must be explained mainly by the interaction of the two sectors, is sufficiently emphasized in the analysis in the subsequent subchapter.

capitalist (or group capitalist, the monopoly company) and not from the point of view of the national economy as a whole, is not the exceptional foresight of the entrepreneur, but partly the emergence of the capitalist form of commodity metamorphosis, and partly, but in connection with the former, the unfolding of the capitalist mechanism of price and income formation. The *former,* to put it briefly, means that the metamorphosis typical of simple commodity production: Commodity–Money–Commodity (C–M–C) is replaced by the metamorphosis typical of capitalist commodity production: Money–Commodity–Money' (M–C–M'), in which, at the end point of the metamorphosis, there is not a concrete kind of commodity aimed at the satisfaction of a certain clearly defined and therefore limited personal need, but the endlessly multipliable money, which may also serve as the starting-point of another metamorphosis. But for this metamorphosis to have a sense at all, M' must be greater than M (M' = M + $\varDelta$ M), a "miracle" which materializes in the process of production on the basis of the appropriation of the labour product of *others*. The repetition of this "miracle", the reproduction of $\varDelta$ M (at the same or higher level) presupposes, however, reinvestment, and therefore this "sacrifice" to be made by the capitalist is the very *precondition* for him to remain a capitalist, i. e. to live on *other* people's work. In this sense, the relationship between his personal consumption and investment decision is a transferred, an *indirect* one. (It appears direct only on the basis of such an irreal, lunatic assumption that the capitalist, contrary to his capitalist existence, would think in a non-capitalist *way,* that, in the interest of the excessive satisfaction of his momentary needs, he would renounce his claim to remain a capitalist, that is, to satisfy his excessive needs at the expense of other people's work in the future, too.) The capitalist's investment, then, as well as the preceding accumulation is in fact not a "sacrifice", *not a deduction* from his own personal consumption fund (by no means in the dynamics of a recurrent process), since the reinvestment of part of the surplus value wrested from other people's work reproduces or even increases in the last analysis his own personal consumption fund. Hence Marx's ironical remark: if the capitalist makes such a "sacrifice", philanthropy requires us to rid him of this "burdensome sacrifice" by socializing his capital.

But the fact alone that the relationship between investment decisions and personal consumption has thus become indirect, cannot eliminate the absolute advantage of investments with quick returns, that is, it does not explain concretely why investments with slow returns do not represent even a relative "sacrifice". The explanation is provided by the mechanism of *price formation*. The formation of "producers' prices", that is the redistribution of surplus value among the capitalists through the mechanism of price formation resulting in average profit, eliminates the relative disadvantages of investments with slow returns and by a process of reduction equalizes the time-horizon. In the case of monopoly prices the undertaking of slow returns with a long time-horizon is even over-compensated.

Under traditional community relations, where production is *directly*[15] under the authority of the producing individuals,[16] or to put it more exactly, is confined to the economy of the producing individuals, the time-horizon is necessarily very short. Long-term accumulations and investments mean the drastic renunciation of the satisfaction of urgent actual needs, or at best, as in the case of exceptionally good harvests, of a permissible relative "comfort". However, in view of the *security system of subsistence* prevailing in communal societies even this cannot unambiguously be justified by the argument of securing a more distant future. Incidentally, it is the fact of belonging to the community which provides security for the individual – beyond the sphere of his own economic decision – which entitles him to share in the institutionalized distribution or redistribution of the means of production (land) and, as a last resort, even in the redistribution of consumer goods – according to traditional customs – in the form of gifts and support from relatives.

The transplantation from outside of the capitalist sector and the outward orientation of its operation have also deteriorated the conditions of operation and the surplus-generating capacity of the subordinated "pre-capitalist" sector. The most direct and most unconcealed of these deteriorating effects was land expropriation widely practised in many countries (especially in South-, Central- and East-Africa), which coincided with the establishment of the colonial commodity-producing economies (plantations, mines), and compelled the "pre-capitalist" farms to make do with smaller areas of usually much inferior land. The consequences of all this are the disruption of the normal rate of the traditional shifting cultivation, the excessive exploitation of the fertility of land and pastures, soil erosion, the diminishing yields of crop farming and animal husbandry, the appearance of "population pressure" in rural areas, etc.

Taxation (imposed by the colonial government representing the "modern" sector) and the demonstration effects coming from the changed economic environment with the new needs and demands arising in their wake, have created, on the one hand, the necessity of acquiring cash-income, i. e. that of transforming the subsistence economy, while on the other hand, the way of carrying it out has been limited and distorted by the character of the capitalist sector. Instead of the final exodus of surplus manpower from the "pre-capitalist" sector and the

---

[15] The direction and supervision of social production in a socialist economy cannot be atomized. Instead of being reduced to the spheres of activity of the producing individuals or groups, it must be a *social* direction and supervision exercised by central organs representing the society as a whole. Increasing the role of the market and decentralizing a considerable proportion of economic decisions to ensure a more flexible adjustment of production to the concrete cunsumption demands, which is a characteristic of recent economic reforms in Eastern Europe, *cannot* affect the fact and necessity of the centralization of long-term investments and the accumulation serving them. In this way, the long-time horizon is to be ensured at a social level, at the level of the national economy.

[16] This is virtually the case in spite of the common ownership of land and the common performance of certain productive activities or operations preparing them (e. g. forest and bush burning, irrigation, etc.).

transformation of the subsistence economy, the migrant-labour system, in association with subsistence economy, has evolved, supplemented by partial and occasional market production. Instead of fulfilling its only possible national function, namely the mobilization of underemployed manpower,[17] the migrant-labour system, owing to the large-scale absenteeism of male labour force, has led to a decreasing intensity of economic activity in the "pre-capitalist" sector, to the deterioration of its productivity and, consequently, to an increase in relative population pressure. Thereby it has also reproduced the necessity of maintaining itself as an additional source of income and subsistence.

While land expropriation, taxation, migrant labour, diminishing crop yields and increasing population pressure, etc., have reduced the marketable surplus-generating capacity of the sector, the necessity of market production and the need for cash, together with the non-productive utilization of the surplus produce, have increased. On the other hand, the greater competitiveness of the farms of the capitalist sector (owing to the better quality of their lands, the state subsidy received, more favourable transport facilities, greater credit-worthiness, the advantages of large-scale farming, the better quality of their products, etc.) has reduced the marketing possibilities of the "pre-capitalist" sector.

The general decline of the cottage industries resulting from the same factors, but particularly from the competitiveness of the goods produced in the capitalist sector or imported from abroad, has further narrowed down the sphere of economic activity and the domestic division of labour, and has limited the possibility of the internal mobilization of the seasonally unemployed, becoming thereby a further contributory factor of the decrease in surplus-producing capacity.

Thus the accumulation possibilities in the "pre-capitalist" sector are limited first of all by the above-mentioned obstacles to creating and expanding surplus. However, even in the case of regular or occasional surplus product formation (depending e. g. on weather conditions) there are such *"built-in diverting factors"* at work which prevent converting the economic surplus into productive accumulation.

Such factor is, among other things, the one which may be called *"propensity to total consumption"*, i. e. the stimulus to use the total surplus for the expansion of consumption, for surplus consumption. This in turn is the consequence, *first,* of the low consumption and nourishment level of the rural population, which usually reaches the subsistence level of basic human needs only by consuming the total surplus occasionally produced and left. *Secondly,* it is the consequence of the markedly subsistence character of the economy, further of the lack of knowledge of market conditions, the technical and economic difficulties of marketing the produce (lack of storage facilities, great distances, lack of means of transport, poor competitiveness), i. e. of circumstances hindering the conversion of surplus

---

[17] Its real function was of course the supply of cheap labour for the colonial capitalist economies.

into cash for accumulation purposes. *Thirdly,* it is the consequence of the lack of producers' goods (e.g. simple agricultural tools) needed for the realization of productive accumulation or the difficulties of acquiring them (the lack of weakness of the corresponding distribution network, great distances, etc.). In addition, it is also closely connected with further "diverting factors".

What are these "diverting factors"?

First of all, we must make mention of the so-called *"propensity to conspicuous consumption",* which is especially strong among the representatives of the "pre-capitalist" ruling strata.[18] But because their income originates mainly from the poor rural population engaged in agricultural production (and not only in the case of feudal landowners, but also of the leaders of smaller tribal communities, chieftains and "witch" doctors), the satisfaction of this propensity stimulates the increasing expropriation of economic surplus and also strengthens the motive of the "propensity to total consumption".

No less "diverting" in its effect is the propensity which is related to religious ceremonies and certain social habits and is under the pressure of the environment, and which may be called the *"compulsory propensity to ritual and traditional expenses".* In traditional environments the celebration of social and family events and religious festivities makes it compulsory even for the poorest strata of society to exhibit the maximum possible degree of luxury. In so far as this practice is penetrated or strengthened by the endeavour to demonstrate (or even improve) the social status and authority within the community, it coincides, to a certain extent, with the "propensity to conspicuous consumption" already discussed. But the expenditures on the events involved are, nevertheless, compulsory even for the poorest population. (It is true, however, that in so far as spendings on religious ceremonies are involved, it is through them that these people, depending of course on the religion they belong to, hope to be happy in the other world, or in the next earthly stage of the transfiguration of the soul.) To this induced propensity belong the relatively immense expenses of weddings and funeral ceremonies, gifts to and maintenance of religious institutions and leaders at a level far exceeding the living standards of those contributing, together with similarly disproportionate, inhuman non-productive expenses in a world of poverty and famine, let alone the huge sacrifices, losses of time and labour force that pilgrimages to "holy" places require. The travelling of Moslems to Mecca from far-away places of the world absorbs not only millions of dollars annually but also the loss of working weeks.

Added to all this must be the losses deriving from the economic consequences of various religious prohibitions. The problem of the "sacred cow" is sufficiently known, but it is by no means confined to India. The observing of the one-week long Rhamadan fast (according to which nothing should be consumed from sunrise to sunset) causes such a weakening of the labour force that at least two

---

[18] We can find an exquisite psychological description of the propensity to conspicuous consumption of feudal landowners in the young Marx's work (*Economic and Philosophical Manuscripts of 1844.*)

weeks must be discounted from the annual working time, which, in the case of the poorest strata, is often accompanied by death or at least its speeding up and sometimes by the spread of diseases, and so on.

The joint influence of "conspicuous propensity" and "propensity to ritual-religious expenses" on the "modern" sector has already been mentioned. Here they are listed among the "built-in" factors as they also pertain to the original characteristics of "pre-capitalist" societies.

A further "diverting factor" is the *insufficiency to meet higher-grade demands* that might stimulate savings and productive accumulation, particularly among the poor strata of rural population. This is also the consequence of unsatisfied, basic needs, i.e. the low income level, which, in addition, goes together with the elastic demand for foodstuffs (more exactly with the "demand" for own products), but is also connected in many places with the lack of knowledge about more sophisticated goods and, consequently, of the wish to acquire them.

This statement may seem, at first sight, to be in contradiction to what we have said when analysing the market relations, about the demonstration effect and the abrupt increase in consumption demands. We must emphasize, however, first, that the demonstration effect asserts itself primarily in the "modern" sector, and if outside it, too, then always *through* the modern sector. Consequently, the dualistic structure, i.e. the existence, in a subordinated function, of a "pre-capitalist" sector alongside the capitalist one provides the explanation how it is possible that while in one sector of the economy it is the satisfaction of needs excessively high as a result of external effects that cause difficulties (both from the point of view of expanding the market of domestic products and of stepping up accumulation), in the other sector of economy it is the lack of knowledge of more sophisticated goods and of the desire to acquire them that impedes orientation towards the internal market and thereby the expansion of surplus production and accumulation. On the other hand, it is the other phenomenon also discussed earlier: the lack of continuity in the development of demand, the "missing links" in its pattern provide the explanation why even at such points where the demonstration effect also asserts itself within the "pre-capitalist" sector, that is, where high-grade products are not unknown, the effect of the demand to satisfy more sophisticated needs on stimulating surplus production and productive accumulation does not make itself felt either.

As a matter of fact, high-grade demands appear only in "traces", not continuously or in a both quantitatively and qualitatively gradually expanding and connected system. As a consequence, they lead either to the typical phenomenon of single "target purchases" already mentioned, or are directed towards such commodities which are inaccessible even under the transformation of a "pre-capitalist" economy into a commodity-producing economy.

The *insufficient knowledge* of how to turn the economic surplus into productive investments and of the way to realize and utilize them, also belongs to the "diverting factors". This insufficiency is connected with the backwardness of economic thinking, generally characteristic of "pre-capitalist" societies, but is also indirectly connected with the quantitative and qualitative insufficiency of public education, the underdevelopment of communication and information services, i. e. also with the weakness of the positive effect of the "modern" sector. The latter factor, to use Myrdal's term, may also be called "spread effect", adding to it, however, that it is not simply the consequence of the low developmental level of the national economy[19], but rather of dualism, the contradictory character of the two sectors. It is commonly known that communication, a wide range of contacts and links has developed within the capitalist sector and particularly between the capitalist sector and foreign countries, while even the simplest achievements of the development of science and technology are, for lack of the "channels" of positive demonstration, not accessible to the "pre-capitalist" sector.

Certain changes in this respect can only be observed in countries where the extension of the educational network to areas of the "pre-capitalist" sector has already made appreciable progress. But even in that case only when the character of school education has also been changed and where – usually in connection with the former – a regular, not campaign-like, so-called "extension service" has been introduced. But even then a rather serious obstacle to the spread of information on investments and production expansion is the simple but very sad fact that the research of international agrarian science is confined, apart from some tropical export crops, almost exclusively to the problems of European and North-American agriculture and their products. As far as the "original" products of tropical agriculture are concerned (including animal stock, e. g. the species of animals substantially differing in characteristics from the European ones), scientific research is still in its infancy. But the solution of the problems of developing tropical agriculture and of carrying out the transformation of the "pre-capitalist" sector in general can be based neither on the expansion of the traditional one-crop exports faced with marketing difficulties, nor on the enforced adaptation of cultivation methods used efficiently in the case of European plants and their production.

As further impediments to productive investments must be mentioned certain *negative circumstances of the transfer of potential investment factors* in the case of marketing
– of land,
– of economic surplus and
– of labour force.

This transfer takes place either within the "pre-capitalist" sector or between the two sectors, or along their contact face. In principle, the exploitation and utilization of land, economic surplus and underemployed manpower[20] – all mean

---

[19] For a detailed discussion and criticism of Myrdal's conception see *The Political Economy of Underdevelopment*, Part One, op. cit.

[20] Nurkse is right in saying that disguised unemployment implies a disguised saving potential as well. (R. Nurkse: *Problems of Capital Formation in Underdeveloped Countries*. Oxford University Press, 1962, p. 37.)

potential investment possibilities. In most cases, however, the specific direction and the way of the transfer eliminate or reduce this possibility.

Thus, e. g., the sale of lands – where it is not prohibited by traditional customs – aims mostly at satisfying the sellers' "propensity to conspicuous consumption", at meeting the needs required by ritual customs, subsistence, or by paying off previous debts (usury!) incurred because of them, that is, they are sales serving consumption purposes. But on the part of the buyers, too, these purchases are made solely in the interest of satisfying their "propensity to conspicuous consumption", or of "hoarding up" their fortune or the expansion of the sources of non-productive consumption.

The sale of economic surplus is often carried out through intermediaries or usurers who not only skim off a substantial part of the surplus, but also eliminate it from the productive accumulation process and use it for their own "over-consumption" or usurious loans serving the same purpose.

At the same time, the utilization of manpower comes up against the limitations of the absorptive capacity of the "modern" sector. Thus, the "physical" transfer of manpower, however temporary in many cases, to the capitalist sector, owing to urban unemployment or employment in non-productive jobs, does not always mean real "labour investment", a greater and productive utilization of the underemployed manpower of the "pre-capitalist" sector.

With unfolding capitalism in Western Europe both the commercialization of land (with the abolition of feudal law) and the marketing of the surplus product (through the careful separation of even the slightest surplus product from the volume of product necessary for reproduction and the bare subsistence of those engaged in agricultural production), as well as the hiring of labour force migrating or rather expelled from the rural economies, fitted into the uniform process of *primitive accumulation*, and the transfer of these potential accumulation factors served the complete transformation of "pre-capitalist" agriculture and the development of a truly viable urban industry. In the developing countries, however, similar phenomena did not result in a genuine primitive accumulation.

Land expropriations preceding the establishment of foreign plantations cannot be compared with enclosures in England, which prepared the creation of a domestic agricultural capitalist class and of a proletariat finally "freed" from its means of production and rural basis. But even where the commodity-producing big estates developed in domestic ownership and where, consequently, the transfer of lands from the subsistence economy to market economy opened up real sources of accumulation, these sources of accumulation remained for the most part unutilized, owing to the lack of other conditions of transformation.

The conditions for either the "English", the "American" or the "Prussian" way of agrarian capitalist development could not come into being in the colonial or dependent countries. Not even the development of the largely specific and mostly capitalized Latin-American agriculture can be regarded as a real "Prussian-type" development. This is not only due to the fact that the transformation was induced from outside and served primarily foreign interests with foreign capital playing a predominant role in it, but because the feudal forms of the expropriation of the economic surplus can be assessed as the specific results of a heterogeneous process rather than as transitory remnants, which, instead of the forceful accumulation of the national agrarian capital, are the factors of stagnation and immobility.

Thus the transfer of lands from an economic form ensuring less accumulation possibility to another, a more developed one, has remained, *on the one hand*, partial, that is, the primitive forms of the economic utilization of land have widely survived (largely accounting for the "population pressure" on land), and, *on the other hand*, it has not attained its real aim: the expansion of national accumulation for productive purposes. This transfer served, on the part of the buyers or expropriators, *either* the accumulation of foreign capital, *or*, instead of the growth of productive accumulation, the non-productive consumption or hoarding up of certain indigenous strata. But even on the part of the sellers, the typical motive for them was not the productive utilization of the resources acquired by the sale of land (or the more rational exploitation, by means of these resources, of the remaining land), but the maintenance or expansion of their consumption.

The same applies, more or less, to the realization of surplus product, too. The greedy and mercilessly rational endeavour in the early phase of European capitalist development not only to concentrate every available surplus but also to convert it into *productive* accumulation could not unfold in the colonial and dependent countries, except for certain spheres of the operation of foreign capital. Instead, the transfer of surplus for consumption purposes has remained typical both of the mostly "occasional" sellers and the exploiting intermediaries of the "pre-capitalist" sector.

The migration (in many places a coercive process at the beginning) of manpower from the "pre-capitalist" to the capitalist sector, may be a form of the productive mobilization of disguised unemployment, or even the starting-point for rural social transformation, which means that this "factor of production" may fit into the process of productive accumulation. But the specific circumstances of this transfer in the countries concerned usually render a real mobilization impossible. The transfer itself has mostly remained temporary or periodical (migrant labour) and could therefore not become the driving force of the transformation of the "pre-capitalist" sector, and could not produce an urban proletariat independent of pre-capitalist ties. Since the exodus of male labour force has been, in spite of rural "over-population", often detrimental to the output of "pre-capitalist" agriculture, the accumulation potential of this sector continues to deteriorate despite the decrease in the number of consumers. At the same time, owing to the limited and slowly increasing absorbing capacity of the productive branches of the capitalist sector, disguised rural unemployment has changed in many places more and more into unconcealed urban unemployment (i.e. into a still less favourable form both socially and also from the point of view of the accumulation potential). And if the labour force that has become redundant for the productive branches of the capitalist sector finds employment

110

in the non-productive branches (usually in domestic service), this again does not mean the realization of the investment potential.

In addition to the obstacles to expanding productive accumulation as summarized in the foregoing and manifesting themselves partly in the "modern", partly in the "pre-capitalist" sector or their interactions, it is worthwhile to mention the troubles arising from foreign trade.

3. THE EFFECT OF THE DUALISTIC STRUCTURE ON THE POPULATION AND MANPOWER SITUATION

"Population pressure" is a well-known phenomenon in the developing countries manifesting itself in the fact that the results of the growth in production and income are rendered ineffectual by the higher rate of population growth. Consequently, there is a constant tension in the field of food supply and employment. The specific dualism of the manpower position of developing countries is also commonly known: a large-scale surplus of unskilled labour, on the one hand, and an acute shortage of skilled labour, on the other.[21]

This time we shall pay special attention again to those aspects of this phenomenon which are connected with the co-existence of the two sectors, with the lack of internal integration.

"Population pressure" as well as underutilized manpower surplus are definitely *relative* phenomena, since they are a function not only of a rapid rate of population growth but also of production growth lagging behind it, and of the insufficient labour-absorbing capacity of the capitalist sector.[22] This relativity and its background become especially apparent if we examine the interaction of the "pre-capitalist" and the capitalist sectors.

The rapid rate of population increase is, as commonly known, due to a decreasing death rate concurrently with an unchanged high birth rate. The decline of mortality is the result of the positive effect of the "modern" sector, or of the better, though far from satisfactory health service the "pre-capitalist" sector received from outside. On the other hand, birth rate is still basically determined, beyond the actual or assumed need for labour supply, by ancient customs and moral-laws deeply rooted in the "pre-capitalist" sector.

It is obvious that the only acceptable human solution, in the interest of a more favourable rate of population growth, can only be achieved by a further *decline in*

---

[21] The fact that in recent years employment difficulties for school leavers (and even university graduates) have arisen and have been increasing in a number of countries, does not mean at all that this acute shortage has come to an end, and the problem itself of employing school leavers is the manifestation and consequence of the disproportions and "missing links" in both the employment and educational system and which, with an acute shortage being maintained, tend to give rise to overproduction and/or oversupply in certain qualified categories.

[22] That it is *not* an absolute phenomenon is proved by the very fact that it may be accompanied by an extremely low and an extremely high population density alike.

mortality rate and a vigorous improvement of the health service in general as well as by an unlimited freedom of conscious and voluntary birth control, together with the elimination of the effects limiting this freedom.

What are the factors and effects that restrict the individual (parental) freedom of birth control, and make for a high rate of population growth?

Such is, first of all, the organization and division of labour of the "pre-capitalist" sector, with *child labour* playing a role in it. But at least of the same importance are those *"compulsory propensities"* which develop in parents due to the influence of religion, ancient customs, moral laws, and under the psychological "pressure" of the clan comprising a large number of relatives. The manifestation of the latter factors are: the social condemnation of barren women; religious prescriptions rigidly subordinating sexual intercourse to generating children (which to a large extent is typical of Christian religions); the social or even religious approval of the husband leaving or rather expelling his barren wife; the acceptance by certain religions (e. g. Muslim) of maintaining several wives and even regarding this practice in some countries as a measure of authority and wealth; the morally approved extension of sexual intercourse within the clan to brothers-in-law, sisters-in-law and relatives of second degree, etc., which, in the last analysis, strengthens the tendency of a high population growth.

The *institution of the clan* itself restricts the decision-making authority of the family in a narrower sense (parents) by sharing with it the burden of maintaining the children and, by doing so, makes the parents' decision more or less independent of and exempt from these expenses.

Apart from the above-mentioned factors and religious prohibitions, the spread of family planning is due, first of all, to the lack of *knowledge* of the methods of birth control acceptable from both human and medical points of view, as well as to the unavailability to a sufficient extent of the necessary institutions and means of health. (Even if, e. g., the existence of the "pills" happened to be already known, and there exists the will to apply them, the difficulties of acquiring them and primarily the exorbitant prices make this method of birth control practically impossible for just those wide masses of population where the conditions for bringing up many children are missing.)

However, it should be emphasized again that the high birth rate (population growth) is but one of the components of "population pressure", of "over-population". It is not an unfavourable phenomenon in itself, only in conjunction with, and in fact *because of,* the lagging rate of the growth of production and the poor labour-absorbing capacity. But while the increase in population is determined in the last analysis by influences stemming from the "pre-capitalist" sector, the growth rate of the economy is basically contingent on the development and expansion possibilities of the "modern" sector. For lack of internal integration, the movements of the two components are not interlinked. This also accounts, in the last analysis, for surplus manpower output.

112

(a) SURPLUS OF UNSKILLED LABOUR

As far as the quantitative aspect of the manpower problem is concerned, unskilled labour surplus is also due to the dualism of the "pre-capitalist" and the capitalist sectors in that the former acts as an abundant and rapidly expanding source of manpower, while the latter as a medium with much less labour-absorbing capacity.

The volume and rate of the labour output of the "pre-capitalist" sector depend on course on the development of the demographic situation outlined above, as well as on the "spatial" and "time" limitations of the labour-absorbing capacity within the sector, i.e. the area of cultivable land and the quantity of other available means of production, on the one hand, and on seasonal changes in labour-intensity on the other. (It should be noted that the latter are particularly considerable, and cause a wide range of fluctuation in the degree of the exodus of the labour force and disguised unemployment where they are confined only to a few crops ripening at the same time. The fact that animal-breading tribes are not involved in the migrant-labour system is due not only to their nomadic way of life, but also to the much evener labour-absorbing capacity and intensity of animal husbandry.)

In determining the size of the outflow of labour from the "pre-capitalist" sector an important role is also played by the effect of the "dislodging" economic and non-economic factors. Such are, e.g., the insufficiency of the sources of subsistence, escape from debts, from the primitive living conditions and customs and from the sphere of feudal, semi-feudal dependence or from the crippling ties of kinship. Account must also be taken of the suction effect of the capitalist sector, which manifests itself in the attraction of the conveniences of urban life, the hope of higher consumption levels and living standards and the expectation of better educational possibilities, etc.

The effect of the above factors, together with the interaction of the labour-supplying "pre-capitalist"-rural sector and of the capitalist-urban sector which should absorb that labour, add up to *the cumulative tendency of an over-supply of manpower*. Though the development of labour surplus depends not only on the supply of labour force by the "pre-capitalist", but also on the absorbing capacity of the capitalist sector, the expansion of the latter is impeded by the well-known difficulties of the growth of the constituent branches of that sector and the limitations of accumulation and unfavourable market relations, or, in the case of the newly established import-substituting industries, by the limitations of the capital-intensive techniques, in addition to the increasing suction effect of the capitalist sector.

As a result of the over-supply of manpower, the increase in productivity in the capitalist sector does not generally result in rising wages, at least not for unskilled workers. (Or if it does, it increases the suction effect and the over-supply.) It leads, instead, to the expansion of production, which usually means the growth of

8 Nyilas

113

the enclaves mostly grappling with unfavourable world-market conditions, or to the import-oriented luxury consumption of entrepreneurs, owners, and possibly of the élite of workers and employees.

(b) THE LACK OF ADEQUATELY TRAINED LABOUR FORCE

The unfavourable *qualitative* structure of manpower, the acute shortage of skilled and semi-skilled workmen is primarily the consequence of the backwardness of public education, though it is also connected with the quantitative development and peculiarities of the movement, the flow of the labour force. The nature and effect of the two sectors are reflected not only in the latter, but in no small measure also in the state and structure of education.

The appropriate quantitative and qualitative development of education and vocational training is limited, or detrimentally effected, by
- the low level of the national income and budgetary revenues (which, in turn, is also connected with the limitations of internal accumulation;
- the insufficiency of the positive incentives of the capitalist sector and the assertion of the negative external effects penetrating this sector;
- the "resistance" or negative effect of the "pre-capitalist" sector;
- the consequences of the co-existence of the two sectors.

1. *The capitalist sector* has not promoted the development of the educational system. Owing to its origin going back to colonial times, to the low technical level of its main and typical branches (agriculture and mining), as well as to the guiding, managerial and skilled personnel formerly entirely and still largely composed of foreigners in many places – this sector has shown very limited demand for *local* skilled labour. It has been based, instead, on cheap unskilled labour. Consequently, the general development of the educational system and vocational training, particularly technical training, did *not* become of vital interest to the productive branches of the capitalist sector, their growth decline remained independent of the result or failures of the local school system. But even the non-productive spheres of the capitalist-urban sector, primarily public administration itself, had no demand for locally educated youth in such a number and composition that it could have induced a sufficiently widely based development of primary and secondary education. Even the education of the few local persons employed in higher posts or requiring specialized training took place in the universities and colleges of the metropolitan country. For occupying the lower posts, however, usually requiring only reading and writing and the knowledge of the official language of the metropolitan country, the few, mostly missionary schools attended by children of the well-to-do and reliable "better families" appeared fully sufficient.

On the other hand, the capitalist sector, as the externally oriented part of the economy closely associated with the economies of other countries, opened up the way for the transplantation of the West-European educational system, in addition

114

to, or reinforced by, similar activities of the colonial governments. This school system was not only the reflection of an economic and social environment entirely different in structure and development, but was already outdated even in its original environment, in view of the requirements of economic and technical development. Its excessively unpractical *orientation* towards the humanities, and the high-reaching but not sufficiently well-founded graduality (i. e. the multitude and confusing character of the successive degrees), as well as the often irrational freedom of choosing courses, together with their great inadequacy of meeting the practical needs of the profession, etc., cannot prove suitable for economic development.

The complementing of the capitalist-urban sector by some new branches differing from the export enclaves (e. g. import-substituting plants based on capital-intensive techniques), as well as the policy of replacing foreign personnel and substituting local labour force for foreign colonial officials particularly in state administration, have brought about *changes* in the structure of labour demand. This has taken place even in such countries where formerly the employment of local labour force in the capitalist sector remained almost exclusively restricted to unskilled (mostly migrant) workers, and the educational system, too, was extremely underdeveloped. But a certain degree[23] of a shift in the demand for labour force towards the skilled categories has not yet resulted in a sound demand pattern which could stimulate the building up of a system of general education and vocational training adjusted to the needs of a dynamic economic development. The *"missing links"* are characteristic features not only in the industrial branch structure but have also evolved in the pattern of manpower. While in the former they prevent the economic linkage effects from coming into operation and strengthen outward orientation, they disrupt the "social linkage effects" in the latter. In addition, they hinder the natural supply of qualified labour and the *joint* upgrading of the entire labour force. This is one of the significant contributory factors of the contradiction – along with the internal deficiencies of education – which exists between the serious shortage of skilled labour and the increasing employment difficulties of school-leavers.

Besides semi-skilled but unqualified workers, experienced only in simple technical operations, the new industries demand a labour force of a *small number* of highly qualified and *specialized* workmen rather than a core of mobile and versatile skilled workers with wide, comprehensive knowledge of, and practice in, their trades. And yet it would be the latter that could fill up their own ranks by training the less qualified and less experienced workers and ensure the supply of the higher grades of labour force (technicians, shop-managers) partly by their own further education.

And the advancing replacement of foreigners in public administration (together, in many places, with the further expansion of state bureaucracy), has

---

[23] This does not affect, or only scarcely affects, the invariably dominant primary-producing branches, and even less the domestic service still playing an important role in employment.

brought about an abrupt and disproportionately increasing demand for administrators, which, together with the income expectations of these jobs, stimulates the over-production of unspecialized bureaucrats.

Thus, while opening up new scope for social differentiation and increasing the separation of a narrow élite within the workers from the uneducated masses and promoting the alienation of a state bureaucratic élite from society, these changes in the structure of the capitalist-urban sector and public education *do not induce* a large-scale development of general education and the formation of a structure of vocational training founded on a wide basis and comprising interlocking vertical grades.

But the spontaneous, inducing effects exert a poor or even adverse influence not only on the sound transformation and development of public education but also on the process of on-the-job training as well. On-the-job vocational training does not develop satisfactorily as it is held back, among other things, by the fear that workers, after having been qualified and trained, will leave their jobs and so the cost of their training will be lost. This is particularly significant in an internally non-integrated economy including enclaves, as in such an economy there is no or scarcely any possibility of replacing a worker who leaves his job by a worker trained elsewhere. It may also occur that a qualified or trained worker returning to the "pre-capitalist" rural sector gets completely lost to the labour market or at least to the trade in question.[24]

2. The "resistance" of the "pre-capitalist" sector to the development of education may manifest itself in a number of ways. Thus, e.g., in the *subjective aversion* of part of the traditional leading strata or even of some heads of families to science endangering traditional institutions, to the spirit of education revolting against ancient customs, and to the education of young people wishing to outdo the old.

But it becomes apparent first of all in the *objective obstacle* that child labour is still fairly widespread and difficult to dispense with in this sector, it being an important part of the productive forces of the family or community.

It further manifests itself in the equally objective obstacle that is characteristic of the sector in general: the territorial dispersion of families and communities and the very limited availability of transport facilities.

The "pre-capitalist" sector exercises a negative effect on the development trend of public education by the fact that – in so far as it takes an interest in, and shows a demand for education at all – (of course within the limitations mentioned earlier and usually only in relations to the children of the well-to-do upper strata), their interest lies primarily or exclusively in legal, political, philosophical,

---

[24] This danger is of course less apparent in the case of the highly specialized (and well-paid) élite workers. This is, among other things, one of the contributory incentives for applying capital-intensive technology, where the other extreme, i.e. the combination of the wide masses of unskilled labour with a small number of expatriate guiding personnel (which is generally the case in the primary-producing export enclaves) does not seem to be profitable.

116

religious, etc., studies needed for administrative, judicial or ecclesiastical jobs, i.e. in the humanities rather than in the teaching of natural sciences or in vocational training.

Feudal monarchs, maharajahs, chieftains, who, owing to their wealth and privileged position, could afford already in colonial times the luxury to give their children higher education, sent them, almost without exception, to the faculties of law, philosophy, theology, political sciences or liberal arts of British or French universities or to military academies. They assigned of course the same role to the local schools of primary and secondary education, in order to ensure an adequate preparation for such university studies. And where local universities came to be established, the members of the traditional leading strata, who, owing to their direct share in political power or through self-government or parliamentary representation, were in a position to influence the character of these universities, they invariably tried to do it in favour of sciences they had studied themselves and wanted to be taught to their children.

3. From the point of view of the development of education and vocational training the *co-existence and interaction of the two sectors* further increase the negative consequences and effects we have already referred to.

First, labour migration and fluctuation, owing to the combined effects of the attractive and repelling forces, assume considerable proportions and show an increase in many places. As a result, even the skills acquired in practice mostly get lost, and regular or longer on-the-job training comes up against serious difficulties owing to large-scale dropouts or to new trainees.

Secondly, the labour market is rather "open" in the sense that not only the volume of inputs but also of outputs is uncertain and constantly changing, which makes teaching and the training of skills on the job rather risky for capitalist employers in general and individual employers in particular.

Thirdly, the intensive and interconnected fluctuations in the size of the labour market and of the internal labour demand and absorptive capacity of the "pre-capitalist" sector also determine the position of those of schooling age and make the measure of enrolments uncertain and the number of intermediate dropouts considerable.

Fourthly, owing to migration and school dropouts, the level of the basic schooling of the employed and of those waiting for employment is extremely different and uneven. This in itself makes further education and on-the-job training extraordinarily difficult.

Fifthly, the one-sided orientation of public education towards the humanities and its non-descript character devoid of all practical features follow from the very nature and effects of each of the two sectors. Though originally the heritage of colonial times, it has later become one of the manifestations of the internal mechanism of the system, of the mutual relationship of the two sectors. The increasing tendency of bureaucratism, also a consequence of the inherent mechanism of the system, constitutes one of the major obstacles to the re-orientation of public education, its shifting in the direction of practical knowledge.

Sixthly, the income relations prevailing within each of, or between, the two sectors bring into motion economic incentives in favour of public administration and of administrative jobs in general, at the expense of productive employments and related practical trades. They channel, therefore, education and intellectual resources in general into an unsound direction.

Seventhly, and largely as a result of the above factors, a considerable part of the demand for skilled labour can be satisfied by means of imports only. This leads, in addition to the danger of neo-colonialist influence, to wage gaps between foreign and local employees or strengthens the tendency of income tensions within the local society.

Eighthly, a substantial proportion of the education of qualified labour materializes through foreign scholarships, which, apart from dependence on such grants, also involves the danger of foreign intellectual influence and enhances the difficulty of forming a homogeneous national intelligentsia.

4. SOME OTHER MANIFESTATIONS AND CONSEQUENCES OF INTERNAL DISINTEGRATION

The tow-sector character of the economy, the lack of its internal integration, makes itself felt not only in the spheres of market relations, accumulation, manpower and education, but in other fields and relations as well. In addition to the development of social class structure (to be dealt with in the next chapter), such are, e.g., the building up of the transport and communications network, the system of applicable economic incentives and social reactions and the way of thinking in general, the development of social consciousness and even such fields as, e.g., the use and effectiveness of foreign assistance.

The transport network is characterized not only by a high degree of decentralization, the predominance of outward-going transport lines (which is closely connected with the export-orientation of the capitalist sector), but also by the extreme contrasts of the means and methods of conveyance. Between the up-to-date and largely long-haul means of transport and the primitive, mainly human means of conveyance of the "pre-capitalist" sector, there are usually no intermediate methods (such as horse- and oxen-drawn vehicles and in many places even pack animals,[25]) which played such an important part, e.g., in the development of the short-haul trade relations of European countries and which could also be made available to the rural primary producers at a relatively low cost. The demonstration effect and the ensuing imitation propensities manifesting themselves through the capitalist sector, as well as the "prestige propensity" of

[25] An objective impediment to the widespread use of saddle animals is of course the danger of tsetse flies infecting large areas.

the young states, induce them to adopt a costly transport development policy (demanding a first-class road network, expensive sea- and airports, etc.). At the same time, for lack of short-haul means of conveyance, simpler and cheaper methods of transportation, an overwhelming proportion of total social labour gets lost in walking to the workplace or to the market.

There is a striking disproportion and contrast between the ways of *communications,* too. Along with developed networks of radio, television (in some places even colour television) and telephones in the towns, communications in many a rural area are still based on personal contacts and primitive signalling (drumbeats, smoke signals, etc.).

(a) THE PECULIARITIES OF SOCIAL REACTIONS AND WAYS OF THINKING

As a result of the interferences of the effects of customs and propensities rooted in the "pre-capitalist" sector and of the influences operating through the capitalist sector, the *social reactions* to economic decisions are of a very heterogeneous character within the society as a whole, too, and are especially different in the two basic sectors. Therefore, the incentives that can be applied in the course of the implementation of the economic development programme cannot be identical in the two sectors, nor can the incentives that proved effective in the developed countries be simply copied even within the capitalist sector. (It is well known, e.g., that in many places wage incentives were not only ineffective but often had an adverse effect, as was also the case with price incentives applied to agricultural produce.)

All this is also connected of course with the peculiarities of the *general way of thinking,* which are not simply some "ancient", "original" phenomena of the societies of developing countries but are the consequences of the "economic environment". Thus, e.g., the false interpretation of the concept of work, or more exactly the vague, erroneous assessment of productive or useful work, is connected with the peculiar characteristics and effects of the two sectors.

In the "pre-capitalist" sector productive and non-productive activities are still largely not differentiated, on the one hand, and, on the other, there is hardly any direct relationship between the quality and intensity of the work and its results.

The administrative and religious functions usually also include some economic functions but mostly in such a way that the latter play a secondary, subsidiary part in relation to the former. (Such is, e.g., the chieftain's right and role to re-distribute the lands as compared to his main function which he as the representative and "mediator" of dead ancestors performs in governing the tribe, a function from which, as a matter of fact, his responsibility to re-distribute the tribal lands constituting the property of dead ancestors follows.) As regards directly productive work, it is usually despised in feudal and semi-feudal societies, while in the primitive societies of tribal community it is often exactly that work, i.e. female labour, on which agricultural production, the growing of food crops is based and thus public supply depends, to which no credit is given at all.

The relationship betwen the work performed and the result achieved is loose largely because crop-yields in the "pre-capitalist" sector, as in backward agriculture in general, are determined to a great extent by natural factors, i.e. by factors independent of human labour. Therefore, primitive thinking considers favourable crops as gifts of the gods or ancestors, or ascribes them to the rain-producing activities of wizards rather than to the labour put into that work. But it would not be just to blame these societies for their resistance and reluctance[26] to increase productive labour and for the ineffectiveness of economic incentives! As long as the objective circumstances are such that the results of strenuous work can be annihilated by weather less favourable than usual, a single dry season or a flood, while at another time idleness is richly rewarded by nature, increased productive work is not the consequence of economic rationality but that of compulsion.

But owing to the integration into the economy and operation of the capitalist sector, even such ways of the development of the "pre-capitalist" sector have got blocked which, as a result of the development of productive forces, eventually led, e.g. in Europe, to the transformation of that sector. The integration of the capitalist sector impeded, on the one hand, the extensive expansion of the "pre-capitalist" sector to keep pace at least with the growth of population, i.e. the realization in economic results of the "extensive" compulsion operating through the increasing number of "hungry mouths", and prevented qualitative change in productive forces that might have been made possible by the increasing number of "working hands". It hindered, on the other hand (by means of the possibility of labour migration and even by laws), or used in its own interest, i.e. monopolized, the "intensive" type of compulsion, which included the manifestation in increased economic exploitation of a hierarchical social order causing the disintegration of pre-capitalist society. This is one of the main reasons why "underdevelopment" cannot be explained by the "original" backwardness of the pre-capitalist society, and why even the primitive way of thinking of the "pre-capitalist" sector, or to put it more exactly, its survival, is not connected with the peculiar character of the capitalist sector.

In addition to what has already been mentioned, the direct relationship between productive work and its results is further weakened by the fact that in many places the distribution and re-distribution of the results of work take place in compliance with the laws of communal society, that is, according to the rules of a primitive egalitarianism. This holds true not only of primitive communal societies in their strict sense but also of the so-called village communities based on

---

[26] Many economists describe this phenomenon simply as "leisure time preference" and, in accordance with the traditions of orthodox bourgeois economics, are satisfied with the explanation that peasants, who for some – obviously psychical – reasons are lacking the "spirit of enterprise", prefer resigning the benefits that can be obtained from production to sacrificing leisure time and comfort. This is the only "explanation" they offer for the socio-economic aspects of the phenomenon! (It is in a similar way, by referring to the lack of the "innovation propensity" of peasants, that they account for the technical backwardness of the "pre-capitalist" sector.)

feudal relations, and of clans that can be found in the multifarious combinations of social formations.

As far as the capitalist sector is concerned, the factors (most of which have already been mentioned) working there against the appreciation or even a clear delineation of productive work, are those which are connected with the role of foreigners, the disproportionate size of the non-productive branches and institutions of the superstructure, and the predominance in general of administrative-bureaucratic activities.

The households of expatriates and of the local élite following in their footsteps, and other institutions destined to serve them, that is, services in general, provide for the local manpower not only the main, in many places the most important sort of emloyment, but also by far more attractive jobs, which are, as far as the working conditions and earning possibilities are concerned, much more favourable than those available to them on the land or in plants. And what is even worse: the concept of income, of making money is not sufficiently tied to productive work, moreover, often and in many places it is not connected with anything at all that could be called "work" or a socially useful activity.

The wages of workers and employees engaged in the productive branches are generally subsistence wages or time wage rates (usually fixed by the week or the month) which are hardly, if at all, connected with actual performance. As a rule, performance norms and targets, the application of any methods to measure performance, or any information service concerning the work performed are very rare exceptions.

In the typical productive branches of the capitalist sector the system of quantitative incentives is, by the way, usually in conflict with the limitations of the given market. This means that they are, without significant structural changes, and thereby without a radical alteration of market relations, not rational at all. Owing to the problem on unemployment generally the governments themselves do not regard these incentives as desirable. This holds true not only of the enclave sectors where increased production, due to the limited world-market demand usually leads to the accumulation of unsaleable stocks, or gives rise to a decrease in prices and returns, but also of the import-substituting sectors producing for the internal market. The too fast increase in outputs in the latter comes up against the limitations of local purchasing power, often even of raw-material supply, storage and transportation capacities, etc.

A clear delineation of the productive and non-productive activities, a sharp distinction between productive and non-productive expenses in general both within the productive branches and plants and within the national economy as a whole, is entirely lacking, especially as the relevant economic indicators and data supply are concerned. This reflects of course the effect of the application and all deficiencies of Western economic theories and "international" economic-statistical methods, but is not unrelated to the natural "self-defence" of an overgrowing administration and bureaucracy either.

121

According to Western economic principles and the methods of calculating national income based on them and almost "legalized" by the UNO, all income-generating activities are "contributions" to the national income, moreover, the spending of incomes has an income-generating effect. The idealization of personal consumption and even squandering as against savings, which eventually follows from these principles, makes it rather obvious that they have been worked out not under the circumstances of, and for, poor societies. What is, however, less commonly known is to what extent these methods of calculating national income and even the "internationally" applied approach of the statistics and planning of national income divert in a wrong direction or make difficult the mechanism of practical economic management. Thus even those who generally oppose the application of the Keynesian multiplier principle readily accept, as a rule, the methodology of calculating national income according to Keynesian principles. As regards employment, its increase constitutes a key question of economic policy and receives a pronounced treatment both in the recommendations of foreign economic advisers to the governments and in textbooks, but it is hardly mentioned anywhere *what sort* of employment is needed, and how productive employment must and can be increased not only be reducing unemployment but also by means of decreasing non-productive employment!

We need not dwell on the "self-defence" of bureaucracy as it is a well-known phenomenon everywhere. What makes it worth mentioning, however, is the fact that such self-defence has greater possibilities in developing countries, partly owing to the largely disguising effect of the above-mentioned principles and methods, partly because bureaucracy itself has become a prominent sphere of the socio-economic and political leadership – at least in relation to the *local* social elements and economic factors – and the principal sphere of the development of the élite, that is, of the local ruling strata. The size of public administration, the magnitude of the state apparatus, the dimensions of the guiding-administrative organs even within the productive sector – in relation to the size of a *controlled* economy and to the dimensions of the administrative economic activities – are all questions that are usually never raised in the developing countries. The growth of the *public* sector, its growing percentage share (in the national income or in the budget), which is normally considered as an indication of socialist or at least non-capitalist development, especially if it coincides with the official declaration of a socialist policy, is very often the consequence of a state "hydrocephaly" and also to some extent of the above-mentioned calculation method rather than of a real shift in the social relations within productive activities. It may mean a certain (if not necessarily a positive) change in income distribution or utilization without a basic change in production relations! The growth (in regard to the number of staff, current expenses and investments) of the state and the so-called parastatal top organs established to control, guide, or co-operate with, foreign or local capital, and their higher participation in the profits of productive units alone does not make production relations more "socialist", and may even curb the productive investments and not the profits of private capital.

122

Favouring non-productive work is also connected with bureaucracy in that administrative posts objectively ensure easier, more rapid and spectacular careers than productive, economically and socially useful occupations. Even a considerable part of those qualified specialists who have performed their studies in technical, natural or medical sciences, tend to obtain administrative jobs, and will sooner or later be in charge of some administrative organ entirely unrelated to their original professions. All this is still further boosted by political ambitions, whose shortest paths also lead through the forest of public administration and bureaucracy. (Productive activities seem to provide far fewer or only exceptional possibilities of getting into political leadership.[27])

Many more features of social consciousness and ways of thinking might still be mentioned which, in one way or another, directly or indirectly, are connected with the distorted structure of the economy and its corresponding social patterns. Not indifferent is, e.g., the influence of the spirit of hierarchy and patriarchalism stemming from the "pre-capitalist" sector but getting further impetus in the administrative pyramid of the capitalist-urban sector. It curbs the spirit of enterprise, the development of a democratic atmosphere, fosters the idolization of political leaders. Especially noteworthy is, further on, how the elements of "racial", tribal, minority or religious consciousness get mixed with the new elements of political consciousness, and how often the criteria of these affiliations are identified with the criteria of political reliability, "revolutionarism" or "reactionarism" in public opinion or in explicit or implicit "official" judgement.

Such identifications are not only more frequently and more rigidly applied here than in Europe (who would deny that they can be met with in Europe, too?), but they also constitute a contributory factor of sudden political changes and coups d'état.

(b) TRENDS IN THE UTILIZATION OF FOREIGN AID

Economic disintegration and the co-existence of the two heterogeneous sectors may come into an unfavourable interaction with the direction and effectiveness of *foreign aid*.

On the one hand, we are faced here with the well-known phenomenon that the suppliers of foreign grants and loans prefer the capitalist-urban sector and mainly its already established enclave branches and/or the capital-intensive import-substituting industries, which have hardly any contact with the "pre-capitalist" rural sector and other branches of the economy. By doing so they enhance economic disintegration and usually the export orientation of the capitalist sector, as well as the import-sensitivity of the economy, together with the other unfavourable effects already mentioned. The capitalist-urban sector is given preference by the creditor countries partly in order to strengthen either old capitalist interests

[27] This is, by the way, one of the contributory reasons for the frequency of "indoor" coups d'état.

123

inherited from colonialism or the new ones, and partly to safeguard their own foreign-trade interests as well as for the sake of investments in aid involving lower costs and lesser risks and promising the realization of spectacular results.

On the other hand, from the very lack of internal integration and the interaction of the two sectors follows the tendency which shifts the utilization of foreign aid in the direction of the "least resistance", and makes it follow the beaten track towards the capitalist sector and its already operating branches. This tendency is brought about partly by objective, partly by subjective influences.

As predominantly *objective* reasons for giving preference to the capitalist-urban sector when taking decisions on utilizing foreign aid and on making investments appear the following circumstances: The easier realization of investments and the lesser need for complementary investments in the capitalist-urban sector; the more or less existing communal services; the network of transport and communications; the given marketing possibilities and labour supply; fewer organizational difficulties; better known and tested technology; the easier way of assessing the profitability of and returns on investments, and – if we disregard the less easily assessable effects – their undoubtedly more favourable indices. The pressure of unemployment in the capitalist-urban sector with all its threats of social and even political tensions also stimulates the increase of investments in this sector.

To all this must be added motives of a predominantly *subjective* nature. Such are, e. g., the personal economic interests of some political leaders in investments made in the capitalist-urban sector or in the development of one or another branch of enterprise in it, or in co-operation with foreign capital operating in this sector. Such are, futher, considerations of party politics in governmental decisions on aid utilization, which usually derive from the pressure of political movements concentrated in towns and from the pressure of urban demands (either of the urban bourgeoisie or workers united in trade unions). Such is also the well-known propensity for making prestige investments aimed at enhancing one's personal reputation or that of the party or the nation, and at having the appearance of quick development, etc.

The often experienced resistance of the "pre-capitalist"-rural sector to everything that is new, as well as the danger of conflicts over questions of authority and ownership in the course of the implementation of development, investments and new projects also shift the utilization of foreign assistance towards the capitalist-urban sector.

As a result of all this, the difference between the two sectors, i. e. disintegration with all its consequences, becomes more pronounced and greatly weakens the aggregate social and economic effectiveness of foreign assistance even if the individual effectivity of the projects themselves shows a tendency of increase.

V. THE SOCIAL STRUCTURE AND ITS CHANGES

1. THE FORMATION OF THE HETEROGENEOUS, DUALISTIC SOCIAL STRUCTURE

The structure of society reflects, more or less faithfully, the characteristic features of the economic basis, i.e. the structure of the economy. Since the economy of developing countries is characterized by dualism, the dualistic nature, the strange symbiosis of the "pre-capitalist" and capitalist modes of production, the composition of society is obviously extremely *heterogeneous*. The two contradictory economic sectors with their widely different characteristics: the "pre-capitalist" and the capitalist sectors, represent two opposed poles with the lines of force of attraction and repulsion between them, which gives rise to innumerable varieties of social formations.

All this seemingly contradicts but in fact corresponds to the lack of clearly delineated class boundaries and, consequently, also to the underdevelopment of social class consciousness. In fact, it would be erroneous to conclude from the survival of a substantial number of elements of pre-capitalist society, or even from their relatively large proportion within society as a whole, that what we have to do with are some sort of undifferentiated societies, more homogeneous than the more developed ones. The very co-existence of the two sectors means a degree of heterogeneity which is unparalleled in the history of European societies, at least in the sense that a "pre-capitalist" sector embodying centuries-old backwardness could survive in large sectors of society in such a way that the capitalist sector, which had gained meanwhile absolute dominance in power, made hardly any effort to transform the "pre-capitalist" society. In the development of Western societies the modern, more exactly the new and more advanced elements of a society, which had usually come into being from "inside", through the gradual transformation of the society *concerned,* had to clash first of all with the old, still dominant elements (not only superior in number but also in power) before they were able to come to power. This power, however, proved firm only if the new forces, as a result of the further transformation of society, grew in number. That is, both the emergence and the coming to power of the "modern social sector" were closely connected with the transformation of the "traditional" sector, or with the transformation of the latter consciously performed by the dominant "modern" sector having gained the upper hand.

In the developing countries the elements of "modern" society came into being, as a rule, *not* as a result of the internal "self-development" of society by gradually breaking away from the old society that had given birth to them and transforming it simultaneously with their own growth, but, like the new, capitalist forms of the economy, were imposed on it from outside, without any previous "organic" relationship, and built into the joints of or upon the structure of the old society out of a foreign environment. The penetration of foreign capitalism, which, in addition, generally took place under aggressive, colonial circumstances, interrupt- ed the natural development and transformation of the indigenous society, making definitely impossible for this process to take the course and develop at a pace determined by the internal laws of its past evolution.

True, the original society found by intruding colonial capitalism was an extremely slow-developing one, stagnant in many countries for centuries, owing to fossilized feudal and religious relations or, as a consequence of these two factors, to a high degree of isolation. The "breaking up" of such a society, the loosening of its rigid joints, the penetration of its isolated position is in itself a positive "historic achievement", though usually a painful one. Unlike such cases, whether in ancient European history or the pre-colonial history of the peoples under discussion, when the imposition on the conquered society of the rule of conquerors representing a more developed, or sometimes only a militarily stronger but otherwise underdeveloped society, led eventually to the complete transformation or organic merger of the two societies, the export of capitalist society to colonial territories did not result in a complete and radical transformation of the original society found there.

Thus colonization, which unfolded in the time and under the circumstances of monopoly capitalism (thus especially the colonization of the central parts of Africa), could not even fulfil the "historic function" of fully transforming and setting in motion the subjugated societies.

This was due primarily to the fact that under the circumstances of monopoly capitalism (when capital property and capital function became separated and the export of working capital predominant) the penetration and establishment of the capitalist economic sector was no longer necessarily accompanied by the final re-settlement of the persons representing and guiding it. Even if the latter does take place, the immigrant elements of society may continue to be appendages of the metropolitan country as long as they control the political and military power of the host country and operate according to the interest of the metropolitan country, and their economic "breeding ground" continues to remain the metropolitan capital. This direct linkage to the metropolitan country is typical not only of the elements staying only temporarily, as it were in foreign service, in the developing country, but also of the resident settlers having lived there for several decades. This linkage realized both by the international proportions of imperialism and those of technology, transport and communications, has made possible the rather general spread in the areas under discussion of the social phenomenon called *segregation*, which is but one extreme manifestation of racial discrimination.

126

As long as the trends of political power and economic activity corresponded to this segregation (i. e. until the new political power and its economic aims[1] did not run counter to it), the effect of the immigrant capitalist sector was unable to start a radical transformation of the "pre-capitalist" sector, and remained not only restricted but in no small measure negative, too.[2]

The predominance of foreign elements in the political and particularly economic field impeded or at least made it difficult for the internal, indigenous social forces to develop or strengthen, which, under the circumstances of normal development, would have been vitally interested in carrying out a radical social transformation. National bourgeoisie, which could have taken an active part in the fight for the capitalist transformation of every sector of the economy and society, was unable either to develop at all or to become a vigorous stratum, and has become a parasitical stratum dependent on foreign capital. Thus neither the basic external, nor the internal forces of development have attained an irreversible and complete liquidation of "pre-capitalist" formations. The objective contradiction itself between *foreign* monopoly capital, on the one hand, which launched and realized, within certain limits (e. g. in the enclaves), *capitalist* development, and the national bourgeoisie, on the other, as the only potential *internal* basis of capitalist development, accounted for the preservation of certain remnants of "pre-capitalist" formations. This process was only strengthened in many countries by the alliance policy of the colonial governments or of foreign capital seeking to strengthen their own power by giving military or financial support to the leading strata of the former "pre-capitalist" society.

Thus, segregation prevented the integration of foreign elements into, or even their intensive transforming effect on traditional society. But the "national motor" of social transformation could not develop under the circumstances of foreign political or economic rule. In addition, the preservation of the old social elements was also promoted in many countries by conscious political actions. In much the same way as the collapse of the old forms of the economy was not followed by an entirely new and complete economic construction, but the old and new forms came to exist side by side, significant remnants of the old structure of society also have survived.

The capitalist element, which, through the penetration of foreign monopoly capital or settlers' capital, became predominant in the heterogeneous structure, affected and restricted horizontally the economic "breeding ground" of the "pre-capitalist" elements: subsistence economy based on the re-distribution of common tribal lands, nomadic pastoral life, village communities or feudal estates. The most conspicuous manifestation of this horizontal effect was the forceful expropriation of part of the tribal lands in such areas where foreign capital brought about plantation economies with colonial governmental support.

---

[1] Or where the interests and endeavour of international capital did not require the opposite.

[2] The negative economic – and partly social – effects of the capitalist sector have already been discussed in the previous chapter.

This *horizontal effect,* however, operated, by its very nature, within a rather limited area, and was far from becoming a cumulative effect capable of removing the "pre-capitalist" elements from the horizon of the economy as a whole. And this was basically due to the fact that the economic growth and horizontal spread of the capitalist element were largely independent (except for its labour sources) of the development of the local economy and society and depended, to a considerable extent, on the development of external rather than of internal market relations. Thus, as far as the market relations determining economic growth are concerned, its further horizontal spread played a rather insignificant role.

In other words, it was impossible for a mechanism similar to the one existing at the time of the enclosures in England to develop when the horizontal ousting of the old mode of production made not only the forces of production available to the capitalist elements but also ensured the transformation of the *market* and thereby the rapid growth of the capitalist element. In the case of the enclosures in England the further horizontal spread of capitalist agriculture proved economically rational even if the lands expropriated from the feudal or independent peasants were not or just partly utilized for a considerable time. This was because land expropriations drastically reduced the number of those living *outside* the market, i.e. of the social strata of the subsistence economy, and created thereby, at least in part,[3] the market conditions for an economic utilization of the expropriated lands.

The capitalist element having gained predominance also exercised of course a vertical effect. The very fact that the economic sphere of the "pre-capitalist" social element has narrowed down and its environment has changed, gave rise to certain vertical processes. Changes in the production and living conditions of the former "pre-capitalist" society, owing to the mere existence of the capitalist sector and of course of its concrete composition, movement and various effects, brought about certain shifts in the "pre-capitalist" social elements and liquidated their "pre-capitalist" integrity by subordinating them to the laws of motion of capitalist sector. But this vertical effect proved weak, too, or got stuck in face of the resistance of the traditional forces, or, instead of launching at least a process in the direction of a complete transformation, resulted in such mixed, unstable transitory formations which later on became themselves obstacles to, or retarding factors of, social transformation.

The measure of the horizontal effect and particularly the nature and result of the vertical effect depended primarily on the nature and composition of the capitalist sector, while the reaction of the "pre-capitalist" sector was determined

---

[3] As commonly known, in the progress of land expropriations and in the development of the English textile industry a prominent role was played by external economic factors, primarily by the export possibilities of English textiles. This, however, does not diminish at all the importance of the fact that the above-mentioned internal relationships did already exist, while their *absence* in the development of societies discussed here throws light on many a phenomenon.

128

by the nature and composition of the latter. Thus, from the point of view of the "final outcome" a more or less clear distinction must be made according to whether

- the capitalist sector of the economy came into being primarily in such fields as capitalist plantations or mines, or trade parasitizing on indigenous agriculture, or only urban services, or possibly industry;
- the capitalist social element is represented mainly by immigrant settler capitalists or other "racial minorities", or the emerging local élite and bourgeoisie, or international companies;
- the "pre-capitalist" sector means feudal large estates (with landlords and serfs), small holdings (with family or tribal communities), or nomadic pastoral tribes.

Both effect and reaction depend first of all on these factors; it is they that determine in general both the character and size of the participation of the local population in the economic and social activity as a whole.

Since, however, the present-day national boundaries, primarily in Africa, do not usually comprise homogeneous units either in respect to the capitalist or the "pre-capitalist" element taken separately, but include a mixed combination of elements differing in respect to the above-mentioned criteria, there can be found within the dualistic structure of society various smaller or larger *"sub-societies"* that present different patterns of effect and reaction. In other words, even within the society of a single country, various elements of the capitalist sector may come into contact with various elements of the "pre-capitalist" sector. Therefore, the effects thus produced are usually not only limited, but also very different in their direction, which naturally prevents their cumulation and also accounts, at least partly, for their weakness. It is obvious, e.g., that conflicts, interference and mutual weakening of these effects take place not infrequently when a dominant role is played in one economic region of the country by foreign-owned export-oriented plantations, for whose operation the migrant-labour system based on the "pre-capitalist" sector is satisfactory, and to which even the narrowness of the home market constitutes no obstacle, while in another region, owing to increasing market production, the capitalization of peasant economies sets in, or even industrialization begins, requiring the expansion of the local market and the stabilization of manpower. Even within individual areas, the reactions of the various ethnic groups, tribal communities, especially if their economies are also different (agricultural or nomadic tribes), will be different when exposed to the influence of the element of a similar nature in the capitalist sector.

Regarding the "pre-capitalist" sector *as a whole,* and not just as its parts displaying different features and reacting in different ways, the vertical effect manifests itself "below" mainly through the labourers of the migrant system, i.e. those leaving the "pre-capitalist" sector for temporary wage employment, and "above" through the feudal or tribal ruling strata, who, in order to get rich, begin to trade in goods, land, labour and money. But this effect proved too weak to induce a complete social transformation, as – also independently of the interference of the effects already referred to – the economic sphere of such a transformation, owing to the character of the "modern" sector, became an extremely "difficult terrain" from the very outset. In addition, the effect itself which in its manifestation "above" meant the appearance of an alien way of life, and in its manifestation "below" meant employment and exploitation by foreigners, was greatly offset by the bonds and cohesive forces of the traditional society (which often became stronger by the very fact of self-defence).

Even in countries such as India, where already before independence the capitalist elements had been considerably expanded by local, indigenous components breaking away from the "pre-capitalist'" elements, these components have either continued to remain in the bonds[4] of the traditional society, i.e. have not really become capitalist elements, or – though being indigenous elements – turned into aliens themselves by coming into conflict with the rules, religions and habits[5] of the traditional society.

Thus, changes in the structure of the heterogeneous society were confined rather to the periphery of the "pre-capitalist" sector bordering on capitalist elements, and all these changes amounted to was their (often only partial) breaking away from this periphery, but not a real internal transformation. Despite this fact, not a single "pre-capitalist" social community has remained *intact* from the effect of colonialism and of the capital working in the capitalist sector, not a single community of this nature has been able to preserve the *original* conditions of its existence and independent development. *There are no real "pre-capitalist" societies in the "Third World"*, only fragmentary, mutilated remnants inhibited in their growth, remnants which have become the subservient, though alien and contradictory accessories of the predominant system of capitalism.[6] Whatever resistance the "pre-capitalist" communities may have put up in some countries against the penetration of *foreign* capitalism, the spread of colonialism, this resistance, though a definitely positive phenomenon from the point of view of preserving and strengthening the *idea* of independence, could not be successful and does no longer represent a positive force in the perspective of social progress *beyond* the regaining of national independence.

Despite the efforts made by the new governments in several countries to revive the traditions of the past, the resistance against and the isolation from the capitalist elements, as well as the defensive strengthening of the traditional ties, began later to slacken to the extent that the open signs of the rule of foreign capitalism disappeared, and the economic and cultural development of the "pre-capitalist" rural sector came to the fore and made progress within the national development programmes. Nonetheless, the vigorous effects of the

---

[4] A case in point is that of Indian capitalists who maintain an extended family (i.e. the whole kinship).

[5] Some Western authors complain that in India the position of capitalists has been a detested one even in recent times, in which Ghandism is also supposed to have had a role to play.

[6] The real nature of Latin-American "feudalism" and its role *within* the capitalist system is clearly described by A. G. Frank (see his study in the December 1963 issue of *Monthly Review*).

130

traditional social behaviour and rules will make themselves felt for a long time yet and will influence the social processes.

The distortion of the social structure, the measure of the survival, the position and role of the "pre-capitalist" formations in society vary substantially from one developing country to another, depending, firstly, on to what historical periods these remnants can *originally* be traced back, i. e. at what stage of their historical development these societies were found by the penetration of foreign capitalism. Secondly, what *changes* these remnants, while exposed to external effects and fitted into the heterogeneous structure, had to undergo, how and to what extent they adjusted themselves to the changed circumstances. Consequently, owing, *among other things,* to original, pre-colonial developmental differences, the distorted *remnants* of the most different periods of primitive communal, slave-owning and feudal societies can be found in the countries of Africa, Asia and Latin America.

2. THE "FEUDAL" ELEMENTS OF THE SOCIETY OF COLONIAL CAPİTALISM

Where the existence and operation of the capitalist sector came into contact with the already existing and more or less developed feudal relations, as in certain areas of Africa (e.g. in Buganda), but particularly in Asia and several Arab countries, its effect, depending on whether this contact remained an essentially horizontal one or was rather a vertical "superposition", the existence of the capitalist sector led either to the intensification of feudal exploitation and to an internal stiffening of feudal relations and at the same time to the incapability and blockage of their further development, or made use of the forms of feudal exploitation in its own interest and at the same time filled them gradually up with capitalistic content.

It also occurred that the capitalist sector itself introduced feudal and semi-feudal forms of exploitation, such as the so-called squatter system,[7] let alone the various sorts of slave labour, especially during the first period of colonialism (but also later in the fascist system in South-Africa and Portuguese Africa). Moreover, feudalism was actually implanted in *Latin America* by Spanish and Portuguese conquerors by means of royal grants of land estates (encomienda) coupled with the institutions of "negro" slavery. This was, however, not the result

---

[7] In the British colonies of East-Africa and some areas of West-Africa, primarily prior to World War II, a relatively large number of "squatters" were employed on European plantations on a contractual basis. As share croppers they also cultivated the landlord's land, and were allowed, with limited rights, to do independent farming on a specified plot of land. Special regulations, in addition to the contract, stipulated the minimum number of days per year they had to work in the landlord's service. This system began quickly to decline after World War II. Its serfdom character no longer corresponded to the requirements of development, and can now rarely be met with, mostly in non-European economies only.

of the contact of the local pre-capitalist society with the implanted capitalist element, but of the fact that the colonizing power itself transplanted feudalism from Europe to Latin America through its own settlers, who later merged with the local population. It is of course another question how this implanted and originally European feudalism was later made use of by North-American capital. At any rate, the system of "feudal" large estates (latifundia) and of the various feudal forms of exploitation[8] still survives for capitalist purposes in the agriculture of Latin America.

In India, however, where the power system of feudalism (maharajahs) had already existed before British colonization, but was based on village communities in conformity with the "Asian mode of production",[9] the adequate ownership relations of feudalism, the feudal title to landed property was introduced by the British colonizers who, establishing a class of landowners from the old tax collectors, the so-called Zamindarys of Indian princes, gave them the lands, from which they had collected taxes, into their private ownership.[10] The institutionalized system of large land estates and the tenancy and usury systems growing enormously in its wake, as well as the rapid disintegration of the village communities led not only to the more intensive exploitation of the rural producers, but also made increased use of the feudal forms of exploitation in the interest of capitalist exploitation.

In the *Arab oil-producing countries,* feudalism, together with feudal ownership relations and the various forms of exploitation, but in co-existence with a nomadic way of life and tribal and minority relations, dates back to an old historical past. Since in these regions oil production, like one-crop economy in other countries, has not changed the structure and organization of production either in agriculture or in any other existing economic branches,[11] the social consequences of the implantation of the capitalist sector, owing partly to the alliance between capitalist corporations and the Arab reigning sheiks, and partly to the income and consumption effects of the capitalist sector, had resulted primarily in the increased power, wealth and parasitic luxury consumption of the feudal leading strata. In connection with all this and also with the spread of monetary economy, the exploitation of the fellaheen has increased, and class conflicts within the agrarian society have sharpened. A further change has been the appearance in the oil sector of a relatively narrow but, compared with the income of other working

[8] For these questions as well as for the distribution of land estates in Latin America see Z. Kollár's study in this volume.

[9] For more detail see F. Tőke: *Az ázsiai termelési mód kérdéséhez* (On the Asian Mode of Production). Kossuth Kiadó, Budapest, 1965.

[10] See S. Surányi's study in this volume.

[11] This does not apply of course to those Arab countries, e. g. to Egypt, where a one-crop export economy (cotton) was introduced, and foreign capital was imposed on a system of feudalism with relatively developed money economy and market relations, "standing on the threshold" of capitalist transition. Foreign capital used the feudal forms in agriculture for the purposes of export production and the development of one-crop economy. (See. I. Kubik's study in this volume.)

132

classes, well-paid stratum of workers and employees as well as the development of the economic and social infrastructure, especially of a fairly well-trained élite in the spheres of the armed forces and the state apparatus.

In other words, the implantation and presence of the capitalist element have not led to the "dissolution" of the feudal leading strata, the big landowners, reigning sheiks, maharajahs and tribal chiefs and to their transformation into a new social class just as it has not led to a radical change in "pre-capitalist" economic relations. What has happened, is only a certain degree of superficial capitalization, and even this manifests itself only in an orientation towards market economy and sharing in the profits of the investments of foreign companies rather than in the field of economic activities. The parasitic character of this stratum becomes apparent not only in the increasing misery of the exploited agricultural labourers and the low, stagnant level of productive investments in agriculture, but primarily in the rapidly growing luxury consumption of feudal lords and owners and in the transfer abroad of a substantial part of their income enjoyed by them in the capitalist sector, too, owing to feudal rights and bribery.

3. CONSEQUENCES OF THE DISTORTED STRUCTURE OF SOCIETY

The distorted, heterogeneous social structure, the co-existence of alien and contradictory elements as well as the interference of interactions weakening or strengthening one another in a negative sense, have impeded of course the progress of social processes. In these countries the vertical dividing lines between the various classes and strata are, *on the one hand,* much less distinct than in Europe, and not only between the capitalist and non-capitalist elements (because of the *partial* separatism mentioned above), but even within the non-capitalist element (between wage-labourers and peasant farmers, between the community and tribal chiefs and feudal landlords, etc.). *On the other hand,* owing to the existence of regional units of different composition and of the great variety of ethnic (and religious) groups, together with the emergence of the above-mentioned sub-societies, the society as a whole is even more complex and heterogeneous than elsewhere. In addition, on the interfaces of the heterogeneous structure relatively wide intermediate strata could come into existence, which may have an important part to play even in politics.

The sence of class affiliation is weakened not only by the blurred character of the dividing lines between classes, but are strongly influenced and offset by *other forms of social consciousness,* such as traditional religion, tribalism, nationality, caste and sectarian interests, nationalism or their various combinations.

This peculiar character of the social structure and processes provides the explanation why the paths of political changes and shifts in these countries may deviate so much from the boundary lines of social classes. The political groupings and certain leading personalities may shift to the right or to the left, in a reactionary or progressive direction, not only on the "political surface" of their "own" class, within the limits of their class interests, but over a much wider area. Thus, without losing their social basis and with the help of the intermediate strata, or with the assistance of other forms of social consciousness, they may embark upon a path leading beyond or even against the interests of the class serving previously as their social basis.

Thus the possibility of unexpected *political turn-abouts* largely independent of changes in real social power relations follow not only from the "open" nature of the economy and, consequently, political sphere, from the wide and deep front of the intervention of external forces, but also from the large-scale *instability* of internal power formations, the mixed composition of groups that have arrived, or are striving to arrive, at the top of power, and from their varied and changeable socio-economic affinities and limitations of consciousness.

The existence and intensity of the limiting effects of tribal, national, "racial", religious, caste, etc., communities also influence the political processes directly, not only through the medium of consciousness, and in many cases also have an impact on the development of the forms of organization and the systems of public administration.

Especially great is the political significance of tribalism nourishing from the remnants of primitive communal society, of provincialism evolving from the existence of "sub-societies" as well as of "racial", religious and caste-consciousness, etc., and the political weight of organizational and administrative forms evolved on this basis when they coincide, in a rather deceptive way and along a relatively wide front, with the lines of force of emerging class consciousness and conflicting class interests. That is, when, owing to some historical peculiarities, the antagonistic contradictions of society seem to coincide with the ethnic or religious dividing lines. What usually results is an increase in tribal, national, "racial", religious or caste conflicts, and all this at the expense of an emerging class consciousness. The consequence is, no doubt, negative even if the decisive fight between the oppressed and exploited and the oppressors and exploiters takes place between really different "races", nationalities, tribes and religions, and this conclusion cannot be altered by the fact that such confrontation gives rise to complementary revolutionary energies for the former.

All possible "tactical" advantages of such a confrontation based *not* on class antagonism prove too insignificant compared with the "strategic" disadvantages and losses which will inevitably ensue later when the antihumanistic character of the ethnic (or religious) antagonisms comes into an obvious contradiction with the perhaps originally progressive objectives, and discredits them once and for all, and when the front lines of real class conflicts more and more deviate from the ethnic (or religious) dividing lines. But just because of this *natural* tendency, the "tactical" advantages themselves are of an utterly doubtful value as the false ideology of ethnic (or religious) cohesion or confrontation can be manipulated in such a way that they conceal the conflicts within the same ethnic group, or prevent the awareness of a community of interests among strata belonging to different groups, but of the same social status.

134

Manipulation with forms of consciousness with a false social content has often been made use of by the colonialists for strengthening their own power according to the principle "divide and rule". Countless manifestations and instances of this manipulation could be mentioned – from fragmentation of countries on a religious basis (e.g. India and Pakistan) through placing public administration and representation on a tribal or "religious" basis and inciting tribal conflicts (almost all over Africa) to the system of privileges and discrimination (particularly in the fascist systems, e.g. in South Africa). But apart from this conscious manipulation, objective factors have also contributed to the intertwining and merging of social (class) antagonisms and ethnic (or religious) conflicts. And such objective factor was not only the European ("white") character of colonization, as a result of which the antagonism of colonizers and colonized appeared in the disguise of the conflict of "white" and "coloured" people – though oppressed and exploited people have always been found in "white" societies just as oppressing and exploiting people in "coloured" societies. In addition to this undoubtedly most important factor, as the reflection of the uneven development of Western (European) and non-European areas and the expression of the antagonism in consciousness between the centre and periphery within capitalism, *uneven development within the periphery* also had a role to play, leading even within individual countries to increasing regional differences, to conflicts between *de facto* privileged and disadvantaged areas, tribes or nationalities. We can find in nearly any country of the developing world such areas – and also communities in these areas – which, for various reasons, but primarily depending on the location of the enclave sector, have developed more rapidly than their environment, and are regarded as privileged spots within the world of poverty. An additional objective factor is the existence and location of immigrants as well as the social allocation of religions introduced by them (i.e. in what social stratum, or ethnic group of that stratum, a given religion has become dominant).

In the post-colonial period the tribal, "racial", religious conflicts, which were either deliberately developed or came into being as a result of objective factors, continued further to sharpen in many countries, owing partly to purposeful neo-colonialist manipulation, partly to the objective intensification of inequalities.

Manipulation by tribalism, racism or even nationalism was also soon acquired by the élite-stratum getting alienated from society. In many countries tribalism or religious fanaticism has become the mask and expression of class privilege or class dissatisfaction. This, in turn, leads to a fragmentation of the unfolding class consciousness of masses, on the one hand, and strengthens, on the other, the tendencies of separatism as against integration. Both make it difficult for progressive governments to operate and, especially, for the social basis of socialist development to be built and organized. Tribal or religious wars often pave the way for the most reactionary tendencies or formations and open at the same time the door to neo-colonialist interventions.

No less disastrous consequences may be involved in the substitution of "racial" or "national" confrontation for social confrontation. It is already a rather general phenomenon, e. g. in Africa, that reference to "African" consciousness, "African nationalism" is used not only for mobilization, often of a slogan-ranting type, against foreign oppression and exploitation, but also for concealing emerging social differences and conflicts among Africans themselves. Elsewhere, the slogan of "nation-building" may serve similar purposes.

In the period following the collapse of colonial rule, the limitations and negative features of the *nationalism* of developing countries under the circumstances of neo-colonialism have come to the fore in many a country. In supporting the cause of independence of territories not yet liberated from colonialism and in the fight against international imperialism, as well as in the struggle for economic independence, nationalism invariably plays a progressive role. Similarly, nationalist solidarity if of vital and positive importance in combating tribal, religious, etc. conflicts and separatist endeavours instigated by neo-colonialism, and in building up the cohesive forces of new nations. Considering, however, the substitution for the open forms of colonial oppression of the more concealed methods of neo-colonialism which disrupt local society and especially the bourgeoisie within it more effectively, as well as the resulting speeding up of social differentiation, the national movements of ex-colonial peoples can no longer, or at least not without reservation, be regarded under neo-colonialism as the natural allies and reserve of socialism. Credit is due to them rather on the basis of the concrete appreciation of their aims and concrete actions, as well as of the social forces behind them.

VI. THE REQUIREMENTS OF DEVELOPMENT AND THE NON-CAPITALIST WAY

1. THE ROLE OF THE STATE IN THE PROCESS OF OVERCOMING UNDERDEVELOPMENT

The task of liquidating underdevelopment within the framework of the national economy is a very complex one. In follows from the dialectic interconnections of its various factors that underdevelopment can only be overcome in a *complex* way as even one single factor left intact will jeopardize the progress made in liquidating all other factors. It is unimaginable to reach lasting results in transforming the economic structure and developing the productive forces without abolishing economic dependence and exploitation. Conversely: without transforming the distorted economic structure, economic independence cannot be ensured. And the liquidation of outdated social remnants is the precondition for any social advance.

Breaking the dominance of foreign capital, ousting it from the key positions of the economy and restricting its exploiting activity is in itself a very difficult task. It is especially difficult when only one or a few monopoly groups control economic life.

It is for this reason that even the most progressive governments handle the issue of nationalizing foreign companies very cautiously. Though only complete nationalization without compensation means the final liquidation of the "direct" form of exploitation by foreign capital, this is only exceptionally resorted to in developing countries. Where it does occur (e. g. in Cuba), it is either the natural concomitant of breaking away from world capitalist economy and of a radical socio-political transformation, or as a political action or reprisal against a particular imperialist power, i. e. when it is confined to a given capital, or, not infrequently, to the time of a conflict only. In many countries, of course, especially in those "small" ones where foreign monopoly capital exercises control over an economy with a rather limited scope, and commands not only production but also marketing, transport and the supply of qualified and skilled labour, the economic and technical preconditions of nationalization, let alone the socio-political pre-conditions, are often entirely missing. Such "national economies" are able to defy and to do without foreign capital successfully only in alliance with a larger economic-political unit and/or with the help of an external assistance that is also of an anti-imperialist content and of sufficient volume and duration to ensure the further operation of the nationalized enterprises and the elimination of bottlenecks. At this juncture it is worth noting that at the beginning the operation of the nationalized sector came up against not insignificant difficulties even in the

European people's democracies, despite the fact that, in contrast to most developing countries, the bottlenecks were less narrow not only owing to the relatively wider basis of the manufacturing industry and the much denser network of intersectoral relations but also from the point of view of the availability of qualified and skilled manpower indispensable for the further operation of enterprises. In other words, these economies had from the outset a larger potential for creating economic independence, not to speak of the fact that the socio-political conditions made it possible for them to embark upon the road of a radical type of nationalization. It is true, on the other hand, that nationalization in the case of the people's democracies had from the very outset a *class content* and appeared, owing to the large-scale intertwining of national and foreign capital, the relative development of the national capital and the basically socio-political nature of the whole process, not merely as an anti-imperialist, i.e. national, but as a *directly anti-capitalist*, i.e. socialist measure. Consequently, it also had to defeat a stronger and wider resistance (i.e. one also comprising significant internal forces).

Today, in a number of developing countries the nationalization of foreign capital appears either as an issue separated or separable from socialization, the nationalization of domestic capital, i.e. as a national task, or as an issue comprising a wide range of compromises and transitory or gradual solutions.

National capital, where it has developed in any appreciable degree, finds of course the possibility in many countries, and after independence to an ever-growing extent, to co-operate with foreign capital. In this sense it enters into a sort of community of interests with foreign capital, in which the often mentioned changes in the investment policy of international monopolies and the coming into prominence of neo-colonialist solutions also have a considerable role to play. But state internvention aimed at crushing the role of foreign capital serves, in the last analysis, the interests of the bourgeoisie, too. The national bourgeoisie expects the state to provide protection and assistance of its interests, the strengthening of its positions in general both in respect to foreign partners and to domestic manpower. Association and partnership relations with the state sector (joint ventures and various parastatal forms) are definitely advantageous, at least temporarily, for the local bourgeoisie: alliance with the state usually renders protection against strikes and "excessive" wage claims of workers, substantially decreases the risks of enterprises and expands their credit and marketing possibilities. It not only provides a certain degree of protection against foreign capital, but in many cases it also establishes the very contact with it, and ensures for the national capital a bargaining or business position, which it would be unable to secure from its own strength.

Thus, the national bourgeoisie is ready to take its share in developing state capitalism, in supporting the policy of state intervention in order to restrict the power of foreign capital, and even in the business undertakings of the state sector itself – at least as long as it enjoys the help of the state temporarily needed to strengthen its position, i.e. until it feels strong enough to seize power to control the national economy, or comes, or is compelled to come, to terms with foreign capital to ensure itself a favourable position or a last resort against the ever stronger national progressive forces.

If it might be in the interest of the national bourgeoisie to break the rule of foreign capital, this holds increasingly true of the working classes of society, primarily of the unskilled masses compelled to take up work at substistence wage level and often exposed to unemployment owing to the investment and wage policy of foreign capital. The same applies to the strata of poor agricultural labourers blackmailed and exploited by various methods of commercial and credit policy.

But very often even those feudal leading elements who enjoyed the support of foreign monopoly capital, in order to carve out for themselves a larger share of profits, or – especially in recent times – under the pressure of internal forces and (nationalist) public opinion – may take a stand against foreign monopoly capital, or at least cannot refuse to support the policy of restricting its influence.

At the same time it cannot of course be ignored that a certain degree of community of interests has also come into being between foreign capital and certain *strata* or elements of almost all classes of society, especially in the development process of the post-independence period, in the wake of neo-colonialist tendencies. The best-known and most conspicuous cases of such community of interests and alliances are those of local businessmen and intellectuals involved in the undertakings or boards of directors of foreign companies, merchants co-operating with foreign capital or even peasant farmers, rich peasants and élite workers enjoying a privileged position in relation to the masses of workers. Such common interests greatly motivate the fact and measure of state intervention against foreign capital and mainly constitute important elements of the socio-political processes determining the further development of state capitalism. But they do not essentially change the general and objective tendency manifesting itself in the national endeavour to break the rule of foreign capital.

Neither the national bourgeoisie nor any other strata of society have at their disposal any *other* or more appropriate means of restricting the power of foreign capital and of a policy aimed at creating an independent national economy than *state* intervention in economic life.

State intervention has of course a wide range of forms and means, of which even the most radical one, i. e. complete nationalization, may have very different class content. Depending on the current socio-political circumstances, the nature of other means of state intervention may even be more varied. Such are, e. g., the legal regulation of partial nationalizations, taxes, customs duties, reinvestment ratios of profits, the restriction of profot repatriation and income transfers, a certain degree of state control over the administration and activities of foreign companies, the compulsory inclusion of the representatives of local employees in the direction of enterprises, the organization of parastatal joint companies, the legally binding character of state plans and plan targets as well as of the various related quantitative and qualitative prescriptions.

These forms of state intervention, however, can only be assessed in the knowledge of the concrete circumstances, and do not in themselves provide the evidence that anti-capitalist or even anti-imperialist tendencies necessarily make headway. Nationalization may mean the takeover of a bankrupt economic branch or enterprise, and even the offsetting by compensation of the losses of foreign capital. The restriction by law of profit repatriation and income transfer is usually coupled with safeguarding a transferable maximum and also with guaranteeing a measure of safety for foreign capital which it could not possibly enjoy without the strict foreign-exchange policy of the state, since the system of unrestricted income transfers also involves the danger of bankruptcy in the balance of payments position as well as of unexpected and drastic restrictions following in its wake. Joint ventures and partnerships with the state, however, may also mean a substantial decrease in business and political risks for foreign entrepreneurs in that they can enjoy, for compensation of their restricted shares in profits, the various forms of "concealed" profits such as managerial and expert fees, large sums for licences, manufacturing know-how, the use of trade and brand names, increased prices for equipment imported form the parent company, etc.

On the other hand, these forms of state intervention can only be assessed in the dynamics of their application, i. e. as means of a *transitory* character depending on whether their application and further development are really aimed at and make progress towards a complete crushing and liquidation of the power of foreign monopoly capital.

It is due to this general tendency and mixed content, depending on the concrete socio-political circumstances and the dynamics of its application, that in a number of developing countries the most different methods and manifestations of state intervention can be met with, which influence the monopoly position and activity of foreign capital. The endeavour to prefer, by means of various governmental measures, the interests of the national economy to foreign capital can also be witnessed in the case of states that otherwise can hardly be called progressive. At the same time, the policy of making use of foreign capital – unter the restriction of the scope and conditions of its activity with the simultaneous provision of guarantees and benefits – can also be observed in the most progressive countries, even those envisaging a programme of socialist development.

To all this it should be added that "militancy" against foreign capital is often aimed at attaining a better bargaining position which greatly limits of course its character, and at the same time the sphere and success of such manoeuvres are restricted by the (no doubt, contradictory) tendency of strengthening the monolithic features of international capitalism, at least in relation to the developing world. The period that followed the loosening of traditional colonial relations provided the possibility of taking advantage of the new international relations made abruptly available by political independence, and of playing off the various capitalist interests, especially the colonial ones and those with a new

140

orientation, against each other, and also gave some evidence of the realization of such possibilities. It soon turned out, however, that these possibilities were of a *temporary* character, partly due to the increasing merging of foreign companies and the internationalization of investment capital making progress in developing countries, and partly and mainly (but in close connection with the former) as a result of the rapid advance of American neo-colonialism. All this makes the struggle against foreign capital more difficult, but at the same time more unambiguous in its content.

The transformation of the distorted, dualistic structure of the economy and society is an even more complex and long-lasting task. As a precondition for economic development, the transformation of the economic structure as well as social integration will sooner or later become a self-evident task for all those concerned with the problems of accelerating economic growth and developing the forces of production, provided of course that their personal interests in maintaining the *status quo* do not prevent them from recognizing these tasks. Unfavourable changes in the world market, and the formation of world-market prices from the mid-1950s up to the early 1970s have fairly convincingly proved the disadvantages of one-crop economies and even the 1973–74 price increases could hardly prove the opposite. And the slow development of the internal division of labour and market, the obstacles to raising productivity and adopting better working and more up-to-date cultivation and technical methods have unambiguously demonstrated the impeding role of a dualistic economy and within it especially that of the "pre-capitalist" sector.

And as far as social transformation is conerned, as long as it is aimed at ousting non-capitalist elements, the "pre-capitalist" remnants, and at introducing democratic reforms conforming to a bourgeois transformation, local bourgeoisie and even foreign capital may be interested in it. Though the views of the representatives of the bourgeoisie differ on the mode, course and mainly the direction of this transformation, as well as on the role of masses taking part in it, and, being afraid of the danger of a socialist transformation, are inclined even to renounce a bourgeois-democratic transformation, they cannot deny the necessity of such a transformation. And the democratic forces of the liberation movement generally urge this transformation, without which they cannot enjoy the fruits of independence.

Resistance to the implementation of these tasks can generally be witnessed where it entails the danger of the collapse of the whole political system, and thus imperialist interest cannot afford taking this risk, or where the ruling class makes a stand against it, or where resistance to foreign colonization has produced a peculiar traditionalism, a sort of insistence on the forms and customs of primitive, ancient society.

Both sorts of resistance, however, also clash with the interests of those putting it up to such an extent that neither can be a lasting and consistent one. In the first case, it impedes capitalist development, which is of far greater interest to the world system of capitalism than any social transformation, and also provides greater possibility for the "feudal" leaders to get rich. In the second case, resistance clashes with the interests of the traditionalists, because anti-imperialist movement becomes formal, aimless if it is not followed by an increase in the level of domestic economy and the living standards of masses, which is not feasible within the framework of ancient forms.

Thus, both the transformation of the economic structure and the removal of the outdated forms of society appear to be, in one way or another, with a greater or lesser intensity, a *general* requirement in developing countries.

The transformation of the economic and social structure means first of all the abolition of dualism, the integration of the socio-economic sectors of different character, of the economic branches developing more or less independently of one another, and their inclusion in a uniform and dynamic mechanism. Following from the criterion of development, this integration can take place only where a radical transformation of the "pre-capitalist" sector is accomplished.

But the spontaneous mechanism of the disintegrated, dualistic economy works against such a transformation. That is, neither the free play of the spontaneous economic forces, and even less the purposeful policy of international monopoly capital ensure the rapid development of uniform, integrated national economies. Consequently, only state intervention opposing spontaneous mechanism (and foreign monopoly capital), a purposeful development of the government can ensure adequate progress in this field. In other words, the allocations of investments, the determination of their direction, character and size cannot be left to the spontaneous activity of private economies, but require a centralized, centrally co-ordinated development policy. But this development policy and its incorporation in development programmes, long-range plans, cannot be confined to the allocation of investments among branches or areas (districts) on the basis of assessing the economic effectivity of individual investment projects. It must also include the tasks and considerations arising from the requirements of socio-economic *integration*.

Consequently, the liquidation of under-development within the framework of the national economy raises requirements, the fulfilment of which brings the growing economic role of the state into prominence all along the line. Neither the liquidation of economic dependence and exploitation, the breaking of the rule of foreign capital, nor the elimination of "pre-capitalist" economic and social remnants is conceivable without the effective co-operation, intensive economic intervention of the state. State intervention is especially necessitated by the play of spontaneous economic forces, which, incidentally, reproduces the distortions of the economic structure and channels private investments into an unfavourable direction. The reorganization of the subsistence economy and the diversification of the one-crop economy, in addition to, but also in connection with, the fact that it also gives rise to economic and organizational forms characteristic of the agriculture of socialist countries, call for comprehensive measures to be taken by the state just as industrialization, too, can be realized only in this way within a historically short period of time and from internal resources. The immense task

142

of the unfavourable and unstable manpower situation and of training cadres also require that the state's guiding and stimulating activity be extended over the economy as a whole. Hence, the precondition for liquidating underdevelopment and removing the obstacles to development is increasing state intervention in the economy.

2. STATE CAPITALISM AND THE SOCIALIST ALTERNATIVE OF DEVELOPMENT

The economic intervention of the state assumes the form of state capitalism. State capitalism, under whatever conditions it may come into being, is virtually nothing else but the restriction and regulation of economic spontaneity stemming from the existence of private capital. It expresses the peculiar relationship of state and private capital which, depending on the socio-economic system of the country concerned, may be of a varying nature.

State intervention in the *developing countries* is evolved for the liquidation of underdevelopment, that is, for the removal of obstacles to the rapid development of the productive forces.

State capitalism in the developing countries differs from state monopoly capitalism in the developed countries primarily because of its different function: instead of regulating – within certain limits – the spontaneous mechanism of the already highly developed forces of production, its aim is rather the creation of the conditions for the growth of the underdeveloped forces of production. In other words, it comes into being at a low developmental level of the productive forces. It also expresses the relationship of state and private capital, but this relationship is not yet determined in itself. In contrast to state capitalism in the developed capitalist countries, this state capitalism may have a *different and changing class content,* depending on the character and change in character of the state.

State capitalism here means intervention extending over the economy as a whole, but since it affects elements of a very heterogeneous character, it applies different methods and means. In addition to the capitalist elements, it extends over the "pre-capitalist" elements as well, but it is also of a heterogeneous nature in relation to foreign and national capital. This system of state intervention is state capitalism in the sense that the decisive, determining element in it is also the relationship between state and private capital (which may equally include the policy of supporting and the policy of restricting this capital) and *state* control over spontaneity arising from the existence of *capital.*

The character itself of this state capitalism, judged by the tendencies giving rise to it, is determined only to the extent that, in the last analysis, in fulfilling its *function,* it also includes among its measures steps to be taken both against foreign capital and feudal elements. This tendency, in case it asserts itself, gives a progressive feature to state capitalism, just as the task of rapidly developing the productive forces is also a progressive one. Since, however, "underdevelopment" is a complex phenomenon, and its liquidation raises manifold and often contradictory requirements, the anti-imperialist and anti-feudal character of state capitalism is not equally pronounced in the individual countries and periods, and may even be suppressed for a relatively long period of time.

Thus, the social content of state capitalism in the developing countries is still of a rather indefinite character. This accounts for the fact that great masses of society, both the national bourgeoisie and the working classes, may be interested in its development.

The national bourgeoisie may also be interested in the creation of an independent national economy and the restriction of pre-capitalist relations. It is for this reason that the national bourgeoisie often takes the lead in developing state capitalism.

But the relationship between state and national capital within state capitalism in the developing countries is contradictory. State capitalism in these countries, contrary to the developed capitalist countries, came into being when capitalism in the economy and society had not yet been completed and firmly established. Therefore, laws different from those in capitalism and arising from "pre-capitalist" remnants also assert themselves and exercise, in turn, an influence on the system of state intervention, too.

The motion and growth of state capitalism take place on the basis of several, often contradictory tendencies, and therefore a countless number of transitory and mixed formations may come into being. Not only the national and comprador strata of the national bourgeoisie, but also the various elements within the national bourgeoisie may have different relations to state capitalism, and this relationship may even be more differentiated on the part of other classes and strata of society.

It should be emphasized, however, that the concepts "comprador" and "national bourgeoisie" under neo-colonialism and in face of the changes in the investment policy of the big international monopolies can only be applied in an extremely *relative* sense, as co-operation between international monopolies and the local bourgeoisie, and the intertwining of some of their interests open up new and temporarily fairly wide areas. This may dampen or even neutralize the basic conflicting interests between the bourgeois stratum with its otherwise national and anti-colonial endeavours and foreign capital.

It must further be added that the attitude of other social forces of the national independence movement to the policy of state capitalism towards foreign capital is not necessarily unambiguous either. Personal and primarily material interests may tie the ruling élite to co-operation with foreign capital, often parallel with their interest in strengthening the national or even anti-imperialist character of political power. Even the attitude of those working class strata and organizations may be contradictory, who, though exploited by foreign capital, might disagree, at least temporarily, with certain measures of state capitalism.

But such and similar, partly secondary, partly transitory phenomena do not change the *national* character of state capitalism destined to liquidate underdevelopment, or eventually the tendency against foreign capital, or the nature and composition of the forces backing it.

The contradictions which arise between state and private capital as a result of the activity of state capitalism aimed at winding up underdevelopment, restrict, if not exclude, the unreserved co-operation of the national bourgeoisie with state capitalism. From these contradictions also follows that in the period of the liquidation of underdevelopment, the national bourgeoisie is but *one*, though occasionally the main force behind state capitalism, and the other social forces, the working classes, and the élite stratum of intellectuals, officers and civil servants also have, from the very outset, an important role to play. National capital and the leading strata representing its interests, e.g. the élite turning bourgeois, often shrink back from the risk of developing state capitalism before it could have performed its task, and tend to come to terms with foreign monopoly capital on the basis of underdevelopment and dependence. This may provide some security for the system based upon private ownership and against a revolutionary social transformation but does not show a way out of underdevelopment, nor does it bring about the unrestricted control of national capital over the national economy.

Thus, the capitalist way of further development of state capitalism, i.e. the possibility of evolving state monopoly capitalism based upon the developed forces of production and upon the hegemony of national capital, is rather limited in the "Third World". It is especially limited in Africa, where the formation of national capital itself is bound to rely on the effective support and fostering of state capitalism. Apart from the contradictions between state and private capital arising in the course of the operation of state capitalism, account must also be taken of the fact that in the changed international political and world-market situation it is unlikely for a new national monopoly capital in most of the "Third World" countries to arise and also to get a place of international exploitation, the field of which has anyway contracted horizontally. On the other hand, the growth and strengthening of such a monopoly capital exclusively from internal sources of exploitation would give rise to immense inner tensions and rely on an extremely unstable social basis. Therefore, even though there are certain initial though not yet "clear" and unambiguous indications of, or new opportunities for, monopoly capitalist development in a few countries (e.g. Brazil, Iran, Saudi Arabia, etc.) and thus of state capitalism changing into state monopoly capitalism, this type of development can materialize (if at all) at best in a few cases, only as a historical exception.

On the other hand, the socialist alternative of the further development of state capitalism presents itself – in spite of all initial difficulties – as a realistic historical possibility. This alternative means that state capitalism performing the tasks of the liquidation of underdevelopment and bringing about corresponding changes in the position of socio-economic forces, eventually leads on to a socialist system of planned economy, that is, gives rise to and performs development in a *non-capitalist way*.

This possibility follows inevitably from the consistent pursuit of liquidating underdevelopment, that is, from the *inherent* tendency of state capitalism performing this task.

The reason for this is, on the one hand, that state capitalism usually emerges in the developing countries *before* its class content is defined and its class basis is established. Moreover, even the building up of national capitalism presupposes, strangely enough, the intervention of the state power from above, i.e. the existence and co-operation of a state power with capitalist character, more exactly with a capitalist tendency. The dominant character of capitalist relations of foreign origin and spontaneity resulting from them lead not only to the preservation of underdevelopment but, as a consequence, also to the survival of the rule of foreign capital. The dominance of national capital, the unfolding of national capitalism, can only be ensured if this process is supported from above, by the national state. Thus, the interconnection is similar in a sense to that in the case of the development of socialist economy, socialist production relations and state power, in so far that the active intervention of the superstructure is necessary for building up the basis.

But the superstructure can only play such a role in building up the basis if it is backed by a *social force*, determining *in advance* the content of the superstructure and growing and strengthening together with the building up of that basis of the same character. If, however, the national bourgeoisie is weak at the time of the formation of state capitalism, then either an external force, i.e. foreign capitalism, stands behind the state power supporting capitalist development, usually at the cost of maintaining dependence, or social forces of a mixed composition line up behind the state power, in the composition of which rapid shifts in proportion will necessarily crop up in respect to the process of economic development and mainly of industrialization. The creation of a genuine national industry is not only the precondition for the unfolding of national capitalism but it also brings about and strengthens the national proletariat. If this process necessitates state assistance from the very beginning, that is, if a *direct* relationship develops between the state power of a still mixed composition and the economic process involving the growth of the working class, then a direct reaction may result from it, manifesting itself in a shift in the composition of social forces backing the state power.

If this shift, as a reaction of the frightened local bourgeois forces, means increasing reliance on foreign capitalism, that is, resorting to external forces, then it will result in the failure of national economic development and beginning industrialization, i.e. in giving up the results already attained in the liquidation of underdevelopment. If, however, this shift takes place in favour of the weight of the proletarian strata, it will gradually force the state power to swerve into an anti-capitalist direction. In this case, state intervention with its aim of economic development, is associated with anti-capitalist measures, and the development of both the superstructure and the basis are united in a mutually reinforcing cumulative process.

146

The mobilization of the revolutionary energies of *peasantry* and the *progressive forces of the élite,* especially if it takes place in a synchronized and mutually reinforcing way, may help the anti-capitalist and/or socialist tendency to come to power, or to consolidate it temporarily even *prior to* economic development (industrialization), and the subsequent social changes could lead to the creation of an adequate social basis for socialist development. The peculiar historic role of the rural revolutionary forces, progressive intellectuals and military officers consists in their promoting the creation and maintenance of a political superstructure, which speeds up the formation of a real basis for socialist development and may lead, in the related process of its own development, to the creation and consolidation of the socialist state.

On the other hand, but in connection with the foregoing, the organic relationship between socialism-oriented development and the liquidation of underdevelopment also follows from the fact that the latter presupposes, as a rule, the restriction of the spontaneity of private capital. In other words, the winding up of underdevelopment is impossible to be achieved on the basis of the spontaneous activity of private capital. The spontaneous economic forces work in the direction of the perpetuation of underdevelopment. Through the necessary restriction of spontaneity and the recognition of the dissatisfactory direction and measure of the activity of private capital, the inner logic of the struggle against underdevelopment may lead those people who examine the question of alternatives from the point of view of national interests to the recognition of the senselessness, unnecessary sacrifices and blind-alley nature of capitalist development.

In this connection great importance must be attached to "communication" and interactions between the progressive elements of the élite and the rural working population. Under the given circumstances the negative consequences of capitalist development, viz. economic spontaneity and social differentiation, manifest themselves primarily in agricultural and rural society. Agrarian crisis as apparent in the structural and technical stagnation of agriculture and the marketing difficulties of export products demonstrates the intolerability of capitalist spontaneity. And the widening gap between urban and rural incomes and living standards as well as rural differentiation, especially if they give rise, both in absolute and relative terms, to social unrest and the threatening movements of the impoverishing agrarian proletariat, call for the necessity of socio-economic reforms setting limits to capitalization and point to the timelines of the socialist alternative.

No doubt, there also exist the possibility and danger of a *bureaucratic further development* or degeneration of state capitalism,[1] that is, of the emergence of a bureaucratic state capitalism ("étatism"). This would be characterized, on the

[1] According to Bettelheim, the main danger to a further progressive development of state capitalism in Africa (besides the strengthening of private capitalism) is bureaucratic degeneration. (See Ch. Bettelheim: Planification Economique en Afrique Noire. *Cahiers Internationaux.* I–II. Paris, 1961, p. 70.)

one hand, by the state ownership of the means of production, the "quasi-social" expropriation of economic surplus by the state and, on the other hand, by the privileged position of a narrow state bureaucratic élite and a system of income distribution, in which the income share would be determined not by capital, that is, property, nor by work, but by the proximity to the state power, i.e. political position.

Though the indications of the development of this sort of structure can be observed in a number of developing countries, yet it can only be regarded – even in the case of its unfolding – as a *transitory* formation among the main alternatives of further development, in view of the impossibility of the élite becoming a separate, independent class, i.e. in view of the unstable and transitory character of such a structure. Instead, it appears justified to evaluate the development and strengthening of the privileged position of the élite as one, perhaps the most important potential source, of the formation of the *capitalist* class, that is, as part of the capitalist alternative, or as a significant but temporary obstacle to non-capitalist development and a final socialist transformation. Therefore, bureaucratic state capitalism under the guidance of the élite can be conceived of only as a transitional stage which, in the final analysis, leads either to the capitalist or to the socialist alternative. Its transitory character, however, does not necessarily mean a short duration of life. Incidentally, its disappearance is also a function of the objective measure of underdevelopment, that is, of the question what the time horizon is of the processes taking place "under the surface", which (e.g. industrialization and the development of public education, and social differentiation in the villages and towns) give rise to significant shifts to the right or left in socio-political power relations, also determining thereby the fate of the élite.

Whether the further development of state capitalism is finally connected with the *socialist or the capitalist alternative,* depends first of all on the *internal* socio-political development of the individual countries and on the formation of the *power relations of classes,* within the limits set by the international political and world-economic relations.

What is, however, specific to the dialectics of the development of state capitalism in the developing countries is the fact that this development is to a great extent *mutually* determined in that internal socio-economic development and the formation of class relations also depend on the direction, sphere and content of the operation of state capitalism. State capitalism in the developing countries is not simply a means of strengthening and preserving a social system already established but it also determines, to a great extent, the emergence of that social system. Consequently, the internal logic of development is much less tied to the actual state of social forces. Thus it may occur that but a slight shift in the political power relations – even within the same political group, e.g. owing to unexpected economic difficulties or to the necessity of revising foreign policy – which otherwise would hardly have any direct effect on the formation of class relations, brings about such quantitative changes in the mechanism of state capitalism, which may turn into *qualitative* changes also determining, to a certain extent, the direction for further social development.

We can come across this *metamorphosis* of state capitalism when economic intervention of the state, without being preceded or accompanied by a social revolution or a radical re-grouping of social class forces, "outgrows" the limits of its original function (i.e. the task of suppressing foreign capital and transforming the pre-capitalist remnants), and also sets limits to the formation and growth of domestic, national private capital. Since this precludes the possibility of the natural[2] formation and coming to power of the bourgeoisie, it may become the overture to socialist development without, or more exactly before, a socialist revolutionary transformation. At the same time it is a historic shortcut, *the non-capitalist way of further development.*

Of course, the over-expansion of state capitalism in itself – it appropriate social forces are not available – is no security for non-capitalist development. If such forces fail to develop or line up behind an "over-expanded" state capitalism, a reversal will usually take place, and the measures to curb the growth of national private capital are cancelled, possibly as a result of a coup d'état.

The metamorphosis of state capitalism as a criterion of and the basis for such non-capitalist development is usually realized in the expansion of the *state sector* of the economy. But nationalization and the predominance of state ownership in the main economic branches are *not* indispensable and exclusive indicators of a non-capitalist development. State capitalism comprises, on the one hand, a wide range of diversified forms of intervention in addition to nationalizations and state investments, and, on the other hand, the expansion of the state sector may also take place for the lack, or owing to the counteracting effects of other factors, in conformity with, or also subordinated to, the interests of local private capital (even without prejudicing the interests of foreign capital). From this it follows that the existence of this criterion of a non-capitalist development can only be analysed and evaluated *in concreto* with a thorough knowledge of the economic relations and the structure of the country concerned. Not only the concrete character of nationalization, but also the content and direction of the operation of the state sector itself may vary considerably. Without the examination of the aims of nationalization and of the interests it concretely serves, as well as of the operation of the state sector, any information on the share of the state sector, however high it may be, is of no practical value.

[2] Unlike the "natural" way of the formation of the bourgeoisie (through commodity production, capital accumulation and differentiation), the process of the "élite" turning into bourgeoisie in conjunction with the reprivatization of the state sector (but only with the two processes going hand in hand) can be conceived of as an *exceptional* road to the formation of bourgeois class and power.

3. THE BASIC SOCIO-ECONOMIC PROCESSES DETERMINING THE DIRECTION OF FURTHER DEVELOPMENT

The fate of state capitalism, or for that matter any genuine socialist transformation or even a return to the capitalist way of development, depends primarily on those concrete internal economic processes which have an effect on social stratification and the position of the various classes. In other words, the direction and character of further development is a function primarily of the basic socio-economic processes taking place in agriculture and industry, more exactly in the villages and towns.

The question is usually raised in this form: is it possible, under the specific international and specific internal conditions, to build up a socialist socio-economic system when its *par excellence* social basis, the industrial working class has not yet developed?

As far as the "international social basis" of a socialist transformation is concerned, it is true that the existence and support of the socialist countries may mean some protection against interventions aimed at a capitalist restoration. The significance of this factor is hard to overestimate, but still it is no substitute for an internal social basis. As long as the liquidation of underdevelopment takes place within the framework of the national economy, i.e. *not* on the basis of a social world revolution, the socio-economic processes too take place basically within the national economy. Thus, the analogy or even conception which projects the role of the urban basis of "socialism" (industry and the industrial proletariat) in determining the socialist transformation of the rural areas to the international plane and denies the necessity of the industrial and proletarian basis of socialism in relation to the developing countries, the "village" of the world, proves to be a deceptive illusion.

No doubt, one of the most conspicuous characteristics of the internal class relations is the wide gap between the living conditions of the rural and urban population, the extremely low income level of the agrarian strata, their great exploitation and their life calling for radical changes. But can these rural strata constitute a long-run basis for socialist development in the absence of the urban proletariat, or instead of the narrow urban strata of workers' élite leading a privileged life compared to that of the agrarian workers? Can rural socialist transformation be carried out in the framework of a comprehensive co-operative movement or in the ancient forms of traditional communities really provide a wide enough and stable basis for the socialist development of the *whole* economy and society?

The question has not only social and political but also economic implications. If the answer is in the affirmative, then the *absolute,* not only the relative and transitory priority of rural development in the economic development programme will follow from it. In this case, state capitalism must ensure the absorption and utilization of surplus which leads, over and above the reduction of urban overconsumption and the correction of existing income inequalities, to the fastest possible development of the agrarian sector, subordinating – in the interest of that sector – the activities of the other sectors and branches to this trend.

Agriculture, however, is unable to play the role of the leading sector in a modern economy. The *general* direction of the development of the forces of production leads from the agrarian and agrarian-industrial economies to the industrial-agrarian and industrial economies. And if socialism is destined to accelerate (and not to paralyse) development, then rural development may be the *transitory* phase and means of a rational preparation of industrialization but not a final socio-political objective. Consequently, economic considerations alone make it imperative for industry to provide the lasting social basis for social development.

At the same time, the processes taking place in the rural sectors of the developing countries and the very development of agriculture make the sufficient and lasting character of the agrarian basis of socialism questionable.

If even in the socialist countries of Europe agriculture meant for a long time a certain source of *capitalization,* then it is all the more true of the developing countries, where it is usually more difficult to raise industry to be a leading sector of the economy. In many developing countries, unlike in Europe, no strong spirit of private ownership has developed. But after the implementation of the agrarian reform, no matter whether it is directed against foreign plantations, feudal large estates or even the primitive pre-feudal forms of land tenure, not only the question is immediately raised which are the economic and organizational forms most appropriate for the liquidation of underdevelopment but also the problem of the future of the private sector of agriculture.

The formation and spread of the *co-operative form* is a fairly general phenomenon. This form, however, may have very different contents depending on the dominant factors determining socio-economic development. The co-operative form itself may assume a great variety of forms, some of which (e. g. the marketing-purchasing co-operatives or the credit-co-operatives) are also suitable to consolidate capitalist economies and accelerate their development. But even producers' co-operatives based on the common ownership of the means of production may become capitalist enterprises, kind of "joint stock companies" with capitalist group ownership.

And transition to commodity production, the increase of external influence within the traditional communities may be accompanied by the strengthening tendency of individualism, including the danger of the spontaneous disintegration of such communities. In addition, in many countries even the apparently communal relations often include relationships of exploitation and subordination concealed[3] in the system of family, clan and tribal relations.

---

[3] ".... (in Africa) the same complex of gerontocratic and familiar traditions and customs encompass the exploited and the exploiters alike (who are, so to speak, often relatives)." (Quoted by G. Arrighi and J. Saul: Nationalism and Revolution in Sub-Saharan Africa. *Socialist Register,* 1969. Mimeographed. Dar es Salaam.)

The "economic environment", i.e. the effect of the other, leading branches of the economy, determining the character of production relations elsewhere too, and, especially if that "environment" is missing or weak, state intervention itself will determine the social content of the co-operatives and the fate of the traditional communities.

Even in the case of the predominance of co-operatives (and communes), that is, of the economic and organizational forms characteristic of a socialist agriculture, the system of large-scale state intervention restricting capitalistic tendencies cannot be dispensed with. It is even more indispensable where the consistent implementation of the agrarian reform has not been completed, which anyway hinders the liquidation of underdevelopment, or where, after the land reform, small peasant holding has become the basic form of agriculture.

Small commodity production, which came into being perhaps as a result of the transformation of subsistence economies by means of state intervention, may become the source of capitalistic tendencies, and the natural law of its development is the *differentiation* of peasantry. Considering that the restriction and prevention of the working of this law was no easy task even in the socialist countries under the conditions of socialist industry, trade and finances, then it is definitely much more difficult in the developing countries, where these conditions are almost entirely non-existent. And the working of this law may have disastrous consequences not only for the labour market, the development of the rural productive forces and the social position of the rural population but it may even block the road to further non-capitalist development.

The dominant role of agriculture in the production of the national income and in employment, and especially its decisive weight in export production make it a real danger in most countries, even if industrial nationalizations and state control over foreign trade and finances have been effected, that with the simultaneous anti-capitalist development in other branches of the economy there may develop and strengthen in this sector, for lack of an intensive and appropriately oriented state intervention, a strong national capital that may stop or hold up non-capitalist development.

From this follows that the rural basis for socialist transformation in a not yet industrialized society can perform "only" a *transitory function*. (This transitory character means not the subsequent termination of this basis but its complementation with something more important.)

The performance of this function depends on 1. whether agriculture succeeds in creating economically, i.e. by expanding its surplus-generating capacity, the accumulation sources of industry; 2. whether rural development is not accompanied socially by a process of differentiation leading to the formation of a rural bourgeois stratum; and in connection with the above conditions, 3. whether the communal forms of the expropriation of the surplus produced become (or remain) dominant against the individual forms of expropriation, and whether the utilization of surplus takes place in accordance with the interests of the working classes of society and in compliance with the requirements of accelerating

152

economic growth (including the task of industrialization). The realization of these conditions requires not only the increased controlling and guiding-influencing role of the state but also the intensive activity of the social and political organizations. If this involves the danger of a possible growth of state bureaucracy and even of strengthening the power and privileged position of the ruling élite, then this undoubtedly indicates the difficulty but does not reduce the real possibility and extraordinary importance of such a transition.

Therefore, even if the rural working strata and the rural economy alone (however revolutionary the character of the former and however rapid the development of the latter may be) are unable to perform this function of a *genuine* and lasting social and economic basis for socialist development, they may, to a certain extent, serve as temporary substitutes for it, facilitating the development of a socialist basis.

The special importance of this transition is due to the fact that the improvement of the living conditions of the rural working population and rural development in general have anyway become, *on the one hand,* one of the central issues of economic policy in view of such problems as the expansion of the internal market, the mobilization of the available sources of accumulation, as well as of the budget and foreign-exchange revenues of the state, solving the problems of public nutrition, the easing of import dependence, open and disguised unemployment, the levelling of striking income inequalities, etc., that is, they coincide with the general trend of acute development needs. *On the other hand,* the transition itself means the utilization of the available social forces which can be mobilized for a socialist-orientated development, instead of waiting idly for the formation of a more appropriate social basis.

Thus, the processes going on in agriculture, i.e. in the "village", are of extremely great, though, in the last analysis, not of a decisive importance for the creation of a social basis for socialist development. The formation of these processes depends first of all on the direction, intensity and effectiveness of the influences coming from outside and, in the case of non-capitalist development, necessarily also from *above,* and besides the results of these processes also make themselves felt *outside* agriculture and "rural" society, exercising their influence not only on the economic and social relations but not infrequently also on political power relations.

As far as intervention in agrarian development from outside and above is concerned (often referred to as "*penetration*" in the literature of underdevelopment), it raises first of all the question of "interveners", that is, of persons who have authority to decide on intervention (on its character, direction, measure and methods) and to carry it out. Since at the upper and outer poles and the starting-point of intervention there is a state which in its class content is *not* yet unambiguously socialist, but a state power of a mixed class basis led by the manifold and variegated élite, therefore intervention itself is not of an unambiguously definite character.

153

Owing to personal or family interests, part of the political élite may be interested directly, or, for tribal or political reasons (as for constituency considerations) also indirectly in keeping intervention rather ineffective and in preventing it from afflicting the well-to-do rural stratum, or in promoting the strengthening of the "rural élite" as a prospective ally.[4]

On the other hand, intervention also raises the question of introducing the organizational and institutional forms available to it, as well as that of its concrete realization. In so far as the implementation of intervention is based mostly on direct methods, that is, if it is attempted to put it into practice without relying on the "local agencies": a decentralized administration, the local state and party organizations and democratic institutions, then it will usually give rise to the rural society keeping aloof or even putting up an indiscriminate resistance to political power. In remembrance of the requisitions, land expropriations, tax collections and manpower recruiting activities of the colonial administration, resentments against "urban people" or "those coming from the towns" are easy to arouse. This may lead not only to ignoring instructions and even helping-teaching advice, but can also make it impossible to gather the necessary information.

If, however, intervention takes place in collaboration with, or through the mediation of "local agents", then the danger exists that a community of interests may evolve between them and the well-to-do rural strata, and that they themselves are recruited from among the latter. And in this case the sacrifices made in the interest of intervention, development investments, credits and other material and spiritual assistance rendered with the aim of raising the poor rural population or even promoting socialist economic and income relations, will be turned to the benefit of the rich peasant strata.

As regards the "external" effects of the agrarian processes, that is, those which manifest themselves in economic sectors other than agriculture, in society and the political sphere, it will suffice to refer to such relationships which exists between the sound transformation of agriculture, the increased production for the home market, the consolidation or (eventual) liberation of the labour force following the rise in productivity, etc., on the one hand, and the industrialization process, the manpower situation, the stabilization, material, educational and organizational position of the industrial working class, etc., on the other. In addition to these effects, largely indirect from the point of view of the social basis of socialism, it is the mechanism of "penetration" and the given channels of political selection which also provide the possibility of a *direct* effect of the agrarian processes in the political sphere. The decentralized units of the state and party apparatus and the local agencies of intervention in general are mostly recruited from the elements of rural society who, through the political capillaries, not only get in direct touch

[4] Writing on the relationship between differentiation and state intervention (on the basis of his experiences gained on the Ivory Coast) S. Amin remarks that "the bureaucratic bourgeoisie (la bourgeoisie d'État) has never eliminated the private bourgeoisie (la bourgeoisie privée) but contents itself with co-opting it or fusing with it". (S. Amin: Le développement du capitalisme en Afrique Noire. *L'homme et la société*. No. 6, Oct.–Décembre 1967, p. 117.)

with those in charge of leadership but may also get into it, either according to the rules of democracy, that is, owing to their actual merits, or according to the laws of political careerism. If at the "local level" the élite products of differentiation, the rural bourgeoisie, or the elements who are on the way of becoming bourgeois, get into the political channels leading on to the top, then it will lead not only to a reversal of state intervention already mentioned but also to a "penetration" into the opposite direction, i. e. to the filling up of the state (and party) apparatus with bourgeois elements "from below".

Therefore, it is obvious that not only the progress of the agrarian processes, the direction and rate of agrarian development, the character and results of state intervention influencing those processes depend on the development of state power and the élite representing it, but it also means that this interaction is to a great extent a mutual one.

It is of course *the urban (industrial) socio-economic processes* which exercise a more direct and decisive effect on the character of state intervention and on the fate of the élite. The possibility, on the one hand, of a joint interest with capital and bourgeois penetration is greater and more direct, and, on the other, the growth of the urban working strata, the shifts within the worker and employed strata in the process of industrialization (the strengthening of an industrial core at the expense of the workers' "élite" and the lumpen-elements), as well as the development of radical groups of intellectuals in many countries have a direct impact on the political processes. Since the construction of socialism is in the long run impossible without its *real* economic basis, i. e. industry, and without its *real* social basis, i. e. the industrial proletariat, the changes implicit in urban-rural processes are of crucial importance both for surplus production and distribution, and also for social differentiation and political power relations.

In addition to, but in connection with, the economic and attendant social processes, i. e. the basic processes of agrarian development, industrialization and the appropriation and utilization of economic surplus in general and the assignment of social functions, there are of course also a number of other social and political factors and circumstances determining further development, which, however, are so specific that they had better be dealt with in studies on individual countries or groups of countries.

The direction of further development is also influenced, in addition to the internal economic, social and political processes taking place in the developing countries, by the processes making advance in *the world economy and world politics,* or more exactly, by their impact on those internal processes. Moreover, the external processes have an increasingly great importance, owing and in proportion to the "open" character of the economy and society, and to the general increase in dimensions and growing internationalization of the modern forces of production, as well as to the development of international communication. With a certain simplification, the external effects influencing internal development could be classified, according to their relations, into *three main categories:*

(a) The extremely complex category of relations and interactions *between developing countries*. In all probability, this will rapidly expand in the future including both positive, i.e. promoting, and also negative, i.e. inhibiting effects.

(b) The category of the effects exercised by the *developed capitalist countries*. This comprises not only the direct and unambiguously negative effect on inherited dependence and neo-colonialist influences, but also the indirect effect of the policies pursued by the developed capitalist countries in other relations, of their attitude to peaceful international co-existence and changes in their internal politics. In other words, these external relations represent an extremely complex category.

(c) The category of the effects exercised by *the socialist countries*, among them those which but recently have embarked upon the road to socialism. Besides the direct and (in proportion to its effectiveness and unselfishness) positive effect of this novel type of economic relations and external assistance, this category also includes such, perhaps even more important, *indirect* effects as follow from the historical role played by the socialist countries in preserving a peaceful international balance of powers, in preventing imperialist aggressions, and also manifest themselves in the experiences obtained and the results achieved in liquidating underdevelopment, as well as in the demonstration of lessons drawn even from certain errors made in their economic policies.

****

From the summary of our investigations into the historical path and the forthcoming period of the developing countries we may draw the following conclusions:

(a) The historic task of liquidating underdevelopment provides an objective basis for the development of state capitalist tendencies and socialist endeavours.

(b) At the same time, the coming into prominence of internal social conflicts and the concealment of external antagonisms in neo-colonialist form reinforce the tendency of the élite in power to become bourgeois in character, and of the élite or the national bourgeoisie to come to terms with neo-colonialism.

(c) Since, however, neo-colonialist solutions mean the betrayal of the historic task of liquidating underdevelopment, the necessity of economic development and transformation gives an ever newer impetus to seeking a socialist solution, and increasingly tends to present the socialist alternative as the only possible one.

(d) Consequently, the historical period ahead of us will in all probability be a *transitory* but presumably a long-term span of time characterized by alternating non-capitalist changes in some countries and attempts made in the direction of socialist development, as well as by a *series* of failures of these attempts as a result of neo-colonialist interventions, internal deficiencies, errors and various interactions.

(e) The general strengthening of socialist tendencies will manifest itself not only in the rapid increase in the number and frequency of such attempts but also in the stabilization of the results attained by some countries, and in the realization of the policy of breaking away from both international and domestic capitalism.

156

PART TWO

ECONOMIC DEVELOPMENT AND PLANNING IN DEVELOPING COUNTRIES

by

József Bognár

I. GENERAL SURVEY OF THE QUESTIONS OF ECONOMIC GROWTH

1. THE MAIN PROBLEMS OF GROWTH STRATEGY

The acceleration of the economic growth of developing countries raises an extremely intricate complexity of problems, difficulties and tensions of an interdependent and cumulative nature. No doubt, the *circumstances of growth* as known to us in the history of mankind have never exposed the world (humanity) as a whole or individual peoples engaged in the process of development to dilemmas so heavily laden with tensions and contradictions as those which will face them in the years to come.

There are *three circumstances* which, from the point of view of the world and mankind, cause the historic period of economic growth to be full of tensions:

1. The *gap* between the economically developed and the underdeveloped countries *has never been so wide and deep* as in our days.

2. Nations that can be regarded as economically underdeveloped *have never constituted such a large proportion of mankind* as at present.

3. Never before in history has the population of the economically less developed countries *so vividly and convincingly been made aware of the glaring differences between their own living standards and living conditions* and those of the economically advanced world as in our days.

Let us examine in brief these circumstances one after the other:

1. According to reliable calculations, per capita national income in the present-day industrial countries was $ 170 in 1850, while it is $ 100 in today's developing countries.

In 1850, the ware of the developing countries – including China – in the world's total income was 65 per cent, while today it is only 11 per cent.

By the end of the 1970s, *per capita gross national product* of the developed capitalist countries averaged thirteen times ($ 3,250) the amount for the developing countries ($ 250). This average does not of course express the difference that exists between the extreme values of per capita national product in the richest capitalist country and the poorest underdeveloped region. Thus, in 1971, per capita national income was $ 5,051 in the USA and around $ 140 in India.[1]

This striking difference began to take shape when the cumulative effects of the industrial revolution began to make themselves felt as gross national product per

[1] Handbook of International Statistics, Budapest 1974, Hungarian Central Statistical Office.

head of population rose by an annual average of 1.8 per cent over 100 years in the advanced capitalist countries as against only by 0.1 per cent in the present-day developing countries.

It would be, however, a static approach if, in assessing the wideness and depth of the gap between the developed and developing countries, we were to take our departure exclusively from the *present* income levels. These differences *in the medium- and long-term factors* influencing economic growth are even greater than the present ones. We only need to think of such differences as the relative *abundance of capital* in the *developed* capitalist countries versus *shortage of capital in the developing ones*, which, after the launching of economic growth, is becoming even more pronounced; 95 per cent of the world's *research capacity* is concentrated in thirty developed capitalist countries, while only 5 per cent can be found in the developing world; there is a relative abundance of *qualified manpower* in the first group of countries, and an immense shortage of it in the second. (It should not be forgotten that there is a correlation of 0.84–0.87 between per capita *national income* and the *level* of education.) Without external assistance and development efforts this gulf would continue to widen for decades.

2. At present, *about 70 per cent of mankind* live in Asia, Africa and Latin America, and this percentage will rise to 80 per cent by 2000. All countries of these continents, including People's China, are involved in economic growth.

Especially grave is the situation in this respect in Asia where, by 2000, 55 per cent of the world's population (excluding the Soviet Union) will live with a density of population of 148 per square kilometre, while Europe's average population density without the Soviet Union (i. e. the world's most densely populated part) will amount to 118.

We must also be aware of the fact that in the immediate vicinity of Asia there is a practically vacant continent (Australia), whose population will hardly exceed 30 million by the year 2000.

3. Prior to the 20th century, *there was hardly any contact between the inhabitants of the advanced and the less developed countries.* As a result, people living in closed communities *did not know* each other's living conditions, and deemed many things that other people possessed as either needless or senseless.

Except in wars or military campaigns, it was only the members of the leading classes, living anyway in better conditions than the rest of the population, who got abroad, and it was not in their interest to inform the poorer strata of the existing differences in living standards.

Owing to the rapid spread and development of the cinema, television and the means of transport, this situation has radically changed. Today even the simplest people in Africa or Asia can see in films how an American millionaire or engineer lives, and can make comparisons with their own living conditions.

Thus, in the decades to come, *desperation* will grow and will of course primarily be directed against the ex-colonizers and neo-colonizers, but dissatisfaction may affect other countries and states as well.

It follows logically from the foregoing that

160

1. *economic growth must be started in every developing country;*

2. considering the present-day circumstances of these countries, *development is likely to raise especially intricate problems* as

(a) *immense economic objectives must be achieved,* and these objectives are derived not from the prevailing economic state of the developing countries but from the present maturity of the world economy, i.e. from stronger and larger economies;

(b) these immense objectives (i.e. those derived from the scientific and techncial levels of more powerful economies) ought to be realized *within a relatively short period of time;*

(c) compared with these ambitious objectives, very *limited intellectual and material* energies (resources) *are available.*

3. Consequently, these immense objectives *cannot be achieved exclusively from internal resources.* It stands to reason that no country can develop without a maximum mobilization of its own intellectual and material energies, but the provision of external assistance is nevertheless indispensable.

4. Since there is such a great disproportion between the objectives and the resources (intellectual and material energies) needed to achieve them, special attention must be paid to a *maximum reduction of squandering these energies* (structural losses of the type of growth chosen).

In any economy conscious human actions will take place. They take place under capitalism primarily in the individual or group spheres (corporations, trusts), while under socialism common social interest has a real representation both in respect to property and power aiming at the reconciliation of group (enterprise) interests and actions with individual interests and actions.

On the other hand, actions taking place in the traditional, individual or group spheres of the economy of the developing countries have not proved efficient enough to start economic growth. Therefore, the acceleration of growth must be ensured by the *central power* (i.e. the state).

This necessity is, in a sence, independent of the ownership relations, which means that economic growth in such a multi-sectoral economy must be launched even if only a small proportion of the basic means of production are state-owned. There exists not only the necessity but also *the possibility* of starting this process as the state, being in the possession of power, is in a position, by taking into account the different laws of the movements and reactions of various sectors, to stimulate both individuals and groups of people to take a definite action.

The fact that the *direct economic power* of the government, as compared e.g. with the socialist countries, is strongly limited, only means that in taking actions it must consider many conflicting interests, and that the number and measure of deviations from the objectives will be greater.

But even under such conditions, the state power, setting progressive social and political objectives, may assume the *supreme guiding role in economic policy and the motive force of economic development.*

The government must endeavour to include the aims, means and the effects taken in their broadest sense of economic growth and development in a system of uniform principles and norms of action at all levels of economic live and for all sectors of the economy. It is in this way that a uniform economic policy, a long-term *development strategy* (conception) will be formulated.

The *long-term objectives* of economic growth can be derived from the socio-political aims of the given power. Political viewpoints and considerations also play an important role in choosing the *concrete objectives* as they are— at least theoretically – in harmony with the long-term objectives.

The concrete aims can only lead to the long-term objectives through a system of intricate processes; therefore, *temporary* contradictions may exist between them.

2. SOME POLITICAL IMPLICATIONS OF THE GROWTH STRATEGY

It should be emphasized that political issues, that is, the internal and external strengthening of the given power, play a paramount role in the formulation of both the *concrete objectives* and the choice of the *means needed* to attain them.

This is not the place to analyse these problems in depth, and we only want to refer to the fact that economic growth is a process comprising society as a whole, and, consequently, every sector, group, social class and individual are equally interested in its rate, implementation and results. Thus, the process of growth induces changes in society which also influence the position, mass basis and evaluation of the political power.

Economic growth brings about *shifts of power* in the state and composition of the leading stratum of society and in its relation to the rest of the nation. In creating the socio-economic conditions for economic growth, social formations existing for centuries or even millennia break up, gradually or abruptly, formations which provided relative security for the rural population even if this process materialized at a very low level.

As a consequence, people are insecure about the future and doubtful whether the security of subsistence that has evolved at a low level will give way to something better.

Thus the old equilibria, both the relative economic and the socio-political ones, have been upset. In a situation like this, when everything is in commotion in society and most people feel uncertain, the political leadership must always endeavour not to transgress the limit of the "greatest acceptable tension".

It must be taken into account that for the time being *apparently* distressing events continue to happen in the economy; the budgetary equilibrium is upset, very often inflation emerges, foreign-exchange reserves are depleted, the balance of trade and the balance of payments become adverse, prices rise and consumption may also decline.

162

But the leadership must understand that optimization in the economy is possible and necessary not only in relation to the objectives set (the increase in national incomes, employment, accumulation and consumption alike may be optimized), but also in relation to the amount of *time* needed for development (i. e. for attaining certain aims). When in formulating a growth strategy it appears that it jeopardizes, on the one hand, the stability of the political power and, on the other, may lead, owing to the economic risks involved, to setbacks, then it is expedient to extend the implementation of the objectives over a longer period of time. At the same time, however, a too slow progress may also become the source of social tensions. This is one of the causes of changes in the political regime in developing countries (e. g. in the Republic Malgas in 1972) or of military coups (e. g. in Dahomey in 1972). And finally, in elaborating the growth strategy, account must also be taken of the future position of the subsequent generation bearing the burden of development. Many start from the assumption that three or four generations will have to bear only the burdens, while later generations will enjoy the fruits of sacrifices made now and to be made in the future. It is not a just and correct conception, not to speak of the fact that on the basis of theory at present it is only today's sacrifices that are sure to be made, and nobody is able to predict with absolute certainty the future course of events. Therefore, it appears to be expedient also to include the consumption optimum in the many optimization possibilities.

In connection with the *external position* of power I would also like to point briefly to a few facts. It is self-evident that these countries are unable to achieve a rapid rate of economic growth without external assistance. In other words, they must pursue a foreign policy enabling them to receive grants and loans. This is of course no easy thing as the neo-colonialist powers make use of providing grants and loans with a view to bringing these countries into a state of dependence and influencing thereby both their internal and foreign policies.

Therefore, the "optimum of foreign policy" must be formulated in such a way that the developing countries

(a) are able to prevent the intervention attempts of the neo-colonialist powers; but

(b) can accept grants and loans not only from socialist countries and international organizations but also from Western countries.

These two requirements are of course contradictory but not mutually exclusive. The struggle between the two systems is going on relentlessly, and the developing countries are not left to themselves in this fight as

(a) they have already received – and at very critical points of time – credits and grants from the socialist countries, primarily from the Soviet Union;

(b) the co-operation of developing countries, especially such continental organizations as the Organization of African Unity, is able to provide a minimum measure of security for all members of the organization;

(c) controversies between the leading capitalist powers can shrewdly be exploited by a cleverly conducted political manoeuvring.

11*

An "optimum of foreign policy", however, can only be formulated in the case of a comprehensive, well-considered and stable internal policy. It may occur, e. g., that the government of a developing country sets limits to the economic activities of a given sector, or initiates changes in the ownership relations of a branch of economy. Such measure may always be necessary and will not lead to harmful consequences if the internal power relations of the economy and the situation that arises after taking that measure are assessed correctly.

If, however, there is a great drop in production and, as a result, supply difficulties arise, then a quantity of goods corresponding to the loss in production will have to be imported. If there is no sufficient foreign exchange available for that purpose, and the socialist countries cannot provide assistance either, then the government has brought itself by its inconsiderate internal action into foreign-political dependence.

It should be repeatedly emphasized that in this chapter the political problems relating to the growth strategy will not be dealt with in detail. With our comments and examples we only wish to illustrate how closely the economic problems are connected – especially at the governmental level – with political problems.

The political situation exerts a great influence on economic actions, but economic growth itself reacts directly, and also through the social structure, on the political situation.

In the last analysis, the citizens of developing countries will judge the capabilities of their governments by their success or failure to stop stagnation and start an economic development which is equally favourable for the country and its citizens.

3. TYPES OF GROWTH

One of the most important factors of economic growth and/or economic policy is the question of *natural-economic endowments*. It is not the problems of growth and stagnation that are raised by the natural-economic endowments, as any country, even those under the most unfavourable natural circumstances, are capable of development. The natural-economic endowments play a very significant role in determining the *type of growth* of the given economy and in setting the direction (objectives) of development.

(a) LARGE AND SMALL COUNTRIES

There are large and small countries, but the classification of countries according to one or the other category depends not primarily on the size of the area concerned but on the number of population.

Large countries have *several advantages* over the small ones:

1. They can determine their growth type more independently of the international political and economic circumstances.

164

2. Possessing a large variety of raw materials, they can introduce various production technologies and industrial structures.

3. Owing to their wide internal market, they can, perspectively, develop almost all industrial branches economically.

4. Given the same developmental level, they have more accumulation possibilities than the small countries.

Their *disadvantages* are as follows:

1. Various areas of the country are as a rule not homogeneous, and the development of the backward areas is expensive.

2. Being "big bodies", they are unadaptable and less responsive to changes.

Disadvantages of the small countries are as follows:

1. Growth types and possibilities in their case are strongly influenced by the changes of world politics and the facts of the world economy.

2. Since they do not possess a large variety of raw materials, only a limited number of production techniques can be efficiently introduced by them.

3. Owing to the narrowness of the domestic market and their raw material basis, they have to create a more concentrated economy; they must develop only a few industries, but this on a *competitive basis*.

Their *advantages* are:

1. Their population is generally more homogeneous, which means that there are no substantial differences between developmental levels.

2. They may be more adaptive and more responsible to changes.

(b) DENSELY AND SPARSELY POPULATED COUNTRIES

The countries in the Far East are usually densely populated, while those in Africa and Latin America are, as a rule, sparsely populated. (An exception is the Arab Republic of Egypt, which is densely populated.) The densely populated developing countries are marked by a large-scale overt and disguised unemployment. Certain Western economists (e.g. Tinbergen) treat the labour force as a "free good", saying that the marginal productivity of labour is equal to nil. Though this statement is theoretically incorrect, the introduction of an up-to-date technology has undoubtedly its rational limitations.

In the case of *densely populated developing countries* economic growth should proceed along the extensive path, i.e. "capital", wherever possible, must be replaced by labour.

There exist good possibilities of achieving this in agriculture, handicraft industry, the light industries and in the building up of the infrastructure.

It must, however, be taken into account that in certain cases handicraft industry cannot ensure the same quality of products as large-scale industry (metallurgy, steel production, the manufacture of alloys, etc.), therefore in present-day economy labour cannot always replace machines.

In the case of extensive growth, optimization takes place essentially in the interest of increasing employment, therefore the rates of growth of the national income and accumulation will be slower. But a planned utilization of manpower may help in preparing the further phases of growth. During the extensive period of development, the foundation may be laid for improving the natural conditions of agriculture by means of developing its most mobile factor, i.e. water supply.

In the dynamic industrial sector *capital-intensive* investments must be effected, however, capital should not be related to labour but to production value.

In the case of abundant labour reserves, the extensive type of growth will dominate for several decades but in the redeployment of manpower to town (to industry) two phases may be anticipated:

1. the one, in which rural manpower may be transferred without endangering agricultural yields, and

2. the other, in which preventive investments must be made in agriculture to release rural manpower.

At the time of starting the growth process, there is also excess labour both in the towns and the countryside in the *sparsely populated countries*. Here, however, manpower will be an *abundant* factor only for a shorter period of time as unemployment will soon be absorbed by industry, the infrastructure and raw-material production. In such countries it is possible sooner to embark upon the path of intensive development, provided it is not hampered by capital shortage.

The introduction of capital-intensive development comes up against two further difficulties. The one is the lack of qualified labour, and the other foreign-exchange shortage emerging in the case of capital-goods imports.

In agriculture, however, in general and for the time being, it is no use further expanding cultivated areas. Instead, efforts must be made to increase yields by improving water economy and soil fertility.

No doubt, the growth problems of the densely populated countries in the Far East are substantially more complex than those in the African and Latin American countries.

4. THE SIGNIFICANCE OF RAW MATERIALS IN THE ECONOMIC GROWTH AND FOREIGN TRADE OF THE DEVELOPING COUNTRIES

In these days, up-to-date industry is becoming increasingly independent of natural raw materials.

In the developing countries natural resources constitute important inputs in organizing economic activities. The role of natural resources, however, is *entirely passive* unless they are exploited.

Raw materials are not decisive either in that they do not tell whether there prevails growth or stagnation in a given economy but they do exercise an impact on the choice of the growth type and on the structure of the emerging economy. History knows of course several instances of industrial development based not only on domestic but on imported raw materials.

Rich natural resources have different effects on strong and weak economies. The natural resources of economically weak countries exercise a considerable attraction on the monopolies of imperialist countries. The nationalization of raw-material extraction is often impeded by the fact that the capacities of repetitive transport and manufacturing processes relating to the given extraction of raw materials as well as their markets are also controlled by foreign monopolies.

But raw materials are *advantageous* in that they

(a) may provide a basis for exports first in the form of raw materials, then of semi-manufactured goods and eventually perhaps of manufactures;

(b) indirectly reduce the importance of the other factors of production;

(c) may serve as a basis for the development of domestic manufacturing industry.

As far as raw materials are concerned, the price rise of oil since the autumn of 1973 (and, subsequently, of other mineral raw materials) has started a new phase in the development of the world economy and opened up new growth-financing sources for the oil-producing countries (and potentially for the world as a whole). This new situation will not bring about any change in the here outlined strategic objectives of the growth policies of the developing countries, yet it will make possible their implementation within a substantially shorter period of time.

5. THE PROBLEM OF EQUILIBRIUM AND THE MAIN DIRECTION OF DEVELOPMENT

The growth and dynamics of the economy largely depend on the relations which the economy in question is able to establish with the world economy. Economic equilibrium, too, is mainly a function of this relationship. We do not of course regard the requirement of economic equilibrium as a dogma since every type of economic growth is accompanied by upsetting the existing relations of equilibrium. Therefore, we are of the opinion that in the first stage of development, growth (i. e. the upsetting of the existing economic cycle) is more important than equilibrium. The development strategy (economic policy), however, is formulated for a fairly long period of time (one and a half or two decades), which means that a *dynamic* equilibrium must be aimed at. The upsetting of existing equilibrium relations by the newly introduced growth strategy does not cause any serious trouble, but if the reorganization of the growth factors results in lengthening rather than shortening the distance from the state of equilibrium, then we are faced with an unhealthy and dangerous process.

How do the equilibrium relations of a given economy, primarily those of the balance of trade and the balance of payments, develop in the course of the growth process?

Growth starts, in essence, by increasing capital accumulation and securing new employment opportunities for the formerly unemployed strata by means of the material and intellectual resources ensured in this way.

167

The creation of new industrial capacities requires, however, new productive equipment to be imported from abroad. Consequently, an increase in imports will be necessary, and the equilibrium of the balance of trade and the balance of payments, based so far essentially on the lack of demand for capital goods, will be upset. But the growth of imports cannot be stopped in the sector of capital goods as *consumption* will also *increase* both in the private and public sectors.

Can the imports of other goods and for other sectors be reduced in such a way that they offset this increase in consumption? This depends, in the first place, on whether the state can effectively restrict the *luxury consumption* of the leading strata.

The restriction of the consumption of the well-to-do strata would

(a) promote capital formation;

(b) reduce inflationary pressure (because at present increasing government expenditures are financed by credit expansion);

(c) distribute more evenly the burdens of industrialization and protectionist policy;

(d) create markets for new industries.

Thus, the solution of this problem would require wide-ranging *social reforms* and the redistribution of incomes. But some of the governments concerned show little interest in carrying them out.

In such countries, however, where there are no feudal strata and even the number of capitalists is very limited, it is the intellectual strata enjoying special benefits who indulge in luxury consumption. The imports of luxuries to these countries must also be restricted, though this measure would not have far-reaching consequences (e.g., it would but little effect domestic capital formation).

It must not be forgotten either that, owing to the still existing international tension, a substantial proportion of the export earnings of the developing countries is spent on importing armaments. Therefore, in order to accelerate economic growth, the "Third World" would be interested in consolidating peace and international security so that it can save the cost of armaments.

It is obvious that import growth cannot be offset exclusively by the restriction of luxury imports and, under the present conditions, of the import of armaments. Efforts must be made, therefore, at equalizing increasing imports by *exports*.

In the developing countries, 90 per cent of the export are agricultural produce and raw materials.

The demand for foodstuffs in countries with high living standards has already become inelastic though reduced prices through the abolition, or a substantial reduction, of import duties would make it possible to draw new strata into consumption. Otherwise, the expansion of exports would lead to a drop in world market prices. The effect of these consequences can be mitigated by such commodity agreements which also provide for a possible expansion or reduction of areas under cultivation.

Owing to technological development, the demand for classical industrial raw materials has relatively diminished – with the exception of oil. In other words: the increase in the demand for classical raw materials considerably lags behind the growth of industrial production. On the other hand, it is commonly known that raw material production without an adequate development of the manufacturing processes heavily depends on subsidies even in the developed countries.

While the price rise in food and oil imports has imposed significant burdens on certain developing countries, the increase in the prices of oil and other mineral raw materials has resulted in a considerable surplus of export earnings for other developing countries, a fact which has further differentiated the economic situation and growth prospects in the developing world. It must be pointed out, however, that though the price rise has made the oil-producing countries "richer" (measuring the concept of "richness" by the amount of monetary reserves), they are still far from being "developed".

Obviously, it is possible to achieve a certain degree of *export growth in such industries* which require not too much capital and have a favourable capital-output ratio, whose basic materials can be produced in the country, and the low level of wages ensures a comparative advantage for the developing countries (e.g. cotton goods).

However, the so-called dynamic industries requiring large capital investments, having a less favourable capital-output ratio and also an unfavourable manpower coefficient, and in which the developed countries also have a technological *monopoly,* can hardly achieve any appreciable exports.

From all this follows that

(a) the industrialization dynamics of the developing countries must not be based on exports (unlike e.g. in 19th-century England);

(b) an increase in the foreign trade of developing countries will be controlled by an inevitable growth in imports.

Consequently, in order to ensure equilibrium in foreign trade, an *import-saving* (import-substituting) type of industrialization must be achieved. Moreover, diversification in agriculture, especially in one-crop economies, should also be emphasized if difficulties in the supply of the domestic population are to be avoided. Otherwise, owing mainly to the rapid increase in population, the imports of basic agricultural products will rise more steeply than the exports of typical tropical products.

Therefore, the first stage of industrialization will be of an *import-saving* (import-substituting) character, as in Latin America, where the share of imports in total national income decreased from 28 per cent to 12 per cent during 30 years (between 1930 and 1960).

An essentially similar type of industrialization was carried out in the European people's democracies, too, in the period from the end of the Second World War to the early 1960s, with the difference that since 1954 the import-substituting character must be understood as relating to the CMEA and not to individual national economies. The significance of this type of co-operation lies in the fact that it provides a wide market for the products of the new industries by means of diversification and specialization. Its difficulty, however, is manifested by the fact that certain disadvantages of import-substituting industrialization (the secured position of the producer versus the consumer, neglecting the requirements of quality and up-to-dateness, etc.) spread like a chain reaction.

But import-substituting industrialization means the cognizance that the products of the given country are not yet competitive on the world market and need to be subsidized (protectionism). Production costs are higher, the quality of products is poorer and the level of the complementary services are lower than those of their competitors in the world market. Therefore, in the interest of protecting the domestic industry, a *dynamic* (i.e. not rigid, not bureaucratic but capable of a rapid adjustment to changing situations) and a *selective* (i.e. considerably varying from industry to industry) type of protectionism must be introduced. But in choosing the investment variants, especially in the case of small countries, account must also be taken of the fact that today's import-saving industries will also have to export tomorrow (in 5 to 10 years). Even in the case of substantial import saving it is not expedient to create industries the product of which will be considerably more expensive and their quality poorer even in 10 years' time than those of other countries (or of foreign companies). But the fact must also be reckoned with – as amply evidenced by historical experience – that over-subsidized industries working in a conditioned environment find it hard to adapt themselves to new requirements.

However, an industrialization programme cannot be interpreted one-sidedly. Industrialization is necessary for every developing country, yet the neuralgic point of the growth process is *agriculture* (high consumer prices and various ways of syphoning off agricultural incomes). It, however, agriculture, where, in addition, a substantial proportion of manpower still live in a traditional environment, is unable to increase production, then it must import more and more agricultural products, which completely upsets the equilibrium of the balance of payments. The difficulties of many developing countries can to a great extent be traced back to their incapability of increasing at all, or but insignificantly, per capita agricultural output. Thus it is obvious that industrial and agricultural production must be developed *simultaneously,* which does not mean that they should be achieved at the same rate but only that the growth rate of agricultural output must reach 5 per cent annually. (The annual rate of population growth being above 2 per cent, the industrialization process also means increased consumption in *absolute terms,* and the export of traditional products must also be stepped up.) And the increase in production – if markets can be expanded adequately – may reach an annual 9 to 10 per cent, which, by the way, would mean that in 60 to 70 years the developing countries will be capable of reaching the present-day production level of today's industrial countries.

Every developing country is extremely sensitive to the world economy. In the *measure* and *content* of this sensitivity there exist substantial differences.

(a) In certain countries (especially in the large ones) exports grow more slowly

170

than national income (Latin America, India). This means that the economy is of a *defensive* rather than of an *expansive* character.

(b) In certain countries (e.g. Japan) exports may constitute in due time a *balancing sector,* because the markets can be expanded in proportion to, or even more than, the possibility of decreasing imports in the case of an import-saving type of industrialization. Such a country can develop exports from a *balancing* into a *dynamic* sector (e.g. England in the 19th century, the Federal Republic of Germany, the USA, etc.).

(c) For the time being, most developing countries are *import-sensitive,* which means that, under normal conditions, imports grow more rapidly than the national income. If such a country makes the decision to decrease imports one-sidedly, then the growth rate of the national income will slow down. (In the mid-1960s, several developing countries were compelled to pursue such an import-restricting policy.)

In such countries, a vigorous increase in imports is the precondition for the rapid growth rate of the national income. It is of course a different question whether exports can keep pace with the unavoidable increase in imports.

6. ECONOMIC GROWTH AND FOREIGN CREDITS

The accelerated economic growth of the developing countries requires credits and aids.

Here we do not wish to deal with the political background to these credits, and only want to mention that the co-operation of the developing countries, the assistance of the socialist countries and the activity of international organizations may create general conditions under which capitalist credits can be drawn upon without any major political risks.

As far as *assistance* is concerned, mention must be made, however, of the fact that there are various bottlenecks in the developing countries:

(a) limited possibilities of accumulation, i.e. *capital shortage;*

(b) shortage of qualified manpower, i.e. *lack of know-how and managerial skill* needed effectively to direct and operate economic life;

(c) backwardness of the economic environment (roads, waterways, vehicles, transport, storage), i.e. the low level of *services;*

(d) serious contradiction between the possibility of increasing exports and the necessity of growing imports, which leads to a disequilibrium of the balance of trade and the balance of payments, i.e. *to a foreign exchange gap.*

These factors are of an *interdependent* character, which means that an increase in but one of them – with all other factors being unchanged, or with a growth rate required by another factor lagging behind – does not lead to the accelerating of development.

From this follows that a favourable loan or grant is always of a *complex character.* We must consider problems that necessarily arise in other fields of the national economy when credits are taken advantage of.

II. SOME QUESTIONS OF PLANNING AND PLAN IMPLEMENTATION

1. PLANNING IN A MULTI-SECTORAL ECONOMY

A *series of economic decisions* assuming the form of a plan and directing the economic processes of a given period are always of, or can be developed into, *a comprehensive social* character. Thus, according to its *viewpoint*, planning encompasses society as a whole, which means that in choosing from among the different variants it always tries to find the optimum in a social (national) sense.

Planning encompasses society as a whole also in the sense that it is the *product of a social compromise*, in that in forming an optimum solution it also considers *the different*, and in certain cases even *conflicting*, interests of the various social groups, economic sectors, orgnaizations and persons.

Therefore, it would be illusory to assume that implementation is merely a technical problem, whose success or failure is exclusively dependent on the *level* of the organs involved in implementation. If deviating or conflicting interests assert themselves in the sphere of decision-making, then they will not only stay, but will also usually get sharpened in the sphere of implementation. It is not primarily decision-making but *implementation* that promotes or endangers the interests of the different social classes (groups), economic sectors, organizations and individuals.

Therefore, the problems relating to the implementation of plans – such as the analysis and mapping of the expected behaviour of the different sectors, the elaboration of the means and methods by which the behaviour of the organizations concerned can be channelled into the desired direction – constitute one of the most important domains of economics.

It must also be taken into account that the power relations reflected by a decision compromise – and this is especially important in societies in which radical structural changes take place – may change until the beginning of, or during, the implementation period, and this will decisively influence the attitudes of the participating groups, institutions, sectors and individuals.

In this respect, a developing economy must be regarded as a *multi-sectoral* economy, in which the interests of the sectors taking part in implementation are different and often even conflicting, and the interests of individuals do not necessarily coincide with those of the various sectors or organizations either.

The government as the guiding organ of economic development has at its disposal means by which it can influence the behaviour of the various sectors, organizations and individuals. But in relation to the tasks of guiding the economy as a whole, the quality of these means is very limited, and in the case of certain sectors entirely insufficient.

But in a multi-sectoral economy both the organizations and individuals are equally used to co-operation in carrying out such actions which promote rather than impede the assertion of their interests.

Consequently, in the behaviour of every sector, organization or individual there is a *critical point* (a threshold value) above, around and below which its behaviour is friendly, neutral or hostile, respectively.

But the location of this critical point is determined not by the benefits that may be enjoyed, or the losses that may be incurred in implementing a single planning measure, as the sectors, institutions or individuals concerned usually evaluate the totality of concrete government policies or assumed intentions affecting them.

Especially important is to take into account the expected activities of the various sectors if within the same industry (or trade) there are organizations embodying very different interests and basic economic units that can be influenced by very different methods.

In the industry, e.g., we usually find state enterprises, representatives of domestic private capital, foreign private capital and handicraftsmen alike. The situation is even more complicated in agriculture because of the simultaneous existence in many countries of large estates, co-operatives, family farms, and subsistence economy.

If a land reform is carried out, attention must be paid that the resources preserved in pre-capitalist forms are utilized in industry. A capital-short economy cannot do without this kind of capital.

Thus, in the course of implementation the following factors must be duly considered:

(a) the relationships between the individual processes of the multi-sectoral economy before making any economic decision;

(b) the motives and characteristics influencing the norms of behaviour of the various sectors;

(c) the clashes and conflicting interests which exist between the sectors operating in the various economic sectors;

(d) the *threshold values,* which change the behaviour of the various sectors from a friendly into a hostile attitude;

(e) the quantity, quality and relative shortage of the direct and indirect means available to influence these sectors;

(f) the level and adaptation capability of the state (public) organizations taking part in the implementation and the interests of the given apparatus as a collective, as well as the individual interests of its members;

(g) the special interests of the local governments relating to plan allocations, and to the decisions to be implemented in their own sphere or elsewhere.

Thus, the problems of implementation have to be worked out in no less detail and with no less thoroughness than the plan itself or the whole growth strategy (continuously in the form of a 20–25-year plan).

173

2. THE QUESTIONS OF PLAN IMPLEMENTATION

The significance of growth strategy lies in the fact that it determines for a long period of time the allocation of the available resources and the reasonable use of the endowments which ensures that the general aims arising out of the nature of the social system can be achieved in a *special way* (i.e. by concentrating the specific resources of the country concerned). In this way, growth strategy is intended to reconcile the movements of the economic and non-economic factors, on the one hand, and, on the other, to create, in view of the interpenetration of the economy and the interdepedence of the various factors, a harmony, and to bring sense into the social activity (work) done in the interest of achieving these aims.

The problems of plan implementation are especially intricate in the developing countries mainly for the following reasons:

1. No doubt, there are relatively by far fewer *resources* available in the developing countries for the realization of the plan objectives than in other economies. Therefore, in influencing the activity of the various sectors, orgnaizations and individuals fewer *material incentives* can, and more constraints or *inhibitions* must be applied. *Constraint* means the prohibition of an undesirable action or the prescription of a desirable action, while *inhibition* means the infliction with a disadvantage of an undesirable action.

2. In working out the growth strategy (economic policy), foreign advisers, too, might be included, as in the advanced countries there is a great deal of experience available regarding economic policy and planning. But the problems of economic policy in the developing countries are substantially different from the one-time problems of the present-day developed countries. Therefore, the planning methods evolved in the latter cannot be applied *without any adaptation* in the former.

3. In the developing countries, the realization of the conception of economic policy usually depends

(a) on such state apparatus and economic organizations which have but little experience, and

(b) for the implementation of plans such masses must be mobilized which have not yet acquired, or even flatly refuse, modern economic thinking.

4. In the economies of the developing countries there are far more *unpredictable factors* than in the developed ones, the solution of which requires a very efficient executive branch. For instance, the formation of world market prices and demand means for them an independent variable. Consequently, any decrease in prices, the reduction in the output of their export crops, the appearance of replacing and substituting materials, etc., constitute almost unsurmountable difficulties for them.

5. When formulating the growth strategy, it is impossible to foresee the quantity of *expected loans and grants,* etc. What the governments can at best do is to assess, under clarified circumstances and in a consistent way, the questions relating to the operation of foreign capital. But they are unable to influence the

position of the capital market, the general policies of the monopolies and credit institutions, which depend primarily on the position and business trends of the leading capitalist countries.

6. In the course of implementation, extremely wide gaps must be bridged between the sectors working in the various branches. It must not be ignored either that an influence can be exercised on foreign capital, domestic private capital, handicraft industries and state enterprises in both industry and commerce by economic measures of a different kind. Even greater differences must be surmounted in agriculture where, along with up-to-date state plantations, co-operatives, family farms as well as subsistence economies are to be found. From this point of view, the sectoral relations of the developing countries present extreme features compared with other countries.

From all this follows that the incentives and other influencing factors to be applied must be chosen in a very differentiated way.

Connected with the intricate problems of implementation is the *danger of voluntarism*. This is because the government and the leading strata are imbued by the desire to accelerate development. The intensity of their desire is extremely great, which is quite natural. They are animated by national enthusiasm, the demonstration of their capability of leadership, the eagerness – suppressed for a long time – to act, the ardent zeal of the masses and international circumstances alike. At the same time, they have but little experience in leadership, and have not yet met with the unexpected effects of their own actions. We also know that the enthusiasm of the masses does not last for good unless they experience improved conditions in their own lives. Thus, a peculiar coincidence of several factors urges them forcibly to attain rapid successes and spectacular results.

The time factor plays an important role in implementation as time is a factor modifying and influencing essential elements in every stage of the process.

The success of implementation is never independent of time, since a substantial departure from the dates set for achieving the plan targets (production, national income, consumption, etc.) is basically a deviation from the aims themselves. Departure from the envisaged time limits may be an error in implementation but also in decision-making.

In the developing countries, where society and economy undergo a rapid transformation process, government decisions introducing a *"new stage of development"* are very common.

A substantial part of economic decisions actually fit into the framework of the given development concept and serve fully to unfold it. Into this category may also be classified the decisions which do not yet aim at bringing about a new socio-political re-organization of power, and which rather mark *shifts in priorities* within the existing development concept. A case in point is partial re-organization of the available material resources, when in the course of industrialization in a country and of the realization of its conception it proves necessary, owing to the changed directions of technological development, to place on a given industry a greater emphasis than before, and to develop it at an accelerated rate.

The introduction of a new development stage is necessary when the growth strategy (long-term conception) or the medium-term (tactical) objectives cannot be reached by *the old methods;* in other words, if a basic re-organization of the material and intellectual energies or a change in the incentive methods are necessary.

As a consequence, the new development phase will result in a new deployment of the socio-political forces and will modify the *traditional structure of income distribution* or *power relations* among social classes and groups.

For example, since the role and activity of private capital lead to negative effects in certain industries, a decision must be taken to nationalize (let us suppose: on the basis of compensation) the given industries, or to form joint ventures with a 51 per cent participation of the state. Or, if the growth rate of agriculture lags behind the needs of industry and the population to a considerable degree, then, in the interest of achieving the medium- and long-term objectives, investments must be re-allocated, and the income distribution between town and village must be modified, etc.

3. THE PLACE OF PLANNING AND CO-ORDINATION IN THE STATE APPARATUS

What is needed in developing countries is not an *indicative* but a *directive* planning organ closely connected with implementation, which is equally responsible

(a) for the content of *economic policy* incorporated in the plans;

(b) for the application and development of the planning *methods;*

(c) for the *implementation* of plans.

It follows from the principle of this triple responsibility that the central planning organ *is not a scientific institution* but a centre of economic policy, which continually makes suggestions and/or takes economic decisions. Therefore, the central planning body is part of the supreme executive power, i.e. the government.

In a developing countries, the *planning organ*

(a) cannot be a mammoth office, as the number of available specialists is limited;

(b) must choose its staff members – as far as possible – not primarily from among state officials (jurists), but from economists, engineers, agronomists, educationalists, and medical doctors;

(c) must have available, as far as possible, staff members who are *versatile*, because, on the one hand, a small apparatus cannot be specialized in the same way as a large one, and, on the other, it is only many-sided people who are able to think in terms of processes and interconnections, which is of course of crucial importance;

(d) must be given international assistance both in the form of obtaining highly qualified advisers and experienced foreign specialists, and of training specialists of their own.

In providing advice, a flexible system must be ensured. Leading economists are unlikely to be able to spend years in the developing countries but sojourn of a few months each year might prove feasible.

Co-ordination has a great role and significance within the new state apparatus. Its aim is

(a) to eliminate certain differences in the actions of the various state organs;

(b) to reconcile the actions taken by the various state organs to achieve concrete common objectives;

(c) to ensure the joint elaboration of certain common tasks. (The latter activity is no co-ordination proper but rather collaboration.)

It is a very common deficiency of present-day co-ordination activities in many countries of the world that they are too *normative* (i.e. tend to delineate the spheres of authority) and too *static*. Obviously, this is not satisfactory, as in the course of co-ordination it is not the problems of the present but those of the future that should be taken into consideration.

The basic questions to be answered are these:

(a) what will be the relative position of the various branches in the period of co-ordination (e.g. within a medium-term period);

(b) what will be the most important interrelations and interdependences which determine the relationship of the two fields of interest during the co-ordination period (i.e. during the time of plan implementation);

(c) what must be done to ensure that growth and development achieved in one field promote the growth in another.

Like economic decisions and implementation, co-ordination is always a *compromise*. The parties involved in co-ordination endeavour to maintain *at least* the same power relations that existed in the phase of decision-making, but they usually make efforts to extend the rights and influence of the organs represented by them.

Though as a result of the official hierarchy and state discipline the various organs accept the decisions taken by higher organs, they do everything in their power to transform the process of implementation according to their own ideas.

However imperfect co-ordination may be in a centrally controlled economy, a co-ordinated action is still better than a non-co-ordinated one.

III. THE ROLE OF SOCIAL INSTITUTIONS IN ECONOMIC GROWTH

The traditional political and social power factors in the developing countries exert, in a passive sense, an immense influence. The essence of this influence consists in a *tenacious insistence* on inherited social institutions, customs and norms, and in an instinctive *resistance* against their violation or annihilation. It follows from this fact that the traditional political and social forces are *unable to accelerate economic growth*. Economic growth can only be triggered off by forces that are *considerably more progressive* than the traditional political groupings and *understand, or partly understand, the requirements of the time and of national development*. The understanding of modern requirements finds expression in the socio-political conception of these power factors, their organizational principles and the norms of their more purposeful actions encompassing and then also permeating the old society. *The national-social dynamics, the initiation* and direction of growth can be represented by various institutions, of which the *political parties* and the *armed forces* have played the most important role in the developing countries over the past decade.

The creation of the socio-political and institutional conditions necessary to initiate economic growth usually begins in many developing countries with a take-over by the *political party* (movement) closely knit in the struggle for independence, or by the *armed forces* (led by radical officers). The fact of a political take-over manifests itself in a number of ways and forms; thus, among other things, in that the new possessors of power proclaim new dynamic objectives – which, by the way, are identical with the conception of the leading political party or of the radical officers –, reshuffle the inherited state apparatus and put new leaders at the head of the country (usually those political or military personalities who in the struggle for independence or for seizing power distinguished themselves, or who succeeded in these struggles in welding a ruling group or even in taking the lead in that group).

It is in this tangible form that the transformation of the socio-economic system begins, and the institutions promoting and fostering economic growth are formed.

1. THE ROLE OF THE STATE IN ACCELERATING ECONOMIC GROWTH

The state has a decisive role to play in the transformation of the socio-economic system and the acceleration of economic growth.

However, the state organization alone is not able to generate those driving energies which ensure the attainment of the aims (ideas) of economic growth and the harmony between these aims, and the everyday, voluntary activity of the masses (without any constraint by the state). Capable of generating these energies are only *dynamic institutions* (political parties, the armed forces under the leadership of progressive officers, etc.).

While analysing the questions of economic growth it is not our intention to tackle problems relating to the philosophy of state administration.

It cannot be denied, however, that the state is the product of class conflicts, and any state represents the interests of a particular ruling class. But this statement must not be interpreted or exaggerated in a biased way. In the course of development the ruling class, either voluntarily or under the influence of power relations, enters into alliances, or the state, especially the state apparatus, gets alienated in a certain sense, that is, it develops also its own interests and own viewpoints. There are, on the one hand, conflicts within the ruling class itself, which also make themselves felt in the regular routine activities of the state, and, on the other, the state is bound, in one form or another, to concern itself with the interests of the other classes, too, as their members are also in the possession of a certain body of knowledge, organization and capabilities.

It may occur, especially in times of strained political situation (e. g. during the period following the seizure of power or in the case of open confrontation of class interests) that the state takes into account only the interests of the ruling class. In the ordinary course of events, however, these matters cannot be settled in such a way, since

(a) the ruling class alone is unable to keep and exercise power and strives, either voluntarily or under the influence of the prevailing power relations, to enter into alliance with the class pursuing similar aims;

(b) conflicts of interest may arise within the ruling class, which affect the activity of the state apparatus;

(c) in order to promote internal consolidation, to speed up economic growth and to make culture flourish, the state must encourage every loyal citizen and organization to join in the great work of national construction.

In this sense, the state also plays a mediating role partly in eliminating the conflicts within the ruling class, partly in creating a relative harmony between the ruling class and the other classes and strata.

What is involved, however, in the case of the developing countries is not simply the fact that the ruling class divides the power with others but also that the pulitical power can only be conquered and maintained if a widely-based class alliance is achieved. Within this class alliance, however, there is often no dominant class. (This statement is of course true only of such countries in which the class relations have not yet, or have hardly evolved.)

Consequently, the mediating role of the state is substantially stronger in the developing countries than in other types of state or economic development.

Finally, the role of the state is also enhanced by the fact that since its coming into being it has been concerned with more and more complicated problems than states with centuries-old traditions. And they have to solve these tasks with relatively little collective experience behind them and suffering from a serious shortage of qualified specialists.

The new state has to evolve, put into practice and establish the norms of social behaviour required by the new relations and objectives. The successful execution of this task is of crucial importance for the stabilization of the new system. The new power relations and the new social aims radically transform the old social value system (moral categories) and the related norms of behaviour, too. Certain elements of the old social value system are in conflict with the new ones and must therefore definitely be discarded. Other elements, however, are of a more neutral nature and do not hamper the state and government in creating the atmosphere needed by economic growth.

It must be taken into account that the spread of the new value system and norms of behaviour depends on the progress of the prevailing socio-economic conditions. On the other hand, it is not reasonable to obliterate the neutral values and norms from people's minds as long as the new ones have not been established. Otherwise, there will be breaks in the development of social moral with the old norms having ceased and without the new ones being accepted. But moral breaks are of a destructive effect as they give rise to cynicism, indifference and relativism. If these phenomena assume serious proportions, they cannot be stopped even after the emergence of the new value system, which means that part of the population will refuse to accept the new norms, too. In such a situation, however, lawful violence (a series of deterrent measures) must be applied in the interest of establishing the new moral, which is a highly undesirable state of affairs.

In establishing the new norms, the state may enjoy the effective support of the dynamic institutions: political parties and mass organizations. Their power lies in their possibility of spreading their tenets and principles by methods of convincing. The case is more difficult if the army is the only legal dynamic institution, because its means are – by the very nature of things – more rigorous than those of the state. In this case, the army must build up certain political institutions around its own organization.

From the very outset, the new state (government) must carry out a wide-ranging economic activity in the multi-sectoral economy. The economic role of the governments in the developing countries may be extremely comprehensive:

(a) the state performs and initiatory role in economic growth by specifying the social aims of development, by making available most of the resources of growth and creating an economic environment conducive to growth;

180

(b) the state co-ordinates the activities of the multi-sectoral economy with a content and in a form corresponding to the social aims of economic growth;

(c) the state establishes enterprises, plants, state farms, i.e., it is also an entrepreneur (the owner of part of the means of production).

2. THE ROLE OF POLITICAL INSTITUTIONS AND PARTIES

The state (government) does not perform these functions alone but in collaboration with the dynamic political institutions.

Let us briefly survey the points at which the *dynamic political institutions* and the functions and practical activities of the *state* coincide or clash in the course of economic management.

The leading political party unites its *membership* and forms its *leading organs* in the spirit of a uniform political action and organizational conception.

At the same time, the outstanding representatives of the leading political party have their seats in Parliament or in the people's consultative body, which is the depository of national sovereignty and the people's will, and exercises legislative power.

Finally, the most prominent leaders of the party are also members of the *government* and direct its activity.

In the case of a military regime the leading military forms a special organization called Revolutionary Council, National Council, Strategic Council, etc., which also controls the government.

Thus, the political party embodying up-to-date development objectives and organizational forms has two great advantages over military leadership as far as the building up of the new society and economy is concerned:

(a) it has a membership recruited on the basis of voluntariness and conviction, and professing a uniform action programme concerning the crucial questions of national-economic development;

(b) it is able to convince the overwhelming majority of the nation (society) of the necessity of an action constituting part of the uniform programme though

– part of the individuals and organizations participating in that action have not yet realized its indispensability or advantageous character;

– the economic (positional) advantage deriving from that action will only materialize at a later date; that is, the energies invested in the action constitute a temporary sacrifice.

We should like, however, to point emphatically to the fact that the political parties enjoy these advantages only if they manage to win and keep in their day-to-day practice the confidence of a great majority of the nation. If a political party becomes bureaucratic, i.e. gives orders and commands instead of convincing people, then it makes itself superfluous since a state apparatus is better suited to give orders, and the armed forces are better qualified to give commands than a party. Nor can a political party fultil its functions properly if it loses the confidence of the masses, since the capability of winning over people is not a matter of magic, nor an oratory stunt, but the result of a systematic activity performed day after day.

Therefore, owing to neglect, mistakes or moral inefficiency, the political parties may lose the advantages which they have gained over the armed forces.

This does not mean, however, that, without any political organizations the army together with the state apparatus were able to govern. Conviction and voluntary sacrifices will be needed in the developing countries for many more decades to come. The army can seize power alone but is unable to solve the tasks of economic growth all by itself. In public administration the government will need the support of the intellectuals (not only of those in the state apparatus), while to cope with the economic problems it has to rely on the economic organizations and common working people alike. Therefore, in administration and in the process of national construction, it will have to apply the methods of conviction so that the individuals should act of their own will, in accordance with the common aims.

Therefore, it is obvious that the armed forces, too, will need such political institutions which ensure, in a democratic form, contacts and relationships between the leadership and the broad masses of people.

It also stands to reason that the leading political parties (especially in the case of a one-party system) and the councils of the leading military officers (in the case of military rule) will seize a substantial part of the legislative power. This development will materialize in two different forms: first, the party decrees are binding for all party members and thus for the M. P.'s, too, and, second, the parties also take decisions on questions which are submitted directly to the government.

The individual responsibility of the representatives will increasingly diminish as the voters generally cast their votes not on individuals but on political programmes. (In this respect Latin America is an exception because the so-called *personalismo* is still very strong in the countries of that continent.)

There is no doubt, however, that the activities of the political parties or Military Councils will not end with seizing a considerable portion of the legislative power since these dynamic institutions will substantially influence the executive power, too.

Also this influencing activity has several established forms.

The leading bodies of the parties and/or the Military Councils also take decisions on questions concerning the functions of the government (the activity of the executive power). These decisions are binding for those members and leaders of the government, the executive apparatus, and the local governments who are at the same time members of the party or the Revolutionary Council.

The extension of the activities of the political parties and Revolutionary Councils to the domain of the executive power – a result of processes of many decades that took place outside the developing countries – is connected with the recognition that the legislative power has lost some of its significance while that of the executive power has increased. Consequently, the control of the state, social and political life can no longer be affected exclusively (primarily) through the legislative power. We should like, however, to emphasize that the loss of the significance of the legislative power, which largely materialized at the expense of political democracy, is not necessarily a final one and is not desirable either in several respects.

There is reason to hope that in the course of the future development of humanity a sounder equilibrium, better corresponding to the principles of people's sovereignty, will come into existence between legislation, i.e. active democracy, and executive power.

In the case of a one-party system or the emergence of Military Councils the question is always raised where the activity of the party ends and where that of the state apparatus begins. No doubt, it would be a mistake if the political parties or Military Councils wished to perform or make formal the activity of the state apparatus. But equally erroneous would be the conception, according to which the political parties or Military Councils should direct governmental activity exclusively from inside (from government positions) and should perform no activity relating to the direction of the state apparatus.

When searching for points of contact and appropriate forms of linkages between the work of parties, Military Councils and the state apparatus, a start must be made from the deviating nature and possibilities of the different institutions.

Under favourable circumstances, there should be creative, dynamic and enterprising minds in the political parties and Military Councils who are able to think in terms of progress and change. However, the state apparatus (bureaucracy) tends, by its very nature, to set up norms of action for society and itself, and endeavours to perpetuate them. As a rule, its point of departure is that the norms introduced by it, especially the last one, is the best conceivable and does not need any changes. Anyway, a change in the norms established by bureaucracy would diminish its prestige, and what would happen to the world if the citizens did not respect the authorities. Even the lowest-ranked official is convinced that he is the most competent expert of his job though his chief is still better informed and has a wider horizon. If the apparatus is convinced that the norms established by it are perfect, it will of course meet with unconcealed suspicion outside attempts to change them.

The political (military) leaders, however, despite their possible weaknesses and errors, think in terms of masses, changes and possibilities, and do not regard therefore the new norms either as ends in themselves. Since bureaucracy does not think in terms of masses and human relations, it is liable to get alienated from the world which gave rise to it, and which it strives to shape and control.

The negative features of bureaucracy stem not from the deficiencies or incompetence of individuals but from its role, position and the laws of its activity. This means, in other words, that the creative and dynamic ideas, initiatives are bound to come from outside.

On the other hand, it is equally obvious that political parties or Military Councils, if they are effectively to control the activities of the executive power, must build up an apparatus. Otherwise, they must only be concerned with basic principles and interconnections, that is, must behave as legislative power. In this case, to convert the basic principles into norms of action and to realize them (or to have them realized) will be the exclusive task of the executive power.

It must not be ignored, however, that an oversized party apparatus is endowed with the same qualities as an oversized state apparatus: it tends to establish and preserve stable norms. In this case, a contradiction develops between the way of thinking and the aim of the real leaders (creative minds) of the party and the established practice of the party apparatus. This contradiction may have the consequence that the realization of the correct ideas of creative minds incorporating the substance of political parties will be obstructed by the party apparatus.

From this it appears logical to draw the conclusion that it is not expedient to build up such a big apparatus which can prevent the party (Military Council) from performing its basic creative functions.

This analysis of the state and party apparatus was designed to make clearer the relationship between these two institutions during the process of economic growth. The merits and possibilities just as the deficiencies and weaknesses of both of them have a common origin. If good co-operation is ensured, the party performs its basic function: it remains a creative and initiatory body while the state apparatus brings about, in formulating and implementing concrete plans, the uniformity of actions between the various organizations, groups and interests. But the state must not act for others as no benefit can be drawn from such practice. This holds true not only of the economic organizations and individuals embodying the public sector but of the state enterprises, too, which must act, in accordance with the prevailing conditions, with a maximum degree of independence and responsibility.

It follows from the relationship between the activities of the party (Military Council) and the state apparatus that the struggle for power within the party also extends to the state apparatus. Moreover, it follows from the nature of the matter that it is easier to agree on fundamental principles and general ideas, however differently they may be interpreted, than on concrete action programmes. This is because the real clash of interests finds expression in concrete action programmes and the methods of their implementation. Consequently, conflicts within the party reach their climax in governmental implementation.

It is also clear that conflicts within the party (unity organization) are unavoidable since these political organizations comprise not only the representatives of the various classes and their deviating interests but also the representatives of the traditional and modern social organizations and formations. This unity – which was mostly conceived in the period of anti-colonial struggle – is also the precondition for the acceleration of social and economic development. It must be taken into account that

(a) the danger of neo-colonialism is still great, and internal dissension (disruption of unity, dissatisfaction of shelved political leaders and similar factors) provide favourable conditions for imperialist intervention;

(b) in building up the new state and economy, everybody must be united in action, from members of rural tribal communities to the workers of up-to-date large-scale enterprises, from rural handicraftsmen to university professors. The range of people taking part in action extends from the man in the street to the most highly educated person. If the unity is broken up, these very different (often opposed) elements fall apart, often leading to social anarchy.

It is conceivable of course that individuals or smaller groups break away from time to time from this unity, but this must never assume extreme proportions. It would be disastrous if the slow and gradual breaking away of the various groups were due not to changes in the objective conditions but to consequences of personal rivalry among politicians. By no means should political leaders strive to suppress different views by administrative-bureaucratic methods. Conflicts within the party (unity organization) are objectively necessary, and real interests cannot be reconciled with the prevention of the possibility of manifesting dissident views. The strength of leadership consists not in preventing the free expression of real differences in interests and views but in merging conflicting interests and views into a unity of action at a national-social level by means of compromises. The coexistence of conflicting interests and views within the unity organization does not weaken but rather strengthens the position of leadership. In the struggles for power fought within the party (Military Councils) the various government posts often figure as substantial objectives.

Owing to the struggle for power, especially in the case of balanced power relations, the cause of certain economic and social reforms may be staved off for a considerable time. The struggle for political-governmental positions is carried on in a more open form (usually at the ideological level) within the political parties, and in a more concealed form in the state apparatus, where the questions at issue take a professional-institutional nature. If these struggles hinder decisions to be made on important material questions, the leadership should quickly intervene and come to a decision.

It is typical of political struggles that they are carried on in a different "time system" and on the basis of other aspirations than required by the nature of economic processes and interrelationships. If in a country the struggle is fought between two political conceptions (e. g. between a progressive party in power and a reactionary opposition, or conversely), then it is justified to wait for a change in power relations, which makes it possible to take action in compliance with our ideas. But struggles for positions within the regime itself should be assessed differently since in that case the masses will put the blame for delaying the necessary reforms or measures on the regime as a whole. And this is not unfair or unjust as it follows from the very nature of a regime that there are struggles for power in it, too. The viability of a regime presupposes, among other things, that it is capable of action even in the case of such struggles. Account must also be taken of course of the fact that a deferred economic action – especially in a centrally controlled economy – will not be solved of itself, and will crop up again later, under more unfavourable conditions.

In general, one of the great advantages of a centrally controlled economy is that it can ensure a more expedient and planned allocation of scarce development energies (resources). However, these advantages can be made use of only if the economic issues are settled as quickly as required by the nature of the economy. In other words: the time needed for economic decisions (transit time) must not be adjusted to the order established in the practice of the party or state organs.

The participants of the struggle within the regime must consider that securing a somewhat better personal or group position is not worth the loss of professional or political authority that the regime as a whole will have to sustain in the public eye.

Therefore, the leadership must interfere in time in important questions which, owing to struggles for power, have been or are likely to be deferred.

It also often occurs that what is involved in deferring essential political decisions is not real position struggles but the assumed prestige of certain politicians. It is in such cases that specialists who would like to promote certain concrete causes get deeply disappointed in politics and politicians.

This remark does not mean of course that we generally prefer specialists to politicians. We do not question the top priority of political and power problems but make a distinction between the crucial problems of a given socio-political system and the prestige questions of individual politicians. In addition, we wish to emphasize again that the central power commits a serious mistake against the community and itself if, in conducting economic affairs, it ignores the methods and time limits that the economic processes require.

In the foregoing we have analysed primarily the social institutions embodying political power as well as the changes and structural shifts in them in relation to one another in the phase of rapid socio-economic transformation. But the functions of power are outward-oriented and can, from the point of view of economic growth, be identified as such, which makes it possible for the economic organizations and individuals to take actions which are in harmony with the economic conception (the plan).

3. THE MEANS AND LIMITATIONS OF THE CENTRAL POWER TO INFLUENCE ECONOMIC PROCESSES

The problem consists in the measure of availability of *resources and possibilities* necessary for the political power (government) to attain its aims.

First of all, we must emphasize that the actions of economic organizations and individuals can only be influenced within certain *limits*. We wish to summarize them in the following:

(a) the economic behaviour (reaction to government measures) favoured (stimulated) by the government must be in harmony with the *interests* of the acting organizations and individuals, or at least – apart from certain very strained situations arising from the introduction of social reforms as e.g. land reform, nationalizations, etc. – should not explicitly interfere with them;

(b) the quantity of economic resources available to the government is very *limited* (scarce resources), and they cannot be replaced in the long run, though their scarcity can be mitigated by political methods (conviction) and administrative measures;

(c) the given state apparatus – for lack of experience – is *unable* to carry out correctly extremely complex *influencing measures* containing a variety of alternatives and requiring delicate distinctions.

When considering the possibilities and limitations of the guiding activity of the government, account must be taken of the fact that the young state administration has to cope with a host of problems, among others things such as budget equilibrium, taxation and allowances, expenditures of infrastructure, balance of payments, investments, credit policy, etc. Therefore, the government performing the task of economic management should not attend to minute problems.

It should also be considered that the over-centralization of economic decisions will lead to the deterioration of the effectiveness of central economic management. The level of economic decisions will drop for lack of time needed to prepare individual decisions adequately, as a result of which the recommendations will not contain a sufficient number of alternatives and cannot extend over the secondary, derivative and complementary consequences of economic action. Owing to the central organs being overburdened, the economic decisions will be deferred for a long time. Therefore, interference in certain processes will take place too late, and the available resources will prove insufficient. Finally, in the case of the over-centralization of decisions, a vast machinery of bureaucracy will be built up between the active economic organs and government (economic leadership), hindering a rational implementation required by the character of economic processes. Obviously, when the spheres of authority of the central organs are established, account must be taken of the levels at which individual matters can be settled in the most competent way. For example: in most developing countries there is already a Ministry of Health, but it would be inconceivable if ambulance cars needed the preliminary permission of the Ministry to take patients to the hospital.

We must also consider that the economies of developing countries are multi-sectoral, where all sorts of economic formations can be found ranging from subsistence economy to foreign-owned monopoly companies. But it is also evident that the majority of the sectors cannot be centrally directed by the state. All that it can do is a purposeful transformation of the economic environment.

Finally, state enterprises must also have a minimum degree of independence enabling the leadership to develop and exercise their creative capabilities. If, however, central management regularly encroaches upon their independence, they will lose their sense of responsibility, their creative and combining capabilities, resulting in a decline in the economic efficiency of the enterprises. In such cases enterprise managers will not act under the impact of market impulses, but will ask for central instructions.

Account must also be taken of the fact that, owing to the general shortage of *qualified manpower*, performing the tasks of public administration and economic management will constitute a bottleneck for a number of decades to come.

In specifying the system and methods (means) of economic management, the limiting factors listed above should therefore duly be considered. It logically follows from these restricting factors that economic management *should not be overcentralized*, on the one hand, and, on the other, its methods should be evolved *by taking into consideration the actual economic situation and processes.*

Economic management has not only its limitations but also its *requirements*. No doubt, below a lowest (minimum) level of these requirements there is no centrally controlled economy. As a minimum requirement (the lowest degree of management), two conditions must be met. The government must reserve the right of making decisions on such questions as

(a) can substantially influence the position and relationships of the political power and the nation and/or the various strata of the nation;

(b) can be summed up and solved for the benefit of the society as a whole only at governmental (national economic) level.

If these two requirements are not met, there is no centrally controlled economy, or it exists in name only.

These two basic requirements involve of course a number of partial requirements, which can be summarized as follows:

1. The government must create an economic environment conducive to economic growth. In other words: such socio-political reforms must be carried out which make people interested in economic growth and reconcile the internal value system of society with the requirements of development.

2. The government must adopt a determined attitude, clearly apprehensible to the economic organizations and individuals concerned, towards the various sectors, including foreign enterprises. This actually means for all developing countries that administrations must co-operate with a great many sectors to achieve economic growth. Progressive governments justly endeavour to ensure a more rapid growth of the state sector, but this should be attained not primarily by curbing the inner dynamics of the other sectors. It stands to reason that the development of the modern sectors will bring about a change in the present distribution of manpower.

3. The government must promote the exploitation of natural resources and ensure the research and economic capacities needed for the geological survey of the country. (A possible form is the technical assistance received from the advanced countries.)

4. The government must create the general conditions needed to raise rapidly agricultural output, such as the construction of irrigation works, the provision of credit facilities, the improvement of infrastructure including education, etc.

5. In order to increase accumulation, expand the domestic market and

administer social justice, the government should ensure an equitable distribution and redistribution of incomes.

6. In the spirit of an expansive financial policy, the state must control the circulation of currencies and curb inflationary tendencies. We include of course the modernization of the taxation system in the concept of an expansive financial policy.

7. The government must pay special attention to economic measures affecting the living standards of the population. With the help of the available statistical institution it must organize a regular and representative observation of the living standards of the various social strata and/or regions, since changes in the living standards are due not only to direct measures but also to various economic processes (inflation of the national currency, shortages in the market of consumer goods, etc.).

8. It is also the duty of the government to harmonize education with the requirements of economic growth. It must see to it that the individual sectors of the economy are supplied with qualified cadres. In addition, it must have analysed the trends in manpower situation so that manpower mobility between regions and sectors can be appraised and controlled.

9. The government must conclude inter-state economic, trade and credit agreements, investigate their effects on the economy of the country and ensure that their conditions are in compliance with the international norms established in this field. To secure the equilibrium of the balance of payments, the state must control the volume and pattern of imports.

10. The government must establish the purchasing prices of agricultural export products in such a way that the producers are able to expand their production in accordance with the demands of the domestic and foreign markets.

The guarantees for fulfilling the partial requirements deriving from the above-mentioned two basic needs lie in the uniform economic conception (national economic plans). When preparing this conception, there is a possibility to consider those requirements or their relationship with one another as parts of economic growth.

Obviously, in the implementation period of a uniform economic-political conception (plan period) many unpredictable events may occur, often resulting in imbalances. Imports may need to be increased or exports to be decreased, the gestation period and return rates of investments may prove to be less favourable than expected, the country may be hit by natural disasters, and even unsuspected political shifts, changes and sudden turns may occur.

Therefore, it will become necessary to review and correct from time to time the objectives and means envisaged by the original economic conception. These corrections must be performed annually even if no spectacular changes have taken place in the economic and political life.

Considering, however, that the results of agricultural production decisively determine the economic processes of each year, it appears expedient to carry out this review and correction after the harvesting period.

4. THE PRECONDITIONS FOR EFFECTIVE ECONOMIC MANAGEMENT

The government cannot discharge its wide-ranging economic tasks unless
  (a) the political power is relatively *stable;*
  (b) the *unity* of the state power is sufficiently ensured;
  (c) the *best specialists* of the country are involved in the *preparation of decisions.*

The first precondition is of course the most difficult to fulfil. Is it possible to secure a stable political power under the prevailing conditions? An unstable government cannot be expected to think in terms of long- or medium-term economic conceptions, yet without this there is not, and cannot be, any economic growth.

One thing is certain: a stable and lasting political power can only exist if the leaders of the government think both in terms of long-term views and of the daily concerns of the people. The stability of power may dangerously be undermined by a too wide gap between the living conditions of the leading stratum and the general economic possibilities of the country.

The unity of the state power (government) is ensured by the elaboration of uniform conceptions and by the formulation of common norms of action designed to put them into practice. If this condition is not fulfilled, the various ministries and economic branches will follow their own conceptions. But the government is more than a total sum of ministries and economic branches. The task of the central government begins not at a time when the individual ministries and economic branches have already formulated their own ideas (subsequent co-ordination), but it is the uniform conception and action programme of the government that must specify the partial task of these organs. Governmental practice based on the realization of these facts is of crucial importance for achieving economic growth.

With few specialists available, these problems cannot be solved satisfactorily unless the government mobilizes all intellectual resources to prepare and implement the decisions. This is necessary because the state apparatus, for lack of sufficient experience, is unable to analyse and work out the problems in such a way that any decisions can be made on them with full responsibility. On the other hand, new methods of management are gaining ground all over the world, as science is already capable of elaborating action programmes, too. It is also common knowledge that in our age all political and economic decisions give rise to an intricate complexity of effects, counter-effects and resultants, and it is also known that without adequate scientific preparation it is impossible to foresee likely developments. Therefore, it is desirable to engage the best own and foreign scientists in the preparation of the most important economic decisions (including the elaboration of possible variants) and in working out action programmes relating to their implementation.

190

The leadership loses much of its positional advantage if it entrusts the elaboration of the economic-political conception or individual programmes exclusively to government officials. It is easy to understand that without adequate scientific preliminary work even the most brilliant leader is unable to take correct economic decisions. For the formulation of economic conceptions and the preparation of the most important economic decisions there is usually sufficient time available – especially under a circumspect leadership.

In politics the situation is rather different, partly because the speed of action is determined by international events, partly because the number of unpredictable factors is much larger. Even if the prevailing circumstances are considered most carefully, it may occur that an event in world politics substantially modifies internal political power relations. The prediction of these international events would require the knowledge of such a vast body of information, data, facts and interconnections as cannot be made available to the leader of small and medium-sized countries. Therefore, in assessing political questions and taking a position on them, instinct, sense of proportion and foresight, i.e. the intuitive elements of decision-making, also have a role to play.

Besides the government, *centralized economic organizations*, primarily *financial institutions*, also play an important part in organizing economic management. We start from the assumption that the bank of issue, one or two major banks and a few important productive enterprises are state-owned.

The question arises how the government should control the operation of state-owned *industrial enterprises*. In many countries, special ministries are set up for this purpose managing industrial enterprises by means of direct instructions. In this case, however, the direction of enterprises is separated from the principle of material responsibility, which may envolve dangerous consequences especially in countries with no considerable economic-industrial traditions, where, consequently, bureaucratic management may lead to inconsiderate instructions disregarding the requirements of profitability and economic efficiency. In addition, new organs of direction have to be organized needing the engagement of qualified specialists, a relatively scarce factor, which will lead to increased bureaucratism.

Therefore, it seems more appropriate to set up, for the direct management of industry, a *centralized economic organization* which has a comprehensive view of all processes of the national economy and controls the most important one of economic resources (money and/or credit) needed for effective management. This solution of economic management makes it of course necessary for the *bank* in question to have technical specialists available with sufficient experience in the technological aspects and requirements of industrial development.

This suggestion is supported by the well-known fact that of all economic organizations in the developing countries the highest level has been attained so far by the banking institutions. There is, therefore, every hope that this organization, which is concerned anyway with industry in respect to financing, credits, interest rates, etc., will be able to attend to its direction without any major

191

difficulties. The bank then becomes an organization concerned not only with providing the means needed to start the production of material goods (capital supply) but also with directing production. Specialized (industrial, agricultural, etc.) banks are especially suited to perform these functions.

5. THE POSITION OF REGIONAL POWER FACTORS IN ECONOMIC GROWTH

The question of individual *regions* constitutes, both politically and economically, a serious problem in any country where the population is heterogeneous in its language and ethnic origin and where there are extreme discrepancies between educational and living standards.

This is the case in most of the developing countries. In Brazil, for example, in the so-called industrial triangle formed by the cities Sao Paolo, Belo Horizonte and Rio de Janeiro, with about 20 per cent of the country's population living in it, per capita national income is about ten times higher than that in the north-eastern regions of the country.

Similar problems can be met with in India, Pakistan and many countries in Africa, where the economic and cultural conditions of the coastal regions are much better than those in the central inland provinces.

The *decentralization of power* in these countries is not merely an organizational problem determined by rational considerations but also a problem of relationship between different peoples, ethnic groups and tribes. Whether *centralization* or *decentralization* is the right path to embark upon in developing countries, where the internal cohesive forces are not strong enough, is a much debated question.

No doubt, a certain degree of *centralization* is needed in all newly independent countries, especially where the forces of cohesion are not sufficiently strong or are obsolete. But it also stands to reason that centralization must not be enforced *in a bureaucratic manner,* at the expense and against the will of individual regions and without its preconditions being secured. An especially careful approach is needed if a region with the best economic and material conditions tries to achieve centralization at the "expense" of the poorer regions. In such cases, the ethnic group (tribe) of the depressed areas will believe that its low living standards and underdevelopment are due to the intentions and measures taken centrally, i. e. by the other ethnic group (tribe). Under such circumstances the population of backward regions will start defending their political rights, language and economic positions against the central power represented by the other ethnic group (tribe).

This situation will result in *weakening rather than strengthening a uniform state.* Therefore, it appears to be more appropriate to grant the provinces (ethnic groups, tribes) a minimum degree of autonomy so that they may assume responsibility for their own economic development. Consequently, the strengthening of cohesive forces should be effected by a better organization of

192

economic and cultural co-operation between the various regions, i.e. by speeding up an internal integration of the economy and not by bureaucratic-administrative methods. As a result of the acceleration of internal integration, an increasing number of comprehensive, national institutions will come into being, such as transport and communications, higher education and, first of all, a national market. The danger of an enforced centralization lies essentially in its assuming conditions which have not yet come into being, as a consequence of which such a centralization cannot take root, and does not mitigate but rather intensifies the ancient mistrust among tribes, a product of past centuries. By internal integration, however, members of different tribes and regions will get to know each other much closer, and also undertake to co-operate in carrying out their common tasks. Nobody can foresee the future at the present time but the chances are that the various tribes will develop into nations, which, later on, will be united in a single state on a federative and voluntary basis. It is the task of the central government to promote this development.

No doubt, conflicts and clashes of a greater or lesser importance between ethnic groups (tribes) will be unavoidable in the future, too. But it is possible to mitigate their intensity and mould the factors giving rise to them.

But this process should not be enforced, in separation from actual conditions. The regional (tribal) system should not be excluded from the government as long as economic contacts with areas outside the tribal (regional) territories are at a minimum level, and the national market has not yet developed, and, what is perhaps most important, agriculture, or economic activity in general, are carried on within the framework of forms of ancient community relations. (By forms of ancient community we understand the inherited system of ownership relations, the organization of distribution and production.)

The *allocation of investments* is of course influenced not only by economic and political factors but also by natural endowments. The location of raw materials or the natural conditions of growing certain varieties of crops within the country obviously determine the regional distribution of investments.

From the point of view of economics it is more advantageous, within certain limits, to invest in the more developed regions because of the lower costs (relatively lesser inputs needed by infrastructure) and quicker returns. It is obvious that investments made in the coastal regions are cheaper than those in the inland provinces. But here we wish to emphasize again that in economics all statements must be qualified: in case certain regions are given exaggerated preferential treatment, others will fail to develop their internal markets and compel the labour force to migration, which leads to the isolation of certain regions from the process of national-economic development.

So far two patterns of development have been identified in the backward regions within individual countries.

In the developed capitalist countries (the United States, the United Kingdom, France, Italy), capital at the outset concentrated in the more developed areas, while the less developed regions (mostly those in the South) had to make do with a lower level of the economy. As a consequence, the migration of manpower began from the less developed to the developed region, which made it even more difficult for the backward areas to develop. At the same time, the events of the past decades, thus, among others, World War II (the building up of the war industry), increasing economic boom, growing labour shortage and appreciable improvement of the profitability of agriculture, have greatly stimulated the development of the underdeveloped (southern) areas in many countries.[2]

By contrast, the Soviet Union and Yugoslavia, for example, have consciously made, from the very beginning of the acceleration of their economic growth, every effort to transfer a substantial part of the intellectual and material resources available from the more developed to the less developed regions (by means of a central allocation of investments) and to speed up thereby their development. Naturally, investments allocated in this way are more expensive, with smaller returns and higher operation costs. As a result, national income will register a slower growth than could have been achieved with more profitable investments, and the export capacity of industry will also fail to keep pace with the increase in industrial production. (The consequences of this phenomenon can less be felt in the Soviet Union, whose foreign trade plays but a minor role in the economy, than in Yugoslavia, which is more sensitive to foreign trade.)

Thinking, however, in terms of longer spans of time, we must see that new economic processes will start in the backward regions, the norms of industrial society, though sporadically at first, will be established, and the market, owing to increasing purchasing power, will expand with the internal integration of the economy making progress. This, in turn, will make the system of relations between the peoples (nations) of different regions sounder and more productive.

It is obvious that the type of integration described here also brings about certain tensions as the population (nations) of the more developed areas will have to make short- or medium-term sacrifices in favour of the people of the less developed ones, which is of course not an easy thing to do. Therefore, it is of crucial importance that the overwhelming majority of the population should adopt the socio-political principles aimed at bridging the gap between man and man.

A country which pursues the policy of achieving a more equitable distribution of goods, incomes and knowledge cannot adopt the capitalist type (pattern) of internal integration. In the course of economic growth this would necessarily lead to a widening of the discrepancies and glaring differences inherited from colonialism, which would of course be impossible for the masses of depressed areas and progressive-minded people to accept.

The second type of integration is not easy to adopt. A "just" (i.e., politically oriented) allocation of investments is rather expensive. In other words: scarce

[2] During the past decade, in order to ease growing social and political tensions, the governments have displayed considerable activity to develop backward regions. Thus, this intervention has been of a subsequent and secondary nature designed to offset already existing imbalances caused by spontaneous power factors.

material and intellectual resources cannot be used with optimum efficiency if they are to be invested in such regions where implementation is more expensive, the returns of investments are slower and the operating costs of plants are higher.

Therefore, at first a certain combination of the two patterns will be necessary and possible if backward areas are to be integrated into an emerging unified national market.

It follows from the complexity of the task that in the course of economic growth a *fruitful co-operation* between the *central* and *local* organs will be needed. Co-operation can be facilitated by the fact that the dynamic political organization (political party) embraces the whole country in the spirit of uniform principles and of a uniform action programme.

To achieve this, tolerance, confidence, mutual understanding and respect are needed on both parts. In addition, it must be ensured by all means that the various regions should be free to use part of their resources and spend them according to their own conceptions. It is of paramount importance to the inhabitants of the various regions to live in accordance with their customs and traditions within the boundaries of the united state. Each ethnic group (tribe) should be encouraged to contribute its valuable traditions, part and parcel of the whole nation, to the new society and economy.

This is the only way to cause the various ethnic groups (tribes) voluntarily and gradually to adopt the whole conception of economic growth. This will make it possible, on the one hand, for economic growth to accelerate, and, on the other, for each ethnic group – and this is extremely important for the future – to enter the new world without resentment, mistrust and resistance.

IV. THE ROLE OF AGRICULTURE IN ECONOMIC GROWTH

Agriculture has a decisive part to play in the process of economic growth. It may be misleading that in relation to the developing countries we speak of the necessity of *industrialization*. But the economic views related to *industrialization* are often one-sided, owing to the fact that economists are considerably better acquainted with the problems of industry than of agriculture. We must not forget, first of all, that the bulk of the population of developing countries are engaged in agriculture (70 to 80 per cent, as against 12 to 25 per cent in the developed countries).[3]

In the case of certain countries (particularly in Asia) there is undoubtedly a relative *overpopulation*, which means that population growth is faster than food production per head of population. According to FAO data, *per capita agricultural output* in the Far East has not kept pace with population growth and, therefore, compared with consumption between the two world wars, a decline has set in. (In Europe, for example, in the 50 years before the First World War population grew by 0.7 per cent and food production by 2 per cent annually.)

The problem of *overpopulation* is closely connected with such questions as the size of per capita cultivated land, capital investments in agriculture and average yields. Per capita cultivated land is 0.4 hectare (1 acre) in Western Europe, 0.8 hectare in the USA and 0.3 hectare in India, where capital investment per unit of land is also considerably smaller.

In an overpopulated country less animals can be kept, and in crop rotation, if such exists at all, no land is allowed to lie fallow, and the peasant is compelled to exploit the land ruthlessly, which results in the gradual deterioration of soil fertility.

As a further consequences of overpopulation, a significant proportion of the rural population becomes redundant compared with present-day labour requirements. According to computations, 25 per cent of the agricultural population in India would be redundant if modern technological standards were applied.

---

[3] In the developing countries the share of people employed in agriculture in the total of manpower can be computed in two ways: on a *wider* and on a *narrower* basis. According to the former, account is taken exclusively of those directly employed in agriculture, while according to the latter, the personnel engaged in manufacturing agricultural machines, artificial fertilizers, antibiotics, etc., as well as the staff of service plants also come under the heading of agricultural labour force.

No overpopulated country is capable of satisfying domestic consumption and increasing exports at the same time. Therefore, countries of this type (e. g. India, Egypt, etc.) should rather endeavour to export industrial goods. This is all the more possible, as, owing to the low purchasing power, the domestic market does not absorb a large volume of industrial manufactures.

But the Latin American and the African countries (with the exception of Egypt) are not overpopulated. There are still large uncultivated lands available (though, according to Prebisch, it would not be worthwile to extend the area under cultivation in Latin America), but the plants and establishments servicing agriculture are rather expensive.

It should also be noted that the unfavourable development of agricultural production in the industrialization period is very dangerous and may slow down industrial growth as a whole. It necessitates the increase in agricultural imports, which may unfavourably affect the import of productive equipment, i. e. makes the whole growth cycle senseless.

As a result of industrialization, labour force will leave the rural areas, usually parting for good from the ancient community (though the ratio of migrant labour is still high in Africa), and thus will easily adopt the new norms and way of life, since even if acting under the pressure of difficult circumstances, the decision to leave the village is voluntary. But those remaining within the old community will follow its customs and will find it difficult to adopt the rational way of thinking conducive to increasing production.

Despite these difficulties *agriculture has a crucial role* to play in the growth process. In the following we wish to examine this role from three aspects:

1. From the point of view of the *economic problems* of agricultural production we shall investigate the additional demands induced by the economy in the growth process, devoting special attention to the export-import relations of agriculture. Then we shall analyse the role of agriculture in the accumulation process and the impact of taxes imposed on agricultural output on production. Discussing the question of ownership relations in agriculture, we shall be concerned with the question whether inherited community formations can fit into the conditions of modern agriculture, or completely new collective associations, co-operatives are needed. Finally, the problems and consequences of rural exodus will be dealt with.

2. Next, we shall discuss what path agriculture has to embark upon to *increase production*. From the *national-economic and technological* points of view, there are different variants in this field. Emphasis may be placed on the *extention* of the cultivated area or on the *increase in yields* per unit of land (extensive or intensive development). *Live labour* may be increased (kept on the same level or slowly decreasing), or preference may be given *to production per agricultural worker* (increase in productivity of labour). Then agricultural investments will be dealt with, especially from the point of view whether they are to be made before or only after a substantial outflow of manpower. Then some complicated problems

relating to the *natural conditions* of agricultural production (climatic conditions, soil qualities, water resources available) will be discussed.

3. Finally, we shall review the role of agriculture from the point of view of the relationship between agricultural production and human nutrition.

1. THE ECONOMIC PROBLEMS OF AGRICULTURAL PRODUCTION

Agricultural production in the developing countries has to perform four tasks concurrently in the growth process:

(a) It has to secure the *food supply* of the fast-growing population (by an annual rate of 2 to 3 per cent) – at least at the previous level.

(b) It must meet the *increasing consumption demand* resulting from the migration of the rural population to urban centres. Unlike the situation in the developed countries, the increment must be understood in *absolute* and not in relative terms (i. e., what is involved is not the *difference* between rural and urban consumption), as the rural community, of which the urban workers used to be a member, does not decrease its consumption. On the other hand, with the low calorie consumption as evolved in the pre-industrial phase, no regular industrial activity can be performed.

(c) It must ensure *the gradual improvement of the nutrition* of the population, especially of children.

(d) It must raise *export* production, because for offsetting rapidly increasing imports, exports must be stepped up, which is possible for the time being primarily (and in certain cases *exclusively*) by means of agricultural produce only.

From this it follows that in the developing countries the annual rate of increasing agricultural production must reach a minimum of 5 to 6 per cent, that is, a considerably higher rate than in the developed countries.

It should be noted that this high rate of increment, the necessity of which we have calculated on the basis of the *needs of the internal economy,* is corroborated by the forecasts published by the FAO on the world's food supply situation. According to trustworthy FAO computations and conclusions, food supply must be increased by 50 per cent by 1975 (as compared with 1953) and *threefold*(!) by 2000. Obviously, this increase must materialize primarily in the developing countries, since by 2000, compared with the years 1957–1959, the population index of the countries with low calorie consumption will be *250* as against *158* in the countries with high calorie consumption.

However, the fulfilment of this task, even if we disregard the specific and complex natural conditions of tropical agriculture, appears to be extremely hard. The main reasons are as follows:

(a) The lion's share of *accumulation* is secured, whether in a direct or indirect form, by agriculture. If it is true that job opportunities other than in agriculture must be created and this, in turn, also improves the production conditions of agriculture, then it is easy to realize that this burden is unavoidable.

198

Taxes imposed on land or exports and even on import products (with the exception of luxuries) afflict agriculture.

To round off the picture, it must also be noted that in countries where agriculture is better supplied with capital and need not develop at such a high rate, it is heavily subsidized, usually in the form of price support.

(b) A further difficulty lies in the fact that, as a result of industrialization, the labour supply of agriculture, if no other factors emerge, will obviously deteriorate, as it is exactly the young age groups of more productive and harder workers and a more enterprising spirit who abandoned agriculture.

(c) Account must also be taken of the fact that *the switching over of subsistence economy to commodity production* is an extremely difficult task requiring a rather long time and much investment. The old rural communities must be maintained, though in a somewhat modernized form, or else an anarchic disintegration will ensue which, owing to capital shortage, cannot immediately be replaced by other motive forces. On the other hand, the maintenance of these communities slows down the pace of transformation. And, further, it is not easy to find those methods and stimulations to which subsistence economy is responsive and which the economy as a whole can afford to bear. And, finally, in the case of the gradual transformation of subsistence economy into commodity production, *the whole agricultural infrastructure* (roads, transport, storage facilities, railway network, etc.) will prove inadequate, and subsequently a lot of additional and complementary investments need to be made.

Even this short survey will reveal that a number of contradictory requirements must be met in the development of agriculture.

It is not realistic to hope – even after purely economic considerations – that the developing countries could be able to solve these tasks exclusively from their own resources.

But apart from this general conclusion, the contradictory requirements must also be collated with the available resources and development possibilities (variants).

2. PROBLEMS OF INCREASING AGRICULTURAL PRODUCTION

As far as the growth of agricultural production is concerned, we must examine the interrelationship of the factors influencing growth.

In discussing the growth of agricultural output, we must consider the following factors:

(a) *land*, scarce or abundant in relation to the number of population, under given but not necessarily unchangeable ownership relations;

(b) *natural conditions of agricultural production*, thus primarily climatic conditions, soil qualities and available water resources (precipitation and others);

(c) *agricultural labour force* (organizers, skilled and unskilled manpower alike), which is usually available in abundance but at a low level of qualification;

(d) *economic and organizational units* in the sense of micro-economics, within which the producer or producers concentrate their efforts on achieving the production targets given or set;

(e) *fixed and working capital* invested or soon to be invested in agriculture by means of which production can directly be influenced;

(f) *economic environment of agriculture*, i.e. the assistance, impulses or economic constraints that agriculture receives or can receive from other sectors.

The aim of the analysis is such an arrangement of these factors which ensures the attainment or the approximation of the socio-economic aims of production.

(a) We examine the *land* factor, as has already been pointed out, in its relationship to the number of population.

A high population density, within certain limits, has its obvious advantages for industrial development. From the point of view of agriculture, however, a high population density is not advantageous, because either all land including the poorest soil should be brought under cultivation, or the available areas sown should be cultivated so intensively that yields cannot grow in proportion to inputs.

This is, however, not the worst of the possible cases, as in the overpopulated countries the cultivated area per head of population is smaller than in the developed countries (see India's example). Apart from the size of the area under cultivation, *ownership relations* also play a paramount role in the development of production.

In this respect it is especially the big land estates that have a negative effect upon production (Latin America and certain Asian countries). In several countries, land rents paid by the peasants have either been reduced or abolished. This brings of course some relief, especially if the decrees are observed, but not a final solution of the problem. Peasants do not invest in anybody else's land, and the landowner is usually not willing to make investments.

A more appropriate solution seems to be *land reform*, which, if a gradual way of its realization is chosen, should be prepared by progressive taxes imposed on landowners. In case the land reform is carried out gradually, commercialized big estates should be left last, since this is the only type of estate the division or nationalization of which causes *temporary* crop losses.

In any case, it is expedient to establish *co-operatives* (land-renting and similar co-operatives), which possess organizational capabilities and credit-raising possibilities, and are able to undertake joint ventures (water economy) and to co-operate both in supplying agriculture with the necessary means of production and in securing markets for it (in creating favourable marketing conditions).

Landed property in the ownership of tribes and clans, however, should not be affected by the land reform because individual farmers are too capital-short and the circumstances too difficult for them to get on by themselves.

(b) *The natural conditions of agriculture* constitute a much more serious problem than generally assumed in the developed world. So far not enough knowledge is available to us concerning *soil and climatic conditions* to formulate well-founded views on a number of basic questions.

200

It is questionable, e. g., if the European production level could be attained in areas that are extremely poor in precipitation. There is a vast area of many million square miles stretching from latitude 30° north to latitude 30° south, where the amount of annual precipitation is not more than 60 to 100 mm. It is also commonly known that the frequency of droughts and spells of extreme cold is not high in countries in the temperate zone.

This is of course not a novel discovery, though it should be emphasized that this situation can only be changed by large-scale and concerted international actions.

It is less commonly known, however, what the tropical and sub-tropical conditions bring to bear upon the quality of soil. Typical of these territories are the nearly equal length of days and nights, a relatively long insolation time and, except for deserts and steppes, abundant but unequally distributed precipitation. These factors determine not only the meteorological but also the *soil climate*, which has its effects on the processes taking place in the soil and, in the last analysis, on *soil fertility and stability*.

The exuberant vegetation of tropical jungles and savannahs is of course misleading. Very often the rich flora is only maintained by the abundance of precipitation on soils which, when under cultivation, will yield surprisingly poor crops and get exhausted within a few years.[4]

In many areas the method of *"bush burning"* is still widely in use. This kind of cultivation has been carried on presumably for thousands of years without any major harmful effects. But this is only possible under primitive conditions when bush burning is restricted to isolated small spots and is carried on for 2 or 3 years only. The termination of bush burning usually results in the soil regaining its natural vegetation. But with the inclusion of large connected tropical areas this mode of cultivation could have fatal consequences (see the story of the Jata colony in Brazil, in the heart of the Amazonas basin[5]).

It follows from the foregoing that the natural conditions of agricultural production need a large-scale, comprehensive study conducted by concerted international action. Methods must be elaborated by which crop yields by hectare can be increased and also soil can be protected against the harmful effect of tropical sun and precipitation.

Of the natural endowments of agricultural production the climatic and soil conditions are the most difficult to control and change, given our present level of knowledge. Therefore, as also evidenced by the economic history of dry and semi-dry areas, water *supply* is the most variable factor. (It is not accidental that the pueblos in North America and Mexico, the Inkas in Peru, the ancient Egyptians and people in China, Bali Island and Hawai had their agricultural

[4] On the various tropical soils a valuable study was prepared by a Hungarian research team in the Congo.
[5] This territory was cleared by modern machines and was made suitable for large-scale farming. Within two years, however, the soil, deprived of its natural cover, lost its fertile top layer and was leached out of its mineral salts. In five years, the soil, rich in iron, became as hard as rock in the scorching tropical sun.

activities based on irrigation systems.) Even today, very understandably, modern development plans are highlighted by projects designed to control rivers and water systems. We only need to think of the control projects on the rivers Amazonas, Volta, Niger, Ganges, Brahmaputra and the Nile. In carrying out river control, account must also be taken, however, of the fact that rivers overflowing their banks in the monsoon season cover with a fresh *mud layer*, the soil which has been leached out of its mineral content year by year. If river control sets too narrow limits to floods, then care must be taken that the vast amount of organic and mineral substances provided by nature in its own way up to that time are replaced by man.

The natural conditions of agriculture in the developing countries require the application of entirely new methods.

(c) *The manpower problems of agriculture* have already been touched upon. In the *overpopulated countries* there will be ample excess labour available for a long time to come. Consequently, the type of mechanization as used in countries in the tropical zone with the primary aim of saving labour force is not needed. The situation is different if by mechanization new territories can be brought under cultivation without the risk of exposing the soil to destruction.

In this case the bulk of excess manpower must be utilized in agriculture – without disregarding the requirements of industrial development – to expand the area under cultivation, to improve the natural conditions and to develop the cultivation of labour-intensive crop species.

In *sparsely populated countries* manpower reserves are not significant, and therefore a certain degree of mechanization will be needed from the very outset. Water economy ought to be improved, so that new and fertile territories can be gained in these countries, too. However, in the execution of construction work and later in cultivation, live labour may not exclusively be relied upon.

(d) *The economic and organizational units* in the sense of micro-economics have a very important part to play in the development of production. The launching of development from above and the related upper (central) management do not mean at all that the micro-economic units have not their own roles and laws of movement in fulfilling these tasks.

What significant micro-economic units have come so far into being in agricultural practice?

International experience provides the evidence that in this respect the various forms of *co-operatives* have proved most successful. They play or may play an important role in the *economic, social and educational* fields alike.

The ILO conference in 1962 laid down as a principle that any re-distribution of land must be effected by the establishment of co-operative institutions. The UN Economic Commission for Africa has referred in this connection to the United Arab Republic, where the big estates have been handed over to agricultural labourers and tenants establishing their co-operatives. The co-operatives draw up their production plans, attend to the irrigation works and organize the common use of machines. In addition, they also perform of course the traditional co-operative tasks such as credit supply, marketing and social services.

Of similar type are the co-operatives organized in the *Sudan* (in the framework of the Gezira Scheme), mainly engaged in cotton growing. In *Kenya,* however, the objective of the land reform so far has been to put an end to the fragmentation of landed property and to the *waste of lands* caused by the uncertainty of ownership relations. Here too, as a result of the land reform, small and medium farms have been established which, by means of forming co-operatives, have successfully switched over to commodity production. Several other co-operative attempts have been made in the developing countries.

Co-operatives exist of course in both *traditional and modern forms*. In certain countries the ownership relations have remained unchanged though the activities of the co-operatives are not confined to performing purchasing and marketing functions only. Where, however, *the land is owned collectively* (as in several countries of Tropical Africa), it appears a simpler task to take it into co-operative ownership.

Much depends of course on the nature of the tasks to be performed. In the case of irrigation farming (Sudan), or where virgin lands are brought under cultivation (Dahomey), the sphere of co-operative activities will be a wide one from the outset.

The growth of agricultural output can be achieved, as we have already pointed out, in a number of ways: by expanding the area of arable land or by higher yields. In both cases, reliance must be placed on co-operatives in such a way that their members invest labour in it (irrigation or terrace farming).

Irrigation farming may also promote the *diversification* of production. Irrigation societies can easily be transformed into producers' or general co-operatives. In any case, co-operatives are suitable media to *channel* state aid into the agricultural sector. Thus, for instance, the distribution of fertilizers and seeds constitutes a serious problem in all developing countries. This requires a high degree of organization, particularly in countries where the natural conditions of agriculture greatly differ from region to region (provinces or republics). It is more expedient to assign such local tasks to the co-operatives (as in Pakistan), which not only enhance the peasants' confidence in them but also diminish the risk of dishonest distribution practices.

In addition, the co-operatives may also participate in *soil amelioration* and in the organization of the *use of machines*. They may also perform an important function in *domestic marketing*.

It must also be taken into account that in the developing countries various ancient communities (village communities) had existed prior to the economic growth and the starting of the co-operative movement. If these communities are deeply rooted and enjoy the support of a substantial proportion of the population, they can be transferred into some kind of co-operative form. Here the Indian village communities, the *ejidos*, may be referred to as playing an important role in the different periods of Mexican development.

If a population living under backward socio-economic conditions are to be transferred to a modern system, the preservation of ancient forms may facilitate the transition.

Therefore, the building of the ancient forms into an up-to-date co-operative movement is *politically* correct in the given case, diminishes the *social tensions* emerging in the course of social transformation and also stimulates, within certain limits, to increase production.

(e) *The volume of fixed and/or working capital to be invested in agriculture* exerts a great influence on the growth of agricultural output. However, agriculture can make investments for production purposes almost exclusively with the help of the government, because capital goods (means of production) to be utilized are here, too, of foreign origin.

In the case of agriculture it must be always borne in mind that its growth does not directly foster growth in the other sectors, and also that a relatively backward agriculture does not adequately react to growth in the other sectors either. The fact alone that industrial production shows a comparatively rapid development and the purchasing power of industrial workers also increases is indicative of the expansion of the market only, and not of agricultural output. The expansion of the market will induce the demand primarily for foodstuffs (excepting the case that the growth of purchasing power is limited to the leading strata only). It would be a mistake, however, to say that the demand elasticity of agricultural products is smaller than that of industrial goods, since this statement holds good exclusively for well-nourished societies only. From this follows that agricultural output must be increased, as we have already mentioned, by 5 to 6 per cent annually.[6]

Therefore, substantial investments must be secured for agriculture. In the highly developed Western countries, where about 20 to 24 per cent of the national income is invested annually, the combined share of industrial and agricultural investments in total investment is 30 per cent. Under such circumstances, the developed capitalist countries allocate only 8 to 10 per cent of their total investments *directly* to agriculture. In the developing countries, however, a higher share must be earmarked for productive investments and for agricultural investments within them.

Investments must be made by the state in the following fields:
– improvement of the natural conditions of agricultural production and the expansion of the area of arable land (irrigation, soil amelioration, cultivation of virgin lands);
– scientific research, experiments and education in agriculture;
– improved seeds and breeds (experiments in breeding new animal species);
– model state farms (possibly affiliated with a research institute or a university).

In addition, the state must ensure the import of capital goods and the provision of credits for purchasing various fertilizers and, when necessary, mechanization.

[6] Rapid agricultural growth has been achieved in the past 20 years by Mexico, where the annual growth rate of output has reached 6 per cent.

Credits are provided of course by banks, with the state undertaking but guarantee for repayment.

Also *credits* must be secured by the banks specifically for co-operatives and if justified for village communities. Credits should usually be given not in cash but in the form of means of production, animals, seeds, etc., i.e. *in kind*.

It is generally advisable that investments with slow return should be made by the state, since individual economic units are unable to raise sufficient capital for slow-returning investments.

Care must be taken – of course without ruthlessly exploiting available resources – that *priority* is given to investments resulting in a quick *increase in yields*.

When specifying the investment objectives, the forms of implementation and the stimulation of production, it should not be forgotten that we are concerned with a *multi-sectoral type* of agriculture, in which every sector requires different methods.

(f) *The economic environment of agriculture* can be discussed from two points of view:

– It is from the economic environment that we can deduce the social aims of production, which can often be conflicting, and therefore an optimum must be sought.

– The economic environment has a decisive impact on agriculture, promoting or impeding the attainment of its aims.

The most serious conflict between the social aims of agricultural production can be found between production for the *domestic* and *foreign markets*.

At present, most of the tropical countries are engaged in large-scale trading in one or two agricultural export products. On the other hand, the same countries, for lack of a diversified pattern of agricultural production, are compelled to import an increasing amount of agricultural products (foodstuffs).

Rapid population growth and the increase in the number of urban population lead to a yearly rise in imports. The process of increasing consumption cannot of course be halted. As a result, the export-import balance of agriculture is becoming less favourable from year to year.

It follows from the foregoing that a considerable proportion of the material resources and available areas must be used for the diversification of agriculture so that a rapid rise in imports can be avoided.

At the same time, care must be taken that by increasing yields per unit of land, more goods are available for export provided they can be marketed at not diminishing prices.

Essential is the *supply* of agriculture with means of production and raw materials. Again, *organization* has here a very important role to play.

In the course of launching the growth process, the *transport* of agricultural products will undergo substantial changes. Formerly, it was only for export products that transport was ensured with good roads connecting the places of production with the seaports. With starting economic development, a large amount of means of production, materials, spare parts, etc., have to be transported for agriculture, on the one hand, and, on the other, agricultural products must be transported from new export-producing regions. Therefore, in order to diversify agricultural production and gradually to integrate subsistence economy into the national economy as a whole, new trunk and access roads and transport facilities will be needed. If they are not available at the required time, the efforts made to increase production may prove ineffective.

To prevent difficulties of this kind, it is expedient to work out a coherent plan for the expected distribution by regions and types of commodities of the countries' agricultural output (geographical mapping of agricultural production) as a basis for planning a transportation network.

3. AGRICULTURE AND THE PROBLEMS OF NUTRITION

Agriculture has an important role to play in *improving the nutrition* of the local population. In the past decades FAO has carried out several surveys of the food supply of the world population, supplemented in recent years by projections for 1975 and 2000.

In the developing countries, *famine and undernourishment* are common phenomena. *Famine*, as defined by international experts, is the state of affairs when the available quantity of foodstuffs is *inadequate* also in terms of *calorie*. After a certain time, famine will necessarily result in a loss of normal weight and deterioration of the physical condition. In the case of children, this manifests itself in insufficient growth and a significant loss in vitality. Undernourishment is due, in the first place, to the lack of important nutrients.

According to surveys made by FAO, calorie consumption as related to the actual needs of individual regions is 90 per cent in the Far East (2,050 calories), 98 per cent in Africa (2,350), 103 per cent for the Middle East (2,450), 104 per cent in Latin America (2,500), 117 per cent in Europe (3,050), 120 per cent in North America (3,100) and 125 per cent in Australia (3,250).

These figures clearly show that calorie consumption in the Far East and Africa is lower, while that in Europe, North America and Australia is substantially higher than needed.

A further, even more serious problem is the fact that per capita daily consumption of animal protein is only 9 grammes, or 20 per cent of that in the economically developed countries.

The calorie share of cereals, tuber crops and sugar in total calorie consumption is 60 per cent in the developed countries as against 80 per cent in the developing world.

Even more alarming are the FAO forecasts for the years 1975 and 2000 if no appropriate measures are taken. The population of the countries with high calorie consumption will rise only to 124 per cent by 1975 and to 158 per cent by 2000, while those of the countries with low calorie consumption to 141 and 250 per cent, respectively, that is, of the expected 6,000 million people approximately 5,000 million will live in the countries with low calorie consumption. According to these estimates, by 1975 only 90 per cent of the *world's per capita need* of foodstuffs will be available, and only 85 per cent of those of animal origin, while by 2000 the respective figures will be 80 per cent and 70 per cent.

This gap, unless effective measures are taken, will obviously be apparent not in the present-day developed but in the developing countries. It is typical, e. g., that the developing countries, in which 80 per cent of the world population will live by 2000, account today for only 20 to 22 per cent of the world's milk and egg production.

These data on world food supply, owing primarily to the immensity of the problem, will corroborate our opinion already expressed in the foregoing, that the gap between the developed and the developing countries can be bridged only by a wide-based international co-operation and concerted action programmes, as well as by urgent internal social changes (land reforms), which cannot be substituted even by the most successful international co-operation.

Therefore, when *specifying the production aims of agriculture,* we must take as a point of departure the actual needs of domestic consumption, projecting them, first, in terms of calories and proteins, then in actual foodstuffs, to the expected long-term growth of population. Realistic seem to be the estimates made by FAO, which establish the following caloric values of the foodstuffs needed: 2,300 for the Far East, and 2,400 for the Middle East, Latin America and Africa. Within these values the ratio of protein and that of animal protein have to be specified separately.

The specific needs of the various age groups, in particular of children, should possibly also be considered.

In addition, account must also be taken of the *kinds of domestic foodstuffs* by which the above needs can be met, as well as of the methods by which their production can be increased. Taking into consideration the limits of domestic production, the forms of meeting these needs should be established. For example, in what staples should cereals be provided, taking into consideration the domestic production possibilities. In a substantial part of Asia rice is being preferred since this continent accounts for 56 per cent of the world's rice output. But in Africa, wheat bread was in great demand in colonial times though this continent provides only about 2 per cent of the world's total wheat production, and certain areas, unless the problem of tropicalization is solved, are absolutely unsuitable for wheat growing. Since the population of Africa actually constitutes 8.5 per cent of the world population, it obviously will depend in the future, too, on substantial wheat imports. In this case the question emerges, how the African countries can pay for these imports. Would it not be more reasonable to switch over, where the consumption attitudes of the population can still be influenced, to rice growing and make it the basis for cereal supply? For the time being Africa's share in world rice output is insignificantly higher (2.2 per cent) than in wheat production. In addition, while wheat yield per hectare in Africa is only 9 quintals, rice yield per hectare is 17.6, which is relatively high.

Similar problems crop up in protein supply (of vegetable and animal origin).

It is of crucial importance to secure a necessary co-ordination between the manipulation of nutrition patterns and the directions in which food production is developed. This work should be founded by a representative survey of food consumption.

4. THE RESULTS AND SOCIAL IMPLICATIONS OF THE "GREEN REVOLUTION"

In recent years, new species of high-yield cereals developed by plant-improving research have greatly contributed, though in certain countries only, to an increase in agricultural production in the developing world. It is due mainly to the conscious application of these new species that India has succeeded in substantially stepping up her agricultural output during the past few years.

In order to step up intensive cultivation, India has placed special emphasis, in addition to the methods known and applied earlier (irrigation, fertilizers, mechanization, etc.) on the great achievements of modern genetics: the development of high-yield plants. The yield per hectare of irrigated land of the new wheat species is 50 to 60 quintals as against the usual 20 quintals. Excellent results have also been attained with the new rice species. Another important factor of the "green revolution" in India has been the increasing use of fertilizers. In 1960–1961 only 300,000 tons of artificial fertilizers were used; in 1968–1969, however, the amount increased to 2 million. At the same time, the area of irrigated land has also grown significantly.

The "green revolution" has considerably alleviated the serious food supply problem in India, and has also contributed to the growth of the national income and to economic development in general. The rise in the technical level of agriculture has also stimulated industrial development: the increasing use of fertilizers, more advanced agricultural tools (e.g. iron ploughs), machines and means of transport as well as of irrigation installations has not only stepped up their imports but has also exerted a stimulating impact on their domestic manufacture.

But the new phase opened up by raising the agro-technical level of farming was not accompanied by a consistent implementation of the plans drawn up for the structural transformation of the ownership relations of landed property. Although the "green revolution" carried out under outdated, archaic social and land-ownership relations has averted the danger of famine, it has not mitigated mass poverty at all. Instead, it has sharpened the old contradictions of capitalist development and has even given rise to new ones. The "green revolution" has remained an experiment in revolutionizing agro-technology without the transformation of social relations.

This fact alone has kept the "green revolution" within very narrow socio-economic limits, and thus tens of millions of agricultural labourers have been left outside the sphere of social transformation. The fruits of the "green revolution" are enjoyed mainly by the large estates and medium-sized holdings, that is, the "green revolution" accelerates the development of capitalism in agriculture. The concentration of cultivated areas in the possession of big landowners is carried out by means of buying up the land of bankrupt peasant farmers, by increasing land rents and expelling share farmers. The expropriation of small holdings has been speeded up, and the economic position of tenants is deteriorating. Tenants in certain states of India are compelled to sell 70 per cent, instead of an earlier 50 per cent, of their crops to their landowners, while the rent of an acre of arable land has increased (as a result of the potential rise in yields) from 500 to 750 rupees.

The increasing forceful separation from land of the peasantry further enhances agrarian overpopulation and prevents a decrease in unemployment and underemployment. Indicative of sharpening social contradictions are the intensified struggle of peasants for land (often finding expression in arbitrary seizure of lands) and the vigorous demand for a consistent carrying out of the promised land reform.

V. THE PROBLEMS OF INDUSTRIALIZATION

It is on the question of industrialization that the sharpest debates have developed in the past decades.

These debates have essentially been centred upon the following five questions:

1. Should industrial development precede or follow the acceleration of agricultural growth?

2. Should industrialization be launched by the production of consumer or capital goods (means of production)?

3. What technology should be adopted? An up-to-date one, or one that has already been superseded in the advanced countries?

4. Small-scale or big industries should enjoy priority?

5. What should be the role of, and the fight and co-operation between, public and private capital (including foreign private capital) in the process of industrialization?

It would not be wise to answer instantly these questions, which are anyway inseparable from the concrete endowments of individual countries.

Therefore, we shall first examine what factors influence the formulation of the industrialization strategy and what conclusions can be drawn from these factors.

We think that six factors should be identified and analysed:

1. The place and role of industrialization in the growth process related to *other sectors* (primarily to *agriculture*);

2. the impact of *population,* the *density* of *population* and the *manpower situation* on the strategy of industrialization;

3. the role of *capital* in industrialization;

4. *raw materials* and the structure of industrialization;

5. investments in industry and *international trade relations* to be established by means of developing industrial activities;

6. the impact of industrialization on *domestic technology, consumers' market* and the *way of economic thinking.*

Let us investigate these factors one by one.

1. THE RELATIONSHIP BETWEEN THE GROWTH OF INDUSTRY AND OF OTHER BRANCHES

In case industry starts developing at a rapid rate, which agriculture is unable to keep pace with, the following problems will crop up:

(a) In order to satisfy increased purchasing power the *imports of agricultural products* must be stepped up, which may render it impossible to import capital goods and endanger thereby the fulfilment of any further industrialization programme.

(b) Owing to shortages in the consumers' market, the *marketing* of industrial products comes up against difficulties.

(c) The *population,* whose anticipated confidence had to be aroused in industrialization and economic growth in general, will experience that the situation has worsened since the growth process started.

On the other hand, if agriculture developes rapidly without industrialization being initiated, then the following problems will have to be faced:

(a) *Excess manpower* will not be transferred from agriculture to industry, which may have tragic consequences especially for overpopulated countries.

(b) The world-market demand for agricultural produce is *inelastic,* while the purchasing power in the country does not grow sufficiently to absorb increased output. This will result in economic crisis and overall stagnation.

(c) *The accelerating factor,* which could promote also the growth of the other branches, will not develop in the national economy.

From this follows that a *simultaneous, proportionate and interrelated growth* of industry and agriculture is needed.

2. THE INTERCONNECTION OF INDUSTRIALIZATION AND POPULATION

The *number* and *density* of the population have a considerable impact on the conception of industrialization to be pursued.

In this respect, too, there exist a number of variants, because the same country may be overpopulated from the point of view of agriculture and insignificant from the point of view of industry.

As a matter of fact, the industrial development and specialization of a *small country* materializes through international trade. This statement applies of course not to all sectors of the economy, since certain sectors, e. g. the building trade and the services, are rather independent of international trade. A large population, i. e. a large market, is advantageous for the metal-working industry and certain supplying enterprises.

Most of the *African countries,* for example, are small; at present the population of only three countries (Nigeria, the Arab Republic of Egypt and Ethiopia) exceeds the 20 million mark.

Anyway, as a heritage of colonialism, Africa is the continent of small countries. The population of twelve African countries is smaller than that of a modern metropolis (2 million), and the number of inhabitants in eight countries is below one million. This makes it obvious that the industrial development of Africa, apart from one or two countries, must be based on a regional or even a wider sort of division of labour.

An especially serious problem is posed by the industrialization of countries which are overpopulated but poor in *raw-material resources*. In this case *high-quality products* may offer the proper way-out in the perspective. Such countries will have to face serious problems for a time, as in the first phase of industrialization the production costs are high and the domestic market is too narrow to absorb the new products. This makes it inevitable to subsidize exports or even to devaluate the national currency (Japan).

It must also be considered that more and more industries are becoming specific "big-power industries" in that they are not profitable enough even for medium-sized countries. But modern technology is developing by leaps and bounds, and the number of these industries is steadily increasing. Therefore, irrespective of their density of population, the small- and medium-sized countries can carry out their industrialization programmes only on the basis of a broad international co-operation.

Not only the quantity but also the *quality* of manpower is a decisive factor of industrial development. Industry requires skilled labour but the training of manpower takes place not exclusively in vocational schools but also in the process of performing actual work in the industry itself. From this point of view the adequate and correct sequence of building up the industrial structure is extremely important. It is advisable to start industrial development in branches in which there have already been performed certain activities in small-scale or handicraft industry, and some production experience is already available.

Graduality can also be ensured by the practice that first the more complicated components or parts of the end product are manufactured in co-operation with a foreign company, and only later will all components be produced locally.

As regards consumer goods the situation is easier, since various textiles, crockery and household goods have already been produced in the small-scale industry before.

A serious problem is posed by the fact that in the initial phase it is not expedient to develop such industries which presuppose a highly developed *economic environment,* a differentiated demand for technical goods.

Ideal is the case when the newly established industrial plants exercise a maximum impact on the economic environment, promoting its development and differentiation without themselves being too dependent on this environment.

3. THE ROLE OF CAPITAL IN INDUSTRIALIZATION

The problem of capital needed for industrialization must be discussed from various aspects.

The first problem in this respect is how, from what sources and by what methods capital can be secured for accumulation. This question is of crucial importance because the countries concerned are all *short of capital*. From this it follows that capital must be treated as a scarce factor.

A further great problem is the *rate of return* (amortization) of capital. The rate of return on domestic investments is greatly influenced by the *time of implementation* (gestation period of investments). Since the country is short of capital, special attention should be paid to stepping up the rate of return and/or the time of implementation. If the organizational capability, indispensable owing to the limited capacity of the building industry and the simultaneous implementation of a large number of investments, has not yet reached the necessary level, then fewer investments should be started and completed within a short period of time. Otherwise, the resources used in investments are tied up for a long time, and the new investments must be started before the old ones start yielding returns. In addition, the slow inplementation of investments also increases the investment costs.

Obviously, when *choosing the investment projects,* several viewpoints must be considered. One of them is the allocation of investment resources among investments with long-, medium- and short-term returns. Since future needs must be duly prepared, investments with slow returns are unavoidable. The state has to realize a great number of such investments; for example in education, public health, communal services, etc. Their returns are usually *indirect* and will materialize only in the distant future. We only need to think of the costs of establishing a university that must be secured now, while its actual benefits will be enjoyed only in one or one and a half decades. Even slower returns must be reckoned with in the case of primary education, whose results will usually begin to materialize only in the subsequent generation.

If, in order to increase agricultural output, we wish to change ·the natural conditions by improving the most variable factor, i. e. *water economy,* and start flood control and building dams, etc., then the *rate of return will also be slow.*

In this connection account must also be taken of the experience that the implementation costs of such big investment projects are always higher than originally calculated. Unless the necessary precautionary measures are taken, the case may emerge that a few investment projects with slow returns will tie up all investment and organizational resources.

To prevent this, investments with quick returns must also be made.

The ratio of investments to the national income finds expression in the capital *coefficient.* If it is high (e. g., 5 or 6), then investments with slow returns have been made in excess of the real possibilities of the country concerned. In such cases attempts must be made to defer investments with slow returns, to postpone the time limits of their implementation. The drawbacks of this solution, however, are only the lesser ones of two bad alternatives; it can give rise to negative effects and consequences but may prevent a major investment crisis.

Both the dynamics and crisis of an economy in the growth process equally stem from investments. It is investments that send, on the one hand, blood into the veins of the economy and make it possible that stagnation is replaced by dynamics. On the other hand, such investments constitute an overstrain on the resources of the economy, cause imbalances between demand and supply, start an inflationary pressure and pave the way for developing an adverse balance of payments.

Certain disruptions, for reasons already mentioned, are inevitable, as also evidenced by experience in economic history. If, however, as a result of investments a new and sounder economic circulation develops, then this overheated state and the imbalances of the economy will be followed by a certain degree of balance and equalization.

4. INDUSTRIALIZATION AND RAW MATERIALS

It is obvious that industrialization must rely on the country's *own raw-material basis*. If in addition to capital goods raw materials also have to be imported, then the new plant, apart from exceptional cases, can hardly be economical.

Therefore, a *geological survey* of the country, presenting a clear picture of its natural resources, is extremely important. This will of course necessitate regional co-operation on a wide basis since, especially in the case of small countries, it is unlikely that all sorts of raw materials needed to develop a branch of industry are available. In Africa, for example, iron ore of an exceptionally high quality (about 55 per cent) can be found, and is being exported today to a number of developed countries. Evidently, iron and steel industry could gradually be built up on this good-quality iron ore basis, but for the time being the lack of coking coal makes it impossible.

By the way, research efforts in Africa should not be concentrated on classical energy sources (though Africa accounts for 40 per cent of the capitalist world's water power potential), as there are indications of the possibility of a large-scale exploitation of geothermic energies and of the intensive utilization of solar energy. But all this does not go to show that no efforts should be made to explore coking coal deposits in Africa, an indispensable precondition for the iron and steel industry. If in any African country coking coal were found in sizable quantities, then the iron and steel production of five or six countries could be based on these coal deposits.

Most developing countries are rich in agricultural raw materials, certain mineral resources, wood and various sources of power. They can also secure the most important basic material of their textile industry: cotton. It would be highly important for them to explore basic materials for the chemical industry, primarily for starting the manufacture of fertilizers (sulphuric acid, caustic soda, chlorine acid, ammonium). Of course, it should first be specified what sort of fertilizers are needed.

Utmost care must be taken in managing *timber resources*. The ruthless exploitation of forests may cause tremendous losses (deforested lands turning into deserts).

5. INDUSTRIALIZATION AND INTERNATIONAL TRADE

The most serious problems of industrialization are those which are connected with the relationship between the country in question and the world economy. We have already pointed out that the first phase of industrialization is necessarily of an *import-serving* character.

In the case of large countries the import-saving character of industrialization may stay typical for a number of decades, in contrast to small ones, where this character can only survive for a short time. After the elapse of a certain time new industries with an import-saving character must be capable of producing export goods and conquer markets for themselves.

Therefore, it is especially important for small countries to establish co-operation among them in the course of industrialization.

For lack of achieving this co-operation, the following difficulties may arise:

(a) overlapping capacities may develop, making inter-state trade difficult and turning, later on, these countries into competitors on the world market;

(b) the period of protection, during which the given products are manufactured for the home market only, will be irrealistically short;

(c) consequently, the products of relatively expensive investments can be sold on the world market only at very low prices and at high transportation costs.

Co-operation, on the other hand, may reduce these unnecessary overlapping capacities to a minimum, prevent the emergence of many conflicts of an economic interest and lengthen the period of protection.

In Africa, for example, co-operation at both continental and regional levels is absolutely necessary as the continent as a whole is very import-sensitive, and its imports account for 33 per cent of the total continental income.

India produces a large proportion of her domestic consumption. In her consumption of manufactured goods, the share of imports does not reach 20 per cent. In Africa, however, the situation is almost a reversed one even at a continental level: it imports about four times the volume of industrial goods it produces. More than half of all African imports are consumer goods. For the time being, the value of imported machinery and means of production constitutes only 12 per cent of total imports, though this is already an improvement on 1950, when it was only 3 per cent. No doubt, textiles and some other consumer goods (their share in total imports being about 20 per cent), metals, chemicals can be produced without major difficulties on the continent and/or in the specific economic regions.

When establishing new plants, in case the equipment has to be imported, the return rate must also be calculated in *foreign* currency. This is a relatively simple procedure: the *foreign-exchange* inputs of establishing a new plant have to be set against *import savings* (also calculated in foreign currency) achieved after the plant has come into operation.

In case productive equipment is manufactured domestically, it is not sufficient to calculate the time of depreciation at current prices only. The consequences of possible quality deterioration in other industries, the loss of time, etc., must also be considered.

Substantial import savings can generally be attained by developing the textile industry. Presently, the total textile output of the African continent covers only 40 per cent of the demand.

No export growth is usually achieved in the first phase of industrialization, but certain countries, such as India, the United Arab Republic, etc., have already registered appreciable textile exports. If domestic manpower and manpower management reach a satisfactory level, these countries enjoy comparative advantages in manufacturing *cotton goods*. With cotton produced locally and manpower being cheap, a comparative advantage can be secured in the not highly capital-intensive industries and in those where the necessary skill can be acquired within a relatively short time.

The production of industrial basic materials can of course also require a certain degree of co-operation, or else a large number of different plant species must be grown on rather inadequately cultivated lands, and this calls for various skills, a wide network of special advisers and purchasing organization.

6. OTHER EFFECTS OF INDUSTRIALIZATION

Industrialization brings to bear of course significant influence not only upon the technological level and the consumption pattern of the given country but also on the way of public economic thinking and organizational capability of its inhabitants. These changes, however, do not of course materialize overnight but generally more slowly than wished or anticipated by the government. Like any other development, industrial growth also has its negative characteristics, and even larger is the number of these features that people, or part of them, think to be negative.

Yet, most important of all changes are those which introduce new principles of organization in the old society and pave the way for rational norms of action in a society based on traditions. Industry has to bring up *new managers* not only for the industry and the economy as a whole but also, and in no small measure, for agriculture.

In this respect it is highly important that the technological level is represented not only by commodities manufactured domestically at the present time but also by imported capital goods to be used by the domestic labour force at the

216

beginning of industrialization. It is of course impossible to supply all plants with up-to-date technology, but efforts must be made to ensure that such plants are *also* available. Therefore, it is imperative to examine all industrial investments for the impact they will make on the technology, production costs, quality of the goods, etc., in all *other industries*.

As far as the priority of the production of the capital-goods or that of the consumer-goods industry is concerned, no generalizations independent of time and space should be made in the process of development. It is evident that a country like India (with a large domestic market, vast raw material resources, immense surplus labour, a low share of foreign trade in the national income) has to develop all industries irrespective of the fact that it is short of capital and qualified labour.

Obviously, the same applies to all other large countries in Asia and Latin America (Pakistan, Brazil). It is of course also necessary for these countries to raise agricultural production by at least 5 to 6 per cent anually, and in fact even at a higher rate if priority is given to the development of heavy industries, owing to a more rapid growth in purchasing power.

This is another problem which cannot be solved satisfactorily in the case of smaller countries if we think in terms of a closed, national economy. International exchange of goods is becoming, on the one hand, increasingly important for the economy of small countries, and it is impossible to develop a favourable economic structure unless we take world-market requirements into consideration. On the other hand, the new industries require ever increasing investments to be made, and therefore even medium-sized countries are unable to manufacture certain products economically unless they can also export them.

As far as world-market relations are concerned, it takes the developing countries a rather long period of time (several decades) to export to the rest of the world machines and other products of the metal-working industry in *large quantities*.

At the same time, in order to ensure their own technological level, they have to import investment goods.

From this follows that owing to *a)* capital shortage, *b)* the narrowness of the market, *c)* the underdeveloped state of infrastructure, *d)* the necessarily limited raw-material availabilities, only those branches of the capital-goods producing sector are economical to develop which, in one or another respect, are competitive, and it is from these technologically advanced branches that the developing countries must gradually build up exports.

They must endeavour to develop certain *dynamic* industries, or else they will be unable to pay for their imports. They have to co-operate in this field with nations living in the same region (on the same continent) to prevent overlapping capacities from developing.

Rapid technical advance in our age makes it imperative to develop such branches which *a)* are advantageous for the national economy, *b)* are co-ordinat-

217

ed within the frame of a regional unit and c) for whose products there is a demand in the rest of the world.

As far as the *choice of technology* is concerned, account must also be taken of the existence of *surplus labour* at the time of launching economic growth. Therefore, methods of increasing production must be found which also ensure a rise in employment.

Efforts must be made that the effects of economic growth can be felt *at all levels of technology* within the given society, or conversely: that every technological level should contribute to speeding up economic growth.

Water economy, the most variable factor of the natural conditions of agriculture, can be improved with much live-labour. In this manner, "outdated technology" can be made use of for paving the way of modern agriculture, without the risk that this technology will spoil the conditions of a good start or progress.

Traditional (inherited) *technology* can also be widely applied in the *textile industry*. The methods of the handicraft or small-scale industry do not deteriorate the quality of the products, they only take more time, more labour input. Given, however, sufficient labour, this will cause no serious problem. The same applies to the pottery industry, and the manual methods used in making various consumer goods, etc.

But *advanced technology* should by all means be used

(a) in plants manufacturing capital goods, or else backward technology will retard the technical development of other branches, too;

(b) in plants producing mainly for export purposes;

(c) in any other case where large-scale technology ensures an entirely different quality than the best handicraft methods (metallurgy).

218

VI. ACCELERATED ECONOMIC GROWTH AND THE WORLD ECONOMY

1. THE GROWTH-INHIBITING FEATURES OF THE PRESENT STATE OF THE WORLD ECONOMY

From the point of view of the world economy, the acceleration of economic growth is an extremely intricate task, owing to several factors.

1. Substituting dynamic economic growth for stagnation has never before in history affected (a) *such a large proportion of mankind* (70 per cent now and 80 per cent by 2000); (b) *so many national economies* (about 80 countries), (c) *such vast territories* (about 60 per cent of the globe).

2. The gulf between the economically developed and underdeveloped countries (the gap that has to be bridged) has never been so wide as in our days. According to rather optimistic estimates, i.e. assuming an annual 5 per cent growth in national income, the less developed countries will need 80 years to catch up with the *present-day economic* level of Western Europe, and 120 years to reach that of the United States.

3. No automatic factors in the world economy are working towards levelling up the extremely uneven distribution of intellectual and material resources. On the contrary, certain elements of foreign trade, capital movement and technological development are acting in the direction of *polarization*.

The political and economic power factors, a heritage of the past (neo-colonialism, hegemonistic endeavours, and economic superpowers), as well as the emergence of small countries running against the requirements of technological development, and a resulting nationalistic particularism make it difficult for a *world-economic concept*, corresponding to the ideas of a new age, to develop. No effective international organizations are available to effect, in accordance with the requirements of development, a more equitable distribution of intellectual and material resources.

Considering the extent to which imports *must* increase if economic growth (especially industrialization) is to be achieved, and the extent to which exports *can* increase, together with the costs of various services relating to the movement of goods, the indebtedness of the developing countries keeps on rising and amounted to 60 thousand million dollars in 1971.

We have already referred to the factors making necessary the widening gap in the balance of foreign trade (payments). Here we only wish to repeat in broad outlines, complement or shed new light upon some aspects of the expected developments of these processes.

219

As commonly known, the *exports* of the developing countries are composed to the extent of 90 per cent of agricultural produce and raw materials.

1. As to the export possibilities of agricultural produce, the following factors may be observed:

(a) *New dynamic elements* have appeared in the process of economic growth as a result of which agricultural products most important for the food supply of the world are no longer exported primarily by the developing countries (grain, fodder, meat, dairy products, etc.).

(b) A heavily protectionist agrarian policy makes production profitable even for farms showing a deficit balance. Therefore, in Western Europe – the main importer region of agricultural produce – in the 1960s grain imports were 21 per cent, and meat imports 24 per cent below the level of the second half of the 1920s.

(c) The socialist countries, too, are making considerable efforts to step up agricultural production as one of the preconditions for their further economic development.

What can be said in the knowledge of the present state of affairs is that the developing countries can increase only the export of their typically tropical products, for which no substitution can be found (coffee, tea, cocoa, tropical fruits, etc.).

The increase in the export of substitutable products (sugar, rice, etc.) comes up, on the one hand, against serious difficulties, and, on the other, it is not sure that efficient surplus will be available for a long time to come.

Since the autumn of 1973, the situation with respect to the export of raw materials has changed. The increase in the prices of oil and other mineral raw materials has significantly raised the export earnings of certain developing countries. These earnings have made it possible for these countries to finance such investments as will enable them to export their raw materials in a processed form, or to use them for the building up of the basis for their own industrialization. At the same time, the economic situation of developing countries poor in raw materials has deteriorated.

In relation to *imports,* however, there are a number of factors that result in a substantial increase of demand:

1. Economic growth implies an inevitable increase in the *import of means of production* (both for industry and agriculture).

2. Services must be imported to a greater extent. (Their scope and nature are very different and range from technical assistance to the need of foreign experts for educational purposes.)

3. The number of population is growing at a faster rate than agricultural production, as a result of which food imports will also rise.

4. Owing to a certain increase in purchasing power, more consumer goods will have to be imported.

5. The state and national defence will develop new needs that can be met only from international sources.

Finally, when assessing the *expected balance of payments position* of the developing countries, the following factors must be considered:

1. Trade-related service capacities show an uneven distribution. (Marine shipping is owned only to the extent of 6 per cent by the developing countries. In addition, their shipping is at a disadvantage, owing to various regulations of the international cartels.)

2. The indebtedness of the developing countries resulting from the interests of short-maturity loans is steadily increasing.

3. Capital flow into the developing countries is heavily burdened with interest payments and profit repatriation. In certain regions the balance of the in- and outflow of capital has even become an adverse one.[7]

This outline description of the present situation will convincingly prove that international trade, capital movement and even certain achievements of technological development have a considerable effect on *further polarization, on increasing existing discrepancies and tensions.* As a contributing factor in this respect must be mentioned the monetary crisis of the early 1970s and the raising of the official gold price and/or the devaluation of the dollar in relation to gold, causing substantial losses to the developing countries. This has more than ever brought to the fore the conflict of economic interests between the capitalist big powers and the developing world.

A new element of technical progress which makes the transformation of technology as a whole virtually dependent on the advance of four or five leading industries (dynamic industries) requiring vast capital investments and ensuring enormous production capacities (atomic industry, electronics, chemical engineering, engineering and motor-car industries) constitutes a real threat of lagging behind even to the industrially advanced small countries. In other words: the factors of polarization are operating not only between the advanced and the developing countries but within the developed world itself (between the large and small countries, and between the dynamic and other industries).

Even apart from the present-day situation, reference must be made to the fact that the exchange of commodities is the result of processes preceding the exchange, and thus all inequalities that can be found in the distribution of the conditions of production find expression in it. On the other hand, the development of the exchange process is greatly influenced by the distribution of the economic power (market power) among the parties participating in the exchange. No doubt, in the past decades such economic superpowers have come into being which are able to control and alter the circumstances of exchange according to their interests, or such international monopolies have developed which manipulate production and the capitalist world market against the interest of the developing world.

Finally, it must not be ignored that the unequal distribution between the party commanding a stronger market power and the economically weaker party of the

[7] For example in Latin America, according to data quoted by Prebisch, the annual influx of capital is 9,600 million dollars, while the amount of annual remittances is 13,400 million dollars.

gains and profits realized in the exchange process further increases the existing inequalities in the conditions of production, constituting a repetition of the exchange process, which is even more favourable for the stronger and more unfavourable for the weaker party.

Under prevailing conditions, no considerable change can be expected in *capital movement* either. Capital invested abroad is *relatively* smaller today than it was before the First World War. A substantial part of it is channelled into the developed regions, or is tied to political (military) strings. Being afraid of threats to its existence, private capital is reluctant to invest in developing countries without government guarantees. The rate of remittances is high. Thus, there is no automatism in capital movement which would make for eliminating the discrepancies.

2. POSSIBILITIES OF IMPROVING THE WORLD-ECONOMIC POSITION OF DEVELOPING COUNTRIES

Is it possible, then, to accelerate economic growth under such unfavourable circumstances? What evidence is provided in this respect by the growth processes realized in the 19th and 20th centuries?

Economic growth achieved since the early 19th century has taken place either (*a*) at the expense of poorer countries (capitalistic type of growth), or (*b*) from *own resources,* through the economic co-operation of a group of countries, overcoming the difficulties caused by the embargo and discrimination policies of the leading capitalist countries (socialist type of growth).

No doubt, neither of these methods can be adopted by the developing countries. There are no poorer countries than they themselves, and thus they are unable to carry out their industrialization programmes at the expense of other countries, as it had been done by the capitalist countries. And their present power relations, the level of their economies and other circumstances make it impossible for them to break away from the capitalist world economy in the most difficult phase of the growth process.

It is also clear that to achieve an appropriately accelerated growth, they cannot do without the resources of the industrially advanced capitalist countries. This presupposes, however, the formulation of a new *world-economic conception* based on the principle of mutually respecting each other's interests. But there are several factors preventing such conception from developing. The most important are these:

1. In our present world there exist *different socio-economic systems,* whose aims, social structures, international political endeavours and economic (development) models radically differ from one another.

2. There are glaring extremities in today's world economy. Discrepancies between the rich and poor countries are enormous and steadily increasing. This gap cannot be bridged either by international trade or capital movement in their

222

present-day sense. This also finds expression in the fact that since 1971 a group of the so-called least-developed countries has officially been formed, constituting a new, even more complicated situation in the field of international co-operation.

3. In the world economy of our days various *regional economic groupings* have been formed, primarily among countries with similar economic systems and developmental levels. They work out the rules of their inter-state trade and co-operation with the utmost care. It should be emphasized that these regional groupings are needed in both the developed and developing world as they can promote a sound distribution of labour, economical production and widening markets for the national economies. On the other hand, autarchic tendencies, trade discriminations imposed on other countries represent serious retarding factors in the development of the world economy as a whole.

4. Owing to the extremely accelerated rate of scientific and technological development, *new tendencies of polarization* also make their appearance between the large and small countries of the economically advanced world. These tendencies can of course be kept within reasonable limits by applying an appropriate economic policy.

5. An important role is played in the current world economy by the *international monopolies,* which are led exclusively by their own profit motives when taking economic decisions also affecting the vital interests of other countries. These international monopolies disregard the national economies of the poor countries both as regards content and form.

6. Today's world economy is composed of *national economies* with conflicting interests. But the national economy is not merely a form in which the discrepancies listed above find expression, but a veritable content as well, the existence and development of which, under the prevailing conditions, are still a precondition for the growth and improvement of the world economy.

But the developing countries, too, are faced with important tasks to solve. At the 25th session of the United Nations General Assembly, eight socialist countries issued a joint statement in which they laid down, in connection with the Second Development Decade of the United Nations, their position on the economic development of the "Third World". They emphasized, among other things, that internal reforms and a maximum utilization of domestic resources are needed in the developing countries.

3. THE TASKS OF INTERNATIONAL ORGANIZATIONS IN IMPROVING THE WORLD-ECONOMIC POSITION OF DEVELOPING COUNTRIES

Thus, the accelerated economic growth of the developing countries calls for substantial foreign assistance, the restriction and/or offsetting of the world-economic processes that are one-sidedly unfavourable for them. Foreign assistance is sufficiently effective only if it is co-ordinated internationally, which is inconceivable without large-scale international co-operation and agreements. From all this follows that the role of *international organizations* in solving the problems of the developing countries must substantially increase in importance. Here we think first of all of the specialized agencies of the UN, such as FAO, UNIDO, UNDP and UNCTAD.

What intellectual and material resources can be mobilized and concentrated in the international organizations to accelerate the economic growth of the developing countries?

It is a matter of common knowledge that the world is spending currently about 200 thousand million dollars on *armaments,* this amount of expenditure being hardly *below the total annual national income* of all developing countries. The share of armament expenditures in the national income of the industrially developed countries is around 8 to 9 per cent. In case these expenses were cut by an annual 20 per cent (which, despite all difficulties, is not a utopy at all), *half the material resources released*[8] would amount to 20 thousand million dollars, which could increase the growth rate of the developing countries by at least 2 per cent. Thus the time needed by the developing countries to attain the present economic level of the West-European capitalist countries could considerably be shortened (from 80 to about 50 to 60 years).

It can be expected that part of the *intellectual and material assistance* provided at present on a bilateral basis can be made international, while the other part of it can be registered with the international organizations. It would be expedient if the loans and aids for the developing countries were distributed by the international organizations after duly considering the development plans of the various countries (regions). (The conversion of all foreign assistance to international assistance poses of course serious difficulties. Some great powers insist on the bilateral system, while quite a few donor countries are willing to provide export credits only, i.e. want to ensure the maintenance or expansion of their own markets by means of credits. But such credits, too, ought to be registered with the continental organs so that they may consider them when allocating international credits. Otherwise it is impossible to realize a certain concentration of development through investment credits. In turn, the co-ordination of investments is a precondition for a division of labour among developing countries!)

At the World Trade Conference in Geneva and at various other international forums since that time, several suggestions have been made – especially in the Prebisch Report – to introduce the so-called *compensatory financing* method (to offset the losses arising from the deterioration of the terms of trade), to improve the activities of the *international credit institutions* (especially of the IBRD and IDA) in favour of the developing countries which, in co-operation with the international organizations or under their supervision, raise new funds for speeding up economic growth.

---

[8] The other half is assumed to be spent by the developing countries on increasing their own non-military investments and raising the living standards of their populations.

And, finally, it is expected that internationally provided funds will be made available as a result of *consolidating debts and lengthening their repayment periods*. It is well known that as a result of the slow increase in exports and the deterioration of the terms of trade the government debts of the developing countries have quickly increased over the past few years (by an annual average of 17 per cent), and therefore the annual burden of interests and amortization rose to 6 billion dollars in 1971.[9]

The consolidation of debts and the lengthening of the repayment time should be ensured in such a construction that these benefits could serve as coverages for the investment programme. If these funds – or at least a greater part of them – were available, then the international organizations should be given a more important role to play in this field, too.

It would be extremely important if the international organizations were able to organize such programmes which are concerned with problems of increasing significance for the *world economy* and affect *vital interests* of mankind. Such is apparently the solution of the world food problem, especially the grain supply, in the next decades.[10]

[9] Especially rapidly grows the indebtedness of countries such as India and Pakistan (their annual growth rates being 38 and 28 per cent, respectively). The growth of debts is closely connected with the *terms of credits*, which came into being under the conditions of the developed countries and cannot objectively be applied to the developing ones. (To say nothing of the very serious problem, also discussed at the Geneva Conference, that the current system of financing impedes the establishment of trade relations among the developing countries.)

[10] This raises in brief the following problems: in 1960, 70 per cent of the world population lived in the developing world, and by 2000 this ratio will increase to 80 per cent. In 1960, the density of population was 17 per square kilometre in the developed, and 27 in the developing countries. By the year 2000, however, according to conservative estimates of the UN Population Department, the density indices will be 28 in the advanced and 62(!) in the developing world. At the same time, 68.4 per cent of the grain, 81.6 per cent of the meat and 79.3 per cent of the protein output of the world are produced in the developed countries, while 31.4 per cent of the grain, 18.4 per cent of the meat and 20.7 per cent of the protein production of the world fall to the developing countrien with 70 per cent (by 2000 80 per cent) of the world population. In addition, several questions of tropical agriculture have not yet been solved. In certain areas wheat cannot be grown at all, there are no high-bred species in animal husbandry. etc.)

15 Nyilas

VII. THE ROLE OF SOCIALIST COUNTRIES, INCLUDING HUNGARY, IN SOLVING THE GROWTH PROBLEMS OF DEVELOPING COUNTRIES

The assistance provided by the socialist countries, among them Hungary, must be aimed first of all at promoting the exploitation of the growth resources of the less developed economies. In the economy of every country there are factors promoting and retarding and/or restricting growth. Their nature is determined by the overall economic position (including the natural endowments) and development of the country concerned.

To put the question in another way: assistance must be intended to restrict the own and complementary effects of the *limiting factors* (bottlenecks) as they retard economic growth.

What *limiting factors* (bottlenecks) can be found in the economies of these countries, and how do the socialist countries help to diminish their detrimental effects?

Accelerated growth is primarily restricted by limited *accumulation* possibilities. In turn, the increase in accumulation (investments) is the point of departure for all economic development. Without increased accumulation neither the volume of the available productive capacities nor the productivity of labour can be raised. In the first period of economic growth accumulation must be increased at the expense of consumption, but its possibilities are insignificant in countries where per capita national income is low and the population (labour force) is undernourished. On the other hand, in the present-day economic structure the accumulation possibilities are liable to fragmentation as very few large-scale plants and enterprises are owned by the state or domestic private capitalists. On the other hand, foreign settlers' capital of colonial origin repatriates most of its profits. The main state revenues are the various taxes (usually indirect ones), which generally suffice to cover only the "classical" state expenditures.

Under such circumstances the economically less-developed countries heavily rely, in addition to the mobilization of their own resources, on *credits* in order to achieve accelerated economic growth. Just to show the proportions, we wish to mention that in the framework of the First Development Decade (1960–1970) the UN wanted to raise a total of 70 billion dollars in the form of credits, while even the present annual level of 15 billion dollars' worth of loans and grants cannot be regarded as sufficient.

According to the *form* of provision, credits, aids and grants may be classified as
(a) bilateral;

226

(b) regional (the development of the member countries of the Common Market for the Associated African Countries, Alliance for Progress, etc.);

(c) multilateral (grants provided by the UN or other international organizations).

According to their *destination,* credits, aids and grants may be classified as

(a) commercial;

(b) serving economic development;

(c) military (e. g. aid provided by the United States to South Korea, Taiwan, South Vietnam, the Philippines);

(d) serving the maintenance of the budget equilibrium (e. g. assistance provided by France to the members of the Communauté).

Foreign private capital invests today primarily in case of government guarantees.

Credits given by the socialist countries represent a successful combination of development and commercial credits. Of a *developmental character* are these credits primarily owing to the fact that they are provided in the form of investment goods, and *commercial,* because they are to be used exclusively for buying the goods of the creditor country.

But the magnitude of the investments is not exclusively a function of internal accumulation and credits. Any country can make investments – under economical conditions – only to the extent of its economic organization (level of economic institutions, number and qualification of specialists, supply of communal services, etc.). Therefore, in the case of building new plants the greatest problem is posed by the transfer of *knowledge and production experience.* Without their transfer, investments are not implemented, and the new plants are not profitable. Therefore, the socialist countries emphasize in an appropriate form the solving of the problems of *technical assistance* (transfer of scientific and production experience in an organized way). (This question will be dealt with later in more detail).

Credits provided by the socialist countries imply many *advantages* for the developing countries. Such are:

(a) socialist countries extend credits exclusively for governments promoting and strengthening thereby the economic, organizational and guiding activities of the state;

(b) socialist credits promote the growth and development of investments;

(c) credits are combined with technical assistance;

(d) credits are provided at a low rate of interest, and the receiver country may repay them by their own commodities;

(e) credits are free from all economic expansion and neo-colonialist endeavours.

The socialist countries are able to provide of course credits far below the actual needs of the developing countries. Therefore, these latter are compelled to accept credits offered by capitalist countries or institutions as well.

But the favourable and constructive terms of credits given by the socialist countries exert a considerable influence on the credit terms of capitalist countries or companies.

Under such conditions, the governments of the national democratic countries can considerably and in various forms restrict the neo-colonialist endeavours.

The degree of economic dependence on the ex-colonizing countries and the import-sensitivity of the underdeveloped economies is the second limiting factor of economic growth. The negative effect of this factor makes itself felt through international trade. Under colonization, foreign capital developed – as we have seen – only the production of such goods in these countries for which the colonizing country represented the largest market. Therefore, their traditional economic relations cannot be broken off from one year to another. The demand for these commodities (primarily tropical foodstuffs and raw materials) is *inelastic* in the world market, which means that, under the given conditions, the market cannot be expanded as fast as production. In the case of such commodities the formation of prices depends on the big purchasing and processing monopolies.

On the other hand, at the time of accelerating economic development, the import needs of these countries grow much faster than their export possibilities (that is why we speak of an import-sensitive economy). It must also be noted that the world-market terms of trade have shifted to the disadvantage of the primary-producing countries during the past decade. And raw materials constitute 76 per cent of the exports of the less developed countries.

In order to diminish their foreign-trade dependence and import-sensitivity, the developing countries should try to enforce the following viewpoints in their economic policy:

(a) They should ensure ever-increasing markets for their existing export products. In this endeavour they are supported by the socialist countries, which buy from them more and more tropical foodstuffs and raw materials year by year.

(b) By political and economic means (e.g. by commodity agreements ensuring the co-ordination of production and consumption) they must succeed in improving the unfavourable world-market terms of trade. The socialist countries support them on all international political and economic forums to attain this aim.

(c) In developing their industry, they should give priority to the import-saving branches. To meet this requirement of economic policy, they can rely on the socialist countries, which help them with technical advice and delivering complete plants.

(d) The requirements of import saving and export expansion are closely interrelated. An import-saving industry of today will be capable of exporting tomorrow. This change will materialize especially rapidly in industries in which the low wages constitute a comparative advantage (e.g. in the cotton textile industry). Of great importance is the fact that the socialist countries will buy to an ever-increasing extent finished products and not only raw materials from the less-developed countries. (Today, the share of finished products in socialist imports from the developing countries is not yet satisfactory.)

228

The low level of the "economic environment" (schooling, public health, roads, water supply, etc.) and especially the shortage of highly qualified labour force is the third factor limiting economic growth.

The acceleration of economic growth does not necessarily mean the concentration and planned distribution of material resources only, but also "human investments". Certain non-economic factors, such as scientific research, education and vocational training as well as health service also exert a considerable influence on the development of economic processes.

VIII. POSSIBILITIES AND PROBLEMS OF THE DEVELOPING WORLD IN THE NEW SITUATION EVOLVING IN THE WORLD ECONOMY SINCE 1973

The price rises of oil and other mineral raw materials since the end of 1973 have opened up new prospects and raised new problems in the developing world. What is involved in this new situation is not merely a simple price rise, but – as a result of the measure of price changes and the character of the goods affected by them – it amounts to a regrouping of power relations in the world economy.

The multiplied export earnings of the oil-producing developing countries would bring about new power relations even if they imported, in exchange for their oil exports, new technology (machines, equipment, fertilizers, etc.) needed for their own development. This will presumably be the case with countries which have a sufficiently large population and territory. For small countries, however, like those around the Persian Gulf, or Saudi Arabia with a small number of population it would not be rational to develop a kind of "national economic structure". Even in the case of a rational economic development, these small and sparsely populated countries would be unable to spend their incomes on their own domestic development.

Under such circumstances, the group of oil-producing countries as a new centre of economic power should decide on how they wish to utilize their available surpluses. This new centre of economic power is peculiar in the sense that its structure is different from the usual one. Its coming into existence means that the economic power *in the monetary field* is divided in a different way in production, technology, the technical science and highly qualified manpower. From this follows that the leading capitalist countries are striving to isolate the new elements which have penetrated into the sphere of economic power, and subsequently to restore the old power relations. The monetary resources concentrated in the new centre of economic power cause a twofold problem for the capitalist world: first, these resources are missing in the capital circulation of the countries in question (e. g. investments and, consequently, consumption will decline) and, secondly, they may give rise to further difficulties by the disruption of international monetary equilibrium. The capitalist world will defend itself against this double danger by applying all possible forms of political and economic pressure (a military form of pressure is hardly possible), but this situation involves at the same time new possibilites for the capitalist owners in the developing countries. The pressure and the offering of attractive possibilities alike serve the aim that the capitalist owners should tie up their capitals on long repayment terms, in other words, that the oil earnings should be recycled in the capitalist economy for a long time. The recycling of oil funds (petrodollars) in the dynamic industries promises high profits, greater influence in the world of finance capital.

Simultaneously, a vigorous *polarization* is taking place in the developing world. Oil-producing countries with a small or medium-sized population may rise to the level of the developed countries within a short time, though their diversified and balanced economic growth (without extreme income differentials) can materialize only if further radical social reforms are introduced. Certain countries with significant oil outputs and a larger population (e. g. Indonesia, Nigeria, etc.) may speed up the rate of their economic growth by oil exports. Those developing countries which have available certain industrial raw materials of importance for the international economy have also come into a more favourable situation. But the economic position of the fourth group of developing countries (India, Bangladesh, the Sahel countries, etc.) has become extremely difficult, almost catastrophic. They have to continue to import oil, which serves primarily production purposes, since such uses of oil as the driving of passenger cars and the heating of flats play a very insignificant part in the utilization structure of these countries.

These countries have also to rely on imports of other industrial raw materials, agricultural products and chemical fertilizers. The development possibilities of this group of countries consisting of 40 nations and comprising one thousand million inhabitants have got stuck, and their nutrition problems have assumed intolerable proportions.

These countries suffering from immense hardships – and *representing 25 per cent of mankind* – can only be saved by a wide-based international co-operation. Part of their energy imports have to be met free of charge, and most of international aid has to be concentrated in them. In the extension of credits and the various aid activities all countries should take part, including – among others – those countries which, thanks to the rise in oil prices, have become able to build up significant monetary reserves. Moreover, efforts must also be made to help these countries by granting them loans in such forms and on such maturity terms as can be met by them with reasonable efforts.

From the point of view of the developing countries the most important feature of the new world-economic situation is the fact that for the first time in history they have been given a financing possibility which creates the condition of liquidating economic underdevelopment as a world phenomenon, – and potentially for the developing world as a whole, at that if the oil-producing countries directly engage in international development financing and invest their capital, in addition to accelerating their own economic growth (instead of directing their funds towards the developed capitalist countries) in financing the growth of the other developing countries, then there is every hope that in the 1980s a decisive change will take place in the situation of the developing world, and that the gap still existing between them and the developed countries will become narrower.

PART THREE

PLANNING AND PLAN IMPLEMENTATION IN DEVELOPING COUNTRIES

by

Mihály Simai

INTRODUCTION

The countries of the "Third World" are immensely different in respect of their development possibilities, structural conditions and the efficiency of their institutions. It stands to reason, therefore, that planning strategies and planning systems can only be formulated and evaluated correctly in the light of the specific circumstances of individual countries. On the other hand, it is also true that certain impediments to the processes of planning and plan implementation are often so recurrent even under different conditions that the common nature of some of their problems cannot be overlooked.

At the end of the 1960s national economic plans were already prepared in nearly 100 countries of the world. About 60 of the "planning countries" are developing countries. There are among them countries in which planning efforts and attempts can be traced back to two decades, and there are again a few, e.g. some countries in Latin America and Turkey, where the history of planning goes back to even earlier times. But the planning practice of the majority of developing countries has only a past of about 10 to 15 years.

The spread of the ideology and practice of planning in developing countries is not merely a technical or organizational question, it is the result of social struggles fought both in individual countries and on the international plane. It is a historic fact that from the early 1950s, i.e. since the problem of economic development came to the fore on various international forums, it is the socialist countries which have suggested the introduction of economic planning for promoting development while the industrially advanced capitalist countries have offered the "market model" for the developing world. Most of their economists and politicians have identified planning with "communism" and rejected it. It is also true that there were economists in socialist countries too who, for a number of years, considered planning as a specific characteristic, a "monopoly" of socialist economy, holding socialism and planned economy to be the only possible practical form of planning, and identified capitalism entirely with the concept of economic liberalism.

At first, planning in developing countries, too, was the slogan only of progressive national forces, a means for pooling their scarce resources, capital and skilled labour, and for liquidating the centuries-old heritage of social and economic rigidity. In this sense, planned economic development meant a revolutionary method of radically breaking away from the past. It was the successes of socialist countries, primarily of the Soviet Union, which made both the ideology and practice of planning popular among the progressive national forces.

Most of the theoreticians and practical experts of bourgeois planning have proved surprisingly forgetful about the origin of planning of the national economy. The American Professor Bertram Gross, one of the outstanding Western authorities on planning, tries to deduce plan preparation in developing countries from the general "planning"qualities of man.[1] In the meantime he ignores the fact that individual and social activities are different. In order to achieve planning at the social level, certain changes need to have taken place.

On the other hand, certain bourgeois economists concerned with planning in developing countries acknowledge the pioneering role of socialist countries and the great significance of their experiences. For example, the Swedish economist Gunnar Myrdal, though not devoting too much room to socialist experiences in his famous work Asian Drama, writes in the chapter on the Spread and Impact of the Ideology of Planning: "...that the ideological influences from the Communist world have been strong is quite apparent. Very generally, but particularly in India, Burma, and Indonesia, the intellectual and political leaders had received strong impulses from the Russian revolution... The five-year plans of the Soviet Union were recognized as the pioneering attempt... to engender economic development..., which has not spent its force."[2]

Some of the Western bourgeois economists have recognized the wider implications of the attractive force of socialist planning. It was due partly to this recognition that in the Western economic literature of the 1960s – as also mentioned by Myrdal – the idea of "democratic" planning made its appearance as an alternative to "communist" planning. Certain bourgeois planning experts have declared this so-called "democratic" planning to be in competition with "Communist planning".[3] *In this way, however, they have reduced the complex social interconnections of economic growth to a faulty alternative.*

Planning as a technical tool has become not only in the socialist and developing countries but also in many developed capitalist countries an important instrument of economic policy, clearly reflecting the fact that the classical mechanisms of capitalism are unable to cope with the immense problems of developing or industrially advanced capitalist countries. In reality, however, the contents and objectives of planning depend on the character of society, the power relations and structure of classes and strata within them. It is these factors that determine the conditions, nature, peculiarities and applicable means of planning.

Planning in developing or in industrially advanced capitalist countries is of course not identical with socialist planned economy. The latter is based on the central management of the national economy as a whole, including the influence exerted on the relationship of enterprises and individuals. The socio-political precondition for a socialist planned economy is the existence of the socialist state

[1] *The Administration of Economic Development Planning.* New York, 1966, U.N., p. 1.
[2] G. Myrdal: *Asian Drama.* Vol. II, New York, 1968, pp. 726–727.
[3] *Planning for Economic Development.* Vol. II, U.N. New York, 1965, p. 20.

and the social ownership of the principal means of production. The function of socialist ownership is exercised, on behalf of society, by the socialist state.

The social and economic preconditions for state planning in non-socialist countries are more limited, and its basis is accordingly narrower.

It stands to reason that in practice the capitalist and socialist systems are very broad categories, and there are considerable differences in the forms and contents of planning even within the framework of the given systems. In addition, the so-called "Third World" greatly differs from the socialist and the industrially advanced capitalist countries, too. Significant are the social and economic differences also between individual developing countries. It is beyond doubt that these differences also influence the characteristics of planning.

Thus the confrontation of and competition between "democratic" and "capitalist" planning is not only misleading but it does not even correspond to today's realities either.

At a certain stage of socialist development the system of administrative planning instructions had many common features in individual countries, and the system of compulsory plan targets broken down to their minute details represented for many planners the socialist form of planning. There were economists and politicians in socialist countries, too, who held this method to be the only possible form of socialist planning and even of planning in general. And the opponents of socialism identified this with socialism. The situation has changed radically during the past two decades.

But even under the system of central directives the planning experiences of socialist countries did not mean administrative methods only, as the formation of this instruction-based planning system was justified by certain circumstances and the concrete tasks to be performed – factors that show similarities with the problems also facing today's developing countries. Therefore, when examining the planning of developing countries, it is worthwhile and necessary to clarify – duly considering the existing differences – what concrete conclusions may be drawn for the developing countries from the planning experiences of socialist countries.

I. SOCIALIST PLANNING AND THE DEVELOPING COUNTRIES

The methods of planning and plan implementation applied by socialist countries have been determined in the final analysis by the prevailing social and political relations. Nevertheless, the impact of socialist planning on countries with different social and economic systems was considerable even in the past. At the socio-political level this manifested itself in the growing popularity of socialism. There is hardly a single country in the developing world that would openly profess itself as a capitalist one, or would set the establishment of capitalist order as the aim of its economic policy. Very often even big capitalist or feudal circles use "socialist" phraseology without making, of course, the least effort to realize anything like an equal distribution of incomes, or to ease the cruel forms of exploitation.

The influence of socialism also manifests itself in the general acknowledgement of the advantages of development planning by the developing countries.

It is also true that in many countries methods have been introduced – with some modifications – which were first tried out in socialist countries, primarily in the Soviet Union. It will suffice here to make mention only of the choice of the five-year plan period, the use of material balances and other methods, the internal organization of planning agencies, planning offices, ministries of planning and their relationship with various legislative and executive organs, and, to some extent, also of the fact that the aggregate plan targets have been formulated and their feasibility ensured in the course of regular consultations with economic organs at different levels.

Bourgeois economists engaged in planning generally emphasize that the conditions under which socialist countries developed their planning systems had greatly differed from those which were now typical of most of the developing countries. This is of course true in many respects. But it is also a fact that the conditions of many developing countries are not identical, nor are those of several socialist countries. The most essential differences between socialist and developing countries lie in their economic and social relations, playing a decisive role in planning and plan implementation. Along with these differences there are also many similarities in fields which are highly important for planning and development policy. Economic underdevelopment must be put an end to within a relatively short time. In order to achieve this objective, the developing countries must bring about enormous structural changes. They must not only break the

238

resistance of forces opposing these changes but must also make broad masses of people interested in carrying them out. At the same time they also have to reckon with the emergence and increasing pressure of many new needs (e. g. in the field of accumulation and consumption). It must be ensured that accumulation realized in non-convertible currency or agricultural products is converted into modern machinery and equipment, etc. The analysis of the planning experiences of developing countries provides the evidence that they could have seen many problems more clearly and could have avoided many pitfalls if they had known and properly utilized the experiences of socialist countries. But this has usually not happened. True, the socialist countries have also failed to do everything to analyse critically their own planning systems and experiences, which would also have been of use to developing countries.

The scope of our study does not make it possible for us to summarize systematically the experiences gained by socialist countries in the development of their planning systems. Obviously, what is of interest and importance to developing countries is primarily the analysis of the initiation, first steps, successes and failures of socialist planning. It was during this period that the heavily centralized system of planning based on instructions and directives evolved, closely connected with the ambitious objectives and the efforts needed to achieve them. The social ownership of the means of production provided good possibilities for the centralized system of plan instructions. And the commitment to build a communist society – as the ultimate aim – strongly influenced the priorities of planning from the very outset. Incidentally, in this respect the position of socialist countries greatly differs from that of the developing countries. The impact of these factors on the implementation of plans was also of great significance. It made it possible for the socialist countries to build up their complex hierarchic system of planning, ranging from the planning office through the economic ministries down to individual enterprises. The targets included in the central plan were passed on to the lower organs in a gradually detailed form by way of compulsory instructions. These instructions were meant to encompass the whole system of economic activities of productive units and also to exercise a direct control over their interrelationships. This system also made it possible for the management to involve all excutive organs in the preparation of state plans. (Needless to say that a certain degree of participation of producers is also possible under other socio-economic systems.)

As already mentioned, the objective directed towards the establishment of socio-economic relations of a socialist-communist society also left their mark on planning. As we regard planning as a tool to transform the economy and society, the impact of political aims on the implementation of plans is significant. The influence of political conceptions on the planning of socialist countries was different in various periods of time. But the general objectives always played a decisive role in strengthening the social ownership of the means of production and gradually increased the share of social consumption in overall consumption

239

(i. e. of a consumption which is placed at the disposal of consumers free of charge, irrespective of differences in incomes).

In the light of the planning experiences of the individual socialist countries it has become clear by now that the methods of plan implementation applied by the Soviet Union during an earlier period cannot be regarded as the only possible way of directing and planning a socialist economy. When examining the question in its historical perspective we must come to the conclusion that at the time of initiating the first planning system there were hardly any alternatives that could have been adopted in the given historical situation.

Some of the lessons that can be drawn from the planning experiences of socialist countries are of an organizational and technical character. Despite social differences there are also some very significant socio-political lessons. Among them the one that the organizational and technical conditions have to be treated in a close relationship with decisions on economic policy, since the process of economic management includes a great many interrelated and interdependent stages: the preparation of economic forecasts, planning, plan implementation, the checking of the results of economic management and the correction of undesirable consequences of the impacts of management on individual projects.

At every stage specific tasks have to be solved, and appropriate organizations have to be established. The individual stages needed to be closely interrelated.

In socialist countries the content of plans developed *as a rule* in compliance with the implementation possibilities and the methods used.

The path of the development of planning is marked with significant successes and occasional failures. But even the failures did not lead to pushing planning into the background and decreasing its weight and significance. It was the socialist countries which evolved the most comprehensive and most detailed development plans. The technique of planning underwent a highly impressive development. For example, in the Soviet Union, in the late 1920s comprehensive national economic plans were drawn up simply by compounding the plans of individual sectors. In the late 1960s, however, integrated multi-variant plans based on simulation were already worked out. They tried to prepare optimum plan variants as a function of the tasks set.

The socialist countries strove to prevent the planning process from breaking away from the policy of plan implementation, typical of many developing countries, which frequently formulate the objectives without taking account of their feasibility and backing them up with further decisions on their implementation.

Further on, socialist planning provides the lesson that the introduction of an active development policy should not be delayed until appropriate data, information and knowledge are available for the formulation of an overall and fully elaborated plan.

The lack or unsatisfactory quality of statistical data were never used as a pretext by socialist countries to give up their planning efforts.

240

In the initial development stages of the Soviet Union the actions of the government were concentrated on strategic tasks which had an important indirect influence on the entire economy. The lack of statistical data and the shortage of skilled manpower, organizational deficiencies and the overall state of the economy made it impossible to prepare in this stage such a comprehensive plan which could be fulfilled in all its details. The operative programmes of the economic policy were designed to solve specific problems. Very often these programmes were connected with current emergency measures rather than with long-term development objectives. Later on, however, the operative programmes were already focused on central tasks deemed to be essential also for long-term economic growth. The efforts to implement limited aims were regarded more important than the elaboration of a comprehensive plan for the fulfilment of which the means were not available.

The technical preconditions for preparing comprehensive plans evolved and gradually improved in the practice of planning and plan implementation. Remarkable in this respect is the development of the plan and statistics.

The view that large-scale state intervention is essential in controlling the economic processes in order to secure the attainment of social objectives in economic management determined every state of the development of socialist countries. The scope of plans, the number of plan targets, the degree and nature of their breakdown as a guideline, an indicator of orientation and compulsory instruction for the central authorities, or as a directive for the executive organs at various levels changed from time to time. In any case, however, even when the compulsory instructions were limited to special sectors or branches, the choice largely depended on the effect they exercised on the economy as a whole rather than on the usefulness of profitability of individual undertakings.

The first long-range plan elaborated in the Soviet Union in 1920 for a 15-year period was concentrated on the development of electric power generation. But even this plan was not treated in isolation from the general problems of economic growth. From the very beginning it served as a focal point, around which other plan targets were also wet. (First, they were targets relating to the means of production needed for the electric power grid, later a more integrated plan was drawn up for the entire economy.)

The first comprehensive medium-term plan was worked out only in 1928. Not unlike the first Soviet plan, the first reconstruction plans of other socialist countries after the Second World War were far less comprehensive than the Soviet five-year plans or their own plans prepared later. Later on, the plans of these countries contained a large number of targets covering, along with the state sector, the co-operative and private sectors, too, which, at the time of the initial stages of planning, were of considerable importance, especially in agriculture. During the period of consistent and detailed planning it also occurred that the implementation of medium-term plans were stopped before the end of the plan period because of the emergence of unforeseen circumstances, or because it was realized that the plans were originally faulty, which became apparent in the course of implementation. It also happened that no new medium-term plans were immediately substituted for the suspended plans. But this did not mean the weakening of an active development policy, as it was directed in these intervals by stop-gap plans.

First in history, the socialist countries made determined efforts – under the system of a complex, comprehensive planned economy – to create the personal conditions for economic and social development by a large-scale widening of their educational systems, a cultural revolution in the strict sense of the term, which made possible the raising of the cultural levels of the widest masses, and thereby an unprecedented increase in their productive potentials. Simultaneously, or parallel with the production priorities, the main fields of the structural transformation of the educational system were also identified. It was only in the late 1950s and the early 1960s that the developed capitalist countries came to realize the outstanding importance of developing the personal conditions. The socialist countries modernized their educational systems at all levels already in the early stages of their development, and linked them up with measures taken to solve the tasks of economic development. These changes found their expression in the significant increase in the number of teachers, the rising ratio of the training of engineers and technicians, the large-scale development of the network of various industrial and agricultural vocational schools, etc. It was these changes that made it possible to decrease considerably the shortage of skilled labour impeding economic development, and to create the conditions for cadre development.

In theory, socialist countries always regarded it as an irrational and misleading practice to elaborate such comprehensive plans which covered all fields and were independent of the possibility or will to implement them. On the other hand, it is also true that the lack of directly available means needed to implement comprehensive plans never led to the acceptance of plans with a narrower basis than that of the previous ones. On the contrary, considerable efforts were made to improve the necessary implementation conditions in every sector of the economy.

This practice has not changed even after the introduction of the reforms of economic management. The reforms have not abolished the system of central planning, they have rather strengthened and improved the scientific character of planning. A number of new methods of central planning have been adopted. At the same time the independence of state enterprises has been substantially increased, and the number of compulsory plan instructions has been reduced. In some countries these reforms have virtually put an end to the planning method based on administrative instructions and are widely applying material incentives with a major role being assigned to market considerations. From the point of view of plan implementation these changes bring state enterprises with respect to their activities into a position similar to a certain extent to those in developing countries. As the formulation of plans in socialist countries is closely connected with the possibility of realizing, implementing individual plan targets, the adoption of new implementation methods also exerts a significant impact on the content of plans, the number, nature and measure of the breakdown of plan targets.

Thus the increased role of market mechanism does not diminish the role of central planning and state intervention in the economic processes, and does not overshadow it. But it brings about important changes in methods. The aim of these changes is to diminish considerably state intervention in the daily activities of enterprises and productive units. Instead, the government increasingly stimulates the enterprises to carry on their activities in the framework of the general objectives of economic policy. In this stimulation use is made of the means of budget and credit policies as well as of price policy and other factors.

As a result of the new system of economic management several questions of economic development have come to the fore, gaining new dimensions by economic reforms. Most important of these questions and also of considerable interest to developing countries are these:

– Should the national plan contain targets that cannot be reached by state instructions or budget financing?

– What should be the degree of direct state intervention?

– Should state intervention be reduced to the means of an overall economic policy or should it influence the economy by a selective policy affecting different areas in a different way?

In connection with these changes it must also be noted that even under the most centralized system the activities of enterprises could not entirely be reduced to instructions. In spite of the fact that nearly all forms of the activities of enterprises were based on directives, the implementation of compulsory plan targets was stimulated by bonuses or their withdrawal.

The organization of the process of plan implementation, the control over implementation can also serve as an important positive lesson for the developing countries. The method of cost-benefit analysis to appraise the effect of inputs celebrated as a new discovery in the economic literature of the recent past, a method going beyond the direct profitability of individual establishments and taking into account social benefit, was also born in the practice of socialist countries and has since gained wide acceptance.

In assessing the planning experiences of socialist countries it is of course necessary to make mention of certain problems that the socialist pioneers of planned economy have not been able, for objective or subjective reasons, fully to avoid.

One of the most important problems was voluntarism, arising out of the oversimplified interpretation of economic processes and the overestimation of the possibilities of planning authorities and their power over the economy. In the elaboration of plans voluntarism became apparent in overestimating the performing capacity of the economy and setting unrealistic development targets with irresponsible optimism. As a result, certain plan targets could not be reached, and serious discrepancies arose.

The source of voluntarism should not be simply traced back to the qualities of individual persons. It is a possibility arising out of the essence of the planning process. Actually, planners are concerned with quantities and establish relationships and linkages which do not yet exist in reality. If no use is made in the course of planning of the checking forces existing in socialist economy and society, e. g. the inclusion of committees of scientists and specialists, and the mechanisms channelling the opinions of masses and organizations participating in the implementation of plans, and no regular dialogue is conducted with them, then the ever-existing possibility of voluntarism cannot sufficiently be stemmed.

Of the negative experiences gained in the course of the planning processes mention must also be made of the danger of red tape. Its incidence is undoubtedly the greatest in the administrative system of plan instructions, but is by no means restricted to this system only. The mechanisms of this planning method may lead to conflicting interests among the organs of economic management. These conflicts manifest themselves, among other things, in disguised reserves and bargainings during planning discussions. They may unfavourably affect the relationship of the economic authorities concerned and may also exert their impact upon the level of planning and plan implementation. Squandering, irresponsible management, the high costs of economic development – these are for planning the principal consequences of the spread of bureaucratic methods.

The main counteracting force against the danger of the bureaucracy is the democratization of the planning and plan implementation processes, the inclusion of wide masses at all stages of planning, plan implementation and control. Socialist countries have done much more in this respect than any other "planning" state. This has become apparent, among other things, in the formulation of objectives clearly understood and supported by the widest masses and their mobilization for implementation. The Swedish economist Myrdal complains that in many Asian countries economic planning is the matter of a narrow élite and gets lost in the general passivity and indifference of the masses. The experiences of socialist countries provide the evidence that correctly set objectives, reasonable plans, whose implementation has a favourable effect on the economic position of the wide masses and the interests of the country in question, can break the passive attitude of people and involve them in the creative process of great economic and social transformations.

II. PLANNING CONDITIONS IN DEVELOPING COUNTRIES

In the relevant literature there has been made hardly any attempt so far to analyse critically the planning practice of developing countries. Thousands of studies have been published on planning in general or its various aspects, in particular. This literature, however, is largely confined to laying down certain principles.[4]

The problems of economic policy are dealt with elsewhere in the present volume. It is unavoidable, however, to comment occasionally on the relationship between planning and economic policy as the objectives and means take shape in a close interdependence, and therefore a certain degree of overlap cannot be dispensed with.

The dependence of the planning process on *economic policy* follows from the very nature of the former.

Economic policy and plan must develop in a close interrelationship in any well-operating planning system.

Logical considerations and concrete analyses also prove that planning conditions show a great deal of variety between individual developing countries.

Different are, first of all, the economic conditions.

The shares of subsistence economy and the market sector as well as the developmental levels of commodity and money relations differ to a great extent. The relative weight of small-scale, cottage and large-scale industries in the so-called market sector are not identical either. In the modern private sector of industry the ratio of national to foreign capital is also different. There are important discrepancies in the relationship of the public and private sectors. These structural changes in the ownership relations in general and land ownership in particular play a significant role in shaping the content and forms of planning. The great share of private ownership and subsistence economy e. g. considerably diminishes the applicable forms of planning and restricts its instruments. It has been realized in many developing countries that the forms of planning applied cannot be, and are not in practice, the passive consequences of the structure of

---

[4] So far the greatest efforts at a comparative evaluation of the planning experiences of developing countries have been made by the United Nations Development Planning Commission and the United Nations Centre for Economic Development, Planning and Prognostics. The U.N. Development Planning Commission has evaluated the experiences of planning and plan implementation in Latin America, Africa and South-East Asia. The author of the present study has taken part in the research on the first two regions, and has made a partial use in this work of his papers written on the subject.

ownership relations. A consequence of ownership relations and of the institutional system corresponding to them is economic stagnation. On the other hand, the introduction of planning to economic life presupposes the stimulation of the economy, the promotion of dynamic economic growth. This process, in turn, exerts an active reaction on the ownership relations.

Developing countries also differ in their political and economic developmental levels. This fact has its implications not only for differences in the objectives of their economic policies but also results in considerable differences in the means needed to attain these objectives. Substantial are these differences both as regards aims and means, depending on whether the country concerned has made any progress in the social and economic structural transformation connected with industrialization, or is just on its threshold.

The determination of aims and means is not only, and not primarily, an economic problem in developing countries. It is substantially influenced by the character of political power, which may have different views on these problems. Accordingly, the priorities will also be different, and so will be the approach to the direct and long-term aims of raising the living standards, and to the various, so-called non-economic aspects of the living conditions. The role of political power in planning is not confined, however, to the formulation of objectives only. Its crucial significance makes it imperative to analyse its role in planning separately.

1. THE ROLE OF POLITICAL POWER IN THE PLANNING OF DEVELOPING COUNTRIES

In any planning system the determination of the general objectives is economically meaningful only if the potential means and methods needed to attain them have been identified. If these objectives are determined by the authorities in power without their taking into account the possibilities and limitations set by the available resources, it is bound to cause serious disruptions and problems in the work of the planning agencies and the plans themselves. This phenomenon is very common in developing countries. In addition to incompetency, subjectivism and prestige reasons, a major role is also played in it by the political groups in power using the plan for political propaganda purposes against the opposition forces and setting irrealistic aims to overbid them. The setting of such objectives is often motivated by impatience and the endeavour to speed up development. Brazil's three-year plan for 1963–1965 wanted to concentrate on a short plan period the slowing down of inflation, the speeding up of economic growth, the rapid development of public education, public health service and scientific research, the diminishing of developmental differences between various regions of the country, the carrying out of a land reform, etc. It is of course impossible to solve such tasks simultaneously, especially over such a short period of time.

In the context of objectives and means essential political problems also present themselves, such as e. g. how to make the necessary material resources available:

246

should the rich or the poor be taxed more heavily, what foreign aid, and under what conditions, should be accepted, etc.

In spite of the fact that some sort of planning is adopted in practically every developing country, there is nevertheless significant *political opposition to planning* even in our days. It is not only the most reactionary forces of the society of the country concerned which are opposed to planning (being afraid primarily of the necessary reforms) but also some local capitalist groups, which think that certain plan targets prejudice their interests. A disguised and even open resistance can often be witnessed against planning in many developing countries on part of foreign capital operating in the extractive industries. When analysing the planning systems of developing countries it is therefore of paramount interest to be acquainted with the political and power relations and centres. It is important to know, e.g., what organs, at what level, of what composition and political orientation are authorized to make decisions on problems relating to the content and forms of the plan.[5]

The length of the plan period, one of the most important techncial decisions concerning planning, is to some extent also a political question, as its implications for the cycles of political life (e.g. elections) are not indifferent at all. A very important political question is the weight and role of the planning agencies and their relationship to the various institutions. The centre of planning are the planning commissions and planning offices, whose authority varies depending on the position they assume in the hierarchy of state administration. *The activity of the central planning organ is more effective if it has come into being as a result of an important reform of administration* and also enjoys a greater political power owing to the fact that it is subordinated directly to the president of the republic, the head of state or the collective body of state administration.

In case the introduction of planning is not accompanied by a significant reform of administration, the most important conflict concerning planning usually develops in the state apparatus between the central planning organ and the Ministry of Finance, which is the traditional depository of the economic tasks of the state apparatus. The practice of developing countries shows great differences in creating the political-administrative conditions of planning.

It may occur that the central planning body operates as an independent entity in direct subordination to the presidential office of the council of ministers (e. g. in Venezuela in the case of the Cordiplan). Sometimes it is only one of the numerous ministries, and there is no relation whatever of sub- or superordination between the planning organ and the other ministries (as in Syria). This solution in itself is a source of serious conflicts, as the other ministries often do not acknowledge the special authority of the Ministry of Planning. This situation is somewhat mitigated in some countries (e.g. in Pakistan), where inter-ministerial committees

---

[5] See in more detail: *Proceedings of the Conference on the Implementation Problems and Government Decisions in the Countries of Black Africa.* Center for Afro-Asian Research. Budapest, 1971, pp. 13–72.

composed of the representatives of economic ministries operate in planning as "collective decision-making bodies".

The Planning Office is often an independent unit which is responsible only technically for the preparation of plans without having any other function (as in Mexico). Thus the central planning body is far away from the power centres, where the essential decisions are made. Experience shows that planning is much more effective if the central planning organ is not merely a technical but also an important political body.

The close relationship between the various ministries, higher authorities and other state organs, on the one hand, and the planning centre, on the other, ensures greater flexibility. It makes it possible to bring about better co-ordination at every stage of planning. But it is also an important question in many developing countries what status the responsible leader of the central planning organ has in the government. If he is only a "technical manager", he is at a disadvantage in relation to the ministers, and this has its harmful effect on the weight of the body he is in charge of.

In several developing countries important administrative changes were also carried out when planning was introduced, and a central role was assigned to the planning commission and/or planning offices. Sometimes special groups, departments were set up in individual ministries or in the bodies of local self-government, which are responsible for the planning activity. These are often in close connection with the planning offices. But this system cannot fully eliminate the troubles arising mainly out of conflicts of authority in the state apparatus of developing countries.

A frequent problem is posed by the central organs becoming bureaucratic, and their too meticulous, operative intervention in economic life. In this respect India's example is not an isolated phenomenon. Mainly at the request of the late Prime Minister Nehru, the Indian government vested the planning commission with wide powers. In the 1950s the planning commission was a highly important organization with great authority. By the 1960s the situation had changed. In the second half of the 1960s, the bureaucratic planning apparatus, in the first place the central planning organ, was blamed for the failure and discredit of the plans. On account of the failure of the third five-year plan and the troubles of the fourth plan, the planning commission was reorganized as it was realized that it had been unable to cope with its tasks. Originally, Nehru was also a member of the planning commission in order to add weight to it. After his death the level of the planning commission gradually declined. Many of its members (especially the ministers) fulfilled their tasks only formally. The staff of the planning commission grew fivefold during 10 years – and this increase was due almost entirely to a rise in the administrative and not the expert personnel. Instead of dealing with long-term problems and structural questions of the economy, the planning apparatus engrossed in operative details. All this contributed to the right-wing attacks against planning.[6] By reorganizing and "rejuvenating" the planning commission,

[6] *Economic and Political Weekly*. Bombay, February 25, 1967.

Indira Ghandi's government tried to restore the authority of the planning commission and of planning in general in India.

Under the conditions of developing countries the *continuity of power* is a highly important political question in respect to planning. In the 1960s the frequent coups d'état in certain African and Latin American countries discredited the planning system as a whole.

Occasionally, the quickly changing political sphere led to the development of peculiar conflicts between specialists and politicians.

The specialists demanded greater independence in planning. They stressed that given their special skills and education they were suited better than the politicians to perform the tasks of economic management, to set the targets of the plans. (No doubt, the planners or planning economists have a major role to play in elaborating the plan and influencing its final process. But the planners, as evidenced by the example of several Latin-American countries, rarely came off victoriously out of the conflict between political power and specialists.) As a result of frequent political changes and the specific consequences of conflicts between specialists and politicians, the opinion was formed in many countries that since the political sphere often changes, the economic sphere should be left to specialists, it should be separated from politics. As a result of this process, some specialists also professed the view that plans should be extremely modest so as not to disturb the existing political order. They must be such as to satisfy the needs of subsequent regimes. (This was the view held by the planners in Brazil and Venezuela in the 1960s.) It is of course impossible to prepare such plans. Planning at the national level cannot be politically indifferent in any country of the world, as there is no politically indifferent state power either.

In some countries of the developing world, as in Latin America, it is of course also very common that *planning specialists are politically more radical,* representing other socio-political forces than the government, and conduct an active fight for socio-economic reforms by means of planning. This conflict also has a role to play in it that certain conservative politicians, mainly in Latin America, oppose planning, or try to reduce plans to insignificant documents, to mere paperwork.

There are also political conflicts of a different kind concentrating around planning. In spite of the fact that, e.g., governments often adopt planning as a means of an interlinked, comprehensive policy, there is no effective agreement in the political sphere on the accepted objectives of planning. Certain forces in the government often regard the plan merely as an instrument to mobilize external financial resources to obtain foreign aid. It is for this reason that special importance is attached to such questions in the plan which have a direct bearing on foreign support. Other groups in the government or the ruling party would like to make use of the plan, both theoretically and practically, as a revolutionary means of social action to carry out the expedient, indispensable social changes in the given country. (The struggles fought in the sphere of home politics in Egypt and Pakistan on the questions of planning in the late 1950s and early 1960s clearly demonstrate these conflicts.)

The role of the political sphere does not come to an end with the drawing up of plans. Planning also needs substantial political support in the stage of implementation. The determination to implement a given plan is a basically political decision. Political support means the mobilization not only of the highest authorities but also of the masses for the objectives of the plan. This also makes it necessary for the objectives envisaged in the plan to become mobilizing slogans that can be adopted by the people.

This is all the more necessary as in developing countries plans often meet with resistance on part of sectors which think they are threatened by the envisaged measures. Not uncommon is the resistance also on part of the "traditional" state administration, which carries out changes in the institutions with a great deal of reluctance. It jealously defends its positions against all regrouping of power that may lead to a reorganization of the structure of administration.

The problem of political support is even more important in countries where the private sector is strong. The resistance of the private sector is unavoidable in such cases when the plan requires the realization of decisions affecting and combatting vested interests. Certain circles of the private sector may also support the plan in so far as it favours them and redistributes e. g. the investment resources of the national income in accordance with their own interests. In Pakistan e. g., where the objectives of the first five-year plan were set well within the economic and financial possibilities of the country, they failed to realize them because the government organs did not support the implementation of the plan. On the other hand, the targets of the second five-year plan, which was given full political support, were overfulfilled. (This second plan was aimed to a lesser extent at social or economic reforms, it was rather designed to stabilize the existing system of income distribution and/or to support big business and the big landowners.)

The planning bodies are often isolated from the political decision-making centres. Planning offices are often entrusted with preparing plans, while the political authorities give them few, if any, instructions. (This is the case e. g. in many African countries.)

A not insignificant problem arises out of the fact that those operating in the political sphere and have power in decision-making, often do not understand what is included in the plan. With linear programming, input-output matrices, operations research and production functions, economic planning has become a very complex task requiring much special knowledge. Moreover, many specialists are inclined to use a sophisticated and hazy technical language even where there is no need for it, just to show off their talents and display their special skills and knowledge. The accepted technical terms of planning are difficult enough in themselves, and presuppose a degree of basic economic knowledge, often lacking with the political leaders of developing countries.

There are also many examples showing that the administrative activities of the central planning bodies are often overconcentrated. Though the centralization of economic power may be important temporarily, or even for a relatively long period of time, but as a result of this a high proportion of planning experts (who

250

are anyway in short supply in developing countries) are concentrated in planning offices, and since the ministries and the organs of local self-government or other state authorities do very little in the interest of planning, even the sectoral and regional plans are worked out in the planning offices.

We have already mentioned that political determination is of basic importance in plan implementation. However, the success or failure of plans also depends on the degree of co-operation maintained in the course of implementation among the agencies concerned in the administration. If planning is overcentralized, the interest of the lower functionaries will necessarily diminish in plan implementation. This case prevails when co-operation is decreed by law for the lower organs of administration. In general, there are two possibilities to change this situation. First, making these lower functionaries more interested by involving them in plan preparation and, second, making them understand the political and economic objectives of the plan. It follows from these conflicts that in developing countries only such plans can get effective support in the political sphere and are suitable to mobilize the masses, which formulate correct, general national objectives.

2. THE PROBLEM OF THE PUBLIC SECTOR

The experiences of socialist and such developing countries which have succeeded in approximating the envisaged targets of the development plans, provide the evidence that the role of the public sector is of paramount interest for the implementation of plans. In most developing countries the public sector consists of infrastructural establishments, productive enterprises, and financial institutions. The laws of some countries (e. g. India) stipulate that only the state is entitled to carry out activities in certain sectors.

In many developing countries the formation of the public sector was stimulated after the Second World War by serious efforts aimed at speeding up economic growth and by steps taken to defend the national economy against the inroad of foreign capital (India, Egypt, Syria, Iraq, etc.). (Nationalizations, formation of state monopolies, etc.) In some countries – first of all in Latin America – the public sector came to be established considerably earlier, at a time when the problem of economic growth was still a far cry. There are still a number of countries which are even now not primarily development-oriented, and in which state enterprises have nothing to do with growth objectives. Traditional "state paternalism" rooted in feudal remnants, e. g. in Latin America, is far from being a thing of the past. Thus planning based on the public sector has not become easier, and the mechanism of plan implementation is not improving.

For the governments of such developing countries the public sector serves almost exclusively as a source of income (sometimes as a source of private income, and in fact also as a source of growing rich). In this respect the public sector is similar to the classical state monopolies.

The objective importance of state enterprises in planning is ensured by the fact

251

that it is through them that production, consumption and incomes can be influenced in the most direct way.

This is the sector to which the state can give, and does give, direct instructions depending on the legal position of state enterprises. In Egypt, e. g., the plan of state enterprises is binding after approval, and as such is part of the state budget. These enterprises pay most of their profits into the state budget and consequently cannot make investments without central approval or having the necessary resources made available to them. The plans of state enterprises are also instruction-based and compulsory in several other developing countries (while such instructions do not apply to the other sectors). But in many developing countries the situation is different.

Though in principle they wish to integrate their plans with the development plan, state enterprises in Argentine and Mexico operate independently of and even outside the plan.

There are countries in which state enterprises operate with a deficit. The reason for this is usually connected with their specific role. In many countries, e. g. India and Pakistan, etc., state enterprises are designed to help private enterprises by supplying them with cheap services, raw materials, by the free transfer of their development achievements, etc. Thus their economic role is far from being reduced to establishments of the infrastructure. For financing their deficits state enterprises get regular support from the budget (direct subsidies or special benefits) on the ground that state enterprises must not go bankrupt in any case (Iran, Nigeria, Pakistan, etc.).[7] In reality, this subsidization often supports the private sector in an indirect way.

The role of the public sector in planning and plan implementation is also weakened by other factors. Such is e. g. the extremely slow improvement in training, selection and payment of the employees of state enterprises with the usual result that the best forces find employment with local private firms or in establishments operated by foreign capital.

Thus the views held by a significant proportion of the population on state enterprises are not always favourable. In many countries, where the people have no confidence in their governments, the public sector is justly considered as a hotbed of corruption, a source of income for the bureaucratic élite, the "empire" of local chiefs and military district commanders.

Therefore, the mere existence of the public sector does not guarantee the implementation of approved plans. Yet it is a condition of vital importance for, and a possibility of, promoting plan implementation. The budget, the scope of state development programmes, the dynamics of implementation, the level of performing the economic, financial, technical, commercial and managerial functions generally react on planning, on the state institutions established for fulfilling the plans, and therefore the public sector is an indispensable element of plan implementation.

[7] *Organization and Administration of Public Enterprises.* U.N., New York 1968, pp. 54–55.

252

3. THE SYSTEM OF INFORMATION

One of the most burning problems of planning in developing countries is the lack of basic information for planning. Economic planning is aimed at exerting direct influence on the economic processes, at channelling them into the required direction, at promoting and accelerating economic growth. Economic life, even in countries at a relatively low level of development, is an extremely complex system, and its planning calls for a great deal of information on man's social activities in the most different areas. Not only statistical data are needed, as e. g. on natural resources, the interconnections of the macro- and micro-economy (such as the amount and sources of investments and consumption, domestic productive capacities, the flow of material goods and financial resources, etc.), but also such "qualitative" information is necessary as the habits, preferences and reactions to certain steps of the population, etc. Also of great importance is the knowledge of international interrelationships (expected export-import possibilities), international comparative data and time series. Indispensable is the availability of information on the techniques applied. The more comprehensive a plan, the more important is a thorough knowledge of the relevant data.

Several developing countries have made serious efforts to improve their information systems. In certain countries it was already the colonial powers that began – mainly for taxation purposes – to set up local statistical organizations. Yet, there are still serious deficiencies in most developing countries in the quantity, quality and time-horizon of basic data necessary for planning.

The large masses of the native population still live in a subsistence economy, usually out of contact with the market. There are often only estimates of the value of non-marketed products, calculated at market prices for comparable products. The so-called organized or large-scale sector, for which comprehensive statistics are available, yield only a fraction of aggregate production. Quantitative information on the much larger "unorganized" or "small-scale" sector is scarce and only partially available. The subsistence sector of the economy is large and comprises an overwhelming proportion not only of food production but also most of the production and consumption of services in general, and also a high percentage of investments, especially in agriculture and housing. In the case of foodstuffs, market demand is, to a substantial extent, the result of non-market factors, but of compulsion exercised by landowners, moneylenders and their agents. In addition, the system of statistics often does not meet the requirements of planning. National statistical offices play, as a rule, a rather subordinate role in the state apparatus. Their employees are paid very poorly, and their personnel is inadequately trained in general. There are of course exceptions, too. In some developing countries, e. g. India, a statistical system of high standard has evolved with highly qualified skilled staff. Similar is the situation in some Latin American countries. This does not apply, however, to the majority of developing countries. Very few statistical offices have adequate financial resources and are equipped with the necessary machinery and equipment, etc. There are also deficiencies in legislation relating to information. In many cases laws do not make it compulsory to provide information, or they extend it only to questions that are of secondary importance to economic growth and development. The various statistical data supplying services at the sectoral, regional or local levels are not co-ordinated sufficiently, and very few countries have uniform statistical programmes developed on a national scale.

There are also problems in the utilization of available statistical data. The organs making use of statistics often do not sufficiently know what data they actually need from the state apparatus and the private sector. They are often unable to make use even of available data when taking decisions. The relations with planning offices and those between planning and statistical offices are usually reduced to the former asking the latter to provide them with data for plans on which they are already working. The relations between planning and statistical offices are not regulated, the flow of data is not organized, which would be necessary for periodical plan revision and evaluation. The experiences of socialist countries in this respect have shown that planning and statistics have to develop in a close interdependence. Along with the organization of the implementation of plans, a reporting system has also to be developed in accordance with the "breakdown" of plans. This reporting system may lay the foundation for securing the data needed to draw up the plan of the subsequent period. In this way, the plan also stimulates the development of statistics in the corresponding fields of the economy.

In developing countries the quality of data is also uneven, depending on the sector they cover. In general, foreign trade statistics are the most reliable. Second to them in this respect are the population figures, while data on domestic trade, general construction, road construction and unemployment are especially poor. When censuses or population surveys are used as a foundation for planning, the continuity of data is generally lacking. In industrial surveys usually new categories are set up instead of modernizing the old ones. Data are processed with great delays. In recent times, the application of representative methods have helped somewhat to improve the reliability of data. A further shortcoming is the lack of regular and continuous time series designed to keep track on short-term changes in the economy. The publication of statistical data takes an especially long time.

4. QUALITY AND CONTENT OF PLANS

When can a plan be considered as good? The answer to this question is not simple at all. Such general answers as "if it is realistic", "if it can be implemented", "if it is quantitatively harmonious" are not sufficient criteria. It is obvious that a plan must be regarded as the means of carrying out given socio-political objectives, which not only helps to promote the realization of these objectives, but also actively reacts on them, indicating in due time their reality and their possible contradictory character. Thus the main plan targets also serve as a signalizing system for economic management. Consequently, the basic precondition for a sound plan is a correct, well-weighed economic policy, a development strategy formulating the most general national aims, taking into account the possibilities of the country concerned, and envisaging various alternatives. From the point of view of the quality of the plan, the methods applied in planning are also of paramount importance.

The national economic plan is, then, a tool to formulate and fulfil a comprehensive economic policy, and is the expression of that policy both in terms of quantity and quality. Consequently, the failure of planning is at the same time a failure to set and implement effective political objectives. But planning is, properly speaking, a technique of social development and cannot replace a development policy. Some people often tend to forget about this truism. The preparation of a plan document cannot be a substitute for general objectives designed to speed up social and political development. Based on economic policy, a plan must be used as a tool to exert an active influence upon the economy and to effect the required changes. The targets set by the planners must closely be related to the objective conditions of the economy. In other words, the objective economic situation always gives rise to problems which must be faced and which also determine, to a certain extent, the objectives themselves. The many-sided character of the objectives and problems calls for a many-sided planning.

The analysis of the experiences of developing countries in planning and plan implementation provides the evidence that the following main factors had a role to play where planning was more or less successful:

(a) the state had at its disposal adequate organizations in the economy (state enterprises, financial institutions, etc.);

(b) planning was given significant political backing;

(c) the availability of information in appropriate quantity and quality on the given country;

(d) the establishment of new, efficient administrative bodies and the improvement of those already in operation;

(e) the planners were capable of establishing organic relations and a regular exchange of views between the public and the private sector and also with the various socio-economic groups;

(f) the preparation of good, rational plans.

However, the quality and content of plans in individual developing countries vary to a great extent, which makes it difficult to evaluate and compare them. (See Tables 1 and 2.)

Analysing the planning practice of developing countries, Waterston, a prominent specialist of bourgeois planning, distinguishes three types of planning:

(a) project-oriented planning (with plans containing only projects, irrespective of their implications and effects);

(b) integrated planning relating to state investments (including the sources and impacts of resources needed for state investments);

(c) comprehensive national economic planning.

255

Table 1

Planned and past average annual rates of growth of gross domestic product*

Income group	Country and average annual rate			Number of countries
	7 per cent or more	5 per cent or more but less than 7 per cent	Less than 5 per cent	
	Annual rate planned for initial years of the decade 1971–1980			
Countries with per capita gross domestic product of $ 600 or more	Argentina 7.0	Venezuela 6.3	Trinidad and Tobago 4.3 Uruguay 3.6	4
Countries with per capita gross domestic product of $ 300 or more but less than $ 600	Lebanon 7.0 Saudi Arabia 9.8 Peru 7.5 Brazil 9.0 Fiji 7.0 Iran 9.9 Colombia 4.4 Ivory Coast 7.7 Algeria 9.5	Zambia 6.8 Malaysia 6.8 Iraq 6.1		12
Countries with per capita gross domestic product of less than $ 300	Syrian Arab Republic 8.2 Thailand 7.1 Togo 7.6 Sudan 8.1 Malawi 7.8	El Salvador 6.0 Paraguay 6.0 Mauritius 6.8 Senegal 5.1 Sri Lanka 6.1 Philippines 6.9 Kenya 6.8 Uganda 5.0 Pakistan 6.5 Nigeria 6.2 United Rep. of Tanzania 6.5 India 5.7 Ethiopia 6.0	Morocco 4.3 Nepal 3.7	20
Number of countries	15	17	4	36

Source: Centre for Development Planning, Projections and Policies of the United Nations Secretariat, based on national development plans and on national and international statistical publications. For titles of development plans see Table 11.

* Data refer to gross domestic product at market prices. The known exceptions, in the case of planned rates are: Algeria, Ethiopia, Mauritius, Nigeria, Sri Lanka, Uganda, United Republic of Tanzania, and Uruguay; gross domestic product at factor cost: Malaysia, Morocco, Pakistan, Philippines and Republic of Korea; gross national product at market prices: India; net domestic product at market prices: Syrian Arab Republic, "net geographical income". Rates of growth have been calculated from data in constant prices.

256

(Table 1 continued)

Income group	Country and average annual rate			Number of countries
	7 per cent or more	5 per cent or more but less than 7 per cent	Less than 5 per cent	
Annual rate achieved during the decade 1961–1970				
Countries with per capita *gross domestic product of $ 600 or more*		Venezuela 5.1	Argentina 4.3 Trinidad and Tobago 4.5 Uruguay 1.3	4
Countries with per capita *gross domestic product of $ 300 or more but less than $ 600*	Saudi Arabia 9.8 Iran 9.2 Ivory Coast 7.1	Brazil 6.1 Fiji 5.9 Zambia 5.8 Malaysia 5.9 Iraq 6.3 Colombia 5.4	Lebanon 4.4 Peru 4.8 Algeria 2.6	12
Countries with per capita *gross domestic product of less than $ 300*	Thailand 7.2	El Salvador 5.6 Syrian Arab Rep. 6.3 Kenya 5.4 Togo 6.6 Uganda 5.2 Pakistan 5.5	Paraguay 4.7 Mauritius 2.8 Morocco 4.1 Senegal 1.2 Sri Lanka 4.9 Philippines 4.6 Sudan 3.3 Nigeria 2.9 United Rep. of Tanzania 4.7 India 4.0 Nepal – Malawi 4.2 Ethiopia 4.6	20
Number of countries	4	13	19	36

The final year of the period to which the planned rates refer is 1976 for Lebanon, Sri Lanka, Thailand, Uganda and Zambia; 1975 for Argentina, Fiji, Ivory Coast, Malawi, Malaysia, Mauritius, Paraguay, Peru, Syrian Arab Republic and Togo; 1974/75 for Nepal, Pakistan, Philippines, Saudi Arabia and Sudan; 1974 for Brazil, Iraq, Kenya and Venezuela; 1973/74 for India, Nigeria and United Republic of Tanzania; 1973 for Algeria, Colombia, Morocco and Trinidad and Tobago; 1972/73 for Ethiopia, Iran and Senegal; 1972 for El Salvador and Uruguay.

Countries have been classified into three groups according to their per capita gross domestic product in market prices in 1970, converted into US $ at the average effective exchange rates of that year. Within each of these three groups, countries are subclassified according to the range of growth rates specified in column headings and listed in each subgroup in descending order of the per capita gross domestic product.

Where information for the full period indicated is not available, the listing of the country concerned in a particular column is based on inference drawn from partial indicators.

Table 2

Planned and past average annual rates of growth of per capita *gross domestic product**

Income group	Country and average annual rate			Number of countries
	4 per cent or more	3 per cent or more but less than 4 per cent	Less than 3 per cent	
	Annual rate planned for initial years of the decade 1971–1980			
Countries with per capita *gross domestic product of $ 600 or more*	Argentina 5.5		Venezuela 2.6 Trinidad and Tobago 2.6 Uruguay 2.3	4
Countries with per capita *gross domestic product of $ 300 or more but less than $ 600*	Lebanon 4.7 Saudi Arabia 6.6 Peru 4.3 Brazil 6.0 Fiji 4.6 Iran 7.1 Colombia 4.1 Ivory Coast 4.3 Algeria 6.1	Zambia 3.8 Malaysia 3.9	Iraq 2.7	12
Countries with per capita *gross domestic product of less than $ 300*	Syrian Arab Republic – Mauritius – Thailand 4.5 Sri Lanka 4.0 Togo 5.5 Sudan 5.5 Malawi 5.1	Senegal 3.2 Philippines 3.8 Kenya 3.6 Pakistan 3.7 Nigeria 3.6 United Rep. of Tanzania 3.7 India 3.1 Ethiopia 3.7	El Salvador 2.8 Paraguay 2.6 Morocco 1.4 Uganda 1.5 Nepal 1.8	20
Number of countries	17	10	9	36

Source: See Table 1.
* See footnote to Table 1.

This classification distinguishes plans from the angle of the plan as a document. The way of implementation, the role played by direct and indirect measures in the implementation process may serve as another basis for classification.

In our study we are concerned, in regard to the quality of plans, primarily with the so-called comprehensive plans covering the given national economy as a whole, irrespective of the concrete ways of implementation.

It is commonly known, however, that the elaboration of the plan as a document constitutes only one single phase of planning. Care must also be taken of measures and a machinery to ensure the attainment of the objectives, the periodic revision of the plan and the supervision of plan implementation, etc. In the

(Table 2 continued)

Income group	Country and average annual rate			Number of countries
	4 per cent or more	3 per cent or more but less than 4 per cent	Less than 3 per cent	

Annual rate achieved during the decade 1961–1970

Income group	4 per cent or more		3 per cent or more but less than 4 per cent		Less than 3 per cent		Number of countries
Countries with per capita gross domestic product of $ 600 or more					Argentina	2.6	
					Venezuela	1.8	
					Trinidad and Tobago	2.0	
					Uruguay	–	4
Countries with per capita gross domestic product of $ 300 or more but less than $ 600	Saudi Arabia	6.9	Brazil	3.0	Lebanon	1.5	
	Iran	6.1	Malaysia	3.0	Peru	1.8	
	Ivory Coast	4.1			Fiji	2.6	
					Zambia	2.9	
					Iraq	2.8	12
					Colombia	2.0	
					Algeria	0.4	
Countries with per capita gross domestic product of less than $ 300	Togo	4.1	Syrian Arab Rep.	3.2	El Salvador	2.4	
			Thailand	3.9	Paraguay	1.3	
					Mauritius	0.4	
					Morocco	1.0	
					Senegal	1.0	
					Sri Lanka	2.3	
					Philippines	1.2	
					Kenya	2.2	
					Uganda	2.6	
					Pakistan	2.3	20
					Sudan	0.4	
					Nigeria	0.4	
					United Rep. of Tanzania	2.1	
					India	1.4	
					Nepal	–	
					Malawi	1.6	
					Ethiopia	2.6	
Number of countries	4		4		28		36

developing world there are many plans, which, for lack of all these conditions, qualify as simple forecasts. Even these plans often foresee significant changes as compared with previous trends, and sometimes also take into account the potentional limiting factors, but they usually remain wishful desires.

There are a host of instances to prove how far plans may break away from real life. The practice of drawing up so-called "paper plans" is especially widespread on the African continent. An important role was played in this by certain Western advisors or expert teams. In setting up an independent economic organization, most of the young African countries had to start from an especially far-away point. In taking the first steps in planning they had to rely on advisors from foreign, mainly industrially developed capitalist countries. Leaving out of consideration, rather irresponsibly, the natural endowments, social problems, economic and administrative capabilities of the country concerned, many of these advisors regarded planning as "econometric practice". In the 1960s, all African countries, with the exception of the Republic of South Africa, had their national economic plans. Several countries worked out or caused to work out alternative plans for the same period. Occasionally, the predecessors of the "paper plans" had already appeared in the colonial period. These so-called colonial development plans included no development strategy whatsoever. They were prepared by colonial officials not familiar with economic questions, and their content was virtually determined by the economic interests and raw material requirements of the colonial power.

Following the attainment of independence, most plans of the "Third World" have been "produced" in Africa. The plan has become in Africa, too, the symbol of the existence of independent state power. The process of planning was similar in many African countries. There arrived a foreign specialist or a team of specialists for the preparation of the plan. Their work consisted in working out a statistical or mathematical model, or they fed into the existing model the collected or estimated data on the country. They compiled input-output tables reflecting sectoral relationships, constructed some simultaneous equations and submitted an internally balanced, comprehensive plan equipped with capital-output ratios, marginal saving coefficients, import elasticities, production functions, and containing the deficit of investments and foreign trade balance. This plan covered the whole of the economy, determined the annual growth rate, resource allocation by sectors, the expected trend of the balance of payments and specified the amount of foreign aid needed. The expert panel handed it over to the government and left the country. The governments put the plan either in the archives, or approved it formally, and invited another expert team the next year and entrusted it with the elaboration of a new plan. In most cases this sort of procedure proved more advantageous for the economic development of the countries concerned since – as also proved by the experience of several countries – wherever these plans were taken seriously and the governments set out to implement them, they invariably ended in failure. The reason for their fiasco was the simple fact that these plans, however correct mathematically, had nothing to do with the actual socio-economic relations.[8] It was only in the late 1960s that, realizing the shortcomings of their "paper plan" periods, some African countries were able to set about elaborating more realistic development programmes. As regards the objectives, methods and the securing of the conditions of implementation, the plans of several African countries prepared for the period 1966–1970,

[8] *The Economics of African Development.* New York, 1967, pp. 209–221.

or rather for the early 1970s, were much better than the earlier ones. Paper plans were typical not of African countries only. There are still a number of paper plans in force in several Latin American countries, too. Very often the plan is an isolated action programme of different sectors. Sometimes it serves the attainment of even more limited aims, as e. g. the rationalization of the activities of the administration (Colombia). Even today, in several developing countries, especially in Latin America, it is an almost steadily recurring demand to put an end to comprehensive general planning and make greater efforts to realize a few, well-planned special projects. Similar proposals have also been made in India.

Concerning the theory of planning in developing planning, several bourgeois schools of thought have come into being.

One of the best known and recognized of them is Myrdal's approach, whose departure in planning for economic countries is based on economic and political considerations of a more general character, and in this respect his theory is not far from the Marxian concept of the problem. In his view, attention must be focused in planning for developing countries on six closely interrelated categories:

1. Production and incomes.
2. Conditions of production.
3. Living standards.

(These are, according to Myrdal, the economic categories.)

4. Behaviour relating to work and life.
5. Institutions.

(These are the non-economic conditions.)

6. Politics, which, in Myrdal's opinion, is a variable containing the objectives and means.[9]

Myrdal criticizes the so-called model approach formulated by Bent Hansen and Jan Tinbergen. The model approach conceives the position of developing countries as a system of structural relations among various variables (economic conditions) enabling governments to regulate certain changes in the structural relations through state intervention.[10] Myrdal criticizes the model approach on the ground that it treats individual areas in isolation, on the one hand, and on the other, because of the unjustifiably contracted character of its categories. In Myrdal's theory the interrelationships of the above-mentioned elements is so close that the economic questions cannot be treated separately as independent variables for manipulation purposes, disregarding the movements of related areas. In addition, he holds the view that the application of the Western conception of macro-economic categories is entirely irrealistic under the dualistic conditions of the economies of developing countries.

It is evident that Myrdal does not fully reject Hansen's and Tinbergen's approach, but regards it as of limited significance. In this he is fully right.

[9] G. Myrdal: *op. cit.,* pp. 1859–1915.
[10] J. Tinbergen: *Development Planning.* Stockholm, 1967.

261

Bourgeois planning theories regarding developing countries virtually try to provide a general framework for analysing individual questions, and to determine the interdependence of certain factors, their hierarchical relationships. But they give much less thought to the structural relationships between the economic and political processes, and to the plan which is to control them, to the efficiency and contradictions of the means of influencing them. But this approach, too, is useful for the systematization of the planning process, for the shaping of the inherent logic of the plan, which is undoubtedly important in developing countries.

But development planning must not be regarded merely as an application of systems theory and computer technology. The quantitative interconnections of plans, the quantitative identification of objectives and the formulation of resources are often thought of as tantamount to planning as a whole. However important and indispensable all this is, planning must also be concerned with the more comprehensive social and institutional conditions as well. Effective means are needed for developing countries to bring about significant changes in their social and economic structures and the system of their institutions. Such actions that can only be expressed in terms of quality often provide the basic preconditions for attaining the development objectives. A plan has no relevance if it does not contain such socially oriented policies as land reform, redistribution of incomes, the ensurance of social discipline, including financial and budgetary discipline. In other words, political will and ability, if they are to exercise effective control over the strategically important activities of the economy, are indispensable in evaluating the quality of the plan.[11]

Consequently, the planning problems are considerably wider and deeper.

In many cases, however, the documents, which are called plans in developing countries, seldom go beyond the quantitative identification of the most general objectives of economic policy, e.g. the aim to encourage investments, curb inflation, control foreign-exchange incomes, stimulate employment, promote the increase in gross national income.

The higher complexity of plans in some countries does not mean that the earlier practice, when the plan simply enumerated the envisaged big projects to be established (which was, therefore, not more than an investment programme), has undergone substantial changes. This so-called project-centred planning involved, and still involves, serious shortcomings. The most important of them is that there is usually no co-ordination among the projects, their effects are contradictory, and the governments are only concerned about how to raise the necessary investment resources. In Egypt, in the 1960s, the doubling of the national income

---

[11] Of the Marxist authors, József Bognár, analysing the conditions of planning in developing countries, examines in his work *The Direction of Economic Growth in Developing Countries* (Akadémiai Kiadó, Budapest, 1967) those economic and socio-political interconnections the synchronization of which constitutes the prerequisites of successful planning. He attaches special importance to the necessity to reckon in economic planning with a "transition period" lasting for several generations, in which, in the case of effective synchronization, economic development may be quicker and evener.

was envisaged by the plan. (See Tables 3 and 4.) At first they set about performing this task by looking for projects in the various sectors that could add to the national income in the shortest possible time. However, they soon were forced to realize that aggregate effect of the projects proposed by the various sectors contradicted the plan objective at the national level.

In some of the developing countries (e.g. Ceylon) initially only general objectives were envisaged by the plan regarding gross national products. This practice did not prove effective enough. At the same time it turned out that the more detailed the way was in which the plan targets were specified under the given social and economic structure, i.e. the more deeply they went in planning, the more problems cropped up. Especially difficult appeared to be the harmonization in the plan of quantities in value and in kind. At first, the specialists of most developing countries could only think in terms of value categories. It soon proved to be insufficient and gave rise to serious disproportions and tensions. They came to realize that it was beneficial, also for other reasons, to a developing economy if preference was given to objectives expressed in terms of a few physical quantities commonly understood and appreciated. Such are the volume of bread-grain output or other vital consumer goods, the number of flats and the capacity of power plants to be built, the number of school children enrolled, etc. Such simple plan targets are also more effective in mobilizing government institutions, the private sector and masses than abstract targets – however desirable – as investment and savings ratios, the decrease in underemployment, etc. (This does not mean of course that a plan could be reduced to a system of physical quantities only.)

Taking into account the great variety of the needs of developing countries, we cannot expect to eliminate the rise of conflicts among individual objectives. What is important, however, is the immediate assessment of conflicts in order to bring about a compromise among them. The possibility of making choices consists, however, not in merely pooling resources in one or another area, but rather in finding an optimum combination of them. It will suffice to refer to the extremely complex problem of employment. Underemployment and unemployment account for about 20 to 25 per cent of people of working age in most developing countries. The problem of unemployment presents itself for the planners simultaneously in two well definable, though closely interrelated fields, i.e. in urban and rural areas. Of the two types of unemployment the one in towns is undoubtedly the more dramatic. The unemployment rate is higher in the towns than in the villages. Though underemployment is significant in the towns, too, rural underemployment is still higher. Thus, in Latin America, in the 1960s, one-third of the rural population were underemployed. This was due not only to the squandering of human resources, but it was one of the main sources of rural destitution. In Brazil, in the 1960s, the income of the poorest 20 per cent of the population amounted to only one-sixth of the national average. The majority of them lived in the country. Rural underemployment is one of the causes of the widening gap between urban and rural incomes. Urban unemployment and rural

Table 3

*Planned and past increase in level of total investment**

Income group	Country and average annual increase in percentage share of gross investment in gross domestic product			Number of countries
	0.7 percentage point or more	0.3 percentage point or more but less than 0.7 percentage point	Less than 0.3 percentage point	
	Annual increase planned for initial years of the decade 1971–1980			
Countries with per capita gross domestic product of $ 600 or more	Argentina 0.78 Uruguay 0.84	Venezuela 0.37	Trinidad and Tobago 0.14	4
Countries with per capita domestic product of $ 300 or more but less than $ 600	Peru 1.70 Iraq 1.16	Brazil 0.50 Fiji 0.33 Iran 0.68 Zambia 0.58 Colombia 0.39	Malaysia 0.19 Ivory Coast 0.21	9
Countries with per capita gross domestic product of less than $ 300	Philippines 0.90	El Salvador 0.32 Paraguay 0.55 Morocco 0.66 Kenya 0.46 Togo 0.65 Pakistan 0.40 United Rep. of Tanzania 0.68 India 0.59	Sri Lanka −0.20 Uganda −0.02 Nigeria −0.54 Malawi −0.43	13
Number of countries	5	14	7	26

Source: See Table 1.

    * Countries have been classified according to magnitude of their per capita gross domestic product in 1970 and average annual change in percentage share of gross investment in gross domestic product during the period indicated. Within each category, countries are listed in descending order of their per capita gross domestic product.

    Planned increase is generally from data in constant prices of base year of plan, and has been calculated by comparing data for final and base years of plan. Exceptions are for Malaysia, Nigeria, Pakistan, Sri Lanka and

underdevelopment are closely interrelated. With miserable living conditions and underemployment in the villages, the town still has its attractive force even if rural emigrants realize that they have to wait for years to get a job there.

The experiences gained so far and the expected tendencies lead us to conclude that urban employment cannot grow fast enough. Towns cannot absorb the millions of rural exodus. In the 1960s the output of large-scale industry in developing countries grew by 7 per cent, and employment in the same sector rose by only 4 per cent, i. e. the gap between the two indicators widened. It is obvious

(Table 3 continued)

Income group	Country and average annual increase in percentage share of gross investment in gross domestic product			Number of countries
	0.7 percentage point or more	0.3 percentage point or more but less than 0.7 percentage point	Less than 0.3 percentage point	

Annual increase achieved during the decade 1961–1970

Income group	0.7 percentage point or more	0.3 percentage point or more but less than 0.7 percentage point	Less than 0.3 percentage point	Number of countries
Countries with per capita gross domestic product of $ 600 or more		Venezuela 0.54	Argentina 0.02 Trinidad and Tobago −1.02 Uruguay −0.45	4
Countries with per capita gross domestic product of $ 300 or more but less than $ 600	Fiji 1.13 Iran 1.05 Zambia 1.02	Colombia 0.43 Ivory Coast 0.40	Peru −0.97 Brazil −0.32 Iraw −0.30 Malaysia −0.02	9
Countries with per capita gross domestic product of less than $ 300	Sri Lanka 0.75 Kenya 1.18 United Rep. of Tanzania 1.10 Malawi 1.36	Paraguay 0.43 Morocco 0.59 Uganda 0.39 Nigeria 0.41	El Salvador −0.16 Philippines 0.22 Togo −0.23 Pakistan −0.31 India −0.15	13
Number of countries	7	7	12	26

Uganda, where plan data are stated to be in current prices. Annual increase during 1961–1970 derived from data in current prices by comparing percentage shares for 1961–1965 and 1966–1970, the percentage share for each quinquennium having been derived by dividing the sum of investment by the sum of gross domestic product during that period.

For India, data on planned change are net of depreciation.

For differences in concepts of gross domestic product and for details on final year of the period to which planned increase refers, see footnote to Table 1.

that in most of the developing countries the problem of securing rural and urban job opportunities has to be solved simultaneously, and it is no good to concentrate on one or the other task only. The development of rural small-scale industry and cottage industry, together with urban large-scale industry may be a solution for many developing countries. In other countries, however, it is only by means of a massive public works programme that these problems can be eased.

In some of the developing countries attempts have been made to utilize input-output analysis and mathematical models in planning and introduce

Table 4

*Incremental capital/output ratio implicit in planned and past increase in level of investment**

Income group	Country and incremental capital/output ratio			Number of countries
	4 or more	3 or more but less than 4	Less than 3	

Implicit in targets for initial years of the decade 1971–1980

Income group	4 or more		3 or more but less than 4		Less than 3		Number of countries
Countries with per capita gross domestic product of $ 600 or more	Trinidad and Tobago	4.5	Argentina	3.5			4
	Uruguay	4.3	Venezuela	3.0			
Countries with per capita gross domestic product of $ 300 or more but less than $ 600	Fiji	4.3			Peru	2.3	9
	Zambia	4.6			Brazil	2.0	
					Iran	2.1	
					Malaysia	2.6	
					Iraq	2.8	
					Colombia	2.7	
					Ivory Coast	2.6	
Countries with per capita gross domestic product of less than $ 300	Morocco	4.0	Paraguay	3.2	El Salvador	2.9	18
			Mauritius**	3.4	Togo	2.5	
			Senegal*	3.0	Uganda	2.0	
			Thailand**	3.8	Pakistan	2.2	
			Sri Lanka	3.3	Sudan**	1.3	
			Philippines	3.4	Nigeria	2.4	
			Kenya	3.5	Malawi	2.4	
			United Rep. of Tanzania	3.3	Ethiopia**	2.1	
			India	–			
Number of countries	5		11		15		31

Source: See Table 1.

* Countries have been classified according to magnitudes of their per capita gross domestic product in 1970 and incremental capital/output ratio during the period indicated. Within each category countries are listed in descending order of their per capita gross domestic product.

Incremental capital/output ratio implicit in recent development plan equals share of gross investment in gross domestic product for plan period as a whole divided by planned annual rate of growth of gross domestic product.

simulation to examine the effects of changes and actions planned to be made in the economy. But the use of mathematical devices and models, partly on account of the limited availability of information, partly because of the narrow basis of the economy, which has made and is still making the relations between variables unstable, has not proved an efficient or possible tool in many developing countries.

Practice has proved that plans prepared by means of econometric models were less reliable than those based on "common sense", logical considerations or on

(Table 4 countinued)

Income group	Country and incremental capital/output ratio						Number of countries
	4 or more		3 or more but less than 4		Less than 3		
	Observed during the decade 1961–1970						
Countries with per capita gross domestic product of $ 600 or more	Argentina	4.7	Venezuela	3.4			4
	Trinidad and Tobago	4.8					
	Uruguay	10.1					
Countries with per capita gross domestic product of $ 300 or more but less than $ 600	Peru	4.5	Fiji	3.9	Brazil	2.9	
			Zambia	3.7	Iran	1.9	
			Colombia	3.5	Malaysia	2.3	9
					Iraq	2.7	
					Ivory Coast	2.4	
Countries with per capita gross domestic product of less than $ 300	Mauritius**	6.0	Paraguay	3.1	El Salvador	2.5	
	Senegal**	9.6	Morocco	3.0	Kenya	2.5	
	Philippines	4.0	Thailand**	3.2	Togo	2.2	18
	Sudan	4.6	Sri Lanka	3.2	Uganda	2.7	
	Nigeria	4.3	United Rep. of		Pakistan	2.7	
	India	4.4	Tanzania	3.1	Ethiopia**	2.7	
			Malawi	3.1			
Number of countries	10		10		11		31

Observed values of the ratio are calculated in a similar manner except that a time lag of one year is assumed between investment and its contribution to output.

Calculations are made from data in constant prices. Exceptions are planned investment for Malaysia, Nigeria, Pakistan, Sri Lanka and Uganda, which are stated to be in current prices.

The broad inference for the incremental capital/output ratio during the plan period of India is derived by adding in allowance for depreciation to the stated data on net investment and net domestic product, but a precise figure has not been included in the table.

For differences in concepts of gross domestic product and for details on final year of the period to which planned increase refers, see footnote to Table 1.

** Countries which could not be included in Table 5, owing to lack of relevant information.

views formulated after joint discussions with the representatives of various strata and social groups. The errors of computations based on models were occasionally twice to three times larger than those arising out of the "traditional" approach.

This does not mean of course that under the conditions of developing countries econometric models were of no use at all. They have proved and still prove, especially in countries with more developed statistical systems, a useful device for planners to evaluate the impact of a concrete policy measure or an idea.

267

Table 5
Titles and time periods of development plans accepted for the seventies

Country	Title	Plan period*
Algeria	Plan quadriennal	1970–1973
Argentina	Plan Nacional de Desarrollo y Securided, Metas para el Mediano Plazo	1971–1975
Brazil	Projeto do I Plano Nacional de Desenvolvimento Economico e Social	1972–1974
Colombia	Plan de Desarrollo Economico y Social	1970–1973
El Salvador	Plan de Desarrollo Economico y Social	1968–1972
Ethiopia	Third Five-Year Development Plan	7 July 1968 to 6 July 1973
Fiji	Fiji's Sixth Development Plan	1971–1975
India	Fourth Five-Year Plan	1 April 1969 to 31 March 1974
Iran	4th National Development Plan	21 March 1968 to 20 March 1973
Iraq	The National Development Plan	1970–1974
Ivory Coast	Plan quinquennal de développement économique, social et culturel	1971–1975
Kenya	Development Plan	1970–1974
Lebanon	Plan sexennal de développement	1972–1977
Malawi	Statement of Development Policies	1971–1975
Malaysia	Second Malaysia Plan	1971–1975
Mauritius	4-Year Plan for Social and Economic Development	1971–1975
Morocco	Five-Year Plan	1968–1972**
Nepal	Fourth Plan	1 July 1970 to 30 June 1975
Nigeria	Second National Development Plan	1 April 1970 to 31 March 1974
Pakistan	The Fourth Five-Year Plan	1 July 1970 to 30 June 1975
Paraguay	Plan Nacional de Desarrollo Economico y Social	1971–1975
Peru	Plan del Peru	1971–1975
Philippines	Four-Year Development Plan	1 July 1971 to 30 June 1975
Saudi Arabia	Development Plan	Around mid-1970 to around mid-1975
Senegal	Troisième plan quadriennal de développement économique et social	1969–1973
Sri Lanka	The Five-Year Plan	1972–1976
Sudan	Five-Year Plan of Economic and Social Development of the Democratic Republic of Sudan	1 July 1970 to 30 June 1975
Syrian Arab Rep.	Third Five-Year Plan for Economic and Social Development in the Syrian Arab Republic	1971–1975
Thailand	Third National Economic and Social Development Plan (Summary)	1972–1976
Togo	Plan de développement économique et social	1971–1975
Trinidad and Tobago	Draft Third Five-Year Plan	1969–1973
Uganda	Third Five-Year Development Plan	1 July 1973 to 30 June 1976
United Rep. of Tanzania	Second Five-Year Plan for Economic and Social Development	1 July 1969 to 30 June 1974
Uruguay	Plan Nacional de Metas Quinquenales	1968–1972
Venezuela	IV Plan de la Nacion	1970–1974
Zambia	Second National Development Plan	1972–1976

Source: See Table 1.

268

As has already been mentioned, the use of more sophisticated methods is aggravated by the fact that plans have to be approved by politicians who are not adequately familiar with economic matters. Plans often have to be drawn up for parliaments, governments and civil servants in a form which hardly contains any quantitative relationships. Therefore, the published regulations of the plan, which have a certain degree of compulsory force, are formulated only in a general way. This state of affairs only underlines the importance of raising the level of economic knowledge in developing countries.

In most developing countries medium-term plans are usually prepared for 4 to 10 years. There are a few countries which also draw up long-term plans (forecasts) for 15 to 20 years. (See Table 5.)

Medium-term plans (e.g. five-year plans) justly play a prominent role if they are shaped within the framework of a long-term development strategy. In some cases a long-term plan may also incorporate a medium-term plan period. On the basis of experiences gained in planning during the 1960s, some specialists of developing countries deny the expediency of planning for a five-year, and generally for a fixed-time period (India). They acknowledge, on the one hand, the essential advantages of planning for a five-year period in the initial stage of planning. Also its simplicity is admitted as a great benefit inasmuch as it urges the government to proceed along a well controllable road and prevents it from slipping. They also say, however, that such five-year periods mean additional administrative rigidity in a system which is already rigid in itself. In the case of unforeseeable events the necessary changes and corrections are not always effected and the adaptation is carried out by inserting periods where economic planning is suspended. Psychologically, the frequent outbacks of plan targets have a demoralizing effect. Partly with reference to the experiences of socialist countries, certain specialists of developing countries suggest therefore more flexible plans. Such is e.g. the introduction of the so-called "rolling-plan" which consists of the following: the plan of the current year, including the budget and the foreign-exchange budget, a five-year plan whose targets, however, may change from year to year, and a long-range plan covering 10–15–20 years.

It is likely that such a system, if it operates well, will have many advantages over a rigid plan, but in relation to developing countries it may also be the source of irresponsible management. It may urge the governments to interpret their commitments for a given economico-political aim in a very "liberal" way.

In developing countries, too, the plans are broken down in a number of ways, partly by units of time, partly by sectors. The problem of a conflict between planning by sectors, industrial branches, on the one hand, and the national "integrated" plan, on the other, i.e. between sectoral and national priorities, has often come to the fore in the planning of developing countries not only as

---

* Plan refers to full calendar years except where otherwise indicated.
** Most targets indicated in the plan, however, are for 1973.

Table 6

*Planned and past average annual rates of increase in
agricultural and manufacturing components of gross domestic product**

Average annual rate of increase in manufacturing (stated as second figure against each country)	Country* and average annual rate of increase in agriculture (stated as first figure against each country)			Number of countries
	4.5 per cent or more	3.5 per cent or more but less than 4.5 per cent	Less than 3.5 per cent	
	Annual rate planned for initial years of the decade 1971–1980			
9 per cent or more	Venezuela 6.1, 9.4	Peru 4.3, 12.4	Algeria 3.0, 13.8	
	Lebanon 4.5, 9.10	Iran 4.4, 13.0	El Salvador 2.9 9.8	
	Saudi Arabia 4.6, 10.5	Ivory Coast 4.1, 16.4	Nigeria 1.8, 14.3	
	Brazil 7.8, 10.12	Mauritius 4.0, 10.3	Ethiopia 2.9, 13.8	
	Zambia 5.4, 14.7			
	Malaysia 8.4, 11.7			
	Iraq 6.9, 11.2			23
	Colombia 5.1, 9.2			
	Syrian Arab Rep. 5.1, 15.8			
	Sri Lanka 4.9, 10.0			
	Philippines 5.3, 9.0			
	Togo 6.7, 9.8			
	Pakistan 5.5, 10.2			
	Sudan 11.2, 9.5			
	United Rep. of Tanzania 5.1, 13.0			
7 per cent or more but less than 9 per cent	Argentina 4.6, 8.4	Uganda 4.2, 7.6		
	Senegal 5.9, 7.6			
	Thailand 5.1, 8.0			
	Kenya 4.6, 8.9			
	India 5.0, 7.7			
	Malawi 5.4, 8.1			7
Less than 7 per cent	Trinidad and Tobago 5.0, 5.0	Fiji 3.5, 4.5	Morocco 2.1, 4.3	3
Number of countries	22	6	5	33

Source: See Table 1.

*Countries have been classified according to magnitudes of annual rates of increase in agriculture and manufacturing. Within each category, countries are listed in descending order of their per capita gross domestic product in 1970. Owing to lack of sufficient information, precise figures for increase recorded during the past decade are not stated in the second part of the table.

For details on final year of the period to which planned rates refer, see footnote to Table 1.

a methodological question but also as an important problem of economic policy, especially in investment planning. (See Table 6.)

Development plans also contain, as a rule, the investment projects to be realized over the plan period. The role of such projects is especially important in the planning of developing countries. Not only on account of the pivotal role of the state investment programmes but also because foreign aid is usually attached to those investments. The investment projects constitute in the majority of developing countries the only item of the plan that is assigned to a given authority.

270

(Table 6 continued)

Average annual rate of increase in manufacturing (stated as second figure against each country)	Country* and average annual rate of increase in agriculture (stated as first figure against each country)			Number of countries
	4.5 per cent or more	3.5 per cent or more but less than 4.5 per cent	Less than 3.5 per cent	
	Annual rate achieved during the decade 1961–1970			
9 per cent or more	Malaysia Thailand	Iran Ivory Coast Togo	Trinidad and Tobago Saudi Arabia Zambia El Salvador Nigeria United Rep. of Tanzania Malawi Ethiopia	13
7 per cent or more but less than 9 per cent	Syrian Arab Rep.	Brazil Kenya Uganda Pakistan	Peru	6
Less than 7 per cent	Venezuela Iraq Morocco Philippines	Lebanon Colombia Sudan	Argentina Uruguay Fiji Algeria Paraguay Mauritius Senegal Sri Lanka India	16
Number of countries	7	10	18	35

In the case of all the other plan targets it is extremely unusual in the planning practice of developing countries that organizations responsible for plan implementation are specified in an explicit, concrete way.

It is also a general problem in planning that the estimates relating to investments, to production are more elaborated than those relating to consumption, the utilization of the goods produced. In the public sector little attention is paid to the utilization of the output of new enterprises, especially industrial enterprises. One of its consequences is the underutilization of the capacities of many Indian state enterprises. (See Table 7.)

It is also a serious problem that in most developing countries the technical preparation of plans – as evidenced by experiences – is very time-consuming, often taking 2–3 years, i. e. about half the average time that a given government is in power.

Table 8

*Expected and past average annual rates of growth of population**

Income group	Country and average annual rate			Number of countries
	3 per cent or more	2 per cent or more but less than 3 per cent	Less than 2 per cent	

Annual rate expected during initial years of the decade 1971–1980

Income group	3 per cent or more		2 per cent or more but less than 3 per cent		Less than 2 per cent		Number of countries
Countries with per capita gross domestic product of $ 600 or more	Venezuela	3.7			Argentina	1.4	
					Trinidad and Tobago	1.6	4
					Uruguay	1.3	
Countries with per capita gross domestic product of $ 300 or more but less than $ 600	Saudi Arabia	3.0	Lebanon	2.2			
	Peru	3.1	Brazil	2.8			
	Iraq	3.3	Fiji	2.3			
	Colombia	3.0	Iran	2.6			
	Ivory Coast	3.3	Zambia	2.8			
	Algeria	3.2	Malaysia	2.8			12
Countries with per capita gross domestic product of less than $ 300	El Salvador	3.1	Mauritius	–			
	Syrian Arab		Morocco	2.9	Senegal	1.8	
	Republic	–	Thailand	2.5	Nepal	1.9	
	Paraguay	3.3	Sri Lanka	2.1			
	Philippines	3.1	Togo	2.0			
	Kenya	3.1	Pakistan	2.7			
	Uganda	3.4	Sudan	2.5			
			Nigeria	2.5			20
			United Rep. of Tanzania	2.7			
			India	2.5			
			Malawi	2.5			
			Ethiopia	2.2			
Number of countries	13		18		5		36

Annual rate experienced during the decade 1961–1970

Income group	3 per cent or more		2 per cent or more but less than 3 per cent		Less than 2 per cent		Number of countries
Countries with per capita gross domestic product of $ 600 or more	Venezuela	3.3	Trinidad and Tobago	2.5	Argentina	1.5	4
					Uruguay	1,3	
Countries with per capita gross domestic product of $ 300 or more but less than $ 600	Peru	3.1	Lebanon	2.8			
	Fiji	3.2	Saudi Arabia	2.6			
	Iraq	3.4	Brazil	2.9			
	Colombia	3.3	Iran	2.8			
			Zambia	2.9			
			Malaysia	2.9			12
			Ivory Coast	2.9			
			Algeria	2.7			

Source: See Table 1.

*For details on country classification, on final year of the period to which expected rates of increase refer and on the listing of countries for which data are not available, see footnote to Table 1.

(Table 8 continued)

Income group	Country and average annual rate			Number of countries
	3 per cent or more	2 per cent or more but less than 3 per cent	Less than 2 per cent	
Countries with per capita *gross domestic product of less than* $ 300	El Salvador 3.2	Mauritius 2.7	Nepal 1.8	
	Syrian Arab	Senegal 2.4	Ethiopia 1.9	
	Republic 3.1	Sri Lanka 2.5		
	Paraguay 3.4	Togo 2.4		
	Morocco 3.1	Uganda 2.5		20
	Thailand 3.2	Nigeria 2.5		
	Philippines 3.4	United Rep. of		
	Kenya 3.0	Tanzania 2.5		
	Pakistan 3.2	India 2.5		
	Sudan 3.0	Malawi 2.6		
Number of countries	14	18	4	36

Even though the plans of several developing countries contain general statements setting the aims of the redistribution of incomes on a more equitable basis, they rarely translate them into action.

There are also serious deficiences in the *social implications* of the plans. Despite the fact that the general, "integrated" concept of economic development, i.e. the close interrelatedness of the economic and social factors, is accepted, these questions are not considered adequately in setting the plan targets when decisions must be made on how much should be spent on social services (education, housing, public health), or on investment in infrastructure and the direct productive activities of the economy. As decisions on these questions are usually made not on the basis of principles, the final targets are often influenced by such factors as the weight of the leaders of individual power groups or institutions in the state apparatus, or temporary political considerations. The social aspects of the plan are often confined to "family planning", to the promotion of birth control and a few questions of public health. (See Table 8.)

External economic relations have a prominent place in the plans of developing countries. The main problem lies of course in the fact that it is impossible to develop, over a short, 4–5 year period, a production structure in harmony with an ever-changing domestic and foreign demand. (Which, by the way, is not an exclusive problem of developing countries.) In the plans of most developing countries the problem of external economic relations is discussed as an issue of the equilibrium of the balance of payments during the plan period.

In the short run, export earnings depend on the formation of foreign demand for exportable goods and also on the home consumption of these commodities. In

18*

275

Table 9

Planned change in dependence on external resources

Income group	Annual increase in percentage share of external resources in gross domestic product or annual decrease in percentage share of national resources transferred abroad during initial years of the decade 1971–1980 (a) (in parentheses projected external resources as percentage of gross domestic product in final year of plan) (b)			Number of countries
	Countries envisaging surplus of gross national saving over gross investment during plan period	Countries envisaging deficit of gross national saving over gross investment during plan period		
		Countries envisaging increased dependence on external resources by final year of plan	Countries envisaging reduced dependence on external resources by final year of plan	
Countries with per capita gross domestic product of $ 600 or more	Argentina 0.12 (−0.5)	Trinidad and Tobago 0.28 (3.8)	Venezuela −0.15 (1.4)	3
Countries with per capita gross domestic product of $ 300 or more but less than $ 600	Malaysia 0.25 (−2.2) Iraq 0.28 (−2.1) Ivory Coast 0.07 (−3.0)		Fiji −0.01 (8.1) Iran −0.53 (0.3)	5
Countries with per capita gross domestic product of less than $ 300		Paraguay 0.31 (4.6) Morocco 0.14 (6.1) Philippines 0.10 (1.5) Kenya 0.10 (5.0) Uganda 0.23 (2.4) Nigeria 0.63 (11.8)	El Salvador −0.02 (4.0) Sri Lanka −0.36 (1.5) Pakistan −0.15 (3.0) India −0.06 (1.5)(c) Malawi −1.05 (10.1)	11
Number of countries	4	7	8	19

Source: See Table 1.

(a) External resources equal excess of imports over exports of goods and services, including factor income. Within each category, countries are listed in descending order of their per capita gross domestic product in 1970.

For four countries listed in the first column, planned change refers to annual decrease in percentage share of national resources in gross domestic product transferred abroad.

For definition of gross national saving and differences in concepts of saving, see footnote to Table 7. For differences in concepts of gross domestic product and for details on final year of the period to which planned increase refers, see footnote to Table 1.

(b) Minus sign indicates outflow of resources or, in other words, surplus of gross national saving over gross investment.

(c) In relation to net domestic product.

a number of developing countries, especially those based on a one-crop economy, export goods are made available to domestic consumption only to a very limited extent. Hence, the restriction imposed on domestic consumption of such goods will by no means increase the export surpluses. Though some export goods are occasionally also consumed domestically, the circumstances of foreign demand are such that, irrespective of the large supplies available for export purposes, the export earnings will not increase. There are also institutional limitations to the extent to which savings can be made during a five-year plan period. (See Tables 9 and 10).

Looking at the issue from the import side, there are generally two problems in the foreground: making economies in the case of imports (also by reducing

Table 10
*Planned and past average annual rate of increase in exports and imports of goods and services**

Average annual rate of increase in imports (stated as second figure against each country)	Country and average annual rate of increase in exports (stated as first figure against each country)			Number of countries
	8 per cent or more	6 per cent or more but less than 8 per cent	Less than 6 per cent	
Annual rate planned for initial years of the decade 1971–1980				
8 per cent or more	Argentina 9.2, 10.3 Fiji 12.3, 11.7 Iran 15.6, 13.1 Colombia 8.8, 10.7 Algeria 11.6, 12.2 Philippines 10.3, 10.6 Sudan (11.0), (8.7) Nigeria 10.5, 11.3 Ethiopia (9.5), (9.8)	Paraguay 7.4, 9.1	Mauritius (4.6), (8.0)	11
6 per cent or more but less than 8 per cent	Pakistan 8.5, 6.0 Malawi 10.6, 6.0	Ivory Coast 6.8, 6.7 El Salvador 7.4, 6.7 Kenya 6.7, 7.5 United Rep. of Tanzania 6.0, 7.8	Uganda 4.8, 6.5	7
Less than 6 per cent		Syrian Arab Republic 6.5, 5.0 Thailand (7.0), (2.8) India (7.0), (1.5)	Venezuela 4.1, 3.5 Trinidad and Tobago 2.4, 2.9 Malaysia 4.6, 5.1 Iraq 2.7, 4.8 Morocco 4.9, 5.3 Sri Lanka 5.6, 3.4	9
Number of countries	11	8	8	27
Annual rate achieved during the decade 1961–1970				
8 per cent or more	Fiji 10.0, 9.2 Iran 11.9, 9.5 Thailand 8.2, 11.9 Philippines 8.3, 11.4		Ivory Coast 5.6, 10.0 United Rep. of Tanzania 5.1, 8.0	6
6 per cent or more but less than 8 per cent		Trinidad and Tobago 7.1, 6.8	Colombia 3.3, 6.4 Ethiopia 4.4, 6.1	3
Less than 6 per cent	Nigeria 10.7, 5.7	Algeria 6.5, −1.4 Syrian Arab Rep. 6.4, 5.2 Mauritius 7.4, 3.0	Argentina 5.3, 2.6 Venezuela 5.7, 4.1 Malaysia 5.5, 4.9 Iraq 5.5, 3.7 El Salvador 5.7, 4.0 Paraguay 3.1, 3.1 Morocco 3.1, 5.1 Sri Lanka 1.4, −1.2 Kenya 5.1, 5.7 Uganda 4.5, 3.7 Pakistan 5.7, 3.0 Sudan 3.9, 3.7 India 2.8, −0.2 Malawi 3.1, 4.4	18
Number of countries	5	4	18	27

Source: See Table 1.

*Countries have been classified according to magnitude of annual rates of increase in exports and imports of goods and services. Within each category, countries are listed in descending order of their per capita gross domestic product in 1970.

Figures appearing in parentheses refer to annual rates of increase in merchandise trade only. Rates have been calculated from data in constant prices. The known exceptions are planned rates for Algeria, Colombia, Ethiopia, Malaysia, Nigeria, Sri Lanka and the United Rep. of Tanzania, which are derived from data stated to be in current prices.

For details on the final year of the period to which planned rates refer, see footnote to Table 1.

imports for luxury purposes), and the import-substituting type of industrial development. Given the rate of investments, their import content may be modified in principle by selecting such sectors and productive procedures which require fewer imported and more domestic products, primarily labour force. But given the technical inadequacies of developing countries, the possibilities of such import substitution are limited, especially in industry. In the case of consumer goods, increased savings may actually result in a reduction of imports. If, however, in the process of industrialization by import substitution such imports have partially been eliminated, then a major saving drive will not lead to the lowering of the import level. If the production of domestic consumer goods calls for imports, then increased saving may lead to a certain degree of import reduction, but will result in unused capacities in the domestic industries concerned. (The problem of import-substituting industrialization will specifically be dealt with in another chapter of this volume.)

Thus it is seldom possible to ensure that export earnings during the plan period should be large enough to finance the import needs of the economy. It can almost be regarded as a normal state of affairs that export earnings during a plan period lag behind estimated or expected foreign-exchange incomes. Thus the problem of planning boils down to the task of finding the necessary conditions which ensure that

1. export expectations envisaged by the plan are met;

2. import expenditures do not exceed the planned level, and the pattern of imports is in harmony with the priorities laid down in the plan;

3. foreign capital is available either as loan or otherwise to cover the expected foreign-exchange deficit. (It is on this condition that some developing countries base 30 to 60 per cent of their state investment programmes.)

It is of course theoretically possible to effect a long-run development of the economy, a production structure, in such a way that the equilibrium of the balance of payments is maintained, parallel with the expanding volume of foreign trade. But to put this aim into effect is extremely difficult even in industrially developed capitalist countries. From time to time these countries are also compelled to take a number of emergency measures to eliminate their balance-of-payments gaps. This is an even more difficult problem in developing countries.

Manpower planning is an extremely complex and unsolved problem in all countries, but particularly in the developing world. No doubt, in this case we have to do with a problem that cannot be solved within, or squeezed into, the framework of one or two medium-term development plans. It is one of the preconditions for liquidating poverty and backwardness to draw a substantial part of the population into the process of "information-collecting and information acquisition". The more backward a given society, the more difficult is this process. As a result of the expansion of public education, well-informed people take an active part in economic development. This process tears down obsolete traditions and contributes to an increase in the individual's labour productivity. The training of a skilled staff in adequate quantity and quality is therefore

278

a further basic condition for realizing the objectives of the development plans of the national economy.

For this reason the rate of development of public education in most developing countries is much faster than capital accumulation or economic growth. But the expansion of education also adds to the number of the army of the educated unemployed. The level of technological development and the environment do not allow to absorb all talents and skills. In societies which are poor by any standards, investments in the development of public education often lead to the further impoverishment of society. Therefore, the effectiveness of investments in public education will be extremely low for society.

The serious deficiencies of the educational system also diminish the effectiveness of planning in this field. The educational system inherited from colonial times does not meet the requirements of promoting industrial growth and industrialization. This system had served the interests of an exceedingly narrow élite, and is unable to satisfy the needs of a modern nation, even in the bourgeois sense of the word.

But the transformation of the educational system is looked upon in the majority of developing countries not from the viewpoint of radical socio-economic changes. There can be no question of a cultural revolution or any radical change similar to it.[12]

In determining the needs of population, the departure is usually taken not from the endowments, the development plans of the country in question but from the occupational pattern of the active population of developed capitalist countries. This is regarded as an optimum. Consequently, they neglect e. g. agriculture. They ignore that in developing countries the town exercised a stronger attractive impact on skilled labour than in the developed countries. They do not pay sufficient attention to the problem of "brain drain", the appeal of foreign countries either. Consequently, the attempt to integrate the educational system with the system of planned economic development has rarely been successful. As a result, the educational systems and policies of developing countries are characterized by serious disproportions.

There is a disproportion between the composition of school-leavers and the occupational structure needed by development at every level, ranging from village schools to universities. Especially small is the number of engineers, economists, agronomists and teachers. There are few vocational schools and

---

[12] The Experts' Report of the World Bank stresses in this connection that in the early 1970s only 44 per cent of all young people of school-age in the developing countries went to school, in spite of the fact that between 1960 and 1967 the number of children enrolled increased by 51 per cent (to 212 million) in developing countries. The Report specifies the main problems as follows: (a) the number of young people of school-age is rising rapidly; (b) the quality of educational establishments is deteriorating; (c) the ratio of apprentices is very low; (d) the educational system is not tied to manpower demand; (e) the maintenance costs of schools are rising; and (f) limited availability of development resources. (International Bank for Reconstruction and Development, October 18, 1971.)

279

technical secondary schools. The teaching materials follow the traditional pattern. There are also serious disproportions within the educational system itself. Efforts are being concentrated on the development of primary schools and universities. The development of secondary education is neglected. As a result, there is a great shortage of teachers in primary schools, and there are few university students. The staff of "medium cadres" is also very limited.

Even the scarce material resources available to the development of the educational network are frittered away for lack of a purposeful, comprehensive cultural policy. The "status quo" not only remains unchanged, but the situation is getting worse. Extension courses and adult education are all but completely neglected.

Thus the educational system and the cultural policy fit into the general "trend", which seeks to find solutions to the burning problems of economic development without effecting any radical social changes.

Moreover, public education is usually too much of an academic character. Curricula have generally been taken over from the advanced countries. It is partly for this reason that students cannot get a training needed by economic development and by their actual employment opportunities. In many countries with a high enrolment the drop-out rate is enormous. There is a shortage of well-trained teachers, and the equipment of schools is very poor. Low payment rates also contribute to the poor quality of teachers. The level of higher education is often very low as universities can often not afford to employ professors in full time, while the number of students enrolled in these establishments is very high.

III. SOME PROBLEMS OF PLAN IMPLEMENTATION

What does plan implementation under the conditions of developing countries mean? It is impossible to give an unambiguous answer to this question in the case of most developing countries. Where plan targets have a "prediction" character, this question is not raised at all. A faulty prediction is not the same as the non-fulfilment of a plan. Implementation can be set as a realistic objective only in the case of technically correct and structurally well-balanced plans. Plan implementation does not mean the endeavour to fulfil mechanically the targets envisaged by the original plan document either, especially not under the circumstances of developing countries, where the original objectives and ideas often prove incorrect and faulty, and new, unforeseen problems often crop up. The main problem of plan implementation is of course to examine what results have been achieved in promoting development in the direction set and assumed to be correct.

1. THE INSTRUMENTS OF PLAN IMPLEMENTATION

Under the social and economic conditions of the majority of developing countries plans cannot be fulfilled by means of instructions. We have already mentioned that in certain cases the government gives or may give instructions for state enterprises, or may compel them to implement the plans. But even this is not general practice, and must rather be regarded as an exception.

Thus governments need a set of instruments to ensure that the plans are duly fulfilled.

It is not enough just to acknowledge that a development programme is a means of action and not merely a diagnostic study or the expression of expectations. Plans cannot be fulfilled if they do not contain the instruments, the clear formulation of actions to be taken.

The co-ordination of the economic-political objectives, the ensurance of their concerted impact working in the same direction, would be a hard job in itself even if all the quantitative and qualitative interrelationships were fully known. This is, however, an impossible requirement even in the industrially highly developed capitalist countries under the current conditions, and given the present-day level of our economic knowledge. This applies to developing countries to an even greater extent. It is unknown what the reaction will be on certain incentives or limiting factors, and the uncertainty is especially great in such fields where the development process gives rise to sudden changes in the behaviour of people and their economic activities in general. Past experience is of little value, simply because it is lacking. Again this is a phenomenon not exclusively limited to developing countries only. Similar experiences have been witnessed in the industrially advanced capitalist and socialist countries alike. But the experience of developing countries also shows that the governments are usually overconfident of the effect that one or another regulator will make. In reality, however, these regulators more often prove insufficient than successful, and do not lead to the expected results. This is due partly to the resistance of the private sector, partly to the fact that in the given economic environment the economic and non-economic factors produce a much stronger reaction than the anticipated impact of the regulators (if it has been anticipated at all). Therefore, when setting certain objectives of the economic policy it is absolutely necessary ro reckon with the effect of regulators, which may be different in intensity at various levels.

In order to implement their development plans, their investments, the governments need adequate financial resources. Consequently, whenever taxes are levied, direct or indirect, account must also be taken of the impact of taxation, how the incomes siphoned off by means of taxes will affect economic growth. Or conversely, how the private sector or the population at large will react upon a reduction of taxes. If the policy is aimed at promoting accumulation in general, then it is more expedient to introduce a kind of tax which will reduce the consumption of the population rather than impose a tax which will curb the investments of the private sector. But it may also occur that the taxation policy aims at restricting the investments of the private sector in favour of the public sector. This, in turn, will call for a different type of taxation.

There is a conflict of interests and a nearly permanent debate in developing countries upon the desirable long-term political objective to be set, and the necessary short-term measures to be taken. Temporary equilibrium troubles often call for stabilizationary measures that are in conflict with long-term political objectives (e. g. the stopping of long-term development investments because of temporary balance of payments difficulties). Hence, an adequate adjustment mechanism is needed to maintain the principles of economic policy. Reaction on short-term needs cannot be avoided. Governments are often compelled to take such measures, because equilibrium troubles may develop in the external economy, which may undermine the long-term objectives of the national economy. It is this factor that gives prominence to the importance of annual planning.

In the chapter on economic policy we have seen that the measures of influencing the economy may be divided into two groups: those representing a direct intervention in the economy and effecting it directly, and those either stimulating or restricting the decisions, and having a special impact on the private sector. In nearly all developing countries. use is made of all available devices.

There is a difference only in the intensity of utilization, the proportions of individual policy measures and the efficiency of the state apparatus. But there is a noticeable tendency that the significance of indirect factors increases with the rate of growth of the economy concerned.

But the choice of adequate instruments of economic policy depends not only on the state and development of the economy but also on the nature of long-term objectives.

A crucial, specific problem of plan implementation in most of the developing countries is posed by agriculture operated nearly exclusively by the private sector, with subsistence economy still playing a not insignificant role in it. It is an almost unsurmountable task to integrate it with the national economic plan, and it is even more difficult to ensure plan implementation. These problems present themselves in an especially sharp form in the most underdeveloped African countries, but also in the relatively developed ones, as the Arab Republic of Egypt. Since the weight of agriculture in the economy is extremely great, often decisive, the deficiencies of the plans in relation to agriculture also determine the possibilities in other fields.

In developing countries the following principal policies of plan implementation were and are applied.

State investments. Productive state investments constitute the most direct measure at the disposal of a government in plan implementation, in setting the direct targets connected with determining the size of national economic investments. Such investments are made for strategic or political reasons as the government wishes to keep certain assets within the public sector. State investments are also made because the necessary skills are lacking in the private sector. Very often the magnitude of investments makes it necessary for the government to intervene in such cases when sufficient private capital is not available. The significance of state investments in developing countries, in their social transformation, is extremely great.

Direct control. The quantitative, physical means of direct control are often used by developing countries for the allocation of scarce resources. This is very often indispensable in developing countries to ensure further progress, to prevent the squandering of resources or their utilization for undesirable purposes not promoting economic growth. Most frequent is direct control over foreign exchange earnings and management, price control, direct state export and import controls, etc. The benefits and drawbacks of direct control are apparent in nearly all developing countries where it is applied. One of the greatest problems is the lack of a mechanism which could apply direct control in an efficient and satisfactory way. In applying direct control it is also difficult to find an objective criterion on the basis of which decisions can be made on the allocation of resources. As the demands are multifarious, they will present themselves simultaneously in various domains of economic and social life. In practice, the danger is very great that, instead of objective criteria – the main targets of the plan

– secondary, political, personal factors or even corruption may serve as a basis for decision-making.

Indirect incentives and regulators. In order to bring to fruition the development objectives of plans, the governments of most developing countries are trying to make their decisions effective by applying means which have an effect on the profits of the private sector and on the conditions of its production. These regulations are designed to stimulate certain activities and restrict others. Most important of these are fiscal policy, customs policy, credit policy and certain wage and price controls. Some of them are highly selective.

Experience has shown that the effectiveness of indirect incentives and regulators depends, partly, on the effectiveness of the market mechanism. Such calculation possibilities must be ensured for those strata aimed at by the regulators, which enable them to measure exactly the impact of these regulators upon their economic activities. This makes it necessary for them not only to know the impact of discriminatory measures or incentives well in advance, but also to be familiar with the alternatives. These conditions, however, are seldom ensured, and, consequently, such regulators have proved of little value for attaining the objectives. In most developing countries the market mechanism is embryonic, the risk is too great, the countries are capital-scarce, and the private sector has not got enough capital to invest when incentives are applied. Therefore, potential profits must be high enough to stimulate investments. Marginal differences are of no use in this case. The impact of incentives on foreign capital and, in general, securing the assent of foreign capital to adopt the plan targets is a rather complicated question. The effectiveness of indirect incentives is also influenced by other factors, e. g., by the simultaneous application of direct policy measures. Under the conditions of developing countries the optimum combination of direct intervention and indirect measures is one of the most difficult and delicate tasks of economic policy and plan implementation.

2. ANNUAL PLANS AND THE STATE BUDGET

From the point of view of the implementation of medium-term plans, *annual plans* are of crucial importance. The significance of annual plans follows from the medium-term plan itself. For one thing, a medium-term plan cannot contain all targets in the same detail as an annual plan. In addition, unless the fulfilment of medium-term plans is not supervised in certain phases of the plan period, it is extremely difficult to keep a tab on the progress of implementation. The mechanical interpolation of intermediate years – as widely applied in many developing countries – is not a solution. Without annual planning, medium-term plans cannot be interpreted. Without it medium-term plans are ineffective.

As also evidenced by the practice of developing countries, it is not easy to establish an organic relationship between medium-term and annual plans.

It is often accepted as a principle that the targets of medium-term plans should be used in evaluating the annual plans, but annual plans must also continuously be made use of in reporting on the progress of the development plan. Under the dynamic circumstances of developing countries plans are subject to continual changes, and substantial alterations are often necessary. However, the re-assessment of the targets of medium-term plans and the taking into account of implementation in the course of annual planning is seldom effected. It is exactly for this double purpose that annual plans should be made use of.

Under the steadily changing conditions an optimum compromise must be sought in annual plans between long-term needs and short-term possibilities. It is a lesser evil, in a sense, if constant and drastic deviations from the medium-term plan targets must be tolerated than if no medium-term plans exist at all. On the other hand, unforeseen changes may lead to a critical situation if rigid insistence on medium-term plans is enforced. In case such changes prove necessary, every effort must be made to effect a best possible adjustment in the annual plans of the implementation measures to the main development objectives.

Another extreme case in the practice of plan implementation in developing countries is the unconditional enforcement of the annual plan and, especially, of the budget. In several countries of South-East Asia, the centre of plans is the state budget. This is connected with the view that state investments constitute the central means of plan implementation in any development plan. The state budget is, in essence, a development budget comprising all state development expenditure that can be regarded as investment or quasi-investment.

The importance of the budget in developing countries is beyond doubt. However, planning covers more than merely investments.

A heavy concentration on the budget is, to a certain extent, the reflection of the standpoint of governments not wishing (or occasionally not able) to plan the national economy as a system, a view which makes it possible for them to avoid planning a connected network of operative controls and operations needed for plan implementation. Such plans seldom pay due attention to domestic or foreign trade, prices, etc. As their attention is focused on investments, the state budget as the centre of planning is orientated mainly on the accounting of state expenditures. If the plan is formulated only in the context of the state budget, it will provide no rational basis for a co-ordination of the development efforts of the economy. Thus budget should not be mixed up with the plan, nor can it be substituted for the plan.

It must also be admitted that in many countries significant analytic work is being done in drawing up the state budget, in the course of which occasionally physical quantities are also taken into account and efforts are made to co-ordinate economic policy, too. Such analytic work is often fragmentary.

In several developing countries, however, the organization of the state budget, whose task it would be to see about the implementation of the development budgets, lags far behind the requirements. Not only is budget discipline entirely lacking, but there is often no continuity in budgeting either. Its composition changes from year to year in individual countries. In several developing countries, given the general weakness of the budgetary system, a large proportion of the public sector, primarily the activities of state enterprises, are not included in whatever form in the state budget. (The budget often includes only such items as represent subsidies for state enterprises.)

Supervision of the fulfilment of the plan also constitutes an important part of implementation. It is one of the weakest links in the planning of developing countries. The main problems in the field of supervision – if it exists at all – are the following:

– supervision is exercised not by organizations independent of the planning and financial organs but by the same agencies which are responsible for implementation;

– supervision is often limited either to extremely complex or mainly administrative questions, such as the observance of formal administrative discipline or similar measures, and is usually not concerned with preventing the squandering of state funds.

The relationship of the supervising organs with legislation is also extremely loose, and it seldom occurs that deficiencies and omissions in implementation are brought before the legislative body. Supervision is not flexible and mobile enough.

The problem is made even more complicated by the fact that it is utterly difficult to form a true picture of the economy itself. Lack of data, problems of co-operation between public and private sectors, great physical distance of some parts of the private sector from the centre, etc. – all these factors add to the difficulties of supervision.

3. IMPLEMENTATION PROBLEMS OF STATE INVESTMENTS

As has already been mentioned, state investments are the most important means of plan implementation in developing countries. Their share varies from country to country, but in most countries, in fact in the majority of the developing world, it exceeds 50 per cent of total investments. The structure of state investments is also different. In most developing countries over 50 per cent of state investments are of the infrastructural type in its broadest sense. In some countries the share of productive investments is often 60 to 70 per cent.

Owing to the great significance of state investments, the micro-economic implications of their implementation are also of primary importance to the national economy. As in all other countries, state investment programmes in developing countries consist of individual investment projects. The implementation phase begins with the approval, and ends with the putting into operation of the project in question. The approval, i. e. the selection of the project and the determination of the order of execution of individual investment projects, takes place before the detailed plans are drawn up. The preparation of detailed technical and economic documentation and execution comes afterwards. The execution of state investments in most developing countries is also encumbered with serious difficulties. These difficulties are very complex and are due to various factors. Usually two deficiencies are criticized in connection with the execution of investment projects in the public sector: implementation takes more time, and the costs are substantially higher than envisaged in the plan. Very often, too optimistic calculations are made with a view to getting more easily the higher organs' agreement on starting the investment. These problems are not unknown in the state investments of socialist countries either, and are actually met with in the private enterprises of industrially developed capitalist countries as well. In the developing countries, where the conditions of adequate technical planning are not available, and whose experience in analysing the economy and the market with regard to the supply of necessary materials and their price formation is limited, these problems stand out in even stronger relief. Sometimes external factors are responsible for them. Such are e. g. price changes in foreign markets, the denial of an expected loan or credit, etc. But the crucial deficiencies and bottlenecks originate in the developing countries themselves: lack of skill, obsolete organizational methods, red tape, inefficiency, disruptions or occasionally deliberate sabotage in certain fields. As a result, incompleted investments grow at a much faster rate than new investments.

The first and most frequent difficulty in the execution of investment projects is the lack of co-ordination. Responsibility for a given investment in the public sector lies either with a ministry, a development company, a state enterprise, or concurrently with several organizations. The services of foreign enterprises have also often to be made use of. In most cases local private enterprises or other state organs also take part in the execution. Therefore, co-ordination is a task of crucial importance, especially in the case of such complex and multi-purpose projects as the Aswan Dam Complex in Egypt or the Damodar Valley System in India. Usually two methods are used in this field. Either a separate company is formed to take care of the execution, or a project board is founded, to which the chief engineer in charge is directly responsible for implementation. It is obvious that even given an efficient organization, the immense and complex task of implementing a project is difficult to cope with, especially if the practice of traditional public works is followed, which is common in developing countries. In India, e. g., implementation contracts were prepared even in the late 1960s according to an Act approved in 1929, which is of course far from meeting present-day requirements. In most Latin-American countries there is no generally accepted legislation on the implementation of state investments, nor are there any appropriate organizations to execute and supervise them. In the initial phase there is the Ministry of Finance or a development corporation, and in the last phase a finished project with nothing in between.

In most cases the problems already begin with the technical designs, which are often very poor in quality. The execution of projects usually starts at a time when the technical designs are not yet available. As a result, changes in the plans in progress are very common, and there is much extra, unplanned work. It often occurs that no account is taken of the necessary infrastructure, labour force and other prerequisites. The shortage of building materials also adds to the delays.

In many countries the contractors are private businessmen. In such cases the government agencies are compelled by law to invite tenders. But they are, as a rule, unable to take decisions as either very few tenders are sent in for the project and the number of competing contractors is too small, or they lack the expertise needed to evaluate the tenders. Bribery is also a common phenomenon.[13]

It is impossible to have access to reliable data that are comparable. What is available is rather a sort of sporadic records, which are, however, typical of the general situation. In India, e. g., in the five years between 1961 and 1966, only 24 out of 228 major state investments were accomplished in time, the rest were finished with more or less delay. Compared with the time planned, the delays exceeded two years in the case of 13 projects, and 6 months in the case of 134 projects. Out of the 228 there were only 66 projects with no significant surplus cost. Unplanned costs amounted to 40 per cent in the case of 93 projects. These problems and proportions are also characteristic of other developing countries.

Obviously, such practice considerably diminishes the effectiveness of state investments and retards the implementation of plans.

4. THE MECHANISMS OF SURMOUNTING UNFORESEEN DIFFICULTIES

The plans of developing countries are often based on too optimistic assumptions. However, even in such cases, when the plan is more or less realistic and exact, many unforeseen difficulties jeopardizing the whole programme may arise in the course of implementation. (We are referring here to economic questions only.)

In the late 1960s, Sussex University (England) held a scientific conference on the theme "Crisis in Planning". One of the participants from a developing country said that the problem lay rather in how planning must be made in a critical situation, "Planning in Crisis" – instead of "Crisis in Planning", because this was one of the principal problems of developing countries. A critical situation may arise from many factors in a developing economy, and difficulties and tensions are inevitable concomitants of planning.

But external problems arising in the course of plan implementation are of greater significance, since developing countries are dependent to a great extent on the import of foreign machinery, equipment and know-how. (External factors may also be different, e. g. changes in export or import prices with the effect of diminishing export earnings or increasing import prices, or the loss of other resources, e. g. a decrease in capital imports, a change in the behaviour of creditors, etc.)

It stands to reason that no single country, not even the industrially advanced countries, are in a position to fully eliminate or neutralize the impact of certain unforeseen, primarily political factors, on the economy. There is a factor of

[13] *Indian Builder*. New Delhi, April, 1965, pp. 30–31.

uncertainty involved in all economic activities, and many countries have sufficient reserves to counterbalance it.

As regards plan implementation in developing countries, a built-in buffer mechanism designed to diminish the adverse effects of these factors is a viable method. This calls for the formulation of the following requirements:

1. In order to diminish the impact of unforeseen difficulties, the programmes of state i vestment projects, especially in countries with less experience in plan implementation, must be made more flexible. General preparations must be made in such a way that certain projects can be postponed until the conditions of implementation are ensured, and the execution of other projects can be slowed down or even stopped altogether. Therefore it is necessary to lay down, already in the medium-term plans, the priorities of individual projects for their significance from the point of view of plan targets.

2. Already in the medium-term plans provisions must be made for the reduction of certain items in state expenditure to ensure the channelling back into the development budget of sums in the case of unforeseen income losses. If such changes take place it is not enough, however, just to build up money funds; a material equilibrium must also be established, including foreign-exchange equilibrium.

3. For the above reasons it is expedient to draw up "shadow budgets", special budget variations in annual breakdowns to determine what changes that are to be effected in the case of an economic emergency do the least harm to the plan, or, on the other side, what new projects should be launched in the case of an unforeseen increase in resources.

4. The special importance of foreign earnings makes it imperative to co-ordinate to the highest possible degree the economic problems of internal and external relationships, especially when emergency measures have to be taken. This makes it necessary not only to ensure a high degree of concentration of foreign exchange control but also to take a number of other political and administrative measures:

– When and where is it vitally important to implement projects with a high import-content? If, for economic and political considerations, it is essential to implement a given plan project, it is expedient to secure foreign financial resources, e. g. a loan, to ensure the unimpeded influx of the necessary machinery and know-how.

– A special reserve fund of foreign exchange must be built up to ensure the temporary bridging of sudden gaps and income losses. The size of such funds must be determined as a function of the import needs of projects deemed to be most important for the national economy.

– As the projects of various types are affected differently by external difficulties (e. g. agricultural projects, communal development, road constructions are, as a rule, less import-sensitive), it is necessary to ensure the temporary regrouping of the labour force for such projects in the case of great international crises, and not to leave the labour force (or certain material resources) unutilized.

– They must also be prepared to find adequate internal or international substituting resources suitable, at least in part, to offset unforeseen losses. If such states of emergency prevail, the resources of the international organizations or inter-governmental capital transfers may also be used.

Developing countries have seldom succeeded in establishing such buffer mechanisms and even less in forming reserve funds. The difficulties caused by unforeseen problems have often led to disruptions in, or even to, the termination of the implementation of their plans. In such cases they have been unable to ensure the continuity of their economic objectives.

5. PLAN IMPLEMENTATION AND FOREIGN-OWNED ENTERPRISES

A not insignificant part of the activities of international super-monopolies is still concentrated in the countries of the "Third World". Many enterprises are the survivals of colonial times, and are mainly concerned with the extraction of raw materials and a certain degree of processing. In the second half of the 1960s, 56 per cent of American private capital and 49 to 50 per cent of British private capital were invested in "mining and metallurgy" and the oil industry in developing countries. Further, not insignificant sums were also invested in the agricultural sector. The volume of the investments of foreign monopolies has increased – though, compared with previous periods, at a lower rate – even after independence was gained by developing countries.

The "global" or "multinational" super-monopolies are faced in the "Third World" with partners whose positions are much weaker than theirs. It is their presence in the developing countries which represents most conspicuously the international system of monopoly capitalism, of imperialist exploitation.

Historical experience provides the evidence that capital export creates relationships between developed capital-exporting and capital-importing countries different from those between developed capital-exporting and economically underdeveloped capital-importing countries, though they are in both cases basically identical relationships of exploitation. But the actual forms of its manifestation in countries where foreign capital completely controls the economy differ from those in countries where the weight of foreign capital in the economy is relatively insignificant.

In the first group of countries the so-called "assimilation" of foreign capital is much more difficult, occasionally impossible, as Hilferding pointed out in relation to economically underdeveloped countries:

"In large economic areas, where capital is, owing to given national conditions, necessarily developed at a rapid rate, the national assimilation of foreign capital took a short time. Thus, e.g., Germany assimilated Belgian and French capital very quickly... In small economic areas, however, assimilation met with serious difficulties as the formation of a national capitalist class was a slower and more difficult process.

290

This became ... impossible as soon as the nature of capital export had changed, and the capitalist classes of the large economic areas (i. e. the leading imperialist powers – *M. S.*) did not strive to establish in foreign countries industries producing consumer goods, but rather to secure raw materials for their own even increasing producer-goods industries. It was in this way that, e. g., the ore and coal mines of the countries of the Pyrenean peninsula were taken over by foreign capital. These countries were deprived of these raw materials to the advantage of British, German and French industries at a time when they might have set about developing the most important branch of modern economies, i. e. their own iron industry. As a result, their capitalist development, together with their political and financial development, got stuck at the very beginning. As they became economically subject to foreign capital, they also became politically second-rate states ..."[14]

It is obvious that international capitalist exploitation, which came into being as a result of relations taking shape in the wake of capital export, exercised the most serious impact upon the economy and society of developing countries.

In the past, the economic subjugation of developing countries was coupled with colonial political dependence. In this way, peculiar forms of imperialist exploitation came into being.

It was the most salient feature of colonial exploitation that the political rule made it possible for the metropolitan countries to exercise full and exclusive control over the economy of colonies and to exploit them. Free capital flow protected by violent (military) means, tariff reductions for the colonizing country, monopolized foreign trade, control over finances, land concessions, the right to prospect and exploit natural resources, and the licensing of other economic activities for the colonizing power and colonial companies, double exploitation of colonial peoples, high taxation with the resulting incomes wholly or partially transferred to the metropolitan country – these were the most common means and methods of obtaining colonial extra profits.

The situation is virtually the same in such present-day economically underdeveloped, dependent, semi-colonical countries where the imperialist monopolies enjoy substantial prerogatives extorted by violence, blackmail, or "more refined, tactful" means, as by setting up and bribing puppet governments, etc. But these prerogatives are much less stable now as the state apparatus is no longer controlled by foreign capital in the same way as in the colonial times, even in systems closely collaborating with the imperialist powers. Foreign capital is compelled to let local ruling strata have their share, and take into account the measures of local legislation. Though in many cases the legislation of the new states regulates the activities of foreign companies, but also seeks to attract foreign capital investments by various tax reductions and other incentives. These incentives supplement the benefits the specific conditions of the "Third World"

[14] R. Hilferding: *Finance Capital* (in Hungarian), Budapest, Közgazdasági és Jogi Könyvkiadó, 1960, pp. 437–438.

291

offer international companies to increase their profits, to have at their disposal raw materials in large quantities, cheap labour, a complete monopoly position in the market of a given industrial product, which in turn makes it possible for them to keep their prices at a high level. It is for these reasons that the profit rate of foreign business companies is higher in developing countries. The average profit rate of foreign investments made by American companies was 14.96 per cent in 1950 (of which the profit rate of companies located in developed capitalist countries was 13.6, and that of companies operating in developing countries 16.3 per cent).

Fifteen years later the profit rate realized by foreign companies dropped to 11.8 per cent (8.7 per cent in developed capitalist countries and 15.4 per cent in the developing countries[15]). Within this, however, the profit rate of oil companies in the Middle East rose from 32.4 per cent to 41.7 per cent. In the same way, the profit rate of British companies operating in developing countries is double the rate realized by them in the developed capitalist countries.

The governments of some developing countries are making significant efforts to involve foreign private companies in the implementation of plans. In this they are led by the consideration that – foreign companies operate as "development leaven" in their economy by transplanting new technology, technical and managerial skills, creating new job opportunities and contributing to general economic development. On account of their greater experiences and widespread international relations, they may promote the expansion of exports. This is certainly true to some extent. But the question is, to what extent, at what price and for whose benefit they promote it.

In the recent past most developing countries have gained unfavourable experiences concerning international corporations, especially in two respects. The one is that foreign super-monopolies are, to put it mildly, "politically not neutral in the country" and have always tried – wherever they have had a chance and possibility – to "settle" local conflicts by open political pressure, occasionally by military intervention, to protect the positions of monopoly companies even in non-colonial developing countries as late as the first half of the 20th century. The ill-famed declaration e.g. of the late American president Coolidge that any property held by American citizens abroad constitutes part of the nation's assets and is therefore under the protection of the state, is still regarded to be in force in the USA.

The economic implications of the issue are at least of the same importance. In the colonial period capital-exporting foreign companies concentrated their activities primarily on the extraction and export of mineral resources and the development of related public works.

The rule of foreign monopoly capital prevented the colonial countries from developing their productive forces and building up their independent national economies.

[15] *Survey of Current Business.* Washington, September 1965.

In the past, developing capitalist economy was based, under the conditions of colonial relations, not on local needs, not on the national market, and was little concerned about the demand of the local population. *The basic aim of the centres of world capitalism was to ensure cheap raw materials of foodstuffs for the extended reproduction process of metropolitan countries.* Therefore, foreign monopoly capital penetrated primarily those sectors (exploitation of mineral resources, production of agricultural commodities) which produced in the first place for the leading imperialist powers, and provided only to an insignificant extent sectors for the needs of home consumption. *Foreign capital investments specialized the colonial countries in producing but one or two products needed by the monopolies.*

One-sided specialization developed a one-crop structure of the economy, which excluded the possibility of independent development and, indeed, presupposed the dependence of the economy of the country in question on the imperialist powers.

The marketing of one or of a few products turned out by the colonial countries depended not on the internal market, not on the size of home consumption, but first of all on the demand for these products of the imperialist metropolitan countries. The realization of the national income is a basic precondition for reproduction. Since it was the monopolies that determined both the wages and the purchasing prices, it was they again that decided what ratio of the national income should remain in the colonial country. This was also regulated by the practice that the finished products the colonial countries were compelled, as a result of their one-sided development, to buy abroad, were also supplied by the same companies at prices specified by them. Foreign monopolies did nothing to promote the spread in the country of up-to-date technology applied by them in their own enterprises. This demand was often not made at all since the indigeneous population was engaged in agriculture, and the extractive branches, if there were any, constituted an alien body in the "technical desert". These characteristics are still the determining factors of the activities of most foreign corporations operating in today's developing countries. Not only do they aggravate thereby planning and plan implementation but also diminish the accumulation ratio of the national income. In view of this situation a few developing countries pursue a radical policy against foreign monopolies. Most of the new states – of which this radical policy is not typical – have been trying since independence to restrict, in one way or another, the investments of big foreign monopolies. The restrictions may assume various forms. The most important forms applied in several developing countries are these: restriction or prohibition of foreign-owned land estates, regulation of the exploitation of mineral resources by foreign enterprises (tightening of concession conditions), laws specifying in what sectors foreign capital may make investments, and stipulating the share of local entrepreneurs in the establishments of foreign capital and demanding that their management be left in the hands of the citizens of the country receiving capital. National planning makes it necessary to concentrate scarce resources on accepted priorities. Foreign-exchange control is introduced with restriction on profit repatriation by foreign companies. New labour laws, strict export and import controls, high taxes, etc., are often also closely connected with the plan objectives. Foreign private capital is often strongly opposing these policy measures.

The restricting measures applied by developing countries, often combined with the danger of nationalization, have considerably increased the risk of foreign companies, and contributed to slowing down the increase in investments of monopoly capital in developing countries. In spite of these restrictions, foreign companies, especially the big ones, can rarely be compelled to endorse the objectives of the national plans. They usually act in accordance with the instructions of their metropolitan centres, especially in the "traditional" sphere, i. e. the extractive branches. In this case it is the national plans that have to adjust themselves to the demands of foreign companies.

In the second half of the 1960s, 56 per cent of all investments made by American monopoly companies in the developing countries were concentrated in the domain of "mining and metallurgy" and the oil industry (49 to 50 per cent in 1950). Almost two-thirds of British investments in the developing countries are concentrated on extracting raw materials and on plantations. In addition, foreign-owned companies are still repatriating the lion's share of their profits, the larger proportion of the fruit of their economic activities. In the years 1960 to 1965, US super-monopolies repatriated over 9 billion dollars' worth of profit against 3,000 million dollars' worth of new investments made.[16]

In the manufacturing industries it is increasingly common experience that some foreign companies are willing to be "integrated" into the national plan. They are prepared to a greater extent than the companies operating in the extractive sphere to subject themselves to restrictions, and are more willing to channel their investments into industries preferred by the plan. They are often compelled to do so by the keen competition among international companies. Only in this way are they able to gain ground in the markets of developing countries. It is usually the small- or medium-sized foreign companies that are forced to take this course of action.

Even if subjecting itself to the national plan, a foreign-owned company with direct access to modern technology, capital and well-trained management personnel still holds very strong positions in relation to local governments, and has the possibility to realize higher profits than the national capital or the state-owned enterprises. This finds its expression not only in higher profit rates. Foreign companies can organize their activities also in such a way that they realize most of the profits from the goods produced in one country in other countries, or possibly in other products too, because they plan their business activities in the context of the entire international system. (Typical examples are the oil companies.) Therefore tax fraud, a practice widely used by the national capital to evade taxation, is not common with these companies. They may hide most of their

[16] *Survey of Current Business*. Washington, 1967.

incomes in exports or license agreements. Moreover, contrary to the possibilities of domestic capital, foreign capital enjoys in several countries of the developing world guarantees against devaluation, currencies becoming inconvertible, nationalizations or wars. These guarantees are usually offered in the centre of the monopoly by governments having authority in the company's domicile to stimulate international operations.

IV. GENERAL EVALUATION

In connection with developing countries the question is often raised whether the efforts made in the field of planning have or have not accelerated economic growth and whether they have rendered it more effective. Only the analysis of individual cases can provide an answer. There are no general criteria to measure achievements in this fields. Very often the results achieved in raising the gross national product are due to the impact of external changes, the success of the export drive rather than to a change and improvement of the structure of the economy. In any case, for lack of adequate statistical data it is extremely difficult to tell what should be ascribed to the effect of the plan. Plan reports are rarely competent in this respect. (There are often no reports at all, or they are very deficient.)

It is beyond doubt that planning has yielded some results in certain countries. For example, in India, Egypt, Tanzania, Algeria and Syria, planning has definitely played a role in promoting and accelerating economic growth, though the plans often had to be changed. Planning has also been successful in contributing to the development of economic research, and in making the economic activities of the state more organized and co-ordinated. It has also had its share in carrying out some institutional reforms, such as the collection of taxes, the mobilization of savings, the better integration of external and internal resources. These results of planning must also be taken into account when evaluating the recent achievements of developing countries. On the whole, the first 10 to 15 years of planning was but a period of learning and experimenting. Most developing countries proved unable to reach the development envisaged by the plans and attain the objectives set by them. As already pointed out, their plans were often mere "paper plans", with no real possibility to implement them. They envisaged a great many aims which had nothing to do with a well-devised development strategy. The planners often tried to evade the problems rather than cope with them and, as a result, the plan did not prove a serious analytical tool suitable to act on the economy. The plan targets were often based to an unduly great extent on foreign aid. If these aids or loans did not substantiate, the investment objectives of the plan could be realized only to the extent of 40 or 50 per cent. Certain plan targets failed because agriculture did not meet the expectations, in other cases because of foreign-exchange shortage. Efforts aimed at a short-term adjustment proved insufficient, and the original long-term plans often had to be abandoned.

The peoples of developing countries looked forward to economic growth with great expectations when the plans were launched. The failures caused some people to feel disappointed in the plan and planning in general.[17] All this, however, does not mean the failure of planning as such, but the failure of an economic policy or politics that was unable or unwilling to bring about the necessary social, economic or administrative reforms, and regarded the plan at best as a "fashion" or as an instrument of political propaganda. We must also be aware of the fact that at the beginning of planning the expectations were, for objective or subjective reasons, geared up too high. Hopes were raised for tasks to be accomplished within a short time, while in reality they demanded the devoted work of generations and the sincere commitment of governments. From time to time the failures of planning also reflect such problems which the economies of developing countries were not, and could not have been able to cope with. These were not only unpredictable internal problems, but also extraordinary political problems, coups d'état, etc. It is also beyond doubt that the events of international political life also often intervened and hampered the implementation of plans. The economic development of Nigeria, for example, was considerably slowed down by the civil war in Biafra. The aggression by Israel exercised a detrimental effect on the economy of several Arab countries. The war with Pakistan, the huge masses of refugees from East Pakistan compelled India to re-allocate her material resources, which had its bearing on the whole system of planning. The monetary crises of the world capitalist system also aggravated the implementation of plans in many developing countries.

But the first 10 to 15 years of planning in the "Third World" has also provided the evidence that the acceleration of economic growth, the easing of accumulated social and economic problems require greater and more sincere efforts. (See Table 11.)

[17] In the late 1960s, "after about two decades during which planning – by which is meant here government planning for economic and social development – gained virtually universal acceptance in the less developed countries, questions are being heard about its usefulness for accelerating the rate of growth... Those who oppose government intervention in the economy, in renewing or increasing their attacks on development planning, have not failed to point to the poor record. To this defenders of the accepted system of planning reply that what is at fault is not the conventional planning approach, but the failure of governments to follow the precepts and prescriptions laid down by planners" – this is the problem as formulated e.g. by Albert Waterston, a well-known planning expert of the World Bank. (*Finance and Development.* December, 1969, p. 38.)

Table 11

Synopsis of international and national targets

Item	Indicative average specified in the International Development Strategy for the developing countries as a whole during the decade 1971–1980	Median value for selected developing countries*		Number of countries to which medium value pertains
		Target indicated in national plans for initial years of the decade 1971–1980	Figure recorded during the decade 1961–1970	
Average annual growth of gross product	At least 6 per cent	6.8 per cent	4.9 per cent	37
Average annual growth of gross product per head	About 3.5 per cent	3.9 per cent	2.1 per cent	37
Average annual increase in population	2.5 per cent	2.7 per cent	2.8 per cent	37
Average annual increase in agricultural component of gross products	4 per cent	5.0 per cent	Less than 3.5 per cent	36
Average annual increase in manufacturing component of gross product	8 per cent	9.7 per cent	More than 7 per cent	36
Average annual increase in percentage share of gross national saving in gross product	0.5	0.4	0.2	20
Average annual expansion of exports	Somewhat higher than 7 per cent	7.2 per cent	5.6 per cent	28
Average annual expansion of imports	Somewhat less than 7 per cent	7.1 per cent	5.0 per cent	28

Source: General Assembly Resolution 2626 (XXV) and Tables 1–5, 7 and 9.
  *Country coverage is not identical for all items, and there are differences in concepts used by a number of countries. For details, see Tables 1–5, 7 and 9.